LW00739441

GUARDIANS
of THE HORSE
II

Edited by Peter Rossdale and Rachel Green

Romney Publications

LIMITED EDITION

No: 320/600

Published by
Romney Publications
351 Exning Road, Newmarket, Suffolk CB8 0AU, UK.

First edition November 2001

© Romney Publications 2001

ISBN 0-9541587-1-7

Designed and Typeset by
Equine Veterinary Journal Ltd, Newmarket, Suffolk, UK.

Printed by
Geerings of Ashford Ltd, Kent, UK.

Front Cover
Bronze of Double Finesse and foal (Valika) sculpted by Penny Wheatley.

Contents

Preface

The relationship of man and horse goes back to before 3500 BC; and covers periods of history from the Hittites to the Assyrians, and from the Ancient Egyptians, Chinese and Persians to the present generations of mankind. The horse may have started this relationship as a source of food, but soon became a partner in hunting, war, transport and, in recent times, a loved companion; the simple love of a child maturing into that for the thrill and satisfaction of sport and pleasure.

The horse, indeed, owes us a debt of gratitude, for without our patronage it might have become an endangered, or even extinct, species. But, on the other side of the coin, has been - and today even more so - the multitudinous means of help and enjoyment provided by the horse to mankind. These extend from early childhood to the days of old age; providing a focus of animal contact that Desmond Morris considered to be of 'inestimable value' in a world ' full of impersonality and urban stress'.

We see, also, hundreds of thousands of individuals employed worldwide in the pursuit of maintaining, caring for and preparing the horse for useful purposes of sport, pleasure and financial gain; and we encounter whole industries that depend upon the horse as a medium for entertainment, spectator viewing and gambling, as well as the ancillary businesses of transport, feed merchants, farriery and saddlery. Remove the horse and consider the loss of pleasure and income for literally millions of people worldwide which would follow.

We are enormously grateful to the authors of the 32 chapters of this book. They not only express their own dedication to the horse and its welfare, but also provide us with a glimpse of the many facets that make the background to all sorts of activities of which many readers may be unaware. The diversity of subject matter - from training and breeding racehorses, to polo and endurance sport, from farriery to equine behaviour, from alternative medicine to the FEI and from an account of the sculptor, Adrian Jones, to the veterinary faculty at Utrecht - illustrates the rich tapestry created in human life around the horse of all breeds and types, from Welsh ponies and Arabians to Suffolk Punches and Thoroughbreds.

Finally, let us not forget, in these turbulent times, how the horse has become a currency of goodwill, bringing together men and women of all ages, of all colours, creeds and race; a currency that helps unite rather than divide members of mankind; and the Guardians of the Horse hold the responsibility of caring for this currency in the day-to-day routine of life.

PETER ROSSDALE and RACHEL GREEN

Acknowledgements

Our profound gratitude goes to authors for their cooperation and support; to the staff at EVJ Ltd for the handling of manuscripts and bringing the publication process to fruition; to Dr Pat Harris for advice on aspects of the text and to Investec Ltd for financial support of the illustrations reproduced in the book.

A little bit of knowledge lingers on

SIR MARK PRESCOTT Bt

Heath House
Newmarket
Suffolk CB8 8DU

Picasso said: *"Anyone who is entirely self taught had a bad tutor"*, in a famous put-down to a bright young artist, who had claimed such self education.

In my profession, racehorse training, it is often said that such groundbreaking trainers as Martin Pipe in England and Joe Crowley in Ireland, were self taught and thus disprove Picasso's theory. However, it is a claim that neither Mr Pipe nor Mr Crowley would make for themselves - for each has a devilishly enquiring mind and at the height of their powers and success, were the first to ask any outsider for information on any new thought or technique. I might also add that they were most generous with their time and thoughts to any who sought their advice.

In my own case, I was fortunate to graduate through the hands of three very different but expert trainers - Sidney George Kernick (1905–1982), Frances Leonard (Frank) Cundell (1909–1983) and Jack Alfred James Waugh (1911–1999). Sadly, all are now dead.

Fig 1: The author, racehorse trainer Sir Mark Prescott.

From Mr Kernick I was taught to think like horses, from Mr Cundell how those horses should be placed and from Mr Waugh how to conduct both myself and my stable.

In their time, the veterinary aids of today, such as endoscopy, tendon and bone scans, x-rays and blood tests, were completely unknown. There were no starting stalls, no all weather racing, no Sunday racing, no camera patrol and such training aids as equine pools, horse walkers and artificial gallops, all now commonplace, were unthought of then. Today, they would not recognise the trade they had plied so successfully. However, not a day passes without my being grateful to one of them for something.

I was taught to ride by a middle-aged divorcée called Frances Selly, who eked out a modest living from her hilltop Devonshire smallholding by teaching local children to ride. A horseracing fanatic, for some reason she became fond of me and refused to send a bill for my riding lessons. Therefore, my stepfather, by way of a thank you, took her to Newton Abbot races and I was reluctantly dragged along. We parked by the last fence. Too small to see over the obstacle, I was captivated by the noise of the horses approaching the last fence, the pounding hooves, the crashing birch, whips cracking and curses flying. The smell of bruised grass and churned mud further entranced me.

A last fence fall by the leader, crashing to the ground only a few yards in front of me, and the sound of the poor animal literally being winded by the impact, prior to rolling over the prostrate jockey, who was then summarily kicked along the ground by two pursuers, took my breath away as well. To my amazement the jockey rose slowly to his feet prior to chucking his whip to the ground. "F***ing hell," he said, and walked slowly back to the stands. What a man, I thought, what a man, and never wanted to do anything else again.

Through Mrs Selly, I was therefore sent, aged 14, to start riding out at local trainer Syd Kernick's Kingsteignton yard, a 6 mile bike ride away. Small, gingery, unfailingly neat and tidy in appearance, Syd had a jaunty carefree nature and a ready, impish smile. Originally a hunt servant, he became a rough, tough, journey-man jockey riding under National Hunt rules until well into his late 40s. He trained about 8 or 10 National Hunt horses and supplemented his income by breaking in difficult horses. His staff consisted of his son Neil, a highly competent jockey, whose career was inhibited by a spectacular stammer and a catalogue of injuries, an old age pensioner called Syddie Gibbs, who was a remarkable handyman with little in the way of tools and supplies to work with, and a cheery local girl with blonde hair and a toothy, flashing smile called Jane Harold with whom I was secretly in love (despite her being 4 years older - a lifetime's difference at that age!).

Meals were provided by Mrs Kernick. Lil was a sturdy dark haired woman, fanatically houseproud, fiery of temper and exceedingly jealous of her husband, probably with good reason. Syd's feckless disregard of time, and her punctilious but suspicious nature, resulted in some spectacular domestic rows.

Winners were rare and hard to come by. No horse was there unless it had a mental or physical problem, and most had both. When a miracle had been wrought, it was seldom acknowledged. We once had a red letter day and a double at Newton Abbot and were so early at the newspaper shop the following morning that it had not even opened. Enticingly on the doorstep lay the day's papers, bound in string. By twisting the bundle sideways we extracted a Sporting Life without breaking the twine. No banner headline proclaimed the Kernick double - instead, "Ryan Price out of luck at Newton Abbott" blazed the headline.

Our owners were local farmers and business men, who expected the lowest rates. Our gallops were fields loaned by supportive farmers and the so-called 'five furlong gallop' was in reality three furlongs and round a turn. For a time, the verge on the newly installed Exeter bypass was our trial ground but this was spoilt, much to Mr Kernick's disgust, by droves of picnickers once the road had been opened to the public. Long canters round small fields and hacking round the lanes was the principal routine and it suited admirably several of the jaded customers that passed through his hands.

One day the phone was ringing in the house as we busied ourselves in the yard at lunchtime and I was sent in to answer it. "Mr Jocelyn Hambro's Private Secretary speaking. Could I speak to Sydney Kernick please?" I shot out into the yard with this exciting news. "Bollocks," said the old man and kept feeding. "I promise you," I pleaded. He went into the house and for the first time in his life took his trilby off, and picked up the phone. "Sydney George

Kernick speaking." "Mr Hambro has asked me if you would take a horse from Newmarket called Barb - he has been very difficult - to see if you can get him going."

A week later, a small chestnut gelding arrived looking well but very light. Neil rode him out for the first few days but he even sweated up whilst being saddled and jig-jogged himself into a lather at exercise each day for a week. "The old man will ride that f***ing thing tomorrow," said the 60-year-old trainer. "He is too much of a man for you kids."

The following morning having legged us up, the Governor then clambered onto Barb himself using a flower bed as a mounting block. This precarious operation resulted in him thundering up the High Street behind us. To our secret delight the horse then proceeded to jar every bone in his body for an hour and a half. As we came back towards the village he paused by an open gate. "Now, whose got all those bloody fags then?" "I've got a packet of 5," I ventured (you could buy Senior Service in fives in those days). "Well chuck 'em here," he said. "What about you Neil?" "Oh I've n...n...n...n...not g...g...g...got any," he stammered. "Oh bollocks, empty your pockets, hand over what you've got" and 20 more cigarettes found their way into the old man's pocket. Filled up now with a supply of cigarettes, he sent us on our way with a cheery "Do as you like with the rest of them," and disappeared into a field of freshly cut straw which was lying in rows adjacent to the lane.

It was about 8.15 on a glorious summer morning and the day was going to get hot. We returned to the yard with the other horses to carry on the day's routine. During the morning, on looking up the hillside, we could see the old man riding full length in a white shirt, red tie, jodhpurs and hacking jacket, riding up and down the rows of straw. Each time Barb jogged he took him back to the beginning again. Whatever the horse did his rider sat motionless, puffing away at one of our cigarettes, apparently lost in a world of his own and completely oblivious of any other ("You see Mark, three parts of the art of riding is doing nothing and that is sometimes pretty hard to do"). Second lot, third lot and lunch went by. In the afternoon, the animals who were being broken in were taken out. Every now and again we glanced up on the hillside above to see the two of them progressing endlessly and relentlessly towards the top of the field, only to look up 20 minutes later to see them back down at the bottom again. At

4.00 pm he returned, the horse having finally accomplished the task of zig-zagging all the way to the top of the field and all the way back down without jogging once. The horse was perfectly cool. "He was glad to walk in the end, but I ran out of fags and had to stop an hour earlier than I intended," he said. The horse never jig-jogged again.

Once he had made his mind up to do a job, Syd Kernick had endless patience - all thoughts of the rest of the day left him - bills, debts, entries, owners, meals - everything was forgotten as he lost himself to the task in hand.

During the winter we received a second call. Sir Jocelyn was to be in Torquay staying at the Imperial Hotel and would like to look round evening stables. "What time would be suitable?" Evening stables! We never had evening stables! A partially disembowelled car was hurriedly pushed into the muck pit and covered with tarpaulin, bales of straw were flung into boxes and banked up the walls (a weeks supply in a day, compared to normal rations, for each horse), canvas headcollars were tossed into the garage and leather ones, long discarded, were buffed and shone to replace them. Mrs Kernick made curly cucumber sandwiches and 'the front room' was readied, for the first time since they had got married. In the meantime, some washed carrots were produced from the kitchen, cut beautifully lengthwise. The horses had never seen such a delicacy before and I was instructed to hand them to the Governor as we went into each box from a feed bowl: "Just like in the big stables - sure to impress him". Just as all was ready, a Rolls Royce crept into the yard and evening stables commenced (for the first time in recorded history). The eight horses were shown in all their battered glory but embarrassingly (being totally unfamiliar with such a treat) each refused all offers of washed carrots, despite Syd trying to ram the vegetable between their firmly clenched front teeth. Sir Jocelyn was then invited into the house. We all fell over each other in trying to offer him sandwiches. "Well, it's been a most interesting afternoon Mr and Mrs Kernick, but we really must be going," said the great man. "But before I go Mr Kernick, I think you should know that this horse, Barb, was bought with a contingency". There then followed a dreadful pause. We all knew that Syd had absolutely no idea what a contingency was, but we all were powerless to help. He scratched his chin; still no rescue came. At last he ventured, *"Well there's plenty of those buggers about these days, but if you give them a good blistering they're normally alright."* Amazed and bemused, Sir Jocelyn thanked us all for our kindness and left. Sadly, the horse proved useless and no replacement followed.

The bread and butter of the stable were the horses to break in and Syd's outstanding reputation for dealing with such horses meant that they came from far and wide. The further they came, the worse they were and the more yards they had been in on the way. In the same way that no matador will fight a bull that has been fought before, so no horseman wants a horse that has already been spoiled by another. The smallest child's pony can do what it likes with anyone. It is twice as strong as a man. It only doesn't do so because it doesn't think it can. Properly broken in, and if no mistakes are subsequently made, all horses should believe that man can do as he wants with them and, as long as man doesn't abuse or overface that trust, it will be happy to do so for the rest of its life.

These horses, however, knew all the tricks and all the dodges; many were extremely dangerous and most had been poorly treated at some time. *"By the time they reach me, Mark,"* Syd said one day, *"it's no good knocking them about, someone has already tried all that. We've got to think of something else, we've got to think of something better."* His method was tried and trusted. On arrival the horse would be put into the top corner box on peat moss bedding. The top door would be shut and locked. The horse would then be left in the dark with no food and no water for 36 hours.

On the third morning, Syd would muck the horse out himself, by hand, into a small basket skip. He wouldn't speak to the horse and, as it started to follow this strange man, who never spoke to it, round the box, Syd would literally barge the horse out of the way and then leave. *"You see Mark, no one has ever been up to it and not spoken to it before. It's alone, it's in the dark, it's hungry and it badly wants a friend and I'm going to be that friend in the end."*

In the evening he would repeat the process, only this time, after mucking it out, he would let it drink from a bucket. *"Sixteen swallows Mark, count its ears moving. It can't swallow without its ears moving and it can live for sixteen days on sixteen swallows, I've proved it!"* The cycle of fear was thus broken. The horse regarded him as the nice man that brought it what it wanted most in the world - water - and not the horrid man that had denied it. Thus, seven thousand miles apart and separated by twenty years, Syd Kirnick and that other great horse expert, Monty Roberts, had developed quite independently their own *'advance and retreat'* method with horses.

He was endlessly inventive. We once had a horse whose party trick was to hurl itself onto the ground as soon as a saddle or roller was put onto it and then refuse to move. It had burn marks all over its side and stomach where someone had set fire to the straw beneath it in a desperate attempt to get it up. An ingenious attempt to counteract this by rushing into the house for a jug of cold water to pour into its ear was only partially successful. It immediately leapt up and, having shaken its ear and removed the irritation, it then flung itself back down on the floor again.

This horse caused the old man some consternation and for two days he did nothing, but full water rations were resumed. On the third day, I was told to take the horse down to a local river, the River Dart at Totnes, and lunge the horse on the side of the banks. I did so for an hour. Eventually a little white van came bumping down the road. *"Take him into the river there, Mark, you will find it is just up to your thighs, and lunge him there."* So I did and he walked round quietly. However, as soon as we put the roller on him, he flung himself down. As with all mammals, horses are peculiarly tenacious of life - the horse disappeared below the surface but, on starting to drown, shortly resurfaced again. Within 20 minutes we were riding it up and down the river with a saddle on and within 30 minutes it was hack cantering in figures of eight on the river bank.

Syd and Lil rowed to the bitter end. When their son Neil brought home a very attractive girl to announce their engagement, he unfortunately chose a moment of some marital tension between the two parents to introduce her. *"I pity you, poor girl,"* said Lil to the prospective fiancée whom she had never met before. *"Neil will be just like his father. He will expect clean white shirts every day; turn out his turn-ups half way up the bloody stairs when you have just cleaned them; go out for an hour to get some cigarettes and come back ten days later - your life will be a misery just like mine is!"*

"I don't know," interjected Syd, pushing his trilby onto the back of his head. *"I'm rather fond of Neil."* *"You would be,"* she said, *"you would be"*. The poor girlfriend was now retreating towards

the kitchen. *"I'll tell you what,"* Lil went on, *"I rue the day that boy was conceived, I rue the day that child was …"* "Nonsense Lil," said Syd. *"I remember it well, you kept on saying 'more, Sydney, more, Sydney, more!'"* "Oh, I never, you filthy pig!" Eventually Lil was to predecease Syd and, as so often in such cases, he was bereft.

I had almost two and a half magical years there, years full of laughter and homespun wisdom. I remember walking back to the car park at Wincanton with the Governor one day after his two runners had been tailed off in a selling hurdle. A top trainer's Gold Cup horse had won the big condition race. The connections were a picture of concern. *"When you look at their faces, Mark, it makes you realise how lucky you are to have nothing but bad horses to train!"*

At Syd's instigation I left Devon aged 17 in my A40 van to join Frank Cundell's highly successful stable at Aston Tirrold, near Blewbury in Berkshire. I left with a lump in my throat and a clear feeling that the salad days were over.

Frank Cundell was a qualified vet. He had ridden with great success in India and had been joint champion amateur on the flat in Britain. A cousin of Ken Cundell and uncle of Peter he had a 50 horse mixed stable with the emphasis on jumpers.

His wife Barbara was a big kindhearted women who swore a great deal. Their two children had only a passing interest in horses. The yard was immaculate. Medium sized, with horn rimmed spectacles, sharp features and darting eyes that missed nothing at all, Frank Cundell had a sense of fun but no sense of humour and certainly none against himself. He was generally followed about by 2 or 3 Jack Russell terriers, who, surprisingly, were allowed to yelp and bark continuously whilst accompanying him up to the gallops in the Landrover.

Les Foster, the head lad, was gnarled, tough and a professional cynic but genuine and kind and with Arthur, the rather effeminate travelling head lad, ran the yard under the Governor's close direction with great skill and considerable devotion. They could anticipate his moods and requirements and he, in turn, was precise in his orders and punctilious in his habits.

His consummate skill was placing his charges to their best advantage. Just before my time he had steered *Crudwell* to his fiftieth victory in a career

that spanned eleven seasons and incorporated winning the Ascot Stakes at the Royal meeting and being placed in the Cheltenham Gold Cup. In *Crudwell's* last two seasons, Frank Cundell guarded his horse's reputation with such skill and care that no outsider could detect his failing powers. Running him sparingly and only where he had the best chance, he preserved his horse's ability to frighten off the opposition, although the gallant horse was but a shadow of his former self. His last victory, the fiftieth record breaking win, occurred in an optional seller at Taunton. Mr Cundell was as versatile as his charges and was equally adept on the flat. *Welshman's* Wokingham Handicap victory was an object lesson in how to handle a high class sprint handicapper. Most of his owners were his friends and he was widely respected by his training colleagues, amongst whom cousins Ken and Michael Pope were his closest friends.

Thursday evenings in those days were sacrosanct. Mrs Cundell and the children were forbidden to be in the house after evening stables, lest there be any noise or distraction during the dreaded 'calendar night'. At that time there was no centralised handicapping system and races closed four weeks in advance. Each meeting had one individual handicapper responsible for all the horses entered that day. Thus, by entering a horse at several meetings, a comparison could be made between various handicappers assessments of each horse, often revealing considerable discrepancies. By running where the horse was *'best in'*, it was possible for a skilful and conscientious trainer such as Mr Cundell to use the system to each horse's advantage. However, it was a laborious and painstaking process and silence was a vital part in the thought process.

My job on Thursday afternoons was to assist in this task. Two Racing Calendars came each week, he would work off one and I off the other, comparing opposition horses against ours in different races at different meetings and with different handicappers. Excitement was intense when it was discovered that, for instance, Mr Price at Wincanton had *Douai*, on average, ten pounds lower than Major Arkwright at another meeting. *"We'll have to run him at Wincanton Mark, if we have to carry him to the start on a bloody stretcher,"* the Governor would say on discovering such a discrepancy, at the same time reaching for the work book.

The office was small. On one side were a row of owners' silks and on the three remaining sides were desks and the inevitable racing photographs and form books. Earlier in the week in question, Mr Cundell must have ventured to suggest to his wife that the office needed cleaning, because one terrifying evening, as we were comparing *Douai's* weights during this sacred hour, the door burst open to reveal the highly significant figure of Mrs Cundell bearing a roaring vacuum cleaner. *"What the hell are you doing here?"* asked the Governor. *"You said the office was bloody well dirty, so I'll bloody well clean it!"* she replied. I crouched silently, and hopefully invisibly, at my desk. *"Well get out of here. It's Thursday, you know this isn't the right f***ing time."* Undaunted, she started hoovering the floor. To my amazement they were both now so incensed that they were completely oblivious of my presence and they grappled with the machine. Failing to wrest the machine from his wife's clutches the Governor then lay across the floor to prevent further progress but she continued, purposefully bashing the machine into his prostrate body. He then pulled off a master stroke and from his prone position wrenched the plug from the socket. Briefly a terrifying silence reigned. *"You bastard,"* she said. *"You've asked for this,"* and with manic speed she changed the nozzle of the machine, switched on the power point and with a terrible sucking and grinding noise hoovered up all the rubbers and pencils off his desk before leaving in triumph. For a moment there was complete silence and then *"Douai, 10 stone 1 lb"* he said and we worked on as if nothing had happened.

Despite greatly admiring his skill and the relentlessly methodical manner in which he conducted his business, I was never able to strike up a rapport with him and my few ventures on the racecourse were singularly unsuccessful and did little to develop a close relationship. Getting caught on the line at Taunton on St John's Day, having hit the front too soon, was the nadir and further undermined my confidence. *"I'm so sorry, Governor,"* I blurted out on dismounting. *"I thought…"*

"You thought?" he interrupted. *"You thought! You've have never had a f***ing thought in your life! When you can think I'll give you a diploma and you can hang it on the end of your bed and it will say 'I, Sir Mark bloody Prescott, am capable of thought' and you*

can look at it every f***ing morning. Until then you can safely assume that you've never had a thought worth thinking about in the whole of your f***ing life!"; and with that he disappeared (this dressing down was probably only bettered by the late Fred Rimell, who once told the now eminent National Hunt trainer, and then amateur rider, Jim Old: *"If Jesus Christ rode his f***ing donkey like you rode that flaming horse, he deserved to be crucified"*).

I staggered into the weighing room to be greeted by our highly competent third jockey Clive Searle (Stan Mellor and John Cook were first jockeys to the yard at this time). *"How did that go down?"* he enquired with a hint of smugness. I gave him a quick résumé. *"How did you get here?"* he asked.

"In the Governor's car," I replied. *"Best you get there quick,"* he advised. I changed and sprinted into the car park. Amongst the rows and rows of cars, only one gap appeared where that silver Mercedes had once been.

Later that season, a crashing fall on the flat at the now defunct Wye National Hunt May meeting ended my riding career and necessitated a lengthy spell in hospital and I was never to return to Aston Tirrold.

Recuperating at home in Devon, a chance meeting with Jack Leach, writer of the justly famous 'Sods I Have Cut on the Turf', a former classic winning jockey and top class trainer, resulted in my being recommended to Mr Jack Waugh as assistant trainer. *"He's tough but fair,"* vouchsafed my go-between. *"That's shorthand for a living nightmare!"* opined my worldly-wise stepfather. But for once he was wrong.

Mr Waugh came from an old and established Newmarket family. Originally from Scotland, his grandfather and father had trained for the Kaiser. His brother and two cousins were training in Newmarket at that time, and another brother was a stud manager in Ireland. It is a measure of how quickly times change that no Waugh today is associated with training racehorses. Having served his time with his father and Basil Jarvis (*"If I ever did anything right with Mr Jarvis, he never told me,"* he once said), he was unfortunate enough to see action in the first two fiascos of the Second World War at Dieppe and Dunkirk. Invalided out of the army, he started training in the latter years of the war and quickly established a high class clientele of mainly owner-breeders at Heath House, later adding a second stable across the Moulton Road at Osborne House.

Tall, erect with piercing blue eyes, his demeanour could change in an instant. Unbending, with a Victorian black and white view of right and wrong, he was a regular churchgoer and a formidable presence. He favoured conservative dress - thick grey flannel trousers, woollen ties, solid rubber soled shoes and Fair Island sweaters were his customary garb.

A quick interview at Newbury racecourse was followed by the offer of Assistant Trainer's position for a month's trial to last six months whilst he got over a minor illness. *"Start the day after tomorrow,"* he said. *"I'll see you at midday,"* and with that disappeared across the paddock to saddle his runner.

I drove back to Devon, packed my bags and said my farewells. The following morning I left the farm at 5.00 am. It was a perfect late summer's dawn, a light mist lay in the valley and I stopped in the lane to look back at the farm I was destined never to see again. If I had left to go to Mr Cundell's with a sense of dread and impending doom, this time my pulse was quickening and I vowed to myself to make a success of this venture and learn from the mistakes I had made at Aston Tirrold. As my stepfather said to me that last evening, *"anyone can make a mistake but only bloody fools make them twice"*.

In those days there was no dual carriageway from Exeter to Newmarket and it took almost 6 hours to battle through the likes of Swindon, Stony Stratford and St Neots. I arrived at Newmarket an hour early and drove to the foot of the heath to see the horses on Warren Hill. A group of touts were standing by the wall observing the passing strings of racehorses. *"Can you tell me, please, where Heath House is?"* I asked cheerfully. Without looking up one of them replied *"You're leaning on the wall"*. *"Thank you,"* I said. *"Can you tell me which Mr Waugh's string is please?"* *"You're looking at it,"* was the monotone reply.

Mr Waugh was riding his hack *Councillor of Trent*, a big raw-boned bay gelding whom I was to learn later terrorised the apprentices in his stable to such an extent that they fed him by standing on the back of the horse in the adjacent stall and pouring the food over the partition. *"Ah, there you are,"* said Mr Waugh, *"an hour early - you'll do. Follow me."* The hack man came out and took his horse away and Mr Waugh led me in through the front door of Heath House. Being a beautiful day, the back door

was also open, and I could see through the house into the paddock, where an early yearling was being lunged on the sand bed. *"This,"* he said, tapping her bottom as she brushed the stairs, *"is the missus - she is the best in Newmarket."* We then swept into the paddock. *"And this,"* he said, *"is Jack Button, and he's the best head lad in Newmarket. If you can't get on with them, you can't get on with anyone; so, by now you will have realised the worse thing about this job is me!"*

I spent the afternoon trying to find accommodation and was disconcerted to meet another stable's head lad, whom I had known when I was riding, in the street. I told him I was looking for a flat and that I had come to work for Mr Waugh as assistant. *"Don't bother with a flat, bed and breakfast will do you, no one could last with that bugger for more than a week,"* was his cheerful summary of my prospects. At 4.00 pm I was back in the stable yard to help Jack Button go round the horses. Mr Waugh emerged at exactly 5.30 pm and then took me round evening stables. Everything was immaculate, I had never seen anything like it in my life. Each headcollar was soaped and polished, each lad's tools were laid out on a white stable rubber, placed on top of a pile of straw neatly made into a box shape in the left hand corner of each horse's stable. By the stable door, straw was neatly twisted in like the end of a roll of carpet. The horses stood knee deep in drum threshed straw. The hay had been rolled out of a circular bale, each stem still unbroken.

As Mr Waugh swept round stables I was reminded of James Robertson-Justice in the *Doctor at Large* films, where he played the surgeon looking round the wards, with Dirk Bogarde, the junior doctor, trotting along behind. Robertson-Justice would give each patient a quick glance and then a crisp comment which had to be written down by the matron. Feeling one lady's pulse, I recall him dropping it onto the bed with the cursory remark *"Soon be dead,"* and on he went.

As Mr Waugh entered each box, the lad took off his cap and each horse was standing to attention facing three quarters to the left. *"Evening, Thorpe"* (all paid men were called by their surnames and all girls and apprentices by their Christian names). *"How's he tonight? God knows why he ran so badly last week."* He would then feel the animal's front legs, then its back, pat the ribs then feel the hind legs before tapping his stick on the wall. The horse would then turn over the other way, the lad dodging seamlessly beneath his neck. *"Put another Animalintex on that speedycut, Jack,"* and on he would go to the next box. After we had looked at all 50 horses he invited me into the house. *"What a nice man,"* I thought. *"How lucky I am. I expect he will want to know if I have got anywhere to stay and probably he will give me a drink."*

We went straight into the office. *"Have you ever done entries?"* he asked. *"A little, when I was at Mr Cundell's,"* I replied. *"Good, here's last week's entry form and this is the extract I make from it each week in pencil on foolscap paper. You'll soon work out all my hieroglyphics. This is next week's entries sheet, here's the pencil, here's the paper, do the same, please, and put it on my desk at 5 o'clock tomorrow morning - goodnight."*

I was staying with Mary Alderman, a tremendously elegant former girlfriend of my stepfather's, on the Fordham Road until I found a flat but I had no time for more than a mouthful of the supper that she had prepared for me. I shot up into my bedroom. It took me until 11.00 at night to make a chart of all the possible shorthand combinations for each possible race description. By 11.45 pm I was ready to embark on the current entry form. By 3.30 in the morning I had completed my task. Anxious to make a good impression, I then ruled off in blue biro the margins and names of horses and in red biro inked in all the meetings. It looked splendid and I slept the sleep of the just for two hours before arriving in the yard at 5.15 am.

I left the result of my labours on his desk and thought to myself how pleased he would be with his new assistant. At 6.30 am Mr Waugh strode into the yard. I was to learn that you could set your watch by his first appearance - what I only discovered later, and to my cost, was that he had normally been round the horses before anyone came to work and already knew the answers to all the questions that he would ask Jack Button and myself.

We rode out first lot. He was charm itself, except for one anxious moment when I got between him and his string. A sharp rap across my forearm with his hunting crop and a crisp *"Never get between a trainer and his horses,"* cured me of that for a lifetime!

On return to the yard we went into the office. *"That's my desk, that's the secretary's desk and that's your desk."* He sat down at his desk and proceeded to read the *Sporting Life* and the *Sporting Chronicle.*

I seated myself at my newly appointed place of learning. The polished surface of the desk was completely bare save for a neat pile of shredded paper arranged centrally as a pyramid. To my horror I could see little bits of blue and red biro on the surviving scraps. Summoning all my courage I asked, *"Excuse me, Sir, was there something you didn't like about the entries I did last night?"* *"I said, do them in pencil,"* came the reply. *"Put them on my desk at 5 o'clock tomorrow morning"* and he returned to his paper. He had established the principles of our relationship straight away - *"You do exactly as I say and we'll get on fine".* And thus began the two and a half happiest years of my life.

Jack Waugh had never had an assistant trainer before. Having cut me down to size in the first morning, he then established my credentials with his head lad Jack Button. *"Never thought I would need an assistant trainer, Jack,"* he explained, *"but with Bunty* [his daughter] *soon to be married and my not feeling so good last year, and you not getting any younger, we could both do with a bit of help and the quicker we get this cove taught the better it will be for both of us".*

Unlike so many head lads who are jealous of both their knowledge and their job - *"another eyes front come to suck my brains,"* one Newmarket head lad had described the new assistant to me - Jack quickly caught onto the scheme and we became great friends and I, his greatest admirer. Small, lightly made with a slightly flattened nose, laughing eyes and sparrow thin legs, Jack Button was always impeccably turned out. A natty dresser in his spare time, he wore his greying hair raffishly long for the period. Jack had been apprenticed to Basil Jarvis when Mr Waugh had been assistant there, and they were together from that day until the day that Mr Waugh retired. As with almost any relationship in the world, theirs was founded on respect. Each was well aware of the other's foibles and each respected the other's privacy, but each held the other in the greatest respect and mutually admired their prowess at their chosen career.

Jack Button was a beautiful natural horseman with an easy horse coper's seat and soft, supple hands. He could pull out almost any horse from the string and it would happily respond to his confident touch by hacking about the heath as if it had been doing it all its life. The staff worked well for him and he liked them although, in common with all his profession, he was endlessly complaining about them. I remember following him down the yard one hot afternoon as he locked up the yard at lunchtime, picking up any grease pots, cotton wool and sweet papers, etc that might have been left behind. Unaware of my presence he was muttering to himself, *"I'm sick to death of valeting these f***ers. Thirty f***ing years I've been valeting them, I don't have to stand for it, I could go anywhere and get a job. They'd miss me, they f***ing well would and so would he in that house too… etc, etc"*.

Jack had been the senior Newmarket vet, Bob Crowhurst's, batman during the war. They had once Hobdayed an enormous number of donkeys in 2 days to stop the unfortunate beasts braying, so that they could subsequently be dropped out of planes behind enemy lines in Abyssinia and not give away their position. It was not something that they relished but something that had to be done, as the saying was at the time: *"Don't you know there's a war on?"* Mr Crowhurst was famed for both his considerable veterinary expertise and a complete absence of a bedside manner. He was strictly practical by nature and one can only imagine what he would have thought of some of the cloyingly sentimental veterinary programmes on prime time television today. For instance, I have a particularly vivid memory of his walking by whilst on duty at a particularly carnage-struck point-to-point blowing into his gun like Wyatt Earp and saying, *"Bit of grief, what? Bit of grief."*

When called out to our stables, mindful of their respective positions in war time, he would stand at the main gates and instead of asking a lad where Jack Button was, he would shout in a stentorian voice across the yard, *"Button. Button. Button!"* Jack would keep walking. *"F*** him, rude bastard, f*** him." "Button. Button!" "I could have shot him during the war you know Mark, and no one would have known."* But in the end, of course, he would relent.

One day, news reached Jack and I of an unusual incident at Ian Walker's stables at Moulton Paddocks, now Godolphin's summer home. A yearling, who had had the tack put on for the first time the previous day, had been particularly fractious and had (quite correctly) had the roller left on overnight. On feeding it the following morning, the head lad had roused it from its sleeping position, but the animal on feeling the restriction anew had exploded, bolted past the head lad along the passage of the cage boxes, in which it

was stabled, and the impetus had been such that it had taken it up the stairs and into the loft. Jack and I had learned that Mr Crowhurst had been called to the yard and had rather enjoyed imaging the scene.

As Jack and I held the first horse for Mr Crowhurst to examine the following morning, we moved into action. *"I hear you had a bit of excitement at Mr Walker's yard yesterday, Sir,"* I said, giving the first ball plenty of air. *"Yes, yes,"* said the great veterinarian. *"Most complex business."* He always spoke in clipped, staccato sentences. *"What did you do, Sir?"* said Jack, giving the second ball even more air. *"Yearling in loft, leaping and bucking when approached. Soon dealt with. Horse sedated. Moon's Plant Hire summoned. In less than an hour the horse was winched to safety."* *"Good Lord, Sir,"* I said, heading towards the door and escape. *"I'm surprised you took so long - from what I've heard I thought you would have Hobdayed it, tied a parachute to its back and shoved the poor thing out of the loft."* *"Not funny - not funny at all. Good Lord, what have you been telling him, Button?"*

My first winter in Newmarket was bitterly cold. Ours was the only stable with water in our area - the Governor having been perspicacious enough to insist on the taps being packed with warm horse dung every evening. Sir Noel Murless and Mr Sam Armstrong's staff, for instance, had to call in daily to churn water to their stables. With no covered rides in those days, our horses trotted endlessly round the straw bed on the paddock, each horse swathed in sheet, rug, night cap and knee boots, each lad in overcoats, gloves, leather waistcoats and scarves. Our trainer supervised operations from a centrally placed muck pit, throwing back the straw, separating that which was usable again to fill in the bare patches on the straw bed. For this operation he wore a trench coat for the first 5 minutes, this was then removed to reveal only a white shirt, sleeves rolled up of course, over the top of which was a sleeveless green Fair Island sweater. He remained there for all three lots, apparently oblivious to the cold, pausing only briefly during third lot to shoot any thirst-crazed rat that ventured out onto the gutters at the top of the stable roof in search of any recently thawed water.

In those far off days, flat racing ended on November 5th and began again about March 20th. There was no all-weather racing. The December sales lasted for only 5 days and the yearlings were broken and doing good canters up sides by Christmas. Most of the trainers were doing a bit of shooting, hunting or coursing, perhaps twice a week, those that didn't enjoy field sports preferring to disappear to the sun in January. It was the time for gelding, blistering, physicing and reschooling the horses ready for the season to come.

During the winter in question, for Major Gibson in Exning, we had an unraced 2-year-old colt called *Grandtully*, a big raw-boned grey by *Fortino II*, a horse who was an influence for both ability and explosive temperament. For some reason he hadn't run as a 2-year-old and had became very headstrong. If the string jumped about for any reason and the lad riding him was ill advised enough to shorten his grip on the reins, the horse would gallop off flat out up the walking ground and into the middle distance. *"Jack and Mark,"* said the Governor in November, *"one of you two better ride this horse for the winter. Hack him about, give him plenty of head and let him get his confidence. I've an idea he will be alright if we can make a man of him".* And so we did, each of us surviving a few moments of intense terror - my own worst being completing four involuntary laps of the yard at Heath House, clattering along the frozen tarmac whilst the rest of the string, trotting in the central paddock on the straw bed, careered across the middle as I hurtled round the perimeter. By the time Warren Hill opened in February he would lead the string pretty well, but we only dared tackle the horseshoe shaped Side Hill canter with him on his own.

Eric Eldin, our stable jockey, returned from India bronzed, tanned and handsome, to start the season in March. Eric was a top class jockey. Strong, tough and stylish in the mould of Joe Mercer, he was second only to Lester Piggott in strength in a close finish. A neat and natty dresser, he had been apprenticed to Capt. Ryan Jarvis and rode with great success each winter in India. Fresh and invigorated by his winter's break in summer climes, his bronzed features made a stark contrast to our ashen white visages.

On our first work morning of the season on racecourse side, Mr Waugh left *Grandtully* to work solo last. *"You hop on that grey horse, Eric,"* he said, *"don't get hold of him. And don't ride too short! Mark and Jack have been riding him all winter, hacking him about, and they have done an excellent job with him. I don't want him spoilt. Let him bowl along on his own*

from the seven furlong marker and don't overdo it." With that he drove off in the Humber to supervise the work from the six and a half furlong pole.

Slightly on edge, having been made to wait whilst the others worked, *Grandtully* began to jig-jog on the spot. Eric who, against the Governor's advice, was winding his leathers round his stirrups to make them even shorter, was running out of his limited patience as well. *"I'll give you Mark and f***ing Jack, you grey bastard,"* he said, digging him in the ribs. With that, *Grandtully* launched himself straight through the car park's wooden fencing and disappeared towards Southfields and was last seen heading towards the Cesarewitch start, leaping paths and aircraft bollards on his way. Eric led him back into the yard at about 9.45 am, as second lot were pulling out. The pleasure that Jack and I gained from Eric's comeuppance was, however, slightly mitigated by the certain knowledge that our winter's work had been undone in a few seconds.

Confined from then on to working alone on Waterhall (the gallop there being away from home and thus less conducive to running away) it became necessary to embark on the dreaded stalls practice with him. Stalls had been introduced for most 2-year-old races the previous year. No one had much idea how to school horses through them and all the trainers hated them with a vengeance.

The first race to be started from the stalls had been run at Newmarket the previous season. Harry Wragg had run three in it and none of them had gone into the stalls, and all cantered back together, but the rest of a large field made a perfect start. As Mr Waugh and I watched through binoculars, fellow trainer Jack Jarvis (conservative to the last) gave vent to the feelings of most of his colleagues: *"Bugger! That worked perfectly!"*

Grandtully would go into the stalls but he wouldn't jump off until the others had gone about 100 yards. *"I'm off to Sandown tomorrow, Mark,"* said the Governor one evening, *"but before I go we'll put that grey horse of the Major's in the stalls and I'll give him a few volts with the buzzer"* (an electric goad), *"that should see him right!"* Before I could venture to suggest it might also result in his galloping off into eternity like the Flying Dutchman, he added, *"and I think you might as well ride him as well, you've always got on with him."*

I always claim I have never lost a night's sleep over a horse, but sleep came but fitfully in my

Exning flat that night. The morning dawned icy cold, grey and wet. *"Real funeral weather,"* commented Jack Button cheerfully as he led me out of the gate to canter up to the stalls positioned as now outside what was then Gondola Stables (where Percy Alden trained) and is now Beechurst of Sir Michael Stoute's. The stalls face up the hill away from the Bury Road and towards the Moulton Road. On the left at the top of the hill is a brick wall shielding Warren Place, ahead, three furlongs from the stalls, is the Moulton Road across which lies Warren Hill wood and to the right a long sweeping descent down Long Hill and worse still back towards Heath House Stables and home.

Grandtully loaded willingly. *"Right, sit tight,"* said Mr Waugh, advancing with the electrical cattle prodder in his hand, the two prongs of which connected with a battery which, when pressed, emitted a buzzing sound and gave the horse an electric shock. Buzz, buzz. *Grandtully* bounced forward, crashing his nose into the front gate. Buzz, buzz. This time he sprang forward and started galloping on the spot. Buzz, buzz. This time Jack Button sprang the gates. The horse launched himself into the air at 45° and then thundered up the hill into the blinding rain towards the Moulton Road as hard as he could lay his legs to the floor. His fear was such that he tried to stride faster than he could gallop and his head kept dipping. Determined not to shorten my reins but sit and suffer, I just sat against him as he gathered still further speed, trying to sound confident: *"Whoah, whoah old man"*. By now there were only 400 yards to go to the Moulton Road and it was apparent that I could never stop him in the time and ground available. Disconcertingly, a Pickfords, blue painted removal van hove into sight along the Moulton Road. If I turned to the left he was too close to stop at the wall and it was too tight to try and pull him round and away from home. If I went straight across the road, even if he didn't hit a vehicle, he would probably fall on the verge, the tarmac or crash into the trees on the other side. I opted to live a few seconds longer and pulled him round to the right. With his home stables in view and a downhill run towards them, if anything his momentum increased still further but he did at least respond to steering, if not braking. We galloped relentlessly downhill towards the walking ground. I pulled him right and now hurtling back towards the stalls we set out to repeat

the same terrifying procedure for a second time. As we flashed past the stalls, Mr Waugh, Jack Button and the two lads looked on with amazement. Mr Waugh, in a trench coat and trilby, stepped forward flapping his arms despairingly and I could just hear as I hurtled by: *"Pull him up Mark, for goodness sake - I've got to get off to Sandown…"* as if he thought this death-defying manoeuvre was some jolly prank such as the victory rolls perpetrated by returning flying aces during the Second World War.

Eventually, both horse and rider weakened by fear and exhaustion, we came to a halt and walked back down the hill. We must have looked a dejected couple - *Grandtully*'s grey coat was blackened by sweat and rain, his head held low, his tail arched. I was slumped in the saddle, soaked inside and out, the oilskins of that period as well as having let in some of the rain having also caused me to sweat copiously beneath them. There was not to be a happy ending. Shortly after this experience, the horse bolted in a solo gallop on the Limekilns and was destroyed in the interests of safety before next lot even pulled out. The phone call later that day to the owner exemplified Mr Waugh's relationship with his owners who had complete confidence in both his integrity and his judgement. *"Good morning, Major, Jack Waugh here. Shot your horse this morning"*. *"Oh right Jack - why?"* *"He'd become dangerous, I'm afraid."* *"Quite right, Jack. We'll have to see what we can get in the autumn. Goodbye."* And that was that.

Mr Waugh radiated intensity of purpose. His duty, as he saw it, was to his owners and nobody else in the world. *"What's right for the owners, Mark is always right for the trainer in the long term"* he used to say, but he brooked no interference - *"Any fool can train a racehorse, but two wise men can't."* He gave all horses time when they needed it. When one owner ventured to suggest that he couldn't afford to wait any longer, the crisp reply was *"you're not rich enough to afford not to wait"*. He was patient and sensitive to a nervous horse but ruthlessly tough when they were fit and racing, and ferocious with one who knew what to do but declined to comply. His stable management was faultless. He was a copy book trainer of his time but perhaps lacked imagination or a bit of flair with the more complex animal.

A great worrier, he was tactfully supported by his wife Mildred who rode him with a silken rein and, however sharp he might be with her, she never took offence as she knew none was intended. Before the sales or a big race, communication between the Governor and the rest of us was cut to a minimum. He would leave me notes of what the horses were to do if he was not present and when he came back he would read the notes that I had written for him, but words came only sparingly. It appears that the same rules applied domestically. *"Has the Governor spoken to you recently?"* Mrs Waugh enquired of Jack Button and I one breakfast with the Derby approaching. *"Not for about three weeks,"* we replied. *"Me neither,"* she said.

Standing on Long Hill one mid May morning during second lot, the Governor on foot and I on *Panjandram*, Mr Waugh put his hand on my boot and said, *"I'm fed up with this. It's a young man's game now. You better train these horses next year. I'll have a word with the owners."* I mentioned the fact that I was only 20 and had thought I was going to train National Hunt horses. *"Don't,"* he said and that ended the conversation. Nothing was mentioned about it again until mid August. *"I've had a word with all the owners. They'll all leave their old horses with you - I don't know about yearlings, but they've bought the yard for you on an interest-free loan and I shall be managing Lady MacDonald-Buchanan's Lordship and Egerton Studs so I'll be able to keep an eye on you."* Thus, in the autumn of 1969, I took over Heath House Stables. Despite this silver spoon start it was to be a struggle to get established. All my staff were older than me and most of Newmarket's 33 trainers (today there are 66) thoroughly disapproved of the *'Johnny come lately'*.

Further, most of the owner-breeders' studs were regrettably in the dying embers of their glory days.

Mr Waugh's last runner was at the October meeting in Newmarket. I was not officially due to take over until November 5th. He had already moved out of Heath House to Lordship but came into the yard each day at his regular time. There was a fine drizzle falling, lads were scuttling about and first lot were due to pull out in about 20 minutes. *"Well,"* he said, *"that's it. I'll leave you to it. I wish you well. However understanding they may be, I'm afraid no owner really quite appreciates that, if you are conscientious, every time a trainer runs a horse a little bit of him goes down to the start with it and in the end there is no more of you left to give. I wish you well."*

Mr Waugh lived on in Newmarket for another 30 years and remained active until his late 80s, pursuing his great loves of shooting, fishing and gun dog training. From his home close to the sales, he acted as a spotter for the British Bloodstock Agency and monitored the success and failures of Heath House, its trainer and jockey, George Duffield, both of whom had served their apprenticeship under his unforgiving eye. After *Pivotal* had won the Nunthorpe Stakes Group 1 at York ridden by George Duffield, the old man rang to offer his congratulations. He closed by saying, *"You know, Mark, I don't miss training one bit, but a day like today makes me feel it was all worthwhile. It's nice to think a little bit of your knowledge might linger on in those that follow you. Makes it all worthwhile you know. Well done to you both. Goodnight."*

Just because you are a vet…

MARK JOHNSTON BVMS MRCVS

Kingsley House
Middleham
North Yorkshire DL8 4PH

"**Y**ou used to be a vet, didn't you?" people ask me on a fairly regular basis. I never quite know how to reply. Sometimes I just agree, for easiness, but sometimes I indignantly state that "I am still a vet".

The fact is that I still feel like a vet. I have been training racehorses on a full time basis since 1987 but I still believe that I am entitled to my veterinary qualification and that I probably use it as much, if not more, than many of those that graduated along with me in 1983.

A friend and fellow veterinary surgeon recently put it to me that, in order to address the current shortage of veterinary surgeons in practice and to help fund our veterinary schools, those that leave the profession should be required to pay back the costs of their tuition. He clearly included me amongst those that had left the profession.

I sympathise in some ways with his views, and

Fig 1: The author, racehorse trainer and vet Mark Johnston.

certainly agree that something should be done to try to ensure that more graduates choose practice as a career, but I was a little upset to be grouped together with those that he believed had abandoned the profession.

No doubt there are some who studied alongside me at Glasgow Veterinary School between 1977 and 1983 (it took me a year longer than it should have) who would go further and might suggest that the tuition was wasted on me from the start. I wasn't the best student, by a long way, and I was a member of the infamous little group that usually returned in September for a second shot at the exams. It would be easy to say that I had my mind on other things, like horseracing, but it wouldn't really be true. I was not a good scholar. I had never been able to discipline myself to study and I was very good at finding excuses to do something else. Horseracing was only one of my many diversions.

My first year at vet school was fun but fairly disastrous from an academic point of view. I can't remember how many exams I failed in June but I know that I gave chemistry the double whammy and failed it for the second time in September. That should have meant exclusion from the course - the boot - but somehow, at appeal, I managed to persuade them that I should be given a second chance. I was allowed to repeat a year in which I would study just chemistry and have one last chance to pass the exam.

I decided, or it was decided for me, that living at home in Aberfoyle (25 miles north of Glasgow) had been one distraction too many and, in order to apply myself to the task in hand, I should move into a flat.

Someone suggested that Gordon Lonsdale, a quiet and studious chap in comparison to me, was looking for a new flat and a new flatmate and I should move in with him. I didn't know him very well but, as he had chosen to move to part of an old vicarage in upmarket Blanefield (still 10 miles north of the city and almost halfway to Aberfoyle), it seemed like a good idea.

Gordon was a very organised person, unlike me, and assumed that we would lead organised lives together, sharing tasks around the home. Sadly, I was not for being organised. I was no more capable of applying myself to Gordon's rotas for cleaning and cooking than I was of studying. I had already met Deirdre, who was to become my wife, by then and I usually managed to divert myself to her house on the way home. I could not be relied upon to cook for Gordon when it was my turn or to turn up on time to partake of his offerings. He rapidly tired of my antics and made no secret of the fact that he felt I was abusing the second chance that the vet school had given me. I, on the other hand, was having a ball; all the fun of first year and and only one subject to study.

As the year progressed, Gordon and I came to the conclusion that we were not suited to sharing a flat. We decided to seek alternative accommodation and, having found it, our friendship (if you could even call it a friendship) would have ended there had it not been for a twist of fate. I passed my chemistry in June and progressed to second year. Gordon failed one exam, anatomy I think, and failed it again in September. He joined me again in second year. We had started together in 1977 and we were destined to finish together in June 1983.

I suppose it is likely that I corrupted Gordon Lonsdale but I can assure you that he didn't need much corrupting. Neither of us worked too hard. We got bored easily in lectures and we were regularly seeking alternative attractions. We became well known for our 'trips', which covered the length and breadth of the country and beyond. We would regularly be tempted from the histology laboratory at Garscube by the sight of snow on the Campsie Hills; and we would sneak out to embark on an overnight journey through the worst of winter conditions to Fort William, Inverness, Aviemore or even Thurso. Anything was better than work.

I am sure we are remembered at Glasgow Veterinary School more for these trips than for any academic achievements. We are, no doubt, remembered most of all for one trip in particular which took place in 1982 when we were in our fourth year. Meat inspection was part of the fourth year curriculum and I am sure that Gordon and I were not the only ones who thought there were better things to do. The meat inspection course took place at Glasgow abattoir on the south side of the city and we had to travel there by bus on a Wednesday afternoon. One Wednesday, Gordon and I failed to arrive. A plan had been hatched in a pub along the way and we had decided that Paris would be more fun than meat inspection. A bus took us to the A74(M) motorway and from there on it was the power of the thumb. That trip alone would fill a chapter or two of this book but suffice to say that we made it to Paris, sent postcards to our classmates and returned by Sunday afternoon.

I hope this small extract from a busy, action packed, period in my life will serve to illustrate the type of student that I was. People could be forgiven then for thinking that I was on a hiding to nothing. It is little wonder that many of those that worked hard and towed the line resented my knack of sneaking through by the skin of my teeth. Yet, even then, I believed that I should be a vet and that I had an aptitude for it that was lacking in some of my classmates. I believed, and still do, that you must have a 'feeling' for animals if you are to be a successful veterinary surgeon; and I do not mean in the soppy, sentimental way that some would-be vets would see it today. I think you need to be able to recognise a fit healthy specimen of any species whether it is a chicken or a bull and I believe that, to this day, I could have a good stab at it.

I knew from an early stage, quite some time before I went to vet school, that I wanted to be a racehorse trainer, but that was only a subdivision of my desire to work with animals. I was always particularly interested in those domesticated species which had become specialised, through selective breeding, for a specific task. I loved greyhounds, kept and raced whippets, enjoyed working with cattle, and greatly admired working dogs like Labradors and sheepdogs. But racehorses were always the biggest attraction.

My father bought his first Thoroughbred mare, for 110 guineas, at Doncaster sales when I was about nine years old. Another followed the next year for the exorbitant price of 210 guineas and eventually, when I was 14, my father splashed out on a horse to race over hurdles and put it in training with Paddy Chesmore, who had recently moved to Drymen near Aberfoyle. Paddy died soon afterwards but his wife, Sue, took over the licence, my father was persuaded to buy a steeplechaser, and I was hooked. I went to Sue's stables at weekends, mucked out, swept yards and, occasionally, if I was very lucky, was allowed to ride round the roads.

It was, therefore, decided before I left school that horseracing was to be my chosen career but, despite my father's ownership of a couple of horses, my family had few contacts in the racing business and no real knowledge of the way forward. We decided for ourselves that veterinary medicine must be the most useful subject to study for any aspiring racehorse trainer and this had the added advantage of providing a safe and satisfying fallback career. And so it was, after two attempts and a great deal of heartache, that I was eventually admitted to Glasgow Veterinary School with the principal aim in my head of training racehorses.

My knowledge of horseracing expanded greatly during my time at vet school thanks to numerous summer jobs with trainers, some time seeing equine practice, and Saturday mornings spent riding out for Tom Craig in Dunbar (a 75 mile drive in the early hours to be there for first lot). However, by the time I qualified in 1983, I still lacked the solid connections in the industry that could provide meaningful employment. I had decided that it would be best to find a position as an assistant trainer from which I could launch myself as a trainer in my own right, but finding such employment proved more difficult than I could ever have imagined. I still have a file full of letters that I wrote to trainers throughout Britain and Ireland. The reply was often the same; 'We are quite happy with our current veterinary surgeons'. I would write back explaining again that I was looking for a job as an assistant trainer but to no avail. By September my parents' patience and the bank manager's tolerance were wearing thin, and I had to accept that I should look for a job in practice. That was one of the best decisions of my life.

As any budding equine practitioner will discover, I found myself in the Catch 22 position of needing experience to gain a job in equine practice and needing a job in equine practice to gain experience. I had no choice but to look at mixed practice with a little equine content and I found such a job with Bob Smith at Newtownstewart, Co. Tyrone, Northern Ireland.

That was a great job. Bob taught me an enormous amount and introduced me to some wonderful people who became close friends. Amazingly, he did this in under six months. He remains an owner in my yard to this day.

No doubt I should have stayed in Newtownstewart for longer but ambition was burning within me and I was determined to gain a route into horseracing or, in the short term, into practice with a greater content of horses. I was looking for jobs almost from the time that I arrived in Newtonstewart and I was to continue that policy until I eventually took the plunge and started working for myself.

My second position was in Yarm, Cleveland, where the content of horses increased to about 75% of my workload and that satisfied me for a year before I moved again to Braintree, Essex where all but about 5% of my time was spent with horses.

Throughout this period, I continued to look for an opportunity to enter the racing industry proper. I applied for jobs as assistant trainer, on studs, as a racing manager, and I began to look at stables to rent or buy. I had no idea how I would finance the purchase of a stable but I continued to look and, on occasions, made ridiculous offers on stables that I could never afford.

As with so many things in life, it was a twist of fate that eventually pushed me beyond the point of no return. Early in 1986, I saw an advert in Horse and Hound for a racing yard in Lincolnshire at an asking price of £95,000. As on so many previous occasions, I sent for particulars and thought little more of it. But that evening I happened to be talking to Edward Stenton, whom I had come to know through a mutual interest in the stallion *Scallywag*, and I mentioned that I had sent for particulars of a yard near his home. Edward was in the life assurance business and hence knew most of the mortgage brokers and estate agents in his area. He asked me who was handling the sale and, when I told him it was Mawer, Mason and Bell of Louth, he said he would make enquiries on my behalf.

The next morning, a Saturday, he phoned and told me not to panic but he had made an offer on the property for me. He had discovered that the yard had been repossessed by the mortgage company and he offered them £37,500, the amount outstanding to them, for it. At this stage I hadn't even seen particulars of the property but I immediately agreed to meet Edward there the next day.

The yard was in a sorry state after being empty for two years, and the beach gallops were invisible due to fog, but when Edward asked me if I wanted it or not, I could see that £37,500 was too much of a bargain to miss and I said yes. Deirdre and I set off back towards Essex wondering what we had let ourselves in for with her eagerly reading aloud the estate agent's particulars that we had been given by Edward. I will always remember turning back after about five miles to search for '*the neatly laid out gravel yard*' and finding it under the jungle of grass and weeds.

Nothing much happened concerning the yard in Lincolnshire or our offer over the next few months apart from Edward phoning us occasionally to say that the amount outstanding to the mortgage company had accrued a little interest and the offer would have to be upped a bit. By mid-summer the price had reached £50,000.

We had almost forgotten about the yard in Lincolnshire and we had committed almost all of our £1,000 bank balance to buying tickets for a visit to Canada, when the estate agent phoned to say our offer had been accepted. My career as a trainer was about to begin whether I liked it or not.

Frankly, I didn't quite know what to do first. I had been thinking about it for years but when the chips were down I wasn't sure where to begin. First, I thought I better set about getting a trainer's licence; a racing stable wasn't going to be much good to me without one. I phoned the Jockey Club and asked them to send me the appropriate application forms but the girl who answered the phone wasn't going to let me off so lightly. She insisted on putting me through to the licensing department.

Kevin Dwyer; that was his name. Secretary to the licensing committee. I'll never forget him and probably never really forgive him. I wonder where he is now or if he ever thinks about that conversation like I do. I didn't expect him to start interviewing me over the phone but there was no way out of it once he'd started. "*Just because you're a vet, doesn't mean you can train a horse,*" he said - the little toad. It was like a red rag to a bull but, as I'd just heard a few minutes previously that I'd spent £50,000 I didn't have on a racing stable, there wasn't much I could do about it. I suppose I should

be grateful to him for letting me know from the outset that it wouldn't be plain sailing; he made me work a lot harder at my application, but I was never really able to see it that way.

Just because you're a vet, doesn't mean you can train a horse; I suppose it's a reasonable enough thing to say. Just because you're a jockey, or a head lad, or a trainer's son, for that matter, doesn't mean you can train a horse either. But I firmly believe that, for Jockey Club licensing purposes, handing trainer's licences to vets would be a pretty safe bet. We are unlikely, if the vet school has done any sort of reasonable job on us, to neglect our animals or to bring racing into disrepute. Jockey Club rules may be complicated and sometimes a little illogical but, in terms of effort required to understand them and memorise the important bits, they'd hardly compare with first year chemistry. So, personally, I believe that just because you're a vet does mean you can train a horse. It may not mean you can train it to win but you should have enough savvy to get by without embarrassing the Jockey Club too much.

Anyway, in 1986, at least, the Jockey Club were not guaranteed to see things that way and Kevin Dwyer made that plain to me from the outset. I realised I was going to have to work hard at my application.

I had to find people that the Jockey Club would respect that would vouch for my ability to train horses. Somehow, with a lot of canvassing, I managed to do that and I assembled a nice little collection of supporting letters including one from Major Michael Pope, ex President of the National Trainers' Federation and a man I had never met or spoken to in my life before I embarked on my licensing campaign.

I also had to find at least a dozen people, preferably current racehorse owners, who would say they would send me a horse. My powers of persuasion were better than I had realised and I managed to obtain 20 promises of horses - mostly from clients of the practices I had worked in. Those promises, no doubt, played their part in persuading the licensing committee but, sadly, they were hardly worth the paper they were written on as only one of the 20 actually came up with the goods when the licence was granted. That one was Paul Venner, managing director of Baileys Horse Feeds. He sent four horses and seven years later I repaid him by training a Classic winner, *Mister Baileys*, for him. Several of the other 19 were later to see the light and follow Paul to my yard.

I also had to ensure that the Lincolnshire yard was up to scratch and that it would pass the Jockey Club inspection. In this I knew there would be one major stumbling block. The Jockey Club, rightly or wrongly, probably wrongly, require every trainer to have facilities to gallop horses on grass. In North Somercotes I would only have the beach and I knew they would not grant me a licence unless I could obtain the use of some grass land. I obtained a local Yellow Pages and, turning to the section on Farmers, looked for a neighbour to my new yard that might have some suitable grass land. Luck was with me again. I couldn't help but notice the letters MRCVS after the name of C.D. Dawson, Grainthorpe - less than two miles from Bank End Stables. Cliff Dawson turned out to be a charming man, joint Master of the local hunt and a point-to-point trainer himself. He didn't hesitate to give me a letter to the Jockey Club saying that he would provide grass land on which my horses could gallop. The land was never needed but the Dawsons became close friends and, to this day, a number of my horses spend the winter or recuperate from injuries on their Grainthorpe farm.

So, after a considerable amount of homework and a touch-and-go interview at Portman Square, the licence was granted in February 1987; and I was under starters orders. The rest is fairly well documented history. I started with the obligatory 12 horses but only six and a half were paying fees; the rest having been borrowed to make up the numbers. I trained my first winner in July of that first year and five more in 1988. I then moved to Kingsley House, Middleham, and the string of horses really started to grow. The first Group winner came in 1992 and the first Classic winner two years later. We have turned out more than 100 winners every year since then and I now train 156 horses from my Middleham base and have another 30 'out of training' at Whitcliffe Grange Farm in Ripon.

My veterinary qualification and time spent in practice has been of huge benefit to me in my career as a trainer. For a start, it gave me a unique selling point which, to this day, attracts owners. It taught me to think things through logically and to be willing to, at least, question traditional methods. But, above all, it gave me an understanding of animal health and welfare and helped me to hone that essential 'feeling' for the animals I work with.

My time as a trainer has, in turn, I would argue, made me a better vet, albeit that I am now a vet with a very specialised and narrow field of knowledge. I have forgotten much of that which I learned at vet school but I have replaced it with far more. I firmly believe that, if I was entitled to my membership of the Royal College of Veterinary Surgeons in June 1983, then I am entitled to it now. I am still a vet.

I hope I have also played a major part in showing Kevin Dwyer, the Jockey Club and anyone else that is interested in horseracing that while being a vet doesn't mean you can train a horse, it is the best formal education you can have for the job.

Veterinary surgeon racehorse trainers

PETER CALVER BVMS MRCVS

Whitcliffe Grange Farm
Whitcliffe Lane
Littlethorpe
Ripon
North Yorkshire HG4 3AS

Over the course of the years, there have been several members of the veterinary profession who have become racehorse trainers. In the first year of the new millennium, it would seem that they hold a more prominent position in this field than ever before, with a veterinary surgeon training the winner of the Epsom Derby and the Arc de Triomphe and another member of the profession breaking the record number of winners trained in a season in Ireland, coincidentally the previous record also being held by a vet. It is interesting to ponder on the reasons for the individual's change of direction, from the relatively secure position of a veterinary surgeon in practice to the markedly more hazardous one of a racehorse trainer. Furthermore, to enquire as to the advantages and, possibly disadvantages, of the skills and knowledge acquired by the veterinary surgeon, has its own fascination. I have endeavoured to pursue this from those currently holding licences and also by enquiries about those who are no longer with us, comparing theirs with my own experiences.

Never myself even having had a runner in the Derby, the achievement of John Oxx in training *Sinndar* to win both the Epsom Derby and the Prix de l'Arc de Triomphe I find breathtaking. John Oxx, in fact, trod a well determined path in that he followed his father into the training profession and always regarded his veterinary training as a means of progression to this end and never actually practised. His father had been a very successful trainer on the Curragh and included the President of Ireland among his owners. On graduating, Oxx junior went straight into assisting his father and, in due course in 1979, took over the licence. It seems to have been a very smooth transition and the successful performance of the yard continued without let or hindrance. While the achievements of *Sinndar* must be the pinnacle, he has also trained three Irish classic winners as well as Breeders Cup and Royal Ascot victors. A most charming and modest man, it is difficult to get him to expand on the benefits of his veterinary education to his prowess as a trainer, as all he will allow himself is that it has all been part of his career structure and that he felt he was needed at home.

It would be natural to assume that with an identical upbringing, with the exception of being at different ends of the Curragh, Dermot Weld's career would have been identical. Surprisingly, this is not so and Weld was not intending to take over from his father Charlie either when he went to, or left vet school. He spent some time with Dr Bill Reed at Belmont Park. At that time there would be few who would not agree that Reed was the leading equine orthopaedic surgeon in the world. Weld's ambition was then to follow the same career which did not include training, even though he also had a spell with Tommy Smith in Australia. He had, however, been leading amateur rider in Ireland on three occasions having ridden his first winner at the age of fifteen; and only some eighteen months after graduating he did take over the licence from his father. This was not before he had had a spell in practice and boasts proudly of his success with a case of porcine dystocia after which he claims the client regarded him as a genius. This may have been due to the fact that Weld was keen to get the race meeting at the Curragh and increased the normal dose of oxytocin, causing the sow to farrow with the urgency more commonly associated with rockets departing from Cape Canaveral. On the very first day he held the licence he trained three winners and has now trained more winners in a flat race season than any other Irish trainer, breaking the record held for more than fifty years by Senator Jim Parkinson who, as previously stated, was also a veterinary surgeon. He has also won Grade I races on four continents and has hopes of including Africa at some time but is less confident of the Arctic or Antarctic. He has been champion Irish trainer on three occasions and, as if to demonstrate his strike rate, has trained the most winners in a season on no less than seventeen occasions. He believes his veterinary education to have been of considerable assistance to him, although in his own words he "*trains their minds*". I am not sure that a knowledge of cerebellar and cerebral function are the basis of this expertise.

The other member of the current triumvirate of outstandingly successful trainers who are also members of the Royal College is Mark Johnston (see p 19). It would be fair to say that his progress towards training did not have the well oiled path of our previous subjects. Johnston's only connection with racing was that his father had had horses in training with the Chesmores in Ayrshire, but this was sufficient to spark his ambition to make a career as a racehorse trainer. With no obvious entrée in this field, he and his father decided that by becoming a veterinary surgeon he would gain access to his chosen career; and it was solely with this view that he entered Glasgow Vet School. After the first year, he doubted if either graduation or a smooth transition to trainer was going to occur but, having drawn a blank at finding anyone to take him on as a pupil assistant, he returned to the battle with first year chemistry and with the singular determination which he has constantly demonstrated, did eventually graduate. He was in practice on and off for four years but was continually endeavouring to break into his intended career. He variously spent some time with Charlie Millbanks, an English trainer in France and John Russell, an English trainer in the US. Having ridden out for Tommy Craig while a student, he had experience of training on the seashore and, in 1987, he felt that he must take the bull by the horns and acquired premises in Lincolnshire which included shore gallops. With some opposition from Portman Square and support from Michael Pope, his career was launched from

here, although initially it looked a fairly forlorn cause. One of his (few) clients was instrumental in his realising that improved facilities were essential if he were to match achievement with his ambition.

He transferred to Kingsley House in Middleham which, in the recent past, had had a fairly chequered existence and had been empty for two years. The previous owner had exhausted his football pool winnings and the resident before that, his owners' credulity. From now forward his career developed with meteoric speed and this year, achieved the fastest one thousand winners, a record previously held by no less than Henry Cecil. His successes have included a Two Thousand Guineas winner and also the Saint James Palace Stakes. He pursues his ambition with what can only be described as passion and displays no regard for the sacred cows of tradition so strongly held by many. In the field of diet particularly, he has pursued an entirely fresh approach which he says he started when training racing whippets while a student. He tends to view the benefits of his veterinary studies more in the line of the classical ideas of a university education in the broadening of his faculties rather than the technicalities, but allows that it is a good basis from which to work.

Of those no longer with us, the loss of Tommy Robson was heartfelt by very many. He was associated with racing throughout his entire life. He started as a very successful amateur rider and won the Foxhunters at Cheltenham. He graduated to holding a professional licence, and I think I am right in saying he is the only veterinary surgeon ever to do so. He won the Scottish Grand National both as a rider and trainer but the pinnacle of his training career was probably the victory of *Magic Court* in the Champion Hurdle. He was also particularly adept at picking up backward horses from the big Newmarket yards and transforming them. After a brush with the authorities he was relieved of his licence temporarily and never really got going again. He was private trainer to a South American whose ambitions appeared to exceed his finances, which was a fairly unhappy experience, and had a more rewarding time assisting Barry Hills. He spent the latter part of his career working at the Sales and was retained by the British Bloodstock Agency (BBA). It would be fair to say Tommy never made great inroads into practice but, throughout his life, was always a model and a source of inspiration to many including myself. A man of great charm, I shall never forget his reply to me when I told him I had a problem with a horse I had at the time which had fallen at the second last in his first three races. In his delightful Cumbrian accent, he told me he was unable to help. He knew of no track which did not have a second last fence. The horse went on to win the Grand National.

I never knew Peter Thrale, who combined an extensive equine practice in Epsom with training. Between the wars he trained a large string and included among his patrons the Lords Roseberry and Norfolk as well as Colonel Harry Llewellyn, for whom he trained *Ego* to be placed in the Grand National before the owner went on to even greater prominence as the owner-rider of the great showjumper *Foxhunter*. Thrale was notable as being involved in both practice and training to a considerable extent and being able to perform each task simultaneously. Among the other well known horses he trained were *Three Cheers* and *Kingsmead*. He also has the distinction of being the great uncle of that outstanding steeplechase rider Richard Dunwoody.

Frank Cundell followed his father into the veterinary profession but went straight into the Royal Army Veterinary Corps. He came from an established racing family as his uncle, Leonard, was a trainer. Most of his time was spent in India, where he both rode as an amateur and acted as a stipendiary steward, so we must presume his military duties were not all encompassing. When his uncle retired, Captain Frank Cundell left the service and returned to England to take over the licence and saddled a winner with his very first runner. However, within twelve months, the gathering storm clouds of World War II necessitated his return to the army and he spent most of the duration in Palestine working with pack donkeys. This was probably not such a rich veterinary education as was Colonel Mouse Townsend's period in Burma where he acquired his pre-eminence in the Hobday operation, performing the operation in profusion on mules to silence them and avoid disclosing their presence to the Japanese. After the war Frank returned to train at Aston Tirrold and trained the prolific winner *Crudwell*, which holds the twentieth century record for the number of wins, being victorious on no less than fifty occasions. Another of this remarkable horse's triumphs was to win a four mile 'chase at Birmingham in a shorter time than

that of the two mile 'chase that day added together. This is a remarkable feat when one considers that if they had started the second race as he finished the first he would have won that as well. Frank was a brilliant placer of horses, as is demonstrated by *Crudwell's* record. He also trained *Celtic Cone* to win a Gloucester Hurdle and go on to become an outstanding NH sire. I remember vividly, as a graduate of only a few weeks standing, being dispatched to Aston Tirrold and wondering whether this vastly experienced practitioner would take the logical course of action and tell me to **** off. He was, however, very tolerant, which is further illustrated by the fact that Roddy Armytage and that figure rapidly becoming a legend in his own lifetime, Sir Mark Prescott, were assistants to him. Elsewhere in this publication (p 7), Sir Mark describes some of his experiences while with him. After giving up training Frank acted as a local steward at Newbury and Fontwell.

Recently, the training ranks have been swelled by the inclusion of James Given (see p 222) who worked as a house surgeon and in practice until answering an advertisement to assist Mark Johnston. He professes that his eyes were opened to the possibilities of racing while he was there; until then he had considered it the province of the very wealthy! There are many of us who do not share that view and consider it more as conducted by the very poor. He now occupies premises in Lincolnshire and from them has been turning out a steady stream of winners and it is to be expected the quality will soon match the quantity. In 2001, he sent out *I Cry for You* to win the Cambridgeshire at Newmarket.

While Given had a brief brush with academia, Jeremy Naylor embraced it much more wholeheartedly. He worked initially with the well known Arundel practice. From there he went to Washington State University for three years and thence to the teaching staff of Bristol Veterinary College lecturing in equine physiology and sports medicine. He was also associated with the Martin Pipe juggernaut. An intimate expertise in the fields in which he specialised must obviously be of considerable assistance to the successful training of racehorses. While at Bristol he became involved with John Bolton who then trained on the edge of the Salisbury Plain at Shrewton, an establishment previously associated with the eccentric Richmond Chartres Sturdy. While deeply interested in the conditioning of racing horses, he had never seriously contemplated actually participating until Bolton decided to give up and asked him whether he would like to take over. Having done so he became the most recently licensed vet/trainer.

Returning to Ireland, mention must be made of 'Bunny' Cox. While he is probably better remembered as a rider than as a trainer, he was nevertheless very successful in the latter role. He remained an amateur in the same way as the Maclernon brothers and Ted Walsh who always said they could not afford to become professionals due the prominence of 'bumper' races in Ireland. All were, however, top rank jumping jockeys. Cox is particularly remembered for his deeds at Cheltenham on *Doorknocker* and *Quita Que*. One of his claims to be a figure of folklore is that of his causing the Rules of Racing to be changed when he performed a tracheotomy operation on a horse on the morning of a race which he won. The authorities were of the opinion that the local analgesic acted as an alkaloid stimulant and assisted its performance. It is further rumoured that his surgical expertise was demonstrated in that the only instrument he employed was a penknife. Those days were more relaxed than now.

Kevin Kerr, brother of the legendary bloodstock agent Bertie Kerr, was also a very successful trainer in Ireland, being responsible for *Green Banner*, winner of the Irish Two Thousand Guineas, and also *Irish Chorus*. His brother, among his remarkable talents, included that of remaining constantly at his post from the entry of the first lot into the ring until the very last. Food and drink were brought to him but I always wondered how he coped with the other functions.

Still holding a licence is John Hassett, who trained *Generosa* to win at the Cheltenham Festival, and very nearly reproduced the feat the very next day. He remains in practice as well after 41 years.

Two in England who combined an active practice with training were Donald Underwood and John Hooton. The latter, although retired, is still with us and acted as a racecourse veterinary surgeon after terminating his training career. He told me that he gave up as he only got sent horses that his clients thought it would be cheaper to have with him than have to get him to visit in his veterinary capacity. He did, however, have two doughty jumping performers in *True Cavalier* and *Flosuebarb*. Underwood's best known horses were *True Song*, which had a reasonably successful career as a jumping sire, and *Drum Major*. It would be reasonable to assume that neither of these two gentlemen ever considered themselves as career racehorse trainers and would have given the greater part of their attentions to veterinary surgery.

What is apparent is that only a small proportion would have said to their careers officers that they wanted to be racehorse trainers and, in the most part, got sucked into it. For my part, from the earliest recollection I wanted to be involved in racing, initially as a jockey. The fact that I weighed ten stone seven at the age of ten failed to convince me of the folly of this aspiration. In fact I have held a permit (only allowing one to train one's own horses) for nearly as long as I held a licence. The other salient factor is that all the major players have delegated their veterinary duties. For my part, I was always loath to do this and the analogy of cobblers' children does seem to have a certain relevance. There can be no doubt that the ability to oversee the role of the veterinary surgeon is valuable but it is probable, in the event of marginal decisions having to be made, that a great advantage is held. Most veterinary surgeons are forced to be naturally cautious and sometimes perception of the 'whole picture' enables a better calculated risk to be taken. It has to be said that employing a veterinary surgeon with a particular aptitude for training injury therapy is more expedient than endeavouring to fulfill that role personally. In my own instance, I feel that a knowledge of anatomy has to be beneficial when evaluating conformation. One's undergraduate training, I hope, enables more balanced judgements to be achieved. In the instance of considering blood samples, I hold the basic premise that ancillary aids are to confirm rather than form diagnoses and thus their significance is better evaluated. The benefits of observation are essential to anyone working with animals and these skills should be maximised by both veterinary practice and education.

Both practice and training have their moments of depression and exhilaration, probably more so in the second instance. I am not sure that nanny would ever have looked on training racehorses as a very grown up job compared with veterinary surgery but I, for my part, am extremely grateful that I have had the opportunity to savour both.

Affinity between horse and man

SHARRON MURGATROYD

Becklyn
Bury Road
Kennett
Newmarket
Suffolk CB8 7PP

It can take many years to gain trust and bond with a horse or pony; sadly it takes only minutes, involving a bad experience, for them to become both wary and nervous. One must remember that every horse is an individual with its own personality - it may be boisterous or timid, precocious or shy, but all can be enjoyed if handled the right way. Like people, some are naturally introverted and need nurturing to bring out the best in them. I feel very lucky to have had ponies and horses in my life, forming strong bonds, bringing joy but also anguish.

> "*Affinity is realised with a poignant sigh, between horse and man something one can never buy*".

My understanding and awareness of trust and communication wasn't realised until I was seventeen. I had worked with racehorses for a year and had been quite in awe of the Thoroughbred.

Brother Bronco (*BB*), a light-framed 16 hh black gelding with a broad blaze and white-rimmed eye, was the first of many challenges, being of a highly nervous disposition. This raw, unbroken Irish-bred 4-year-old had come into the yard the previous year. Recently backed, he remained startled at the slightest thing - running back when tied up, wary around the head and ears, alarmed by sudden movement or noises. Although I was one of the youngest members of the team, the Boss considered me capable of the initial quiet handling and patience required with him in his stable.

During the following weeks we built up a rapport - my first actions when entering the stable with a headcollar involved stroking around the head and neck, getting in close, talking reassuringly and then rewarding with a mint - not easy, as the paper rustling caused him to back away. Soon he made the move to come forward, took it from my hand and the bond had started to form. One evening, when entering the yard with grooming kit, to my surprise and delight he appeared to be waiting for me, the only one in a row of 8 with his head over the door. As I approached, a welcoming whicker confirmed it was for me.

Up until now he had been ridden by a more experienced lad. Between the two of us, the horse's wariness was fading and confidence growing so much so that, one morning, my turn had come to ride him - this is where the true sense of affinity was founded. Slowly, many of his idiosyncrasies (i.e. two handlers for mounting, the cat-like dropping of his hindquarters and high head carriage) lessened and he became one of the best rides in the yard. I was now the regular partner in his daily work, a joy to ride, even when we apprehensively took him on 'The Blackpool Run', our regular excursion to the beach for winter exercise.

The teamwork was rewarded when *BB* won a Novice Hurdle at Kelso at the third time of asking. Dismay followed when the owner took out a permit to train and informed us that he intended to take *BB* with him. It was a sad day when I loaded him into the horsebox, although a phone call 3 days later saw him returned. But what emerged from the horsebox was a startled, wary, white-eyed horse with his cat-like walk. Apparently, on his first night away, the rug slipped, he stood on it, panicked and next morning it hung from his neck with most buckles ripped off. For two days he remained, untouchable, unfed and unwatered.

Back to square one! Well, almost... He obviously remembered me as I quietly took the mints from my pocket, he watched but stood tensely at the back of the stable. Soft words were needed to reassure him before I made any move forward. I ate one of the mints myself letting the paper rustle hoping to remind him that this was something he had enjoyed. I wanted him to make the first move but, although after a few seconds he seemed settled, I had to take the initiative.

Talking gently, I took a step towards him, feeling confident he trusted me as he stood his ground. Slowly, palm outstretched, I offered the mint but I could see by the look in his eye he was still unnerved. Undeterred, my next step took me straight to him. He accepted the mint as I stroked his neck and immediately nudged for another one. This was a poignant moment for me and I felt sure he knew he was safe.

I was surprised at his readiness to trust again, especially as I started to notice the physical knocks he had taken over the last few days; a large graze above his white eye was red and sore, rubbed withers where the rug had chafed, numerous abrasions on each leg and, as he let me examine him further, a nasty gash on his offside hip (obviously caused when leaving the other stable). These superficial injuries required attention and he tentatively let me bathe, clean and anoint each whilst loose in the stable -

our mutual bond was restoring.

Two days of confidence-boosting ensued, involving leading him out for a pick of grass (reintroducing the bridle took a little longer than I expected because his eye was swollen), grooming and general handling. The only setback occurred when I left him tied up - something startled him and he pulled back, breaking the piece of string connecting headcollar and shank.

The Boss decided enough progress had been made and it was now time for him to be ridden. *BB* did not object to the pad, exercise sheet and saddle but, as often in the past, he arched his back and aggressively bit at the wall when I did the girth up. An initial ten minute lead around the yard was sufficient time to gauge his reaction before I was legged into the saddle. This posed no problem and four of us left the yard for a quiet walk and trot up a leafy lane just off the main road. Ears pricked and buoyant he was enjoying the hack. Without hesitation, he took the lead heading for home earning the tribute from the Boss's wife that *"he's very happy to be back!"*

After I had untacked, groomed and put the rug back on (for the first time since he had returned) he instinctively followed me to the doorway and nudged for a mint which he took unconditionally. This gave me time to reflect on how bravely he'd overcome adversity and the gift he'd given me in return - an affinity which was almost palpable.

Animal therapy - how it all began

ANNA JOHNSON MCSP SRP GradDipPhys

Langloan
Woodlands Glade
Beaconsfield
Buckinghamshire HP9 1JZ

The Association of Chartered Physiotherapists in Animal Therapy can trace its history back to 1939 when Lord Mountbatten persuaded pioneering animal therapist Sir Charles Strong to treat not only himself, but his polo ponies. At this time, other CSP members were also treating the occasional animal as well as their human patients.

After receiving veterinary permission for this, Sir Charles decided to form a recognised group, but only managed to sow the seeds of the idea. He developed a Transeva machine to use as a treatment aid in the application of rhythmical muscular contractions and was the first chartered physiotherapist to have his results on horses used for a published paper by the veterinary surgeon Dr Fraser in the *Veterinary Record* in 1961. Many chartered physiotherapists have since followed in his footsteps, using his machine among other electrotherapy and manual techniques.

Over the next twenty years, practitioners struggled independently around the UK, individually trying to follow the rules of conduct for the profession of chartered physiotherapists, substituting veterinary surgeon for medical or dental practitioner. They also had to make their own insurance cover arrangements as the CSP believed it was unreasonable to extend the Society's professional liability policy to include veterinary work, due to the small number of physiotherapists working with animals.

One of the leading physiotherapists working in the field during this period was Mary Bromiley, who was able to draw in a number of interested parties during the 1980s. She became concerned when told by a sales person demonstrating electrotherapy equipment that it was possible for anyone to call themselves a veterinary physiotherapist after a day's course using the equipment. She immediately arranged a meeting with Pen Robinson, who was then professional adviser of the CSP, to discuss the situation.

Around this time Pen had been receiving a number of complaints from the Royal College of Veterinary Surgeons (RCVS) who were concerned about some individuals who were styling themselves physiotherapists, and the extent to which electrotherapy apparatus was being used. There were also a number of enquiries from chartered physiotherapists requesting information on their position if they were to treat animals.

In the spring of 1983, the RCVS welcomed a suggestion from the CSP that a committee be appointed to discuss the possibility of accepting physiotherapy as an adjunct to veterinary medicine.

ACPAT was formally inaugurated on 9th March 1985. Members would have to have two years post-qualification experience in the human field, a working knowledge of animal anatomy and two references from practising vets. This was defined as Category A membership.

By law, chartered physiotherapists can only work with veterinary permission to ensure adequate protection to the animal. Permission is gained directly from the vet prior to an appointment with a chartered physiotherapist.

A chartered physiotherapist can be recognised by the letters MCSP (Member of the Chartered Society of Physiotherapists) and SRP (State Registered Physiotherapist). Their credibility can be checked by calling the CSP.

After completion of the 3 year degree in human physiotherapy and 2 years postgraduate clinical experience, candidates who wish to become Category 'A' members of ACPAT can now do an MSc at Potters Bar Royal Veterinary College as well as the 6 months apprenticeship, also obtaining a fully completed practical skill assessment book.

Physiotherapy is not an alternative, but often an essential adjunct to conventional veterinary medicine. A variety of musculoskeletal injuries can be treated successfully which may present themselves as back and neck, soft tissue or peripheral joint problems, often considered 'performance' problems because the horse is performing below its normal ability.

The role of the physiotherapist is to return the equine athlete safely to full function following injury. Accurate diagnosis by the veterinary surgeon and, subsequently, the physiotherapist is essential for effective and efficient treatment. Tissue rebuilds at a genetically predetermined rate - physiotherapy will purely aid the healing to ensure the best possible repair with minimal scarring, tissue elasticity and maximum joint range of movement to give the equine athlete the suppleness and strength to perform at his peak.

Physiotherapy is most appropriate for:

- All soft tissue injuries e.g. joint capsule, muscle lesions, tendon, ligament, myofascial restriction
- Any restriction of movement
- Spinal/cervical spine problems (including atlanto-occipital)
- Undiagnosed lameness i.e. no veterinary findings
- Reduced level of performance, again with no veterinary findings
- Rehabilitation following surgery or a period of box rest or time off

There are many treatments available and all clinicians will use methods and techniques they prefer, typically:

- Manual techniques to perform joint and soft tissue mobilisations and manipulations

- Passive movements and stretches
- Massage
- Reflex work using stretch reflex to stimulate spinal movement
- Rehabilitation programmes
- Electrotherapy

Once referred by the veterinary surgeon, a full assessment is carried out by a chartered equine physiotherapist, to include the following:

i) Initially, a subjective assessment is performed:

- History of present condition
- Past medical history
- Traumas, e.g. falls/being cast
- Medication
- Use of horse (or expected potential use of horse)
- Behaviour when being shod, i.e. difficulty in lifting a certain leg
- If teeth have been checked (i.e. could mimic an upper cervical problem if it is a tooth problem)
- Saddle fitting, has it been fitted to the horse, recently checked, etc

ii) Assessment of the horse when moving:

- **Walk**, straight line in hand, fluid/equal stride
- **Trot**, straight line in hand, foot fall, symmetry, e.g. pelvis
- **5 m circles,** looking for any restriction from atlanto-occipital to tail
- **Rein-back**, ability, stride length, fluid, symmetry, change of weight
- **Square**, symmetry, checking for atrophy/ enlarged joints, areas of swelling
- **Lunged 20 m circles hard/soft**, looking for soundness, fluid, symmetry
- **Ridden**, if necessary, to establish weakness of a limb/how problem occurs. Also, it is useful to see position and competence of rider, can actually be rider causing problem or purely lack of competence by the rider to work the horse and hence they will perceive this as the horse having a problem

iii) **Passive limbs** are assessed for range of movement, crepitus, pain

iv) **Palpation** of horse from atlanto-occipital to tail:

- Muscle spasm
- Thickening/swelling
- Heat
- Pain
- Myofascial trigger points

v) **Spinal movements**:

- Use reflexes to see dorso-ventral lift
- Range of movement
- End of range feel

vi) **Tail**:

- Loose/tight/one way
- See movement of sacrum using tail

Once problems are identified they can be treated appropriately, usually with a combination of manual (hands on) techniques, stretches for the owner to continue with and rehabilitation exercises either ridden, lunged or in hand, as well as electrotherapy.

Electrotherapy is a subject in itself but to briefly summarise the available and most commonly used modalities:

Laser

- Acronym for *'Light amplification by stimulated emission of radiation'*

- Tissues absorb light which activates cell excitation >>>> chemical energy >>>> stimulates cell repair:
  "Starving cells are more photosensitive than well fed ones" (Karn 1987)

Ultrasound

- A mechanical wave form which can enhance the rate of healing and quality of tissue repair. We mainly use the *non-thermal* properties of ultrasound.

Pulsed electromagnetic therapy

- Affects the cell membranes and, therefore, the transport of ions across the membrane. Damaged cells have reduced cell membrane potential and therefore cell function is disturbed. Pulsed electromagnetic therapy restores normal membrane potential and transport of ions.

Muscle stimulation (use of neurotrophic stimulator)

- Trophic electrical stimulation = healthy nerve signals applied electrically to a muscle with the specific purpose of influencing its metabolic pathway and preventing or reversing the changes of atrophy.

TENS - Transcutaneous electrical nerve stimulation

- A pulsed signal is delivered via skin electrodes which blocks pain signals (Pain Gate Theory). Delivery of the frequency can be altered - supposedly above 60 pulses per second, suppresses the transmission of pain. At lower frequency a muscle 'ripple' will occur which will improve local circulatory flow, reduce local spasm and assist in absorption of excess tissue exudate.

Cryotherapy - ice!

- If bleeding occurs after injury, cold promotes immediate vasoconstriction and makes the blood more viscid, hence diminishing flow and thereby reducing the amount of inflammatory exudate around an injured site.

After approximately 5 minutes dilation will occur and may last 15 minutes before being replaced by another episode of vasoconstriction. This alternation of constriction and dilation is called 'Lewis's Hunting Reaction'.

There is histological evidence that cooling can lessen the inflammatory reaction; experiments on pigs investigating the effects of ice on injured ligaments showed less inflammation when ligaments were cooled compared to controls (Farry et al. 1980).

The physiotherapist should work closely with the veterinary clinician in charge of the case; also where appropriate, the farrier/saddler/nutritionist/

trainer and obviously vet to gain the best possible results in returning a horse to competition or its normal work (i.e. hack, driving horse, police horse etc).

With regard to physiotherapists at a competition, the main role is to enhance performance. The majority of the work is prophylactic as, at a competition, especially team championships, the horses are selected for their soundness and good performance.

As the physiotherapist to the British Equestrian Team (attending European and World Championships and Olympic Games), I liaise with the vet/rider/groom and any other member of the support staff, e.g. farrier/nutritionist/saddler, to achieve the optimum potential physical peak of that horse.

My routine work would involve massage, stretches, exercises and muscle stimulation to maintain suppleness and good muscle tone and obviously relieve any pain.

Once in competition, the objective is to keep the horse in the competition and ice and electrotherapy modalities are used routinely to ease the effects of hard or soft ground/galloping/jumping or dressage.

Typical injuries can be cuts/over-reaches/bruised and cut stifles/knees/thorns in knees and obviously muscle strain and fatigue leading to stiffness and pain.

My aim is to maintain an optimum level of suppleness - if I can affect 1 to 5% of the horse's ultimate achievement it will have been worthwhile. It is great to be involved when the teams do well. Obviously, I am not directly responsible, but it is a nice indulgence to think I have helped.

The Chartered Society of Physiotherapists can be contacted by telephoning: +44 (0) 207 242 1941.

Researching the past: archival sources for the history of veterinary medicine

PAMELA HUNTER
38 Raffles House
Brampton Grove
Hendon NW4 4BU

Introduction

In 1997, the Business Archives Council agreed to undertake a three-year survey of historical records relating to veterinary medicine. It had long been recognised that veterinary medicine was one of the more neglected areas of medical history, partly because of the lack of information regarding sources. No one really knew what, or how much, material had survived. The survey, therefore, funded by the Wellcome Trust, aimed to locate and list extant archives dating from earliest times to the present day.

During the course of the survey, a wide range of organisations were contacted: practices, companies, schools, research institutes, zoos, charities, the armed forces, professional associations and government agencies as well as county record offices, museums and libraries. Each was asked to provide details of the types of records it held and their covering dates. Information received, either from questionnaires or visits, was entered onto a database along with a brief history of each organisation. By the time it was handed over to the Wellcome Library in December 2000, the database contained over 600 entries. Together, they do much to reflect the vital and wide-ranging role played by veterinary surgeons and their predecessors in all aspects of British life - in science and research, leisure and education, public health, the development of the colonies and warfare.

Any study of the history of veterinary medicine or the veterinary profession will inevitably involve the horse. Since early times, the horse has played an invaluable part in British life; the horse as transport, taking passengers from A to B, goods to markets, armies into battle; the horse as an industrial tool, in collieries and breweries, on farms, canals and railways; the horse as entertainment or sport. As horses became more valuable, it made sound economic and practical sense for owners to do all they could to preserve their health and strength for as long as possible. Gradually, therefore, a highly skilled profession emerged, able to meet the growing demand for expert care and treatment for horses as well as for a range of other animals. By examining the records left behind, it is possible to find out more about how and why the veterinary profession evolved.

Early history

Some of the earliest surviving records refer to the care of the kings' horses. Medieval and early modern monarchs spent much of their year moving from one royal residence to another, partly for their own comfort and amusement, but also to make their presence felt amongst their subjects and administer their kingdoms more effectively. With them went vast retinues, along with furniture, decorations, clothing, etc, all transported by large numbers of horses. Horses were also necessary for warfare - strong, heavy animals, capable of carrying bulky equipment, supplies and armour-laden men. Monarchs such as John, Edward III and Henry VIII went to great lengths to improve the country's horse stock, importing stallions from overseas and setting up their own studs[1]. Accounts for the Royal

Household give some idea of the amount of money being spent on horses and their upkeep, while occasional, more specific documents have also survived: *'Expenses of the King's horses at Chester in the keeping of Richard Farrier,'* 11 Edw I, *'accounts of William the Farrier, keeper of horses south of Trent'*, 18 and 19 Edw III and *'account of Haniball Zynzan, marshal farrier of the royal stable, for medicines and ointments for the King's horses 1546/47'*[2].

Prior to the emergence of veterinary medicine as a recognised profession, the care of all animals was somewhat haphazard, plagued by superstition and ignorance. When an animal fell ill, its owner could either treat it himself, or call upon the services of a cow-leech, horse-doctor or farrier. Cow-leeches were confined mainly to rural areas and the vast majority had little skill or knowledge. Preserved in county record offices and libraries up and down the country are vast numbers of *'cures'*, *'charms'* and *'spells'*, many of which would have passed down through the generations. Examples include *'a charm for curing cows 1773'*[3] and *'a variety of recipes, charms and spells 1770–96'*[4]. While some *'cures'* show remarkable foresight, others are capable only of prolonging the agony of any beast unfortunate enough to come into contact with them. Many would never have been written down at all, but passed from father to son, from teacher to apprentice, by word of mouth.

Since cow-leeches were generally so ineffectual, and their remedies often well known, most people were accustomed to treating their animals themselves. Remedies can be found, scattered amongst culinary and still room recipes, in the notebooks kept by housekeepers, farmers' wives and householders. Surviving examples include notebooks belonging to Anne Glydd 1656–1700[5], the Countess of Stradbroke c1820[6] and Morgan and Mary Ann James of Haverfordwest c1825–81[7].

While cow-leeches operated mainly in rural areas, the horse-doctor and the farrier were to be found in towns and countryside alike. Although they regarded themselves as superior to the cow-leeches, and talked of practising *'the art of farriery'*, their skills and knowledge were equally dubious, as a glance through a few of the many treatises on horse care which were produced shows. Those who preached sound advice, such as James Clark, whose treatise on *'Prevention of Disease'* was published in 1788, were the exception rather than the rule.

Bleeding was widely regarded as a cure for all ills and there was much talk of miasmas and humours. Like the cow-leeches, horse-doctors and farriers used prescriptions passed down from earlier generations. Surviving examples include *'a good purge for a horse'* c1730[8], a recipe for *'green salve for any green wound in horse or beast'* c1818[9], a cure for *'horse belley hake'* 1800–66[10], and a remedy for *'grease in a horse'* c1914[11].

Concern about the quality of care being given to horses was apparent from early times. As far back as 1356, the Mayor of London was calling upon all farriers within a seven mile radius of the City to form themselves into a Fellowship which would enable them to regulate their trade more effectively. Out of this emerged *The Worshipful Company of Farriers*, granted a Charter in 1674 and raised to Livery Company status in 1692. In an effort to improve standards, the Company decreed that all farriers wishing to work within the seven mile radius had to first serve a seven year apprenticeship then register with the Company. This proved impossible to enforce, although from the 1750s the Company greatly increased the number of prosecutions against unqualified practitioners. Compulsory registration of farriers was not achieved until 1975[12].

Although comparatively little is known of the Company's history over the first three hundred years, virtually all its records having being destroyed in the Great Fire of London (1666), later records contain much useful information. Registers of freemen (1709–1864) and apprentice bindings (1619–1862) give details of individual members while the Court minute books (1718–1962) chart the Company's struggle to regulate its trade and improve standards of care. Additionally, an examination of the registers of freemen clearly illustrates the emergence of the veterinary profession. While in 1800 all the freemen listed described themselves as farriers, with the odd bizarre exception such as a hat maker, by the 1820s a few had taken to calling themselves veterinary surgeons. By the time the RCVS had been awarded its Charter in 1844, virtually every member of the Worshipful Company of Farriers described himself as a veterinary surgeon[13].

Developments in *'the art of farriery'* can also be traced by looking at patents held by the British Library's Science and Reference Service. Many relate to horseshoes and shoeing techniques, and include such examples as William Woodman's *'Bevilled Healed Expanding Shoe'* dating from 1823 and 'Benjamin Rotch's *'flexible elastic horse shoe'* registered in 1816. Others relate to tools, such as *'artificial frogs to be applied to horses' feet, for prevention of contracted hoofs, thrushes and canker'* patented by Edward Coleman in 1800, or *'apparatus for taking the measurement of horses' shoes or hoofs'* registered in 1849 by Richard Hobson. There are patents too for remedies, including one for *'Major's Celebrated British Remedy'* which claimed to remove spavins, ringbones, curbs, splints and other unnatural ossifications and humours from horses in 1855. In 1774, Thomas Johnson patented his *'preparation for staining horses so as to make them match in colour, also for preserving cattle from flies and other insects, and for making marks on animals as cannot be effaced without injury to said animals'*[14].

The development of the veterinary profession

As the veterinary profession developed, some became concerned that too much emphasis was being placed on treating the horse. The eighteenth century had seen the introduction of a number of agricultural innovations and improvements, including the enclosure of land, crop rotation and large-scale drainage schemes, all of which enabled farmers to preserve more of their livestock through the winter months. This, in turn, stimulated an interest in selective breeding and a number of breed societies were formed. Yet the standard of veterinary care remained low and veterinary education, particularly at the Royal Veterinary College (established 1791), still focused on equine medicine. An idea of what was being taught at the RVC and William Dick's school in Edinburgh can be gained by looking at lecture notes taken by students of the time.

The institutions which backed the two veterinary schools - the Odiham Agricultural Society and the Highland and Agricultural Society - had, from the outset, intended that they would produce better educated veterinarians offering a higher standard of care than was hitherto available. Moreover, they intended that this increased knowledge should benefit not only horses but also agricultural livestock. Their feelings were echoed by the Royal Agricultural Society of England, established in 1838, which stated at its first general meeting that it should actively seek *'to take measures for improving the Veterinary Art as applied to Cattle, Sheep and Pigs'*[15].

Pressure to provide improved veterinary care increased during the nineteenth century. An expanding population and increased urbanisation meant that more food had to be produced. In an effort to meet demand, the restrictions on the importation of live animals for food purposes were relaxed in 1842, while the introduction of Free Trade in 1846 allowed them to be imported duty-free. Yet these developments came at a time when the monitoring of livestock was particularly lax. Disease was inevitable and several contagious diseases were officially noted for the first time, including foot-and-mouth disease (1838), pleuropneumonia (1841) and sheep pox (1847)[16]. Alarmed by these developments, and the apparent inability of the emerging veterinary profession to counter them, the Royal Agricultural Society of England in 1842 endowed a Chair in Veterinary Pathology at the Royal Veterinary College, followed in later years by grants to a number of research institutions.

Many of the earliest qualified veterinary surgeons came from farriering backgrounds. Their fathers and grandfathers were smith/farriers and as they qualified, they very often returned home to work at the family forge. Most of the oldest surviving practices grew out of or alongside forges. This relationship can be clearly seen by looking at Census returns, available in reasonable detail from 1841. The 1851 Census for Rackenford, Devon, shows that Michael Rawle (b. 1788) was practising as a *'veterinary surgeon to horses'* at Chapelcourt. Next door there was a smith's shop run by Thomas Matthews (b. 1788), while living next to Thomas was Aaron Matthews (b. 1817), who also described himself as a veterinary surgeon. Similarly, the 1871 Census for Spofforth, Yorkshire, shows that John Sanderson (b. 1819) and his son Joseph (b. 1844 d. 1912) were living and practising together in Castle Street, next door to a forge run by George Bailey. John was known to be practising in Spofforth in 1857, while Joseph Sanderson qualified from the Royal Veterinary College in 1867.

Practices were carefully situated. Until the mid-nineteenth century, the most favourable position would have been on one of the roads leading in or out of a town, close to the business generated by coaching inns and posthorse stables. The practice of Walker, Glanvill and Richards, now based in Hook Norton, originated in Long Compton, a shrewd choice of location, since nineteenth century Long Compton marked the halfway point on the main coaching route from London to Birmingham via Oxford. At one time the area boasted four coaching inns. The arrival of the railways led to a decline in long distance coach travel but in no way diminished a practice's business. Far from reducing the number of horse-drawn vehicles, railways actually increased them, since goods (and people) still had to be conveyed to and from railway stations and markets. Even the railway companies themselves kept horses to collect and deliver goods. Papers recording the maintenance of railway company horses by veterinary surgeons can be found at the Public Record Office[17].

By the time horsedrawn transport had reached its peak in 1902, there were reckoned to be around half a million private carriages and 133,000 public transport vehicles. Additionally, the volume of goods traffic also rose, reaching half a million vehicles by 1902[18]. As the demand for horses grew, prices increased, and people became more inclined to squeeze every last drop of usage out of their animals. At the same time, the roads, many of which were in poor condition, became unbearably crowded. The horses, inevitably, suffered.

Their plight, however, was a visible one, and led directly to the establishment of a number of leading animal welfare charities. By examining the charities' records, particularly their minute books and annual reports, it is possible to chart their development and the measures they took to help animals. The Scottish Society for the Prevention of Cruelty to Animals, for example, formed in Edinburgh in 1839 particularly to improve the condition of the working horse, installed drinking troughs and carried out formal inspections of pit ponies and Highland coaching horses. Within a few years of its foundation, the Society was able to report a marked improvement amongst the horses on the street, and a corresponding rise in the number of unfit horses being sent to the slaughterhouse[19].

Similarly, Our Dumb Friends' League (later the Blue Cross), founded in 1897 to encourage kindness to animals, also worked hard to improve the lot of the working horse. Its annual reports show that it provided trace horses to help pull heavy loads up hills and awarded prizes to responsible drivers and stablemen. The League's Blue Cross Fund opened nine hospitals in France for the treatment of horses during World War One, and maintained a network of ambulances across London and beyond for the removal of injured horses from the roads.

As transport and industry became increasingly mechanised during the twentieth century, the forges that had been so dominant during the nineteenth century inevitably went into decline and virtually disappeared after World War II. By this time, most practices were seeing mainly agricultural animals, and, increasingly, small animals, a shift clearly shown in the day books and ledgers of practices up and down the country. Clues, too, can be detected in other records such as Dangerous Drug Books and order books. The Dangerous Drug Book for one practice shows that in 1968, 69 operations were carried out on dogs. By 1980 this had risen to 210, with a corresponding drop in the surgical treatments carried out in large animals, particularly horses[20]. In recent years, however, with the rise of the 'leisure horse', many practices are now offering equine care once again.

The leisure horse

Horses have played an important role in man's leisure pursuits for centuries. Richard I is believed to have unsuccessfully tried to establish racecourses across the country, while Charles II frequently raced at Newmarket. During the seventeenth century, James VI and I introduced the first recorded Arab stallions into the country in an effort to breed lighter, faster horses[21]. General interest in horseracing increased during the latter half of eighteenth century, culminating in the establishment of several of the classic races including the St Leger (1778), the Oaks (1779), the Derby (1780) and the 2000 Guineas (1807), and the Jockey Club (1752)[22]. With money, pride and reputations at stake, there was renewed interest in breeding. Weatherbys Stud Book first appeared in 1791, while numerous examples of private stud books survive in libraries, estate offices and record offices. Records from the Duke of Hamilton's racing stables during the eighteenth and nineteenth centuries include bills and receipts for medicines, ointments and visits by farriers and veterinary surgeons as well as correspondence relating to the health of the horses and the running of the stables. Seen as a whole, they give a valuable insight into the running of a stable at that time[23].

Advances in veterinary science have also been encouraged and supported by the racing world, which was quick to realise the benefits veterinary science could offer in terms of reducing the occurrence of infertility, abortion, early death and career-ending injuries. In 1943, the Bloodstock Industry Fund was launched by Messrs Tattersalls specially to raise money for the Veterinary Education Trust (now the Animal Health Trust)[24].

Hunting, too, has been popular since early times. During the nineteenth century, hunting increased by 300–400% and by 1900 it was estimated that 200,000 horses were being kept exclusively for hunting[25]. Leicestershire Record Office has records relating to a number of hunts, including a veterinary surgeon's 'hunter account' for the North Athelstone Hunt dating from 1938, which gives details of injuries to horses and hounds as well as the treatments given and their cost. Additionally there are records relating to the Quorn Hunt - bills and receipts from chemists for medicines and liniments and from veterinary surgeons for treatment dating from 1886 to 1980[26]. Further records are to be found within the personal and estate records of keen hunting men.

Conclusion

The history of the relationship between man and horse is a long and varied one. Fortunately, the records that have survived allow us to glimpse this relationship at many different times and in many different guises. These same records can also be used to chart the development of veterinary medicine and the veterinary profession, from the simple remedies of the past to the advanced scientific techniques of today. Although man's dependence on the horse would seem to have lessened, the relationship continues to evolve and flourish, providing much for the historian of the future to look forward to.

References

1. Trew, C.G. (1953) *The Horse Through the Ages*, London. pp 47-50.
2. Public Record Office, Refs: E101/97/2, E101/102/35,36, SP46/1/fo9.
3. Lancashire Record Office, Ref: DDX 611/4/8.
4. Gloucestershire Record Office, Ref: P218 MI 1.
5. British Library, Department of Manuscripts, Ref: Add Ms 45196.
6. University of Hull Library, Ref: DDHO/19/5.
7. National Library of Wales, Ref: NLW Ms 22747A.
8. Manchester Central Library Local Studies Unit, Ref: L1/46/9.
9. East Riding Record Office, Ref: DDX 128/17.
10. Birmingham City Archives, Ref: Ms 2091/1.
11. Gloucestershire Record Office, Ref: D6843/2.
12. Prince, L.B. (1980) *The Farrier and his Craft: The History of the Worshipful Company of Farriers*, J.A. Allen, London. pp 1-3.
13. Manuscripts Department, Guildhall Library.
14. British Library Science Reference Service - Refs: 4841, 4025, 2370, 12900, 387, 1060.

15. Records for RASE held at Rural History Centre, Reading University.

16. Scott Wilson, J.A. (1939) *The History of the RASE 1839-1939*, London.

17. Public Record Office, Refs: RAIL, AN35.

18. Thompson, F.M.L. (1970) *Victorian England: the Horse Drawn Society: An Inaugural Lecture*, London. pp 12-14.

19. SSPCA Annual Report (1938) '*A Short Historical Account of the Growth and Work of the Society Since its Inception in 1839*'. pp 1-23.

20. BAC/Wellcome Survey entry no 450.

21. Trew, C.G. (1953) *The Horse Through the Ages*, London. pp 47-58.

22. Moss, M. (2000) *The RCVS and the Development of the Veterinary Profession*. p 3.

23. National Register of Archives, Scotland, Ref: NRA(S) 2177.

24. Onslow, R. (1992) *A History of the Animal Health Trust*.

25. Thompson, F.M.L. (1970) *Victorian England: the Horse Drawn Society: An Inaugural Lecture*, London. p 15.

26. Leicestershire Record Office, Refs: DE/3031/142/142-143, DE/3030/1-511.

Useful contacts

For those contemplating research, the following addresses may be of interest.

National Register of Archives: Administered and maintained by the Historic Manuscripts Commission, the NRA holds copies of lists of records submitted both by record offices and private custodians. The indexes are available for consultation at Quality Court, Quality Court, Chancery Lane, London WC2A 1HP or on-line at www.hmc.gov.uk The National Register of Archives (Scotland), administered by HM General Register House, Edinburgh provides a similar service.

Public Record Office: Records created by government with many relevant to the veterinary profession and the emergence of state involvement in the provision of veterinary care. Most records are subject to minimum closure periods of thirty years. Catalogues can be consulted at the PRO, Ruskin Avenue, Kew, Richmond TW9 4DU or on-line at www.pro.gov.uk

Other repositories: National Libraries, museums, university libraries and county record offices hold a rich variety of records. Details of repositories can be found in 'Record Repositories in Great Britain', edited by Ian Mortimer for The Royal Commission on Historical Manuscripts.

Wellcome Library for the History and Understanding of Medicine: Books, manuscripts, deposited papers etc relating to the history of medicine. The Business Archives Council databases on records relating to the pharmaceutical industry and veterinary medicine are held here. Address: 183 Euston Road, London NW1 2BE. Website: www.wellcome.ac.uk

The role of osteopathy in the treatment of the horse

JULIA BROOKS DO(Hons), CHRIS COLLES* BVetMed PhD MRCVS FWCF and ANTHONY PUSEY DO FECert

Awbrook Lodge
Lewes Road
Haywards Heath
West Sussex RH17 7TB

*Avonvale Veterinary Group
Ratley Lodge
Ratley, Banbury
Oxon

History of osteopathy

Osteopathy originated in the United States with a Kansas frontier doctor, Andrew Taylor Still (Fig 1). These were times when heroic medicine, with its bloodletting and purgatives, was the norm. Like Mark Twain, Dr Still was a thinker and a reformer. He spent much time in the study of anatomy, examining the cadavers from Indian burial grounds. Finally, he *"flung to the breeze the banner of osteopathy"*, basing this on *"the perfect works of the creator"*. He was silenced by his peers and even ejected from the church. His experience was to mirror that of the great William Harvey, whose theories on blood circulation caused him to fall *"mightily in practize, and that t'was beleeved by the vulgar that he was crack-brained"*[1]. Like Harvey, Still's recognition was to come later. News of his success spread and, in 1892, the first school was chartered in Kirksville, Missouri. His statue now stands in the Town Square.

In the early 1900s, a group of American trained osteopaths came to practice in Great Britain and, in 1917, the British School of Osteopathy was founded. Today, a 4 year undergraduate training leads to a BSc in Osteopathic Medicine. The title 'osteopath' is protected and can be used only by those with appropriate training, currently numbering around 3000.

What is osteopathy?

Dr Still envisaged a system of the healing art, which placed chief emphasis on the structural integrity of the body as being most important in the wellbeing of the organism. In other words, if the structure is fine then the function will be fine. His difficulty was proving his point, at a time when knowledge of neurophysiology and neuroanatomy was in its infancy. His anatomical studies led him to look at the problems he encountered in terms of 'subluxations', blockage of blood vessels and traction or pressure on nerves. However, as imaging techniques have improved, it has become clear that another explanation is required, as clinicians frequently encounter cases of pain, loss of performance, alteration in function etc where no such pathology can be identified.

It was with the work of the early physiologists Magendie, Bernard and Sherrington that new ideas about the way the nervous system worked began to develop. A concept evolved of the nervous system as an information network constantly changing and adapting in response to sensory information from

Fig 1: Andrew Taylor Still (1828-1917) father of osteopathy, with author, Mark Twain (left).

the body and the environment. This knowledge allowed a move away from early ideas of pressure and subluxation towards a concept of 'somatic dysfunction'. This, to use a computer analogy, is more a problem with the software, rather than the hardware problem presenting as tissue pathology[15]. To extend the analogy, osteopathy may be thought of as a form of reprogramming.

Neurophysiological basis of osteopathy

The concept of somatic dysfunction is fundamental to the osteopathic approach. It describes a problem within the neural network. Somewhere in the course of entering information from the environment and body, processing the information in the central nervous system, and then generating a motor response, something has gone wrong. Clinically, this may present as a horse with a range of symptoms such as stiffness, loss of performance and poor coordination, but where no pathological process can be identified. Osteopathic treatment is directed at muscles, fascia and joints and, by changing the signals from these structures into the neural network, the way sensory information is processed and a motor response generated in the central nervous system is influenced.

The way these neural networks behave is the key to understanding somatic dysfunction and the role of osteopathy in the treatment of neuromusculoskeletal problems.

Generating a motor response

In order to interact successfully with the environment, the body is constantly making small adjustments that are largely unconscious. The basic motor pattern is one of mutual inhibition of flexor/extensor neurones, providing a balance between agonist and antagonist[9], as in the arm stretching out to lift a pint of beer (Fig 2). If this local reflex arc was the whole story, however, movement would resemble that of a robot in a low budget movie, and much beer would be wasted. Fortunately, sensory nerves relay a constant stream of information about, for example, the grip on the glass and its position in relation to the lips. As these nerves enter the spinal cord, they send off sprays of ascending and descending collateral fibres. These,

Fig 2: A simple movement requires not only flexor/extensor activity but also a myriad of postural adjustments.

in turn, synapse on interneurones that have many connections within the spinal cord segment, with other spinal segments up and down the cord and with tract cells up to the brain stem. The result is a network of neurones processing information from the body and the environment, which generate flexible patterns of motor activity (sometimes referred to as central pattern generators or CPGs)

In this way, a pattern can be generated which smoothly lifts the glass to the lips while making automatic adjustments in the other limbs and the midline postural (axial) muscles throughout the spine, so preventing the weight of the outstretched limb from tipping the drinker off the barstool. Alongside this skeletal motor activity, autonomic changes such as alterations in blood flow are incorporated into this response to provide the necessary humeral environment.

It is the variety of interconnections, determined by the cellular and synaptic properties of the neurone, together with the balance of excitation and inhibition, which allow the CPGs to generate many different motor patterns.

Another feature of these patterns is that they are built up over time by a process of learning and development. The tentative gyration of the learner golfer becomes a confident, automatic swing to produce the perfect drive after many hours of practice - theoretically! A process of chemical changes, new connections and 'fast tracking' result in a consistent and reproducible pattern of motor activity.

The performance of the horse in all disciplines will be determined by the effectiveness and appropriateness of the motor responses generated in the central nervous system. This, in turn, will depend on the quantity and quality of incoming (sensory) information.

Processing of sensory information

The ability to generate rapid and appropriate patterns of motor responses to environmental demands depends on sensory information. Imagine trying to operate a radio-controlled car from the next room. It is still possible to generate a motor response, but without sensory cues the result will be somewhat haphazard if not disastrous. For the horse, these sensory cues come from an appreciation of the current position of the body (proprioception) and conditions prevailing in the outside world (exteroception). Both inputs will significantly modify the activity in the CPGs.

Proprioception

Proprioceptive information from muscle spindles and Golgi tendon organs provides continual feedback on the position and activity of the body. Significantly, the greatest concentration of proprioceptors is found in the upper cervical spine[2], which is a vulnerable area when a horse falls. Joint stiffness and muscle spasm following an injury will reduce or alter proprioceptive feedback from this level. This affects the ability of motor pattern generators throughout the spinal cord to modify activity in response to alterations in body position. This may produce changes ranging from subtle gait disorders to ataxia.

A well known professor of neuroanatomy at the New England College of Osteopathic Medicine and Surgery wakes up his students with a practical demonstration of the importance of musculoskeletal input on coordination and balance (Fig 3). The students stand confidently by processing information from the eyes, the labyrinth of the ear and the proprioceptors of the musculoskeletal system. He then gets his students standing on the non-dominant leg (usually the left in right-handers). Wavering in the ranks begins. He has narrowed the point of contact with the floor and reduced a source of sensory input from the other foot. The students then close their eyes. The wavering becomes hazardous, with the foot, the limb and the postural muscles making

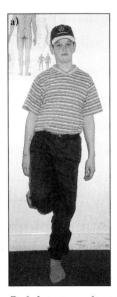 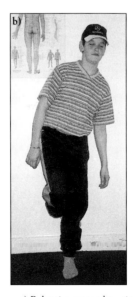 

Fig 3: Importance of proprioception in balance. a) Balancing on one leg using information from eyes, labyrinth and proprioceptors of the joints and muscles of the body. b) Eyes closed. Balance becomes difficult as information from the eyes is lost. c) Neck fixed in sidebend. Upper cervical muscles are now fixed in length, and proprioceptors which rely on subtle changes in length to monitor position, can no longer provide adequate information on position in space. Balance is impossible operating on labyrinth alone.

increasingly unrefined adjustments, because of the now incomplete information. If any are left standing by this time, he delivers the *coup de grâce*. By tipping the head on one side, the neck is held rigid and the all-important proprioceptors in the muscles of the top of the neck are no longer free to monitor position in space from changes in muscle length. Information from the labyrinth alone is insufficient to maintain balance and the students fall. This must be very satisfying for any lecturer, although history does not relate the level of his indemnity insurance.

Clinically, these effects can be observed during movement of the horse with upper cervical stiffness. There is often an impression that all 4 limbs are moving independently and, in turning, there is a lack of fluidity and an element of uncertainty in the placement of the feet. This may not result in overt symptoms, but it seems logical to assume that it will affect the horse's potential for achievement and leave the horse more susceptible to acute injury.

Exteroception

While body orientation is monitored by proprioceptors, environmental information is provided by exteroceptors. These modify patterns of neural activity in order to initiate an appropriate response, which may be anything from an awareness of a horse nuzzling your jacket to a sharp withdrawal as he sinks his teeth into your arm. Exteroceptors are continually sampling external conditions either by precise localising receptors of the A-afferent system, such as those responding to fine touch (the nuzzling), or by the more primitive, poorly localised, pain (nociceptive) pathways of the B-afferent system (the bite).

In a clinical setting, it is the effects of the B-afferent system that are commonly encountered. A painful stimulus from, for example, a joint strain or laceration, will be conveyed to the spinal cord from the periphery by the small calibre fibres of the B-afferent system (A-δ and C fibres). From here, it will pass to the brain to register pain, stimulate motor neurones in the ventral horn resulting in paravertebral and peripheral muscle spasm[5] and stimulate sympathetic activity in the lateral horn, causing reduced blood flow to the skin[13]. The result is a perception of pain which will be felt by the horse, muscle spasm which may be felt on palpation and reduced cutaneous blood flow which may be imaged using thermographic techniques.

However, to avoid a constant state of discomfort, a control mechanism exists at the level of the spinal cord. This is mediated both by the A-afferent input of discriminatory touch and proprioception, and by descending inhibitory pathways (opioid peptides of the periaquaductal grey and serotonin of the raphae nuclei). A-afferents are largely inhibitory and create a 'gate' for nociceptive (potentially painful) stimuli. This is well illustrated as you rub your arm frantically (A-afferent stimulation) to ease the pain in the region of the teeth marks (B-afferent). It is the balance between these two systems which determines the activity of the interneurones and the sensory, motor and autonomic responses they generate (Fig 4).

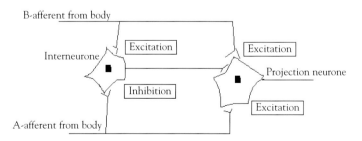

Fig 4: Modulation of signal output in the spinal cord to control transmission of pain. Whether the projection neurone transmits a sensation of pain or not depends on the balance between A-afferents (inhibits the interneurone) and B-afferents (excites the interneurone). If A-afferent input is reduced, as in, for example, decreased activity of joint position receptors around a stiff joint, this will favour transmission of pain sensation from the projection neurone.

This balance can be affected in a number of ways

- A-afferent activity will be reduced from joint receptors when there is restricted movement (a stiff joint). This means that the inhibitory effects of the A-afferents on the interneurones are reduced, and any B-afferent activity which might, under normal circumstances, have been blocked (inhibited) now registers as pain. In effect, pain may exist as a result of joint stiffness rather than direct stimulation of peripheral pain receptors. Physical treatments to increase mobility will restore the A-afferent input and reinstate the gating effect.
- B-afferent activity if intense or prolonged, causes changes in the chemistry and even structure of the interneurones[7]. These can be traced for 3–7 days after only 45 minutes of fairly intense nociceptive stimulation[8]. These changes reduce the threshold for interneurone firing in a process called 'wind-up' or facilitation. In this state, they are supersensitive not only to afferent input, but also to internal network activity within the spinal cord. This is the mechanism underlying hyperalgesia.

Facilitation is interesting for 2 reasons. Firstly, the peripheral endings of sensory nerves feeding into these sensitised interneurone pools actually produce pro-inflammatory neuropeptides themselves[10]. Anyone subjected to stiff shirt collars in their school days will identify with this. The mild rubbing of the collar on the neck at the beginning of the day gives way later to a feeling of intense discomfort and a red ring of inflammation along the collar line. Here, the initial contact is not sufficient to break the skin, or even register as pain. However, with time, the neuronal pool becomes sensitised and the nerve endings release inflammatory neuropeptides which are really quite inappropriate for the severity of the stimulus. This might explain some of those cases of recurrent and apparently inexplicable joint and soft tissue swellings. They may respond to cortisone injections, which reduce inflammation at the local site. However, if sensitisation of the central interneurone pool remains, the inflammation will return.

The second point of interest is that even when afferent activity has been blocked by sectioning the dorsal (sensory) root, a sensation of pain and the autonomic and motor responses may still be present, driven by the output of these sensitised interneurones. This is of clinical significance, as it shows that pain may persist long after the original injury has resolved. Even when pain is no longer felt, the neuronal pool remains highly sensitive to nociceptive inputs which will produce a pain response inappropriate for the magnitude of the stimulus. It is worth noting that this population of interneurones will be vulnerable to inputs not only on a segmental level, but also from a distance, given the span of nociceptive fibres over several segments.

These mechanisms may explain some of the 'non-specific' lameness and back pain which tends to recur for no apparent reason. In these cases, although a diagnosis may not be possible in terms of tissue pathology as defined by x-ray, scintigraphy or nerve blocking, the motor patterns generated by the facilitated segment may be detected. Gait disturbance may be observed and muscle spasm, joint stiffness and tissue texture changes may be appreciated by palpation and passive motion testing. One diagnostic tool which accords well with this concept of somatic dysfunction is thermography. In the 'normal' horse, a reproducible thermographic pattern is observed, which reflects cutaneous blood flow[4]. Where facilitated segments exist, sympathetic activity in the lateral horn acts on the blood vessel walls to drive blood away from the surface, giving a distinctive segmental strip of cooling. In addition to these local changes, the pattern may be disrupted throughout the length of the spine, giving a visual record of information processing dysfunction in terms of inappropriate autonomic response. There is accumulating evidence that the activity of the sympathetic nervous system has an important role in the maintenance of pain states[6].

This integration of sensory input occurs at many different levels and incorporates many different systems. There have been significant advances in our understanding of the way these neuronal networks influence neuroendocrine immune control[14] and the viscera[12] in response to external and internal conditions. These too will influence the way a horse responds to the environment and, therefore, a history which includes information such as previous operations and illnesses may be a useful consideration alongside gait analysis and levels of facilitation.

What does osteopathy do?

From this review of some aspects of the interconnections of the nervous system, a number of the concepts key to the osteopathic approach may be understood.

Osteopathic treatment aims to reverse changes in these areas of somatic dysfunction. Essentially, most techniques are directed towards restoring movement to stiff joints to optimise maintenance of postural position, active movements, passive movements and provide the homeostatic conditions in which these activities may be carried out. The treatment may take a number of forms, including soft tissue, articulatory, mobilisation and functional techniques, the mechanics of which have been described elsewhere[3].

Soft tissue and articulatory techniques stretch the skin, fascia and muscles to improve pliability of and nutrition to the periarticular tissues. They also allow the joints to move in a full range. This increases afferent input from the muscles and joint structures which act to inhibit or 'gate' incoming pain signals.

Mobilisation techniques involve taking a joint with poor mobility to the point of maximum resistance (the restrictive barrier) and pushing through this barrier with a short amplitude, high velocity thrust which may be accompanied by a cavitation sound or 'pop'. This will result in immediate relaxation of the muscles and improved mobility. This is because a sudden increase of mechanoreceptor activity stimulates the large fibre A-afferent system, thereby inhibiting the interneurone pool and blocking the B-afferent (pain) signals.

A useful approach in long-standing, complex cases is functional technique. This uses the idea of 'ease' and 'bind'. A normal joint will reach a point, usually at the middle of its range of movement, where there is minimum tension on the capsular ligaments and the overlying muscles. This is the point of 'ease' (Fig 5). Any movement away from the point will increase tension or 'bind'. This information will be relayed to the central nervous system, where it is processed to map joint position

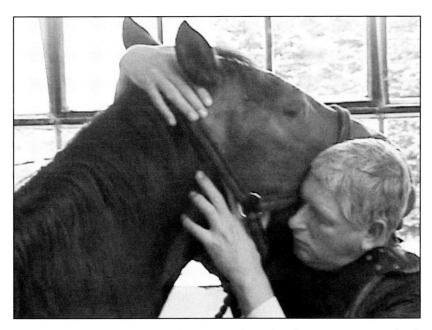

Fig 5: Assessment of neck in a sedated horse: Moving the upper cervical spine through movement ranges to isolate the point of 'ease' in the sedated horse (photograph courtesy of A. Wahba).

and to generate an appropriate pattern of motor activity. Where the normal relationship between the joint structures has been disturbed, this point of ease will be offset and afferent information from that joint will be changed at rest and for any given movement. Difficulties arise with imposing new reference points on well-established networks and the joint is less able to perform appropriately or to coordinate movement with other joints.

This new abnormal point may be isolated by testing each range of movement (flexion/extension, sidebending, rotation, translocation from side to side, traction/compression). With the joint held in this position there is minimum tension and, therefore, minimum afferent input into the spinal cord. This appears to reduce conflicting information

entering the network and allows the old pattern to reassert itself. This pattern is preferred by the system as, over time, neuronal connections have been created that fire more readily to generate a learned response (as outlined in the discussion on motor patterning). However, it is of interest that there is a clinically challenging subgroup of 4–6-year-old horses that develop clinical symptoms as they begin to work or as the work becomes more demanding. It is tempting to conjecture that some form of perinatal injury may have occurred, which has prevented the normal patterns from developing. They frequently undergo more treatment, and require careful rehabilitation.

This overview of certain aspects of neurophysiology shows that it is helpful in some

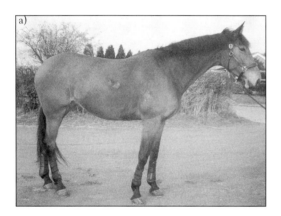
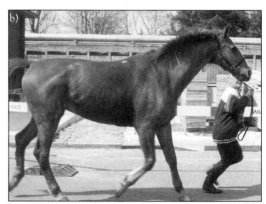
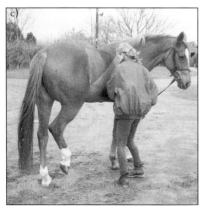
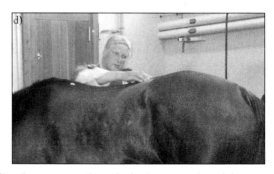

Fig 6: Osteopathy in practice. a) Standing examination: looking for symmetry of muscle development and weightbearing. b) Active movements: looking for fluidity of movement as it is transmitted from the head backwards along the spine. c) Observation of the short turn: neck dysfunction will result in the early replacement of the foot or a rotation element to the sidebend as movement starts going through the region of discomfort. d) Palpation: running the hands down the paravertebral muscles to locate areas of muscle spasm.

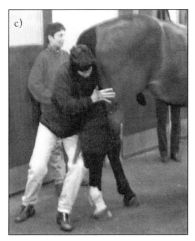

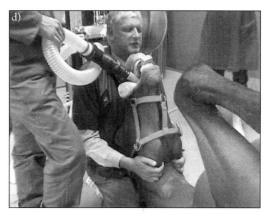

Fig 7: Treatment. a) Functional technique on occipito-atlantal joint complex (photograph by Sheila Gutteridge). b) Functional technique on atlantal-axial joint complex (photograph by Sheila Gutteridge). c) Inhibitory technique on muscles of pelvis and femoral region. d) It is sometimes only possible to appreciate and treat joint stiffness under general anaesthesia (photograph courtesy of A. Wahba).

cases to look at musculoskeletal problems in terms of somatic dysfunction rather than tissue pathology. It is also necessary to look at the function of the spine and limbs as a whole, rather than just at the symptomatic level. Osteopathy offers a complementary approach in the treatment of recurrent 'non-specific' lameness and back pain.

Osteopathy in practice

Once pathology has been excluded and a veterinary referral is made, the process of making an osteopathic diagnosis begins. This diagnosis will be in terms of somatic dysfunction, i.e. how the component parts of the horse work together as a whole and how different areas of dysfunction will contribute towards the presenting problem.

The case history is the starting point. This will give an idea of the type of work the horse is expected to do and the level which it is expected to attain. It will also highlight any past injuries and illnesses that the horse may have suffered. Further questioning may reveal idiosyncrasies in behaviour or movement which, while noticed by the owner, had not interfered with performance sufficiently to be a cause for concern. When considering the history and the function of the horse as a whole, these subtle disturbances in motor function may, in fact, be early warning signals for the coming crisis.

Examination begins by looking at the standing horse for muscle development and distribution of weight through all 4 limbs (Fig 6a). Foot placement and wear on the shoes are also significant in the process of locating areas of dysfunction.

In movement, it is balance and fluidity with which movement is transmitted from head to tail, alongside stride length and foot placement which give further clues (Fig 6b). How the horse copes with long turns and short turns help to identify problems with lateral flexibility (Fig 6c).

Observation will give an impression of how the horse moves as a whole and indicate which areas are functioning poorly. Looking at individual joint movements is also useful. Running the hands down the paravertebral muscles from the occiput back to the tail, areas of muscle spasm and tissue texture changes can be felt (Fig 6d). Moving the joints through the relevant ranges will identify those that are stiff.

Diagnosis requires consideration of past injuries, the way the horse moves overall and dysfunction in specific areas. Initially, it will be a working hypothesis. Where problems have been present for some time, the horse will have had to develop patterns of posture and movement in order to work round poorly functioning areas, and there may be involvement at several levels.

For this reason, treatment may also have to be at several levels (Fig 7). It is useful in these cases to sedate the horse. Like the effect of a couple of large sherries when visiting the mother-in-law, it makes the horse less concerned with its environment and more able to relax. This is particularly helpful when using functional techniques, which monitor subtle changes in joint position.

In a small number of cases[11], the problem may be so ingrained and widespread that a general anaesthetic may be needed to facilitate assessment and treatment. The anaesthetic is light, the horses are in good health and the risks of the procedure are therefore minimal. By this means, assessment of individual joint complexes can be made throughout the spine. It is remarkable how often gross dysfunction of these complexes can be detected under general anaesthetic, which previously had been very effectively concealed by the body's capacity for setting up compensatory mechanisms.

It is hoped that this brief overview shows the potential for osteopathy in a complementary role alongside veterinary science in the treatment of neuromusculoskeletal problems in the horse.

References

1. Aubrey, J. [b.1626 d.1697] (2000) *Brief Lives*, Penguin, London

2. Bakker, D.A. and Richmond, F.J.R. (1982) Muscle spindle complexes in muscles around upper cervical vertebra in the cat. *J. Neurophysiol.* **48**, 62-64.

3. Brooks, J. and Pusey, A. (1999) Osteopathy works for animals too. Part 3: Treatment. *Osteopathy Today* **4**, 14-15.

4. Colles, C., Holah, G. and Pusey, A. (1994) Thermal imaging as an aid to the diagnosis of back pain in the horse. In: *Proceedings of the 6th European Congress of Thermography.*

5. He, X. *et al.* (1988) Acute inflammation of the knee joint in the cat alters responses of flexor motoneurones to leg movements. *J. Neurophysiol.* **59**, 326-340.

6. Kidd, B., Cruwys, S., Mapp, P. and Blake, D.R. (1992) Role of sympathetic nervous system in chronic joint pain and inflammation. *Ann. Rheum. Dis.* **51**, 1188-1191.

7. Mantyh, P.W. *et al.* (1995) Receptor endocytosis and dendrite reshaping in spinal neurones after somatosensory reshaping. *Science* **268**, 1629-1632.

8. Patterson, M.M. and Wurster, R.D. (1997) Neurophysiologic system: integration and disintegration. In: *Foundations of Osteopathic Medicine*, Ed: R.C. Ward, Williams and Wilkins, Baltimore. pp 137-151

9. Pearson, K. and Gordon, J. (2000) Locomotion. In: *Principles of Neuroscience*, 4th edn., Eds: E. Kendel, J. Schwartz

and T. Jessel, McGraw-Hill Co., USA. p 744.

10. Pernow, B. (1983) Substance P. *Pharmacol. Rev.* **35**, 85-141.

11. Pusey, A., Colles, C. and Brooks, J. (1995) Osteopathic treatment of horses - a retrospective study. *Br. Osteo. J.* **16**, 30-32.

12. Sato, A. (1992) Reflex modulation of visceral functions by somatic afferent activity. In: *The Central Connection: Somatovisceral/Viscerosomatic Interaction*, Eds: M.M. Patterson and J.N. Howell, American Academy of Osteopathy, Indianapolis. pp 53-73.

13. Sato, A. and Schmidt, R.F. (1973) Somatosympathetic reflexes: afferent fibres, central pathways, discharge characteristics. *Physiol. Rev.* **53**, 916-947.

14. Willard, F.H. (1992) Introduction. In: *Proceedings of the International Symposium on Nociception and the Neuroendocrine-Immune Connection.*

15. Williams, N. (1997) Managing back pain in general practice - is osteopathy the new paradigm? *Br. J Gen. Prac.* **47**, 653-655.

Acupuncture in the horse

DIETRICH GRAF von **SCHWEINITZ BSc DVM MRCVS**

Equine Veterinary Clinic
Greyfriars Farm, Puttenham
Guildford
Surrey GU3 1AG

Introduction

My first exposure to acupuncture in the horse came in 1981 while still a student at the University of Georgia's Veterinary School. Here, I observed Janet Steiss (now a professor at the Tuskegee University) conducting an acupuncture clinical trial on horses with chronic lameness, from either laminitis or navicular disease. This was published and the results, on the one hand, could be regarded as encouraging, while on the other, were statistically insignificant[18]. Janet highlighted the difficulties in conducting controlled clinical trials in equine acupuncture by reviewing her work at the 1999 Congress of the International Veterinary Acupuncture Society (IVAS) in Lexington, Kentucky.

Two years later, in my first job as a veterinary surgeon, came my first personal experience with the related therapy *Shiatsu* (acupressure), which came about as the result of a severe kick to my hip from a horse. The spinal shock rendered me unconscious for a short while and I was taken by ambulance to the local hospital where I had an examination, including x-rays. I was discharged with a pair of crutches, free of any fracture but with a firm swelling the size of a grapefruit on the side of my right hip and unable to take any weight on my right leg due to pain.

Additionally, I was given a course of strong pain medication (Darvaset) plus anti-inflammatory drugs and instructed to stay confined to bed for 3 weeks with my leg elevated with frequent ice compresses for the first few days.

The inconveniences included the fact that I was due to start a locum position for a solo equine practice in five days and I dreaded the notion of disappointing a practitioner looking forward to his much-needed holiday.

One of my equine clients at the time, Michael Farley, held acupressure clinics at the local medical centre and, fortunately, was able to fit me in two days after the injury. In spite of medication, it was still very painful to be upright and excruciating to put the slightest weight on my right leg. Michael applied firm thumb pressure for about two minutes at each of approximately 12 to 15 points, many of which were located around and on the swelling, and as he predicted the local sensation was one of exquisite piercing pain slowly fading to a vague numbness.

After about 30 minutes and a few expletives, my right hip felt numb and I was able to stand on it and walk, albeit with quite a limp. On the next day I returned limping but without crutches and only half a 'grapefruit' on my hip. He repeated the acupressure treatment, mobilised the limb and instructed me to go out and jog about three miles. In spite of my protests, I did as instructed and found the swelling completely resolved and I was able to ambulate almost normally. I went away very impressed to act as locum as planned; and Michael went on to become well known in the US as a human and equine acupressure therapist and for developing a range of equine orthotics including the Farley Boot.

A few months later I attended an introductory equine acupuncture workshop hosted by the University of Pennsylvania's Large Animal Veterinary Teaching Hospital at the New Bolton

Center. This was a practical demonstration on the anatomical location of some of the more important acupuncture points and treatment techniques in diagnosing and treating back pain.

Professor Alan Klide and clinician, Martin Benson of the University, had recently conducted controlled trials on treating chronic low back pain in performance horses with acupuncture[11]. At the time, I had a perfect experimental 'guinea pig' at home; *Patton*, my Thoroughbred hunter gelding, in his late teens, who had acquired a chronically stiff and stilted low back and pelvic action over the past few years. He also had collapsed heels and flat soles and was frequently slightly lame due to foot soreness. While this lameness would resolve when put on butazolidin, the low back and pelvic stiffness did not respond.

When I practised locating the appropriate acupuncture points for low back and pelvic pain on *Patton*, I was amazed by how much local muscular spasm and evidence of pain could be elicited by simple digital pressure on very discrete locations. I excitedly punctured five very tender acupuncture points (Bladder 25 and 26, and animal Bai Hui at the lumbosacral site) with ordinary hypodermic needles (21 gauge x 1.5 inch) and injected 2 ml of vitamin B12 solution into each point (a technique popular in the US, referred to as aquapuncture).

Three days later, I was astounded to see him turn out into the paddock after his night in the stall with a youthful and exuberant gallop and series of playful bucks which I hadn't seen from him for many years. This rejuvenation extended to being ridden, where suddenly I could feel a looseness in his lower back and an impulsion coming from his hindlimbs; he was obviously enjoying feeling so well and the ride was wonderful. This effect faded out over the course of two or three weeks, but it was reinstated each time I retreated him.

I became increasingly aware of two quite separate categories of pain, one responsive and the other unresponsive to nonsteroidal anti-inflammatory drugs (NSAIDs), the latter responding to a physical and natural medicine. I also noted a strong connection between the acupuncture-controlled pain and behavioural adjustment.

Acupuncture origins

The origins of acupuncture lie in prehistoric times and may have originated in cultures outside China. Evidence for this recently came to light with the investigations of the largely preserved frozen corpse of the 'Ice Man, Oetzi', who has been dated to approximately 5500 years. Oetzi has clearly identifiable dark stained points on his skin independently confirmed by several acupuncturists as classically described Bladder channel points at sites along his arthritic lumbar spine. He has other clearly marked classical acupuncture points on his legs and around his arthritic ankle[21]. It is not certain that Southern Alpine man, in that era, had access to Chinese medicine practices, assuming these had already been developed in China at that time.

The earliest written records of acupuncture are usually credited as originating from the Han dynasty in China around 3000 years ago. The Chinese *Nei Jing* texts from about 300–100 BC and the *Nan Jing* from the first century are regarded as the most important written documents from the historical context.

These works described their observations and theories of anatomy, physiology, pathology and treatments that included acupuncture and moxibustion (heat treatment by burning mugwort). They marked the genesis of medicine as distinct from religion (demonology) in China and focused on symptoms as somatic rather than supernatural[1]. During this period, the emphasis on environmental factors causing disease had largely replaced the more primitive notions of demons and spirits inflicting disease. The main threats to health were seen as excesses of the environmental forces (*Yi qi*) of wind, cold, damp and heat entering a body deficient in its defence forces (*Wei qi*). The theories incorporated their already long-standing universal principles of *yin-yang* (opposites) and the concept of five phases (correspondences with the elements of fire, earth, metal, water, and wood) which are still taught as integral parts of traditional Chinese medicine (TCM). There was also recognition of the importance of balance and interaction with the environment.

At that time, the human body's internal anatomy was described as composed of 11 organs: the five solid (*yin*) organs of the heart, liver, spleen, lungs and kidney, and six hollow (*yang*) organs of the

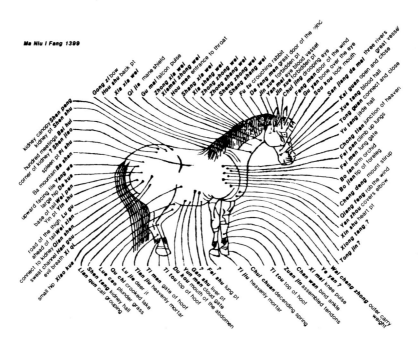

Fig 1: 14th Century Chinese equine acupuncture chart (reprinted with permission from Mosby).

gallbladder, stomach, small intestine, large intestine, bladder and the 'triple burner' (made up of the pleural and peritoneal cavities). A 6th solid organ, the 'heart governor' (translated as the pericardium, but without literal relation), was added later, perhaps as much for symmetry as functional need. These organs were all linked to particular muscular and dermal distributions identified as 12 regular channels (*Jing-luo*) with 135 acupuncture points located bilaterally. The dorsal and ventral midline 'extraordinary' channels with another 25 points were also described.

The physician would use the system of correspondences between the organs and their superficial channels firstly to diagnose the condition of the organs by palpation at certain points over the body and of the pulse in the radial and other arteries and secondly to treat any imbalances or illness using acupoints which could influence their activity. It is now known that viscero-somatic reflexes account for many of these observations.

The Systematic Classic of Acupuncture and Moxibustion, 282 AD, described 649 (300 bilateral) acupuncture points on the 14 channels with treatment indications, needle depth and retention time for each, and introduced the emphasis on disease prevention. Around this time, Chinese medicine was making its way into other Asian countries including Korea, Vietnam and Japan. Sun Si-miao, a famous Chinese physician at the turn of the seventh century (Tang dynasty) refined and modernised the format of acupuncture charts which described more 'extraordinary' channels and systematised the measurement system for the accurate location of acupuncture points still used today. He also described the use of painful points (*a-shi* points) in conditions which modern Western medicine has recently described as myofascial trigger points in myofascial pain syndrome (MPS). *'Puncture wherever there is tenderness'* (Sun Si-miao).

Veterinary acupuncture history

The first known veterinary acupuncture book was written in the 6th century and described the treatment of more than 40 diseases in farm animals including the horse[2]. More than 30 veterinary acupuncture books were written during the period of the Sui dynasty from 590–617 AD. The most famous veterinary acupuncture text came from 1608, which remained very influential in China to the present day.

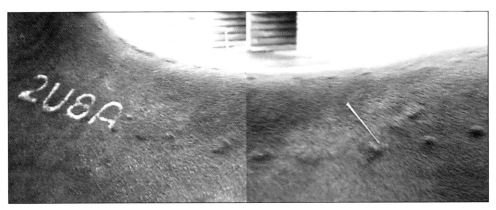

Fig 2: Author's case treated for myofascial pain syndrome. Pilomoter response along the bladder and governing vessel channels during acupuncture; the focal spots of raised hair occur precisely at the acupuncture point locations along the thoracolumbar distribution of points described in Figures 5 and 6, and develop along numerous vertebral segments some distance away from the nearest points actually needled. This demonstrates segmental and non-segmental somato-sympathetic reflexes from the needle response (see also Fig 4).

Interestingly, none of the traditional Chinese veterinary acupuncture texts described acupuncture channels in animals as were described in man and only up to 167 acupuncture points in the horse with location and specific action were documented (Fig 1). Some of these points were named the same as the human equivalent with the same indication but were located quite differently anatomically, e.g. the organ association points. The Chinese names of acupuncture points give information regarding point location and indication, requiring knowledge of Chinese idioms. Learning these by their translated Western name or a simple numeric code is too problematic for most.

In the 1970s, due mainly to demand from Western veterinarians, animal acupuncture charts were devised with the 14 main channels and acupuncture points transposed from the human charts which allows for the use of the international alphanumeric acupoint designation agreed by the World Health Organisation.

Traditional Chinese veterinary medicine (TCVM) also never described the system of five-phase treatment in animals. This requires the precise location of the five command points (i.e. a 'wood' point, 'fire' point, etc) for each of the 12 regular channels which in man occur from the elbows and knees distally. Due to the anatomical variation between man and animals, their transposition becomes very contentious, especially in the horse, with only one digit compared to man's five.

Veterinarians have experienced excellent results using this transpositional system and it most definitely facilitated the teaching of acupuncture in the West, but it has led to many disputes about the validity and specificity of animal acupuncture points as well as the issue of adopting the human channels system. It has also demonstrated the flexibility and ability of acupuncture to undergo further development and modern Western veterinarians have brought many other useful innovations into the practice.

A significant practical problem is that of reporting and documenting acupuncture treatments in order to provide information which can be tried and tested independently. Most Western veterinary acupuncturists will be familiar with the transpositional system, where each point is identified with an alphanumeric code relating to its position along the particular channel. For example, BL 20 refers to the 20th point along the bladder channel, which is regarded as the association point for the spleen (SP) channel. It is located in the last intercostal space in man and is transposed to the 17th (last) intercostal space in horses along the border between the *longissimus* and *iliocostalis* muscles.

This point is, however, recognised as the large intestine (LI) association point in the traditional Chinese equine acupuncture charts. At least in this instance, the indications for the LI and SP association points are very similar, but in other cases there are genuinely significant discrepancies. Allen Schoen discusses this controversy in his book when introducing the section on large animal acupuncture where he decided to include chapters detailing both systems[16].

In 1974, following a trip to China, a group of predominantly American veterinarians formed the *International Veterinary Acupuncture Society* (IVAS) to host annual international conferences, regular training courses leading to certification in veterinary acupuncture, and advanced TCM acupuncture and herbology courses. IVAS now has a worldwide membership and their courses are held in several countries each year. The *Austrian Veterinary Acupuncture Society* and Veterinary College in Vienna hosted a very successful 26th IVAS Congress 2000 and focused on science in acupuncture.

I was delighted to be included as one of the speakers and enjoyed meeting veterinarians from around the world who have made important contributions to the greater understanding of the effects of acupuncture. The veterinary school in Vienna has a long tradition in investigating veterinary acupuncture, going back to 1833.

The Association of British Veterinary Acupuncturists (ABVA) was founded in 1987, with Jill Hewson as Secretary, the late Robert Allpress as Treasurer and John Nicol, a former president of BEVA, who led as President of the ABVA until 1998. The ABVA has grown to approximately 100 members and holds 2 meetings annually, including a spring meeting in conjunction with the annual BSAVA congress and an autumn meeting held in conjunction with the British Medical Acupuncture Society.

We (in the ABVA) have run the IVAS training course in England since 1997 and now have approximately 45 members who have become certified and another approximately 40 veterinarians enrolled in the current course being held at the Bristol Veterinary School's teaching hospital. The requirements for IVAS certification includes attendance at all four of the four day modules, 40 hours of seeing acupuncture practice with certified members, a detailed case report and passing a written and practical examination.

Traditional theories, their interpretations and debates

A detailed discussion of the traditional Chinese medicine (TCM) theories is beyond the scope of this chapter. However, it may be helpful to consider a fundamental aspect of TCM presentation in the West to understand the debates which occur both within the acupuncture community at large and with the conventional medical world. The popular Western discussion centres on the notion of *Qi* as '*energy*' or '*life force*' circulating with a metaphysical form of blood through a system of meridians or channels. This 'energy flow in meridians' cannot be measured or discovered in terms of medical science and therefore the entire basis for acupuncture becomes untenable in Western medicine.

This interpretation leads to some TCM schools teaching that acupuncture can be understood only by accepting a belief system of a metaphysical nature based on Taoism, with other schools teaching TCM as a system of paradigms which gives guidelines to the selection of an appropriate therapy, and other schools (particularly Western medical) dismissing all TCM principals. But this energetics story does not accurately reflect TCM and the more realistic translations put it much closer to 'real medicine'!

In China, there is no gulf between the modern medical approach and the use and study of acupuncture. Many Western-manufactured TCM advocates see medical research as an anathema and insult to acupuncture which, they argue, is proven by virtue of the test of time. Unlike the situation in veterinary medicine, Western 'energetics' TCM schools in the UK and some other countries train and certify non-medical lay people to practice on human subjects. They feel under threat by the medical community, which argues that acupuncture should only be practised by the medically trained. They also often feel they are the true defenders of acupuncture as they have not been 'contaminated' by Western science. Many veterinary TCM enthusiasts have bought into the energetics story and teach it as the 'alternative' rather than the 'complementary' view of health. This approach can only help keep acupuncture at the fringe of medicine.

To help explain the translation dilemmas I approached a well-known TCM expert and teacher, D.E. Kendall OMD PhD, who wrote:

"As a practitioner serving the public's needs, there is a moral obligation to always search for the truth in what you are doing. To just say

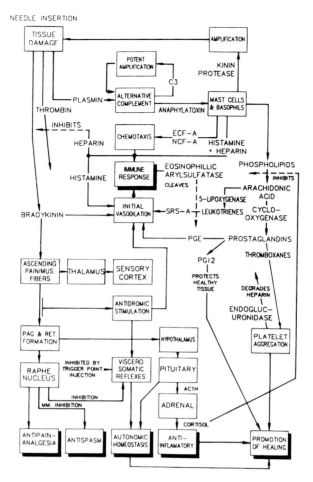

Fig 3: D. E. Kendall's simplified block diagram illustrating the physiological interactions involved in needle stimulation to produce the beneficial responses to acupuncture (published in the American Journal of Acupuncture[9]*).*

acupuncture works on energy, without any explanation of it, is not doing the public any service. After the Chinese started doing research into how acupuncture works, it became obvious that the mechanisms do not involve mysterious energy, but involve extremely complex physiological mechanisms that are explainable by Western terms. This research is still continuing... As for the Chinese word 'qi', any Chinese school kid can tell you that it fundamentally means air. However, air contains a vital element, that we now know is oxygen. This vital air qi is needed for most bodily function and is critical to activating nutrients (ying) and defensive substances (wei). The Chinese language is highly sensitive in terms of context. For this reason, many early and present translations are flawed. Besides, one cannot translate TCM without knowing something about TCM and something about physiology. Chinese use simplified writing conventions when the context is understood to be known by the reader. Consequently, it is a practice in Chinese writing to use 'qi' to mean vital air, but since it is needed to activate bodily processes, especially nutrients and defensive substances as well as substances of vitality (shenjing), the character 'qi' is sometimes substituted for all four of the items. Hence, if the reader understands the context of either the sentence, paragraph, or chapter, then the correct meaning can be discerned. So qi can

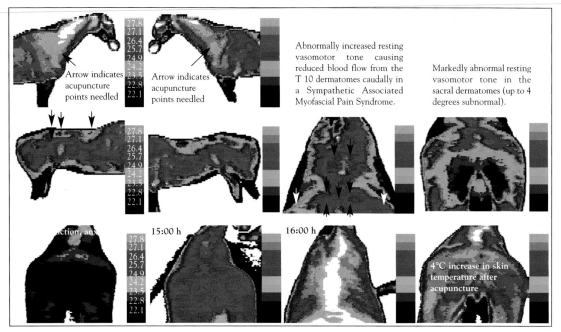

Arrow indicates acupuncture points needled

Arrow indicates acupuncture points needled

Abnormally increased resting vasomotor tone causing reduced blood flow from the T 10 dermatomes caudally in a Sympathetic Associated Myofascial Pain Syndrome.

Markedly abnormal resting vasomotor tone in the sacral dermatomes (up to 4 degrees subnormal).

...ction, anx...

15:00 h

16:00 h

4°C increase in skin temperature after acupuncture

Fig 4: Acupuncture: LI 16; BL 18, 25, 26; GB 28; Bai Hui (arrows). Initially increased sympathetic tone due to needle anxiety in this individual (lower left). Progressive normalisation of the abnormal vasomotor tone over a 3 hour period (below right, 16.00); restores homeostasis in autonomic function via somato-sympathetic reflexes (first documented thermographically in horses by the author).

mean vital air, or it can collectively refer to nutrients, defensive substances, vitality substances and vital air. Qi can also mean function. So you can have a condition of qi stagnation, *which can refer to impaired dispersement of nutrients by the liver, or it can mean impaired blood delivered vital substances to an area or internal organ. As far as qi xu, this can mean a deficiency in any of the vital substances, it can mean impaired lung function and, since qi is used to indicate function, it can also mean functional impairment of an internal organ. The critical point is, one has to understand the context in which these terms are used. Without this crucial test there is no way to understand correctly how to translate TCM.'*

(Personal communication)

The other fundamental translation debate concerns the notion of meridians instead of distribution and collateral vessels (of the vascular system) representing the *jing-luo.* D.E. Kendall

explains that in the *Nei Jing* great emphasis is placed on classifying the vascular circuits in terms of deeper, transitional, longitudinal, collateral and fine vessels. Confirming this fact is the importance placed in TCM on the palpation of the pulses detected in the arteries at 11 specific areas on the body, including over the radial and carotid arteries. Acupuncture points were placed where finer branches of a specific distribution vessel supplied the superficial regions.

The idea of meridians appears to come about from several factors, including the superficial lines drawn up linking certain acupuncture point distributions, the phenomenon of propagated sensation along the particular pathways reported by strong responders to acupuncture, and experiments demonstrating lower skin electrical resistance along these pathways. Birch and Felt also give very detailed and carefully analysed accounts of these and other interpretation dilemmas in their book, *Understanding Acupuncture.* Clearly, once TCM is expressed in a competent and physiologically aware manner, it offers a great deal of medically valid insights into health maintenance; and a great deal

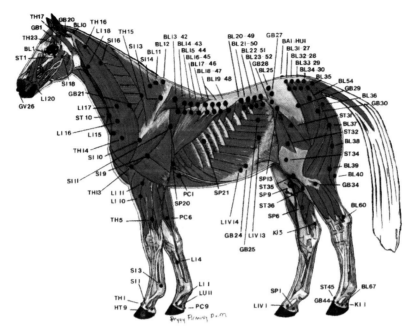

Fig 5: Transpositional equine acupuncture chart.

Acupuncture in modern medicine

Anatomical and histological examinations of acupuncture points have demonstrated important features, which help explain their unique nature. The most significant element involves the nervous system in the form of free nerve endings, neurovascular bundles perforating the superficial fascia, sympathetic fibres of the local vessel, muscle spindles and tendon organs. Neurophysiological studies demonstrate that acupuncture stimulates A-delta and C nociceptive fibres along with mechanoreceptors which elicit complex segmental spinal and central reflexes that initiates a descending control. Segmental spinal effects involve inhibitory enkephalinergic responses while centrally there is a release of beta-endorphin and a descending serotonergic and adrenergic response. The analgesia produced by acupuncture can be blocked by naloxone and also by local anaesthesia of the acupuncture point.

Autonomic nervous system responses from

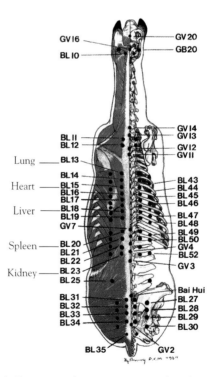

Fig 6: Transpositional equine acupuncture chart. Some of the organ 'association points' are labelled; note the correlation to segmental visceral location and innervation. Compare to the distribution of the pilomotor response shown in Figure 2.

acupuncture occur via somato-sympathetic and somato-visceral reflexes[3,8,17]. A-delta visceral and somatic fibres have a similar distribution in the dorsal grey matter and tract of Lissauer in the dorsolateral funiculus; and visceral and somatic inputs also converge in the spinothalamic tract. These afferents can induce antidromic activation of each other, giving rise to the phenomenon of **referred pain**. This provides for a mechanism of autonomic modulation by acupuncture stimulation. The author has demonstrated this phenomenon in horses with chronic segmental vasomotor disturbance by thermographic studies before and after acupuncture. Acupuncture resulted in the normalisation of vasomotor tone which is under sympathetic/autonomic control[5] (Fig 4).

Local immune and inflammatory defence reactions are activated by needle stimulation through histamine, bradykinin and other inflammatory mediators and the complement system. The neuro-humoral and other physiological responses to acupuncture are illustrated in Figure 3.

Certainly, there is a great deal more scientific research required to understand fully the effects of acupuncture and to determine the most effective acupuncture technique for any particular problem. There are, however, many inherent problems in the scientific evaluation of acupuncture, particularly in the application of the randomised control trials. Traditional acupuncture requires individualised treatments, even within a group of patients sharing the same condition, and there is a valid point to be taken by the fact that each individual has a unique response and adaptation to any particular disease.

Controlled trials require standardised treatments, which means the use of precisely the same points for each patient at each treatment. This is referred to as 'cookbook acupuncture' and is regarded as inferior by most acupuncturists. The author agrees with this and will always treat even the same patient using different acupuncture point combinations in follow-up treatments based upon the acupuncture assessment at each occasion. Many other issues including differentiating sham acupuncture from placebo effects are discussed in detail by Lewith and Vincent[10] and by Jaggar[7]. An additional problem confronting any research including acupuncture research in the horse is the problem of adequate sample size and adequate funding.

Chronic pain problems

Acupuncture is best known for its use in treating pain. Perhaps it is taken for granted that the veterinary surgeon would have a clear understanding on the subject of pain and pain relief, and what could be more fundamental than providing relief from pain? However, I was shocked at the inadequacy of my working knowledge on the subject since undertaking a detailed review of pain research, and noting how little of it was/is taught in primary and secondary veterinary education. Clearly, the level of knowledge determines the level of competence and hopefully all of us wish to be competent in pain recognition and management! The following is a brief outline of some important elements of pain mechanisms taken from *The Pain Series*, published by The Lancet. If you find much of that highlighted in italics unfamiliar ground, then you may agree that much more attention should be given to this subject. Understanding these concepts also forms the basis for understanding the mechanisms of acupuncture.

The CNS mechanisms that control the perception of a noxious stimulus include: *afferent integration in spinal cord, upstream processes and downstream modulation from the brain*[14].

Nociception
- Detection of tissue damage transmitted up A-delta and C fibres
- May be biased by the 'inflammatory soup'
- NSAIDs modify the 'inflammatory soup'
- Blocked by local and regional anaesthesia
- CNS downstream modulation

Perception of pain
- From nociception
- From lesions in the peripheral or central nervous system
- May be in the absence of nociception
- *Intensity of chronic pain may bear no relation to the extent of tissue injury or other quantifiable pathology*

Central sensitisation effects
- Enlargement of the area where stimulus will activate neurons

- Increased response to stimulus
- Lowered threshold to input
- From changes in function, chemistry and structure of neurons (*neural plasticity*)

Symptoms of neuropathic pain
- Persistent or paroxysmal
- Shooting, lancinating, or burning
- May depend on *sympathetic nerve activity* (Sympathetic Associated Pain Syndrome) (Fig 4)
- Stimulus-independent paresthesias (spontaneous A fibre activity) and *hyperaesthesia* (abnormal sensitivity to sensory stimuli)
- Stimulus-evoked *hyperalgesia* (extreme sensitivity to painful stimuli): mechanical, thermal
- *Allodynia* (pain from non-noxious stimulus): can occur in absence of ongoing tissue damage or previous injury, *e.g. low back pain*, *headache*, *myofascial pain syndrome and complex regional pain syndrome*

Findings from diverse studies have indicated that activity in axons located in the lumbar sympathetic chains contribute to the activation of spinal pain pathways and to *low back pain*. These findings from nocireceptive neurons serving lumbar paraspinal tissues suggest that low back pain may be exacerbated by activity in both efferent and afferent fibres located in the lumbar sympathetic chain, the efferent actions being mediated indirectly through sympathetic-sensory interactions in somatic and/or visceral tissues[4]. This is why I believe a great deal can be learned by thermographic scanning of horses with suspected back pain, or indeed any cases of a pain-driven performance problem. The information gained portrays the physiological state of the sympathetic nervous system in vasomotor regulation. I have found a very high correlation in the presence of persistent segmental vasoconstriction and vasomotor asymmetry in chronic back pain cases as has been demonstrated in thermography studies in humans[6].

I have also documented thermographically the effective normalisation of vasomotor function from acupuncture in many horses with these faults (Fig 4)[5]. Another phenomenon that graphically illustrates the somato-sympathetic reflexes and verifies the specific location of certain acupoints is the pilomotor response occurring in some horses during acupuncture. Compare the case illustrated in Figure 2, demonstrating this reaction, with the acupuncture charts from P. Fleming's '*Equine Atlas of Acupuncture Loci*' (Figs 5 and 6).

Finally, *myofascial trigger points* (MTrP), which give rise to *myofascial pain syndrome* (MPS), deserve special mention. These are defined as highly localised and hyperirritable foci within a palpable taut band of muscle with focal tenderness, a local twitch response from stimulation, and a referred pain zone elicited by compression[20]. A 71% degree of correspondence between the location of MTrPs (always in the endplate zone) and traditional acupuncture points in man has been reported, along with the treatment recommendation of trigger point injections or dry needling[15]. This subject, more than any other, provides the introduction and a large focus for most Western medical acupuncture training courses. It is, equally, an excellent starting point for any veterinary medical acupuncture training. In my opinion, most performance horses (as most people) suffer a varying degree of MPS and the successful identification and treatment of the affected muscles will relieve the pain and enhance performance.

The prerequisite for identifying MTrPs and practising acupuncture is a thorough and careful palpation technique. The systematic examination of approximately 100 acupuncture (motor) points bilaterally in the horse provides the most important information for the selection of appropriate points to treat. Chartered physiotherapists are trained to recognise and treat these sites by other means, including acupressure, stretch and myofascial releases and electrostimulation. Equine practitioners, without acupuncture exposure, can learn from them the palpation skills required in locating these sites.

Equine acupuncture practice

Many Western veterinarians find it easiest to start practising acupuncture using fine gauge hypodermic needles to inject a solution (1–10 ml) such as normal saline, vitamins (especially B12), mild irritants, local anaesthetics and steroids. This can be an effective way to relieve tender myofascial trigger points and is perhaps the easiest introduction to the practice of acupuncture.

Practitioners shy of the word acupuncture and TCM concepts may prefer to describe this as trigger point needling or intramuscular stimulation (IMS), for which there is relatively widespread acceptance in western medicine. Many defenders of the traditional theories of acupuncture also insist on differentiating this practice from acupuncture. It is fair to say that this is the most simplistic level of performing acupuncture and does not reflect the skills and knowledge required to practice acupuncture across the full range of medicine. The tools used may vary between practitioners and, in addition to using hypodermics, include traditional acupuncture needles of differing lengths, electroacupuncture units, lasers, moxa and implants, e.g. gold beads, catgut suture or skin staples.

Physical examination techniques include the palpation findings of a large group of '*diagnostic points*'. These occur mainly along the face, neck, back, thorax, abdomen and hindquarters and includes the '*back shu*' and '*alarm*' or '*recruitment*' acupoints. The examiner notes the underlying muscular tone and whether any pain is demonstrated by either light or deep pressure applied to each of the acupoints. Painful points indicate either a local problem or a referred pain problem occurring either segmentally or along the channel distribution of either somatic or viscero-somatic origin. Additional signs, such as a local muscular twitch response, sustained muscular fasciculation or muscular spasm indicates a suspect myofascial trigger point response. The nature of the horse, in terms of its underlying anxiety, fear, or other psychological status, is taken into account and can obviously affect palpation findings, so skill is required in the examination approach. TCM recognises that excesses or deficiencies in an individual's 'spirit' insults the health and is an important element in the overall assessment and treatment.

The skilled practitioner can apply acupuncture to virtually any disease. Once one recognises that acupuncture primarily promotes and restores the body's own neuro-humoral adaptive systems, then one can apply it to any condition where these homeostatic mechanisms are impaired. In some conditions it can be the sole treatment, in particular chronic syndromes that have a poor response to conventional therapies and where there is a significant risk from undesirable side effects to long-term medication.

For example, consider the case of a 15-year-old Arabian gelding referred to me with chronic obstructive pulmonary disease (COPD) who lived outside permanently, had become refractory to oral clenbuterol medication and was exercise intolerant. On my first examination, his resting respiratory rate was 42 and he had all the hallmarks of chronic advanced COPD. Tenderness was detected at acupoints recognised as reflecting (referring) lung pathology (located segmentally relative to the chest's innervation). These were acupunctured with Chinese acupuncture needles, along with distal limb points like the 'Master Point' for the chest, Pericardium 6. Within 15 minutes of leaving these needles *in situ*, the respiratory rate fell to 22. He was receiving no therapy other than the same strict dust management as before and, on the next visit a fortnight later, he was reported as markedly improved. His respiratory rate was recorded as 24 and during acupuncture treatment it reduced to 12. He was put back into light ridden exercise, treated once more after three weeks, and has had no recurrence of COPD symptoms for over 18 months since his last treatment.

In many other cases, acupuncture is best used in conjunction with conventional therapy and other physical therapies. Acupuncture treatments can be successfully applied to chronic musculoskeletal pain and to neurological, dermatological, reproductive, respiratory, digestive, ophthalmological and behavioural disorders. Not only are there a large number of empirical acupoints described in the literature for most of the common chronic conditions in equine practice ('cookbook acupuncture'), but there are also physical examination techniques and TCM paradigms that help determine the acupuncturist's selection of acupoints.

In my experience acupuncture practice enables one to:

- Gain further useful information on the condition of the horse
- Develop a holistic examination procedure
- Aid identifying pain and dysfunction in poor performance syndromes
- Develop a handle on cases where conventional diagnostics are often without useful findings
- Demonstrate that the great majority of horses with acquired training resistances and bad

behaviour suffer painful conditions
- Provide a very effective complementary therapy based on provoking and fostering the natural adaptation and homeostatic mechanisms
- Provide clients wishing to avoid (e.g. under competition rules) or minimise the use of drugs; an optional alternative therapy with negligible risk of side effects.

It is unfortunate, in my opinion, that many Western acupuncturists prefer to relate this information in terms of 'a *Qi* ('energy') blockage or stagnation in the Meridian' rather than in the current medical context. It is also unfortunate that some influential equine acupuncturists, especially in America, gave rise to the notion that pain at certain points was specifically diagnostic for lameness localisation and for certain infections, particularly herpes and EPM (equine protozoal myelitis).

Firstly, these observations were anecdotal and not tested until fairly recently, when it was shown by two independent veterinary acupuncture researchers that the 'diagnostic point' specificity in lameness localisation was very poor[12,13,19]. Secondly, the unsubstantiated claims made by certain equine acupuncturists provide an easy target for the acupuncture critics and damage the overall image of acupuncture as a serious medicine. Let us not forget that medicine is an art and a science, not a pure science.

In spite of the efforts by some acupuncturists to resist Western medical scrutiny, and the efforts by some within the Western medical community to dismiss acupuncture outright, there is genuine progress being made in understanding the legitimate opportunities for integrating the ancient art of acupuncture into advanced medicine. It is encouraging that several of the veterinary colleges in the United States, including Florida State, Tufts, Cornell and Colorado offer veterinary acupuncture courses to postgraduates.

There is a long way to go before veterinary acupuncture is officially recognised along with a standardised certification by the *American Veterinary Medical Association*, the *Royal College of Veterinary Surgeons* and other national veterinary bodies. This is a goal of the ABVA. The study and practice of acupuncture in the horse is very rewarding in all respects. It has genuinely enabled me to provide improved healthcare and a greater understanding of the nature of health problems. One can only hope that funding will become available to help clarify questions of acupuncture technique and efficacy.

Acknowledgements

The author would like to thank David Jaggar and Deke Kendall for their helpful comments on this text.

References

1. Birch, S.J. and Felt, R.L. (1999) *Understanding Acupuncture*, Churchill Livingstone. pp 3-42.

2. Bossut, D. (1990) Development of veterinary acupuncture in China. *International Veterinary Acupuncture Society Congress*, Holland.

3. Bowsher, D. (1998) Mechanisms of acupuncture. In: *Medical Acupuncture, A Western Scientific Approach*, Churchill Livingstone. pp 69-82.

4. Gillette, R.G., Kramis, R.C. and Roberts, W.J. (1994) Sympathetic activation of cat spinal neurons responsive to noxious stimulation of deep tissues in the low back. *Pain* **56**, 31-42.

5. Graf von Schweinitz, D. (1998) Thermographic evidence for the effectiveness of in acupuncture in equine neromuscular disease. Acupuncture in medicine, *J. Br. med. Acupunct. Soc.* **16**, 14-17.

6. Graf von Schweinitz, D. (1999) Thermography in equine back pain. *Vet Clin. N Am.: Equine Pract.* **15**, 161-177.

7. Jaggar, D.H. (2000) The clinical evaluation of acupuncture. In: *Proceedings of the 26th IVAS World Congress on Veterinary Acupuncture and Related Techniques.* pp 167-172.

8. Kendall, D.E. (1989) A scientific model for acupuncture. *Am. J. Acupunct.* **17**, 251-265.

9. Kendall, D.E. (1989) A scientific model for acupuncture. Part II. *Am. J. Acupunct.* **17**, 343-360.

10. Lewith, G.T. and Vincent, C.A. (1998) The clinical evaluation of acupuncture. In: *Medical Acupuncture, A Western Scientific Approach.* Churchill Livingstone. pp 205-224.

11. Martin, B.B. and Klide, A.M. (1987) The use of acupuncture for the treatment of chronic back pain in horses: stimulation of acupuncture points with saline solution injections. *J. Am. vet. med. Ass.* **190**, 1177-1180,

12. McCormick, W.H. (1996) Traditional Chinese channel diagnosis, myofascial pain syndrome and metacarpophalangeal joint trauma in the horse. *J. equine vet. Sci.* **16**, 566-567.

13. McCormick, W.H. (1997) Oriental channel diagnosis in foot lameness of the equine forelimb. *J. equine vet. Sci.* **17**, 317.

14. Melzack, R. and Wall, P.D. (1965) Pain mechanisms: a new theory. *Science* **150**, 971-79.

15. Melzack, R., Stillwell, D.M. and Fox, E.G. (1977) Trigger points and acupuncture points for pain: correlations and implications. *Pain* **3**, 3-23.

16. Schoen, A. (1994) *Veterinary Acupuncture, Ancient Art to Modern Medicine*, Mosby, Philadelphia. pp 345-346.

17. Smith, F.W.K. (1994) The neurophysiologic basis of acupuncture. In: *Veterinary Acupuncture, Ancient Art to Modern Medicine*, Ed: A. Schoen, Mosby, Philadelphia. pp 33-53.

18. Steiss, J.E., White, N.A. and Bowen, J.M. (1989) Electroacupuncture in the treatment of chronic lameness in horses and ponies: a controlled clinical trial. *Can. J. vet. Res.* **53**, 239-243.

19. Still, J.E (2000) Ear acupuncture in the horse. In: *Proceedings of the 26th IVAS World Congress on Veterinary Acupuncture and Related Techniques.* p 157.

20. Travell, J.G. and Simons, D.G. (1983) *Myofascial Pain and Dysfunction: The Trigger Point Manual*, Vol 1., Williams and Wilkins, Baltimore.

21. http://www.akupunktur-arzt.de/oetzi/bilder.htm

Further reading

The Pain Series (1999) *The Lancet*, Vol. 353.

Medical Acupuncture, A Western Scientific Approach (1998) Eds: J. Filschie and A. White, Churchill Livingstone. ISBN 0-443-04976-9.

Veterinary Acupuncture, Ancient Art to Modern Medicine (2000) 2nd edn., Ed: A. Schoen, Mosby.

Acupuncture in Medicine, Journal of the British Medical Acupuncture Society and Swedish Medical Acupuncture Society. ISSN 0964-5284.

www.medical-acupuncture.co.uk

Proceedings of the 26th IVAS World Congress on Veterinary Acupuncture and Related Techniques. Copies may be ordered from: IVAS, PO Box 271395, Fort Collins, Colorado 80527-1395, USA.

Adrian Jones (1845–1938): Army veterinary surgeon, painter and sculptor

SHERWIN A. HALL MA DHMSA MRCVS

14 Huntingdon Road
Cambridge CB3 0HH

For almost ninety years the massive statue of Peace descending on the Quadriga of War has stood atop the Wellington Arch at Hyde Park Corner. During that time it has been seen by millions and admired by many but few would know that the sculptor was Adrian Jones MVO MRCVS FRBS and fewer still would know that he was a veterinary surgeon. Jones has an entry in the *Dictionary of National Biography*; he published an autobiography in 1933, but he has been overlooked by the art historians and it seems that even the veterinary profession has scant knowledge of him. He deserves wider recognition. (Since submitting this text I have learned that an article by Steven Brindle on 'Adrian Jones and the Wellington Arch Quadriga' will be published later this year in the *Sculpture Journal*).

In 1997, the arch and quadriga were on the register of Buildings at Risk but over the past year English Heritage has spent almost £2 million restoring the arch and cleaning the 38 tons of statue to its original, bronze sheen. It is a masterpiece of statuary and one of London's greatest landmarks (Figs 1 and 2). The early history of the arch is clouded in some confusion as to its purpose, position and design, but in an age of triumphal arches in the capitals of Europe, it was originally conceived as part of a grand western entrance to London in a scheme by George IV to remodel Buckingham House as a palace. By the time the architect Decimus Burton submitted his designs in 1825 and 1826, the arch was to be an entrance to the King's Palace from Hyde Park. Construction work began in 1826 and was well advanced by 1828, but then the Treasury refused to sanction the expense of the decorative sculpture work, so it was still not complete when George IV died in June 1830.

His successor, King William IV, had little interest in the arch and proposed that it should become an entrance to Green Park. One of the features of Burton's decorative work that was not executed was a gilt-bronze quadriga surmounting the entire structure. Eventually a statue was erected on the attic of Burton's arch but he had had no say in the matter. It was a huge equestrian statue of the Duke of Wellington by Matthew Cotes Wyatt which stood 27 feet high, was wholly out of proportion to the arch and only erected in 1846 after nine years of controversy. It lasted less than forty years and was taken down when the arch was moved in 1883 as part of a road-widening scheme. Once again it was proposed that the arch should carry a quadriga.

By this time, Adrian Jones, although still a serving soldier, was on the threshold of his other career as a painter and sculptor. As a schoolboy at the grammar school in Ludlow, Shropshire, he had enjoyed drawing and painting but his secret ambition to become an artist was sternly discouraged by his father who told the young Adrian that he was to become a veterinary surgeon. On qualifying from the Royal Veterinary College in 1865 he had no intention of going into practice; instead he joined the army and was posted to India in 1867. He was well suited to the army life, which enabled him to indulge his love of racing, hunting and, of course, painting and sketching. He was still in the army, having just returned from the First Boer War in 1881, when he took a studio in Kensington and entered the world of artists. He struck up a friendship with Mr Charles Bell Birch, ARA, who taught him the elements of sculpting

Fig 1: The Quadriga on the occasion of the unveiling on November 8th 2000 following restoration by English Heritage (The Independent/Tom Pilston).

and, recognising his talent, suggested that he should take it up professionally.

> *"That",* said Jones, *"acted like fire in a powder-magazine. It blew up all my doubts, hesitations and uncertainty and behind them I saw what I took to be my real destiny."*

Fig 2: Restoration work proceeding on the Quadriga, July 2000. Note the elaborate decoration on the wheels and the sense of scale imparted by the human figure (English Heritage Photographic Library).

The first work that Jones produced under Birch's tutelage was a statuette of one of his own hunters which he called *'One of the Right Sort'*. It was accepted for exhibition at the Royal Academy in 1884 and in the same year he was awarded the first prize of the Goldsmith's Company for a statuette of a huntsman and two hounds in a composition called *'Gone Away'*. He was on active service with the Camel Corps on an expedition to the Nile when he received news of this award. On return home he sculpted a statuette of *'The Camel Corps Scout'* from sketches he had made in the Sudan. This was followed by another statuette entitled *'The Last Arrow'*, depicting an American Indian on a galloping horse. It was exhibited at the Old Grosvenor Gallery, Bond Street, in 1888 where it aroused much interest and was about to set Jones on a course that led to the *Quadriga*.

The success of *'The Last Arrow'* prompted the gallery to propose that Jones should sculpt a big group of a four-horse chariot, a quadriga, driven by an Assyrian. He accepted the challenge but the Old

Grosvenor Gallery closed before he could complete it. Perhaps this was a fortunate twist of fate. He altered the composition to suit his own taste and submitted the work to the Royal Academy where it was exhibited in 1891 under the title of 'Triumph'. It was highly acclaimed and, more importantly, it attracted the attention of the Prince of Wales who saw it at the Academy Banquet. He sent for Jones, to whose astonishment the prince suggested that the Decimus Burton arch at the top of Constitution Hill would make an ideal site for a quadriga modelled on the one he had admired at Burlington House. It was an enormous compliment but it raised some daunting questions. The site would demand a statue on a scale far grander than anything he had attempted before, and at this stage he had not even produced a life-sized horse. He experimented with photographs and drawings and developed his ideas as a sketch-model which went on exhibition at the Royal Academy. Seeking support for his scheme he called on the President of the Royal Academy, Sir Frederick Leighton, hoping that he might put in a good word for him if the opportunity arose. He got short shrift from Sir Frederick who said that 'he had his own friends to look after' and that Jones had not got the experience in modelling a group on this scale. Ignoring the damper, he told the president that he would submit a life-sized group for the next exhibition of the Academy.

Duncan's Horses

Jones did have some second thoughts but he was now committed and, in a flash of inspiration, he decided that his group would be modelled on Duncan's horses from Macbeth, Act II, Scene 4

> Duncan's horses
> Beauteous and swift, the minions of their race
> Turned wild in nature, broke their stalls
> Flung out
> Contending 'gainst obedience as they would make
> War with mankind

His final design was of three horses, of which one was beneath the other two. It was not possible to pose a live horse in such a position so he arranged with a knacker to set up a dead horse in the required, contorted manner while he modelled the details. The work was in plaster and was finished in time for the Royal Academy Exhibition of 1892. 'Duncan's Horses' was a magnificent evocation of Shakespeare's words. It was larger than life so Jones had proved his competence, but in so doing he had antagonised the academicians. They were jealous of somebody who had burst upon the scene as an amateur, an army vet, an outsider who was winning acclaim and, worse, commissions. 'Duncan's Horses' sparked off what became known as 'The Great Art Scandal'. In the July 1892 issue of the Magazine of Art, there was a scurrilous article to the effect that a prominent work at the Royal Academy was not the true work of the putative sculptor but one that had been ghosted by an assistant. The sour-grapes tenor of the anonymous article came to a climax in the last sentence:

> It was necessary for us to point the matter out in view of the success of at least one prominent work at the Royal Academy; but the artist world, which has already recognised and pronounced upon the trick, needs no enlightenment as to the persons who, lacking alike artistic intelligence and honesty, seek by their questionable but commonplace manoeuvres to acquire the honours and advantages that come so hardly to so many a genuine artist, with his patient life of unrequited toil, of neglected talent, and unmerited poverty.

News of the scandal spread to the national press but in neither the article nor the newspapers was Adrian Jones named as the impostor. The identity was no secret in the art world and a letter addressed to the Secretary and Gentlemen of the Committee of the Savage Club, of which Jones was a member, did name him as being publicly charged with dishonourable conduct in his profession. The committee demanded the charges to be substantiated or withdrawn; they were withdrawn. Jones could not seek legal redress because there was nobody bold enough to face him in court.

Following the exhibition at the Royal Academy, 'Duncan's Horses' was put on display at the Crystal Palace. The Crystal Palace had been built for the Great Exhibition of 1851 in Hyde Park and was notable for the speed and ease of its construction using pre-fabricated cast-iron girders. In 1852 it was taken down and re-erected in Sydenham, south

London, where it was destroyed by fire in 1936. 'Duncan's Horses' escaped serious damage in the fire but it had to be moved, so Jones offered it to his *alma mater*, the Royal Veterinary College. In 1937, an appeal was launched in the *Veterinary Record* to raise funds to have the group cast in bronze but the Second World War broke out before the casting could be made and by the time the war finished the funds would no longer cover the cost. For thirty years or so the plaster sections were held in store in Maples depository in Camden Town.

In the early 1960s, when the Royal Veterinary College was expanding the newly acquired field station at Potters Bar, the Principal, Dr R.E. Glover, proposed that 'Duncan's Horses' should be restored and put on display. He had been advised that the plaster group could be weather-proofed by a coating of glass fibre. He hoped it could be done in time for the ceremony of the opening of the new buildings by Her Majesty the Queen Mother in 1965, but it was not to be and Dr Glover had been retired, two years before the work could be completed. On 12 July 1967, Lord Harding of Petherton, Chairman of the Horserace Betting Levy Board, unveiled 'Duncan's Horses' on the lawn of Hawkshead House.

The weather-proofing was not a success, however, and, once again, 'Duncan's Horses' was in danger of being destroyed. By 1979, over £1,000 had been spent just to keep the statue together and there were doubts as to whether it could be saved. Some temporary repairs were made, but the only long-term solution was to have it cast in bronze, the cost of which was estimated to be £30,000. In the *Veterinary Record* of 15th January 1983, there was a special report entitled '*Last chance to save RVC art treasure*' which gave an account of Jones and his work and made an appeal for funds. The numerous contributions that were received included a generous donation from Mr Paul Mellon, the American philanthropist, art collector and horse breeder and at a ceremony on 26 June 1985, attended by Mr Paul Mellon, the Duke of Edinburgh unveiled the bronze casting, 93 years after Adrian Jones had sculpted it (Fig 3).

Jones' second career

Apart from the Great Art Scandal, Jones was enjoying life in London. He had retired from the army in 1889 or 1890 and, in 1891, had got married for the second time and taken up residence in Church Street, Chelsea where he had a large studio constructed in the garden. He felt on top of his form, his star was rising and the commissions were coming in but, as yet, there was no follow-up to the interview with the Prince of Wales about a quadriga for the Burton arch. Having proved himself with 'Duncan's Horses', he produced two more life-sized groups in quick succession. In 1893, 'Maternal Care', a dramatic composition of a mare protecting her foal from a wolf, was exhibited at the Royal Academy and in the following year he exhibited '*The Rape of the Sabines*', another dramatic piece of a Roman on a plunging horse carrying off a Sabine woman. In the decade from 1891, most of his commissions were for paintings, for which he was acquiring as big a reputation in France as he was earning here. His work was also much admired by the Prince and Princess of Wales who commissioned several paintings in this period. *Persimmon*, the horse which won the Derby for the Prince in 1896, was a particular royal favourite and Jones was commissioned to paint his portrait and make a statuette. Some years later, in 1905, after the Prince had ascended the throne, the Jockey Club commissioned an over-life-sized statue of *Persimmon* for presentation to the King. He chose to have it erected at Sandringham where it still stands.

The turn of the century marked a turn in Jones's career and, within a few years, he had developed a reputation as a sculptor of large memorial works. In 1900, the Royal Marines opened an appeal to erect a memorial to the memory of their officers and men who had recently been killed in China and South Africa. The appeal committee reported that an eminent sculptor had volunteered his services and advice and had furnished a design for a monument. The eminent sculptor was Adrian Jones but the committee voted to reject his design. Instead, they asked him to prepare an alternative to include two human figures, one representing a wounded Marine falling to the ground with the other standing over him with bayonet fixed. Jones did as he was asked and was awarded his first commission for a large work. The statue was erected in the Cambridge Enclosure in St James' Park where it was unveiled by the Prince of Wales (the future King George V) on 25 April 1903. In 1940 the statue had to be moved to make room for the Citadel, the big

Fig 3: Duncan's Horses on the lawn of Hawkshead House, Royal Veterinary College.

on working fast. Even so, he had to work day and night to have the maquette ready but he got the commission. It was cast in bronze and shipped to Australia. The people of Adelaide must have been well pleased with their statue because they commissioned another one from him in 1916. It was to the memory of Captain Sturt, a famous Australian explorer who is depicted shading his eyes with his hand while looking into the far distance, a composition that catches the spirit of an explorer superbly well. Almost one hundred years later, we can search the internet websites and find that Adrian Jones still has two statues in Adelaide, one in King William Street and the other in Victoria Square.

In the aftermath of the second Boer War, General Redvers Henry Buller VC was reviled by some for his ineptitude in the field and he was dismissed from the Army in 1901, but there were others who championed his cause and wanted to raise a statue in his honour. It was Adrian Jones who got the commission in 1904 for an equestrian statue to be funded by public subscription. The finished work was taken by rail (Fig 5) from the foundry in Thames Ditton in Surrey to Exeter in Devon, the county of Buller's birth, where it was erected on the

Fig 4: An artist's impression of the Marines' Memorial taken from the appeal brochure for the restoration and enhancement of the site (reproduced by kind permission of the artist, Mr David Hoare).

concrete building next to the Admiralty, to house the wartime operations and signals headquarters. It was held in store throughout the war and in 1948 was re-erected on the north side of the Mall, just to the west of the Admiralty Arch, where it stands to this day. On 29th October 2000, there was a ceremony of unveiling and rededication of the memorial following a refurbishment of the statue and the enhancement of the site by the addition of floodlights and a large, circular, bronze inscription set into the ground around the pedestal (Fig 4).

His second commission for a large public statue came from Australia in 1904. A committee from the city of Adelaide came to London to see Jones and asked if he could prepare a sketch model for a memorial to the Australian soldiers who had been killed in the second Boer War. They wanted to see the result by the end of the week, "*a large order even for a rapid worker*," said Jones, who prided himself same day as the unveiling ceremony, attended by General Buller and thousands of well-wishers. It can still be seen at the junction of New North Road and Hele Road and there is a photograph of it on the *Crediton Courier* website.

Two more commissions followed in quick succession. The first, in 1905, was a war memorial to the Carabineers which took the form of a bronze panel showing a Carabineer scout in South Africa. It stands in the grounds of the Royal Hospital, Chelsea where it can still be seen from the road. The second, in 1906, was important not only for its subject but for its position; it was to commemorate the Duke of Cambridge by a statue to be erected in Whitehall. A committee invited several sculptors to submit designs in 1906. Jones won the commission with his favourite composition, an equestrian statue, which was regarded as the most fitting for the former Commander-in-Chief of the British Army. It was a windy, rainy day in June 1907 when King Edward VII was due to unveil the statue. The flags covering it were sodden and did not fall clear when the king pulled the cord, but Jones had shrewdly positioned four soldiers to ensure that they did come down with no further embarrassment (Fig 6). A few days later, Jones was ordered to Buckingham Palace where the King appointed him MVO (Member of the Victorian Order, an honour awarded by the sovereign).

At last, the Quadriga

In 1907, it was sixteen years since Jones had been summoned to Marlborough House by the Prince of Wales to hear the suggestion that a quadriga should be mounted on the Burton arch. Thereafter, he was regularly reminded by the Office of Works that the scheme had not been forgotten but that a lack of funds prevented its being followed up. When Jones was eventually approached in 1907 by Lord Farquhar, the Controller of the Royal Household, to produce an estimate for the job, he was understandably irritated because he had already submitted several plans over the years to no effect. This time it was different. The Royal Household had found a suitably discreet donor in Lord Michelham who, as Herbert Stern, had

inherited a fortune from his banker father and had become one of the Prince of Wales' circle. In 1905 he was created Baron Michelham of Hellingly and in 1907 he chose to defray the costs of the *Quadriga*. Jones did not know this when Lord Farquhar called but he was so keen to get the commission that, in his own words:

> "*I agreed at once, for I knew that if I could succeed with the* Quadriga *it would be the biggest work of my life, and whatever may be said of my ambitions, none will charge me with having disguised them, either from myself or my friends. Having received my assurance, Lord Farquhar at once began to discuss the question of cost, and what he did not know about economizing was not worth learning. The difficulty of estimating for a work of the size proposed was, of course, considerable, but my heart was set on the job, and the canny Scotsman, small blame to him, was not long in finding this out, so that eventually I found myself agreeing to complete the work for a sum which was quite inadequate. In fact I had to dig pretty deeply into my own pocket to complete it to my own satisfaction.*"

The government was not as generously motivated as was Jones and pointed out to Lord Farquhar that they had not agreed to bear any part of the costs which would have to include a modification to the arch and that "*they would be glad to hear from him that the funds necessary for this minor service will be forthcoming…*"

Fig 5: The statue of General Redvers Buller leaving the Thames Ditton foundry to be taken to Exeter by railway (Elmbridge Museum).

Fig 6: The statue of the Duke of Cambridge in Whitehall.

The challenge for Jones was to reconcile his artistry with the mechanics of mounting a heavy statue 62 feet above the ground. It was not simply a matter of scaling-up a model. He had to consider how the figures would appear to a spectator at that distance from the ground and the fact that they would be seen from different viewpoints, sometimes as a silhouette. The winged, celestial, female figure had to be especially large but still retain an ethereal quality of alighting *on* the chariot rather than travelling *in* it and the group as a whole had to have an airiness. The reining-in of the horses which conveyed the effect of Peace stopping the chariot of War also helped distribute the load. By having the horses' hind legs well under their centres of gravity, each horse was able to support its weight unaided. There is no doubt that Jones' design for the quadriga of Peace was derived from his 1891 group entitled '*Triumph*', but Jones has given no mention of how the composition was conceived and one wonders if he were inspired or otherwise influenced by other quadrigas which could be seen in the capitals of Europe. The Brandenburg Gate in Berlin has one; there is one in Vienna and the National Monument to King Victor Emanuel II in Rome has two. There is one on the Arc de Triomphe in Brussels completed in 1905 and the Arc de Triomphe du Carrousel in Paris has a quadriga by Baron Bosio, sculptor to Napoleon I, which has a strong similarity to Jones' composition.

Work on the statue began in earnest in 1907. The studio was not large enough to take more than one horse at a time so it was not possible to see the entire work before it had been cast in bronze, by which time it would have been too late to alter it. The process began with clay being thrown onto a structure of metal and lathes called an armature. This provided a rough shape of the figure which Jones could then model to his satisfaction. Each horse stood about 10 feet high and used 7 or 8 tons of clay. The chariot was larger still, its frame measuring 9 feet by 18 feet and each wheel was 8 feet in diameter. The finished product of this stage was a clay figure which was exactly of the form and detail that Jones required. To convert that to a bronze equivalent required four more processes.

First, a 'negative' mould had to be taken of the clay 'positive', by covering the clay figure with plaster of Paris. When this was dry, it was removed in sections and a second, 'positive' model was made by pouring plaster of Paris into the 'negative' mould. The product was like the original, clay figure but, being of plaster, was more durable and could be sent to the statue foundry. There the process was repeated; the 'positive' plaster form was used to make a 'negative' mould of sand which could then be used to produce the final, 'positive' form in bronze. Each horse was cast in seven pieces at the foundry of A.B. Burton & Co of Thames Ditton and it is not to be wondered that the whole job took them three years. In February 1911, the consulting engineer for the Office of Works, Mr William Dunn, visited the foundry and reported that the pieces had not yet been assembled and that:

"...the bronze horse which has been set up in the Founder's yard is poised on two hind legs, in the attitude of rearing. It was held up by wooden props under the breast and these could not safely be withdrawn. Neither sculptor nor founder had any clear idea of how this horse, which is a type of the others, is to be held up on its hind legs, and no scheme has apparently been sufficiently thought out for the setting up of the large figure on the chariot, or for maintaining it in place."

Jones had some difficulty in convincing Mr Dunn that the horses would not fall over, so he and A.B. Burton retained their own consulting

Fig 7: The Quadriga erected and posed with the staff of the Thames Ditton Foundry in 1911 (Elmbridge Museum).

engineer, Mr Alexander Drew, who advised them on how to provide the stability required to satisfy the '*most exiguous requirements of the Board of Works*'. King Edward VII took a personal interest in the project and occasionally visited the studio to inspect progress. On one occasion he asked Jones what the principal figure represented; Jones explained that it was '*Peace*', an allusion to the king's contribution to the Entente Cordiale of 1904.

In 1910, it was the king's dying regret when he realised that he would not live long enough to see it finished. The casting was complete by July or August 1911 when the *Quadriga* was assembled in a shed at the foundry and photographed together with Burton's workforce (Fig 7). In November, the statue was dismantled and the pieces were transported to

Hyde Park Corner on a horse-drawn boiler carriage which had to take a route that would ensure adequate clearance under the bridges. It was erected in January 1912. Jones had expected that there would be a ceremony of unveiling for which he had devised an '*original, ingenious scheme*' and when he realised that there was to be no such ceremony it cost him '*quite a lot of money to get out of the contract into which I had entered with a view of carrying out my ideas*'. King George V and Queen Mary drove to the *Quadriga* on 2 April 1912 where Jones, Burton and Lord Michelham were presented to them. In 1914, a small bronze plaque was added to the arch to commemorate Lord Michelham's donation, but there was no reference to the artist who had created the *Quadriga*. In 1921, Jones' name was added in a

Fig 8: The Cavalry Memorial in Hyde Park. The Dragon has a moustache which is said to represent that of Kaiser Bill.

barely legible, small script.

Any commissions after the *Quadriga* must have seemed small beer, but Jones was kept busy with portrait work. When war was declared in 1914 he was aged sixty-nine but feeling very fit, so he tried to join up, thinking that at least he could serve in the Remount Department, but although he got a hearing, they turned him down. Despite the war, he was busy in his studio with new commissions and it was in 1916 that he modelled the statue of Captain Sturt, the Australian explorer, mentioned above. After the war there were commissions for memorials. His Bridgnorth memorial was unveiled in March 1922. The Uxbridge memorial was a figure of Peace, bearing a strong resemblance to the celestial figure on the *Quadriga*, mounted on a granite column 26 feet high. No doubt it was an imposing piece when unveiled in 1924 but, sad to say, it is nowadays somewhat lost among the overgrowing trees and the base of the column looks neglected. For the *Cavalry Memorial*, his last big statue, he chose to model St George, the patron saint of cavalrymen, in the moment of triumph. The horse stands over the slain dragon while St George holds his sword aloft in his right hand. The dragon's face has been given a moustache, supposed to be that of Kaiser Bill. It was unveiled in 1924 at Stanhope Gate, Hyde Park, but

was moved a few hundred yards westwards in 1961 when Park Lane was widened and it now stands just north of the Serpentine Road (Fig 8).

Jones was never elected to the Royal Academy. In 1935 he was awarded the Gold Medal of the Royal Society of British Sculptors, the veterinary profession honoured him as an Honorary Associate and he was made an honorary member of the Incorporated Association of Architects and Surveyors. He died on 24 January 1938 and his obituary in the *Veterinary Record* depicts a vivid image of his later life.

> *A picturesque figure, he was rarely seen out without a flowing black cloak lined with scarlet, which he wore through the Abyssinian campaign, the Nile Expedition and the Boer War. "So much of my life is wrapped up in my cloak that I could never bear to part with it", he said.*

This remarkable, flamboyant character deserves to be well remembered and his works to be better known (Fig 9).

Fig 9: Portrait of Adrian Jones from the Veterinary Record *of 1933, the year his autobiography was published.*

Fig 10: A painting of foxhounds in the possession of the Royal Veterinary College (Reproduced by kind permission of the Principal, Professor Lance Lanyon).

Bibliography and acknowledgements

This account of Adrian Jones and his works has depended almost entirely on his autobiography, *Memoirs of a Soldier Artist*, London, Stanley Paul & Co Ltd, 1933. The source which has provided complementary details is the monograph entitled *The Wellington Arch, Hyde Park Corner: A History* by Dr Steven Brindle of the Government Historic Buildings Advisory Unit. I have also read a small book by Selwyn Hodson-Pressinger which he published in 1997 to draw attention to the 'delitescent but gifted sculptor'. I am grateful to Mr Roger Dillon for a summary of the history of the Royal Marines National Memorial and for permission to publish the illustration that was used in the appeal pamphlet for the refurbishment and rededication of the memorial in 2000. I am equally grateful to Captain C.J. Sayer MBE for some items on the history of the Cavalry Memorial. Mr Michael Rowe of the Elmbridge Museum, Weybridge, was very helpful in providing records of the Thames Ditton statue foundry and Mrs Janet Pickstock of the Royal Veterinary College, London, kindly provided a photograph of the painting of the foxhounds (Fig 10).

As it is difficult to find a copy of Jones' autobiography, the following is a listing of all the works mentioned or illustrated in his book.

Year	Title and description
1884	*One of the Right Sort.* Statuette in bronze, modelled from Jones's own hunter. Exhibited RA 1884.
1884	*Gone Away.* Statuette of mounted huntsman with two hounds. Awarded First Prize in competition of the Goldsmiths' Company.
1885	*The Camel Corps Scout.* Statuette reproduced in bronze and silver. Copies purchased by the officers. Modelled from a drawing made while on the Nile Expedition.
1888	*The Last Arrow.* Statuette in bronze of a North American Indian on a galloping horse. Exhibited at the Old

Grosvenor Gallery 1888.

1891   *Triumph.* Four-horse chariot(quadriga), presumably in plaster. Modelled for Old Grosvenor Gallery but instead was exhibited at the Royal Academy in 1891.

1890   *Sainfoin with Watts up.* Picture of the Derby winner of 1890 with jockey. For Sir James Millar. Jones described this as one of his earliest pictures.

1891   Statuette of Master, Mr William Oakley, capping on three hounds. For the Committee of the Atherstone Hunt. Presented to Mr Oakley at Cliff House, Atherstone.

1893   *Sheen and Gold.* Picture of the horse. For Prince Soltykoff. Sold at auction by Philips, 1984.

1893   *Amphion with Tom Cannon up.* Picture of the horse and jockey. For General Byrne.

1893   *Forager.* Life-sized model of foxhound of the Pytchley Hunt. Forager was a favourite of Earl Spencer.

1892   *Frontin.* Picture of the horse. For Monsieur Menier, painted in France.

1892   *Rueil.* Picture of the horse. For Monsieur Edmond Blanc painted in France.

1892   *Reverend.* Picture of the horse. For Monsieur Edmond Blanc, painted in France.

1892   *Julius Caesar.* Picture of the horse For Comte de Marois, painted in France.

1892   *Frisky Matron.* Picture of the horse. For Comte de Marois, painted in France.

1892   *Why Not.* Statuette of the winner of the Grand National. For Captain C D Fenwick.

1892   *Duncan's Horses.* Larger-than-life statue in plaster. Exhibited at Royal Academy 1892. Was at the Crystal Palace 1892–1936. In store from 1936–1967. At The Royal Veterinary College from 1967 to the present day. Cast in bronze in 1986. A maquette of Duncan's Horses can be purchased from the Royal Veterinary College.

1893   Statuette of a mounted Royal Standard Bearer cast in silver. Commissioned by the Officers of the 2nd Life Guards and presented to the Duke and Duchess of York on the occasion of their marriage.

1893   *Maternal Care.* Life-sized statue of a mare and foal being attacked by a wolf (material not specified). Exhibited at the Royal Academy in 1893. In his autobiography (1933) Jones said that it may be seen on the lawn of Borman Court near Salisbury.

1893   *Cloister.* Picture and bronze model of the winner of the Grand National.

1894   *The Rape of the Sabines.* Life-sized model of a Roman on a plunging horse carrying off a Sabine woman. Exhibited at the Royal Academy in 1894. Lent to the Alexandra Palace and Jones said that it was still there in 1933.

1894   Two pictures of three horses at grass. For Lord Wavertree.

1895   *Viva and Plumpie.* Painting of hack and dog, favourites of the Princess Alexandra of Wales.

1896   *Persimmon with Watts up.* Painting of the Derby winner. For the Prince of Wales.

1896   *Persimmon.* Statuette in bronze of the winner of the Derby. Commissioned by Princess Alexandra of Wales for presentation to the Prince on his birthday.

1896   Memorial plaque in white metal of Capt Berkeley Piggot on Laing's Nek. Erected in Winchester Cathedral.

1896   *Changing Ponies at Hurlingham.* Painting for Lord Wavertree.

1896   *The Soarer with Captain Campbell up.* Painting of the winner of the Grand National for Lord Wavertree. Was also made into statuettes of silver and bronze.

1896   *Merry Gal.* Painting of the horse.

1896   *Magic.* Painting of the horse.

1896   *Cherry Lass.* Painting of the horse.

1897   *Lactantius.* Painting of the horse for Mr Leopold de Rothschild.

1897   Painting of General Gore mounted.

1897   Painting of an Irish hunter for General Gore.

1898   *Persimmon.* Bronze statuette for the Prince of Wales. Persimmon was a great favourite of the Prince.

1900   *Diamond Jubilee.* Painting and bronze statuette of the Derby winner for the Prince of Wales.

1900   *Ambush II with Anthony up.* Painting and bronze statuette of the Grand National winner for the Prince of Wales,

1900   *Persimmon with Watts up.* Painting of the Derby winner. Commissioned by the Prince of Wales for presentation to the Tenth Hussars.

1902   Royal Marines Memorial. Two human figures in bronze. Commissioned by the the officers of the Royal Marines. Unveiled by Prince of Wales (King George VI) on12 April 1903. Enhanced, restored and rededicated in 2000.

1903   Colonel Afsun Dowla. Statuette in bronze. Exhibited at the Royal Academy 1903.

1903   *Crusader.* Statuette of a knight on horseback. Exhibited at the Royal Academy 1903.

1904   Boer War Memorial. Equestrian statue commissioned by the City of Adelaide. The original plaster model was presented to JonesŒ town of Ludlow.

1905   *Persimmon.* Over-life sized statue in bronze of King Edward's favourite horse. Commissioned by The Jockey Club for presentation to King Edward VII who had it erected at Sandringham where it still stands.

1905   Buller Memorial. Equestrian statue in bronze of Sir Redvers Buller VC. Erected by public subscription in the city of Exeter where it still stands.

1905   Carabineers' Memorial. Bronze panel mounted on stone and bricks. Commissioned by a committee of Carabineers (spelt 'carabiniers' on the bronze). Was erected in the grounds of the Royal Hospital, Chelsea where it can still be seen from the street facing Chelsea Bridge.

1907   Duke of Cambridge Memorial. Equestrian statue in bronze. Erected in Whitehall. Unveiled by King Edward VII in June 1907.

1912   *The Quadriga.* Jones' *magnum opus*, a massive statue in bronze of Peace descending on the quadriga of war, mounted on the Burton Arch at Hyde Park Corner. The costs were defrayed by Lord Michelham. There was no ceremony of unveiling. Restored by English Heritage in 2000.

1913   *Lord Roberts.* Life-sized equestrian painting. Exhibited at the Royal Academy, 1913.

1913   *Enid and Geraint.* Painting but no other details. Exhibited at the Royal Academy, 1913.

1914   *Lord Roberts.* Portrait (second one), life-sized equestrian painting, mounted on his Arab pony, Voney.

1916   *Captain Sturt.* Bronze memorial statue for the City of Adelaide.

1921   *Action Front.* Large statuette in plaster of a group of horses and guns. Exhibited at Royal Academy in 1921. Was subsequently cast in bronze. Jones thought this to be one of his best works.

1921   *Tetrarch.* Statuette of the stallion for Major Dermott McCalmont.

1921   *Lord Cavan.* Portrait on his favourite hunter. Presented to Lord Cavan by the members on his retirement from the mastership of the Herefordshire Hunt.

1921   A painting of a group of four foxhounds. Presented to Lord Cavan by the farmers on his retirement from the mastership of the Herefordshire Hunt.

1922   *Earl of Lonsdale.* Bronze statuette of Lord Lonsdale mounted on his favourite hunter. Presented to Lord Lonsdale by the committee on his retirement from the mastership of the Cottesmore Hunt.

1922   *Hunter.* Statuette of the horse in bronze. Presented to Lord Lonsdale by the farmers on his retiirement from the mastership of the Cottesmore Hunt.

1922   Bridgnorth War Memorial. Statue in bronze of a soldier. Unveiled 9 March 1922.

1924   Cavalry War Memorial. Equestrian statue in bronze of St George, Patron Saint of cavalrymen. Unveiled 21 May 1924 at Stanhope Gate, Hyde Park but removed in 1961 to a site to the west, just north of the Serpentine Road.

1924   Uxbridge War Memorial. Figure of Peace in bronze mounted on granite column. It was unveiled on 9 November 1924.

1929   *The Empty Saddle.* The Iniskillings Memorial Statuette in bronze. Unveiled at York in May 1929.

The following works are also mentioned or illustrated in Jones' autobiography, but their dates are unknown.

- *Lord Kitchener.* Life-sized equestrian portrait, date uncertain. Presented to the town of Ipswich where it is still hanging in the Town Hall.
- *Steward.* Presumably a portrait of a foxhound. Presented to Captain Brassey of the Heythrop Hunt.
- Lord Allenby. Life-sized equestrian portrait. Date uncertain.
- The Queen's Bays Memorial. Mounted trooper in war kit. The memorial was transportable in cases.
- *General Smuts.* Equestrian portrait. Illustration in Jones' autobiography but no details are given.
- *Lord Annaly.* Equestrian portrait in the hunting field when he was Master of the Pytchley Hunt. Illustration in the autobiography but no details and the date is uncertain.
- *Bechers Brook.* Statuette of a horse falling on landing. Illustration in the autobiography but no details are given and the date is uncertain.

Homeopathy for horses

ALAN SLATER BVMS MRCVS DC DAC DVetHom DHM
Sunnyside Holistic Centre
The Coach House, Main Road
Narborough, King's Lynn
Norfolk PE32 1TE

Introduction

I have been using homeopathy for several years, initially on the conditions that conventional medicine cannot treat and now on (almost) everything.

I came to it with a mindset of *"That won't work! That's homeopathy!"* when a colleague suggested it for an animal I was treating. The horse had got gradually worse for two weeks with my treatment. I begrudgingly used homeopathy and was very annoyed when, after three days, the horse had made a full recovery. Since then I have become a little more open-minded.

Why use homeopathy?

Many people commonly use it as First Aid for both animals and people. Whether they tell you or not, a lot of your clients are already using it on their own animals with varying success. The degree of success usually depends on what they use it for, how knowledgeable they are and how conscientious they are at dosing. This is where the vet comes in, with their expertise and knowledge. I believe that it is a therapy that all vets can use, if they wish to; obviously, I am biased. It is not a panacea, but then nothing ever is[22,25]. I know this to my cost in treating mastitis where, on one farm, it was completely ineffectual.

Homeopathy can be used on animals only by vets or by their owners. This is a short introduction to hopefully help you understand the subject better.

I have included some of the odd words that, often, are a hangover from the 18th century German in which the original literature was written.

As a taster, I have given a few examples of cases I have treated successfully. Some of these may sound like 'cook-book' therapy rather than the correct method of ascertaining the remedy, but it is a less complicated way to start. It is the way I learnt. These cases should then give you the confidence to use homeopathy on a more classical level.

Common misconceptions

- It is not a form of faith so you don't have to believe in it. This therapy does work on animals that don't know or care what the tablet is
- Similarly, if it were a placebo effect, then it would not work on animals. The only placebo effect I find with animals is a negative one directed at me as 'the vet - who might be carrying a syringe'
- It is not a form of herbalism. Herbalism is a very good therapy in the hands of an herbalist. It can be lethal if incorrectly used and many herbs are very poisonous. Some of the homeopathic remedies are used as mother tinctures (concentrated solutions) and here the remedy is very similar to a herb

History

Homeopathy has a long history. The idea of 'like curing like' probably stems back to prehistory.

Throughout I have used the spelling Homeopathy. This is the American spelling and has just been accepted (2000) as the norm; the original spelling of Homoeopathy has been dropped for ease of international use.

Hippocrates wrote about healing with contraries and similars. Paracelsus used a similar form at the beginning of the 16th century. However, the accepted 'father of homeopathy', who first used the term, is Dr Samuel Hahnemann (1756–1843). He considered his contemporary physicians to be dangerous (blood letting, purging, mercury poultices, etc). In fact, he decided that he, personally, would get little profit from practice, as he was *too conscientious to prolong illness or make it appear more dangerous than it really is*. He did consider that vets were much more responsible and conscientious in their therapies than were doctors. He left general practice and became a pharmacist, chemist and scientific translator. Here he shone, and many of his publications were considered the best of the time.

However, he changed his ideas and life when he translated a treatise by Dr Cullen on the treatment of malaria with cinchona or Peruvian bark. Dr Hahnemann didn't believe that this was effective simply because of its tonic effect on the stomach. To prove his hypothesis, he took cinchona (now known as China) himself and found that he developed the symptoms of malaria. He then suggested that the cinchona was effective because it caused the same symptoms as malaria in a healthy person. This was repeated on other subjects to make sure that it was not a fluke. This method of testing a remedy is called a proving and is how all remedies are arrived at. Incidentally, you may remember that cinchona is the source of quinine.

Initially, friends and relatives were taking these drugs (or remedies) in their original form. These included strychnine, arsenic and mercury, so the danger was quite obvious. Hahnemann was worried about this and, therefore, reduced the dose progressively. As you would expect, the remedy stopped working as the dilutions became weaker. However, he decided to shake the liquid remedy vigorously whilst hitting it against a book (the Family Bible). This 'shake with a sudden stop' was called succussion and caused the remedy to gain in strength the more it was diluted. One way of understanding this is that the kinetic energy, from the shaking, is being 'stored' as potential energy in the remedy. These dilutions were called potencies.

Potency

A remedy is made by dissolving the original material initially into a solvent such as water or alcohol as a concentrated solution. The material used can be anything at all. Some of the more common include *Bryonia* (white Bryony), *Arsenicum Album* (arsenic) and *Apis Mel* (bee). This solution is called the mother tincture and is written as $\emptyset$. One drop of this tincture is added to 99 drops of a liquid, usually alcohol. This is considered a 1c dilution (1 in 100 or centesimal). This procedure is then repeated using one drop of the 1c to produce a 2c dilution. If the dilution is 1,000c then this is written as 1M. (On the Continent, decimal or 1 in 10 dilutions are used and written as x or D). These dilutions can continue *ad infinitum*, although 1M and 10M are the usual limits.

A potency coming into its own is the LM series where the dilution is 1 in 50,000 (L = 50, M = 1000). This series goes from LM1 to LM30. All of these potency sequences were devised by Dr Hahnemann.

If the original remedy is insoluble, then it is ground up with lactose powder (trituration). The same dilutions are followed using this sugar rather than a liquid and by 3c the material is soluble.

After 12c, by Avogadro's hypothesis, there is unlikely to be a single molecule of the original compound left, i.e. this is not a material medicine but an energetic therapy. This can be difficult to accept. In one review, the author[14] concluded that homeopathy worked but they didn't accept the theory so it couldn't work! This is my translation of their summation. The other aspect of potency that is difficult to appreciate is that the higher the potency (the greater the dilution) then the more potent or 'stronger' the remedy becomes. The common potencies used in Britain are 6c, 30c, 200c, 1M and 10M.

Homeopathy is only completely safe as OTC (over the counter) remedies. These are restricted to 6c and 30c potencies. However, the higher potencies can cause proving symptoms, aggravation and apparent illness. Remedies cannot kill but there are remedies that can allow animals to release their hold on life or cause severe aggravation in an already sick animal. Some of the very low dilutions are also potentially dangerous as they are made from poisonous substances (e.g. strychnine) and may still retain their capacity to kill.

Philosophy

Conventional medicine or Allopathy uses the opposite in treatment, e.g. antibiotics to kill bacteria. Homeopathy uses a remedy that, in its original form, would cause similar symptoms. A useful example is *Apis Mel* (bee). This is often used for swellings; yes, including bee stings. Thus like is curing like - or, in Latin, *similia similibus curentur*.

Dr Hahnemann's idea was that two similar diseases could not exist in the body at the same time; the stronger one would take over. The remedy (as an artificial disease) is perceived as the stronger by the body so it triumphs. However, as an artificial disease, it doesn't really exist so the body can easily overcome it. This overcoming probably explains the fact that, in some cases, the patient initially gets worse - the aggravation of homeopathy.

It is important to remember that homeopathy is believed to work via the immune system so, if this is not functional, the remedy will not work. Both corticosteroids and antihistamines can suppress the immune system and homeopaths can be quite vehement in their opposition to these drugs. I have used homeopathy along with such conventional drugs and the response has been muted but still present (personal opinion). In a similar way, if an animal's immune system is non-functional (autoimmune disease or severe overwhelming disease), then homeopathy is less likely to be of use.

The laws of homeopathy

This is a scientific therapy, worked out empirically first and then the theory proven. Thus, there are certain facts or laws that can be stated.

1. The first is the *Law of Similars* already stated, i.e. any substance which can produce a certain group of symptoms in a healthy person, can cure that group of symptoms in a diseased person, or like cures like.

2. It is considered that only one remedy should be given at a time (*classical homeopathy*). This is in the ideal world and my personal opinion is that this is very difficult in animals. I therefore do use more than one remedy at a time but that is a personal decision. This is called *complex homeopathy*. Some ready-made commercial complex homeopathic compounds are already sold directly to vets.

3. The law of minimum dose. The least amount of remedy should be given that will achieve a cure. Hahnemann said that one dose should be given and not repeated until the effect was waning. Again, in animals, this is hard to judge so I tend to give remedies on a daily basis. Other homeopathic vets may consider this wrong, but all I can say is that it works for me and I rarely get the anticipated aggravation.

4. The *Laws of Cure* or Hering's Laws state that as the patient is cured, the symptoms clear from within to without, from above to below and from now to the past. Examples would be:
   • A heart condition may show bowel or skin symptoms, as there is improvement
   • A skin condition would start to clear in the centre with the feet, face and tail clearing last - 'it drips off the body'
   • An animal with a chronological list of diseases during its life may regress back through this list in reverse order, fortunately in reduced form. They do not need to be treated. Clients need to be aware of this as panic can set in otherwise

One example I had of this recently was a horse that I was treating for Cushing's disease. As this improved, the symptoms of a previous respiratory disease (believed to be pneumonia) flared up for a day. The next day this had gone but there was lameness in the left hind foot. This also lasted a day and cleared. As the owner had bought the horse as a foal, she was able to confirm his history of these diseases.

Diagnosis

Contrary to public opinion, it is more difficult to use homeopathy than conventional medicine. This is because two diagnoses are required. The first is the one the vet is used to, the diagnosis of the specific disease. The second is unique to homeopathy and requires a diagnosis of the unique remedy for that particular horse, i.e. treat the patient not the disease. Knowing the specific disease is not enough; it is essential that you know how the individual case is reacting to that disease.

For example, if fifty people all developed influenza, they could well end up with fifty different remedies. To continue the example, if one developed a green nasal discharge then the remedy could be *Pulsatilla* (if in plaques) or *Kali Bich* (if stringy and sticky). The other symptoms that each individual is showing would also be taken into consideration. These symptoms could affect any part of the body or mind, *Pulsatilla* for example being a friendly but shy creature with symptoms never the same twice.

Conversely, sometimes homeopathy can be used if no initial diagnosis of a specific disease is made or can be made[2]. This does allow for very early treatment to avoid disease damage. It can also be misused to cut corners.

Repertorisation

There are two types of books to help you with this diagnosis or 'repertorisation'. The *Materia Medica* is known in 'normal' or allopathic medicine also. It is a list of remedies (drugs) with all the symptoms that the particular remedy produces. I believe any conventional vet should also have a copy of a homeopathic *Materia Medica*, as many remedies are very poisonous in their original form. The *Materia Medica* thus lists the symptoms of many poisons, helping to ascertain which poison is involved. This has caused some poorly informed people to state that homeopathy is poisonous. It is not. It is totally safe in the usual potencies sold OTC (over the counter) and in the hands of a trained homeopath.

The second book is, I believe, unique to homeopathy and is called a *Repertory*. This is almost the reverse of the *Materia Medica* insofar as it is a list of symptoms. The symptoms are classified as to which part of the body is affected, and on what level (physical, mental and emotional). Incidentally, this has been misconstrued that homeopathy only hides and doesn't treat the symptoms - the opposite of the truth. It is impossible to memorise the whole book but useful 'rare and unusual symptoms' should be so memorised; e.g. 'fear of forthcoming events' is often treated with *Argentum Nitricum* (silver nitrate). There are now several computer repertories that do ease the chore of repertorisation.

Here we come to the first hurdle of using homeopathy on animals. Dr Hahnemann stated that there were three levels of symptoms. These are Mental, Emotional and Physical. By and large, the first two are out of our reach. George McLeod always used the physical only in his books. This means that the physical must be examined more deeply. This is not to say that the vet doesn't already do this but unusual behaviour or symptoms may be considered unimportant. Thus, for example, if a horse with liver disease showed flaring of the nostrils this would probably be ignored as unimportant. To a homeopath, this could suggest *Lycopodium* was the remedy of choice. In fact, I did see a horse that was unable to walk from cirrhosis (believed due to ragwort poisoning) that actually responded dramatically to *Lycopodium*, being apparently normal by the next day. It lived another 5 years of normal life before the liver cirrhosis caused another bout that was considered untreatable.

A second hurdle is that all these remedies were tested on humans. This is indicative of the degree of scientific research that went into the promulgation of the homeopathic principle. On the other hand, this means that most of them have not been tested on animals. Usually this is not a problem as the symptoms are the key issue independent of species. Human individuals don't, however, have hooves, tails or herbivorous alimentation, and they walk upright. This may be confusing when using the repertory. Nevertheless, most disease patterns are present in all mammals. At all times, it is important that the whole of the symptoms are taken into account, i.e. it is a whole body treatment, not just of the apparently affected areas.

The proof

As each treatment is unique to the individual, trials are difficult to arrange. There is very strong anecdotal evidence from many sources. A lot of homeopathic vets would be happy to talk about their cases. In my case, it is often difficult to shut me up! A specific organisation in this country is the *British Association of Homoeopathic Veterinary Surgeons*. This has quite an arsenal of case studies. The BIH case notes also contain many such cases. George McLeod, sadly recently deceased, has written several books on homeopathy, including one specifically on horses. In this he lists the remedies that he has found useful. Some journal articles have been written[24] and some papers published on horse problems[25, 26].

There are few experiments involving animals, as the original therapy was comprehensively based on human testing. By this I mean that Dr Hahnemann tested the remedies on healthy people to see what symptoms they could elicit. They recorded these as provings. I accept that these were not double blind trials. Jeremy Sherr, a well-known contemporary homeopath has carried out provings on new remedies such as Scorpion and Hydrogen. These have been double blind trials, at least in part. I have included some references for other species, including humans. There are some on laboratory animals and *in vitro* tests showing an obvious effect on the animals or cells, respectively[3, 11, 18, 21, 24, 26]. *Aconite*, for example, has been to show a strong analgesic postoperative effect in children[1].

There are many articles in journals that have been written about homeopathy. Most are based on anecdotal evidence. Christopher Day, for example, has written letters to the *Veterinary Record* stating cases and group cases that he has treated. Some of these cases have been blinded trials.

The remedies

There are over 3000 remedies in use, as anything can be a remedy. This includes plants (about 60% of total), animals (part or whole, healthy or diseased), minerals and even conventional drugs. I stock about 500 and probably only use about 150 regularly, with about 50 of these on a daily basis. I will suggest a few that can be used on a day-to-day basis to gain confidence and belief and to test the water.

The remedies can be supplied by many homeopathic pharmacies. These include Weleda, Helios and Ainsworth. They can be supplied as tablets, liquid or, less commonly, as injections. I

purchase the liquids to medicate my own tablets. Initially, I only bought tablets, until I became more sure of my ground.

Dosing

The remedy can be given as a liquid, tablet or powder. As the remedy can be absorbed via any mucous membrane, injections are rarely used or needed in Britain. One exception is Iscador, manufactured by Weleda for cancer therapy. On the Continent, injections are much more common.

Homeopathic remedies are not robust, so care needs to be taken in giving the medication. Certainly, for human individuals this requires the remedy to be given away from food and not handled. George McLeod advised putting the remedy on a piece of bread or in an apple. This seems effective, as does dissolving the remedy in the drinking water. The amount of water is not important. As the tablet form carries the remedy on the outside, handling the tablet will remove it. This will not affect the handler but will reduce the effectiveness of the treatment.

If the remedies are stored away from sunlight, strong smells and in a cool place, then it is considered that they will last a long time, possibly indefinitely. It is hoped that Dr Benveniste's work (reported in '*Memory of Water*') will result in qualitative and quantitative tests. In these experiments he and other independent workers postulate a theory that water can form 'coherent domains' containing millions of molecules. They further suggest that these are the reason that water can 'remember' previous contact with other molecules. Their reproducible experiments seem to confirm the theory. A lot of controversy is involved in the issues. However, Dr Benveniste is continuing with refining his experiments to prove the issues completely. He is a well known scientist with a strong *bona fide* background.

Treatment

This is a short suggestion list of conditions that I treat routinely. It is important to remember that, although I have put these down as specific diseases, homeopathy treats the whole patient, not just the present disease pattern.

Aconite can be used postoperatively with *Arnica* to reduce bruising, pain and improve healing. Please make sure that these are not given preoperatively. *Arnica* reduces bruising by increasing the size of blood vessels and will result in bleeding at the surgical site if already present. Our local (human) hospital plastic surgeons have recently found this out to their cost (personal communication) with their patients having increased bleeding, especially after facial treatment. *Aconite* is also very effective in shock, from whatever cause, reversing the effects as rapidly as they came on.

Wounds are a regular occurrence, in veterinary practice, that respond well. *Arnica, Staphisagria, Silica*[17] (soft tissue injury), *Apis*[4] (skin oedema and erythema), *Symphytum* (bone or tendon damage), *Rhus Tox* and *Ruta Grav* (ligament and tendon damage), *Ledum* (penetration wounds) and *Calendula* lotion are the remedies I use commonly. *Calendula* is really herbal, but is so effective in healing wounds that I use it often; the wound must be clean or the lotion will seal in the infection, forming an abscess.

Arthritis is a common and chronic condition that usually responds well to homeopathy. If the stiffness, or difficulty in moving, eases off with exercise, then the usual remedy is *Rhus Tox*. I use the 1M potency (1000c). If the stiffness worsens or stays the same, then try *Bryonia* 1M. This remedy is also useful for respiratory and some skin problems, i.e. it is a polycrest (has multiple uses). Homeopathy has been shown to be effective on rheumatoid arthritis in humans[9, 10].

Laminitis usually responds well. In the acute form, *Aconite, Apis Mel, Nux Vomica* or *Belladonna* are often effective. In chronic cases, I often use *Bryonia* or *Calc Fluor*.

Foal diarrhoea, either chronic or acute, can be a major problem, as it is in children[14]. *Nux Vomica/Carbo Veg* in combination or *Arsen Alb* can be very effective. Normal rehydration must always be used, although China is also helpful in this respect. I treated a 2-year-old Shire that had suffered with chronic diarrhoea for all its life, despite treatment from many vets. I used *Nux Vomica, Carbo Veg* and *Merc Sol*. The horse recovered in seven days with no recurrence.

Colic is obviously an emergency and all cases need to be treated quickly, safely and with all available means. The diagnosis is essential in order that cases requiring surgical intervention are treated as soon as possible.

I believe that homeopathic remedies add another dimension, another set of braces to the belt. If the condition were of very sudden onset, with fever and sweating I would use *Aconite* immediately. This in itself is often enough to stop spasmodic colic and could be administered by the client whilst the vet was *en route*. *Belladonna* is also useful in the same kind of case if the horse is very excitable. *Colocynthis* colic cases are likely to have a lot of pain with flatulence and watery diarrhoea. Any symptoms from incorrect or overfeeding often respond to *Nux Vomica*. On a similar gastrointestinal note, however, I have had little success on internal parasitic disease[25]; other vets have and there are many remedies for this.

Metabolic diseases can also be helped with homeopathy[15]. Obviously, any deficiency disease must receive the correct missing nutrient; homeopathy seems able to help the body absorb this nutrient more efficiently[5]. In fact, a specific form of Cushing's disease has recently been treated successfully in dogs with *Quercus* and *Corticotrophin*. I have used the same combination in horses with an improvement in the clinical signs in 4 out of the 5 cases I have seen.

Upper respiratory tract infection can respond well[7, 8]. I often use a sequence of *Hepar Sulph, Pulsatilla* and *Silica*. These are given one after the other, each for 10 days. In my experience, aggravation is common and followed by recovery, even in chronic cases. One case I treated this way had been treated for 2 years conventionally, including washing out the guttural pouches three times weekly. In humans, homeopathy has also been effective in some cases of 'hay fever'[18] and allergic asthma[20].

Skin problems can respond well to homeopathy[6]. It is almost a cliché to suggest *Sulphur*, although this works best on conditions that are hot, itchy and worse for wet conditions. Incidentally, I find *Sulphur* does not work below 200c potency. Ringworm I have treated successfully with *Bacillinum* and *Chrysarobin* together.

Mastitis usually responds well, but this is such a multifactorial condition that great care must be taken[22, 16]. I can vouch for this somewhat ruefully.

Homeopathy is also being used in place of the

conventional vaccinations with nosodes. This is at least partially because of the client's fear of vaccinosis (adverse vaccinal reaction). I am unable to say how much of this is hype and emotion or reality. I do know that there are genuine fears in the general public on the issue. A nosode is a homeopathic remedy taken from a diseased animal or human. It can be used to treat that specific disease (or diseases with similar symptoms). However, in the vaccinal procedure, there is no disease present and the remedy is being used prophylactically, i.e. like is not curing like. Homeopaths argue among themselves about the correctness of this form of treatment. It would certainly appear, in my experience, that it is as effective as the vaccine in preventing disease. This may be due to several factors, such as the disease not being present or the horse already being immune. No testing has been done into their efficacy. I use nosodes regularly with apparent good effect.

Thus homeopathy can be used both as treatment and as prophylaxis[22]. It can be used in all species and, I believe, is effective, safe and rewarding.

Training

This can be like my initial 'training' of self taught empiricism with much reading. I would not advise it, as it is easy to get lost up many a dead end. The *British Association of Homeopathic Veterinary Surgeons* run a course resulting in VetMFHom (Veterinary Member of the Faculty of Homeopathy) accepted by the Society of Homeopaths. *The British Institute of Homeopathy* runs a correspondence course resulting in DVetHom (Diploma of Veterinary Homeopathy), accepted by the Homeopathic Medical Association.

Summary

I am biased insofar as I had homeopathy used on me effectively and have used it effectively on many species. I recommend you try some of the remedies I have suggested (if necessary in tandem with conventional medicine for your own peace of mind); I believe that you will be pleasantly surprised. Homeopathy is not a denial of scientific veterinary knowledge but merely a different form of therapy, another tool in your armoury.

Finally, to quote Dr Hahnemann:

> *"The physician's highest calling, his only calling, is to make sick people* (in our case, animals) *healthy - to heal as it is called... The highest ideal of therapy is to restore health rapidly, gently, permanently; to remove and destroy the whole disease in the shortest, surest, least harmful way, according to clearly comprehensible principles."*

This is, after all, what all good vets and other therapists want.

References

1. Alibeu, J.P. and Jobert, J. (1990) Aconite for postoperative pain and agitation was 95% effective in children. *Pediatrie (Bucur)* **45**, 465-466.

2. Altman, M. (1994) Fever of unknown origin cured by homeopathy. *Harefuah* **126**, 317-320.

3. Begum, D. *et al.* (1989) Plumbum Met and Opium were partially effective in recovery of delta ALAD activity in lead intoxicated rats. *Ann. Pharm. Frol.* **47**, 24- 32.

4. Bildet, G. (1989) Oedema, erythema and pruritis in the guinea pig (produced by UV irradiation) were treated successfully with Apis Mel. *Ann. Pharm.* **47**, 24-32.

5. Cook, T. (1998) Selenium deficiency in sheep (Libya 1975) was treated with Selenium and Selenium 6x. *BIH Notes.*

6. Davies, C. (2001) Treatment of a pony with skin allergy. *Br. Hom. J.* **89**, 41-42.

7. Ferley, J.P. *et al.* (1989) A homeopathic preparation improved recovery from influenza-like symptoms in humans. *Br. J. clin. Pharmacol.* **27**, 329-335.

8. Gassinger, C.A. *et al.* (1981) Aspirin and Eupatorium Perf were equally effective on the common cold in humans. *Arzneimittelforschung* **31**, 732-736.

9. Gibson, J. *et al.* (1978) Homeopathy was more effective than salicylate on rheumatoid arthritis. *Br. J. clin. Pharmacol.* **6**, 453-459.

10. Gibson, J. *et al.* (1992) Homeopathy was effective on rheumatoid arthritis. *Ibid* **9**, 343-345.

11. Harisch, G. (1992) Both Conium and Merc Phos were shown to have a positive effect on liver function in rats. *Deutsche Tierärztl. Wochenschr.* **99**, 343-345.

12. Harman, J.C. (1994) Homeopathy in Equine Practice. *Equine Pract.* **16**, 16-18.

13. Jacobs, J. *et al.* (1996) Homeopathy was found to be useful in treating acute childhood diarrhoea. *Pediatrics* **93**, 710-725.

14. Kleijman, J. (1991) Meta analysis of controlled homoeopathic trials in humans showed 81 with good results and 24 with poor results although most trials were of poor standard. *Br. med. J.* **302**, 316-323.

15. Manchenko, P. *et al.* (1992) Homeopathy proved useful in reducing glycosuria and hyperglycaemia in (human) *Diabetes Mellitus. Vrach Dalo* **11-12**, 74-76.

16. Merck, A. *et al.* (1989) Acute mastitis (especially E. Coli) in cattle responded well to homeopathy. *Berliner Münchener Tierärztl. Wochenschr.* **102**, 266-272.

17. Oberbau, M. (1992) Silica effective in wound healing in mice. *Ibid* **123**, 79-82.

18. Poitevin, B. *et al.* (1988) Lung Histamine nosode and Apis Mel were effective at inhibiting, in vitro, immunological degranulation of human basophils. *Br. J. clin. Pharmacol.* **25**, 439-444.

19. Reilly, D. *et al.* (1986) Homeopathy was helpful in helping control hay fever. *Lancet* **2**, 881-886.

20. Reilly, D. *et al.* (1994) Homeopathy was effective in treating allergic asthma. *Ibid* **344**, 1601-1606.

21. Santini, C. (1994) Cuprum Met reduced the facilitating action of neostigmine in intestinal transit in the mouse. *Cr. Seances Soc. Biol. Fil.* **184**, 55-58.

22. Schutte, A. (1994) Homeopathy resulted in decreased morbidity rate in housed pigs and dairy cattle. A specific complex homeopathic compound Laseptel was as effective as oxytetracycline and a potentiated sulphonamide. There was no effect on chronic mastitis. *Berliner Münchener Tierärztl. Wochenschr.* **107**, 229-236.

23. Sommer, H. (1988) Treatment of 'Tying-up' Syndrome with Flor de piedra and China was effective. In: *Animal Clinical Biochemistry - The Future*, Eds: D.J. Blackmore, P.D. Eckersall, G.O. Evans, H. Sommer, M.D. Stonard and D.D. Woodward, Cambridge University Press, Cambridge. pp 323-331.

24. Sukul, N.C. *et al.* (1986) Gelsemium, Cannabis indica, Graphites and Agaricus all enhanced restraint induced catalepsy in the rat. All lasted different times; the higher potencies lasted longer. *Psychopharmacol. (Berl.)* **89**, 338-339.

25. Taylor, S.M. *et al.* (1989) Homeopathy (as the specific nosode) was ineffective in prevention of parasitic bronchitis in calves. *Vet. Rec.* **124**, 1577.

26. Wagner, H. *et al.* (1986) Four homeopathic preparations were injected into volunteers (2 trials) and 1 *in vitro* trial. All showed enhanced phagocytosis. *Arzneimittelforschung* **39**, 421-425.

Further reading

This is a taster and by no means complete. It is often useful to get a popular book to attempt to grasp the essentials. These are books that I have found useful and ones that many of the veterinary clinician's more interested clients will already have. The ones marked (*) I think are essential to understand homeopathy. The ones marked (#) are more related to the scientific explanation.

Boericke*; *Materia Medica and Repertory*
Christopher Day*; *Homoeopathic Treatment of Small Animals*
Samuel Hahnemann*; *The Organon* (6th Edition), Ed: Wenda Brewster O' Reilly

George MacLeod*; *Treatment of Horses by Homoeopathy*
George MacLeod*; *Veterinary Materia Medica and Repertory*
James Tyler Kent[#]; *Other Books on Theory and Practice*
George Michel Schiff[#]; *The Memory of Water*
Vithoulkas[#]; *The Science of Homoeopathy*
K.J. Biddis; *Homoeopathy in Veterinary Practice*
James Tyler Kent; *Homoeopathic Materia Medica*
James Tyler Kent; *Homoeopathic Repertory*
Dr Frederik Schroyens; *Synthesis (Synthetic Repertory)*
Meredith Snader *et al.*; *Healing Your Horse*
Ian Watson; *Guide to the Methodologies of Homoeopathy*

International Equestrian Federation (FEI) - the role of the veterinary profession

PROFESSOR LEO JEFFCOTT MA BVetMed PhD FRCVS DVSc VetMedDr

Veterinary School
University of Cambridge
Madingley Road
Cambridge CB3 0ES

Introduction

The Fédération Equestre Internationale (FEI) is an important organisation because it has overall control of all equestrian sport worldwide. It is the organisation that formulates the rules and regulations for all international equestrian events in the jumping, dressage, eventing, driving, vaulting, endurance riding and reining disciplines. This includes the supervision and maintenance of the health and welfare of the horses taking part, as well as promoting principles of horsemanship. Since the FEI was formed over 70 years ago, it has concerned itself very much with the welfare of the horse and in 1991 produced a Code of Conduct which specifically deals with welfare in all equestrian sports. The FEI takes its responsibilities extremely seriously and continuously strives to improve the role of the horse in sport throughout the world. There is a large and important veterinary side to all FEI activities.

The primary mission of the FEI is to advance the growth of equestrian sport around the world by promoting, regulating and administering international competition in traditional equestrian disciplines and by helping the sport to evolve in ways that enhance its attractiveness, both for the participants and the public, while still respecting the ideals and principles of horsemanship.

Its main functions are to:

- Act as the sole authority for all international events in Dressage, Jumping, Eventing, Driving, Endurance Riding, Vaulting and Reining
- Establish rules and regulations and to approve programmes for equestrian competitions at Championships, Regional and Olympic Games, and to control their technical organisation

History of the FEI

Horses in racing and other forms of sport have been part of our heritage for hundreds of years. However, it was not until the late 19th and early 20th century that equestrian sport gained widespread popularity with the public. There was little organisation of international competitions until the equestrian events (Dressage, Jumping and Eventing) were accepted into the Olympic movement for the 1912 Games in Stockholm. After this it became clear that some internationally recognised rules for these disciplines were essential. In May 1921, delegates from 10 national equestrian organisations met in Lausanne to discuss the foundation of an international federation. Representatives from United States, France, Japan and Sweden decided on the constitution of an International Equestrian Federation and the first congress was held in Paris in November 1921, where Baron du Teil from France was elected the first President of the FEI.

Management of the organisation

The FEI is made up of a large group of affiliated National Federations from around the world. These national governing bodies have representatives that sit on committees and advise on the policy and future direction of the organisation. Affiliation to the FEI is open to all national governing bodies which have effective control of the Olympic Equestrian Disciplines and preferably those recognised by their National Olympic Committees. There has been a steady growth from the eight Federations that started the FEI in 1921 to over 120 today.

The general structure of the FEI stems from the General Assembly made up of representatives from each affiliated National Federation. The General Assembly is the supreme authority of the FEI and meets in Ordinary Session once a year (Fig 1). The National Federations are divided into nine regional groups; these regional groups are established for promoting and co-ordinating the development and the activities of the equestrian sport within the Group area.

The Bureau is the main committee and is responsible for the general direction of the FEI. It consists of:

- President of the FEI
- 1st and 2nd Vice-Presidents
- Secretary General and Assistant Secretary General
- Treasurer
- Chairmen of the Technical Committees for dressage, jumping, eventing, driving, special disciplines and veterinary matters (i.e. Technical Chairmen)
- Chairmen of the Regional Groups
- Chairmen of the Judicial and Marketing Committees, participating in the Bureau in a consultative capacity
- Chairman of Strategic Planning Committee

The executive board is responsible for dealing with current matters of policy and day to day management which cannot be held over until the next Bureau meeting. It sets the guidelines for the development of the sport and monitors the

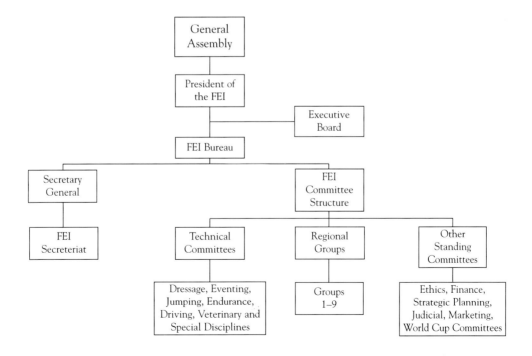

Fig 1: Overview of the organisational structure of the FEI.

Table 1: Some historical facts of veterinary involvement in FEI

Veterinary Committee founded 1966

1966–1990	Chairman	Prof. Igor Bobylev (RUS)
1990–1998	Chairman	Dr Peter Cronau (GER)
1998–present	Chairman	Prof. Leo Jeffcott (GBR)

Veterinary Department founded 1982

1982–1995	Head	Dr Alex Atock (IRL)
1995–present	Head	Dr Frits Sluyter (NED)

---

management of the Secretariat. Membership consists of the President, two Vice-Presidents, Treasurer and one Group Chairman. The Secretary General attends Executive Board meetings in a consultative capacity.

The Secretary General acts as the FEI's chief executive officer and is responsible for the organisation and administration of the Secretariat at its headquarters in Lausanne, and for the financial management of the Federation. The Secretariat is divided into seven departments: Administration and Finance, Jumping and Driving, Dressage and Special Disciplines, Eventing and Olympics, Veterinary, Legal and External Relations.

FEI veterinary matters

The veterinary profile of the FEI was rather low to start and a Veterinary Committee was not established until 1966. The first edition of the Veterinary Regulations was written by the President, The Duke of Edinburgh, in the early 1960s. The Veterinary Department in the FEI headquarters was not established until 1982 (Table 1).

The real veterinary work for the FEI is done in the Veterinary Department under the leadership of Dr Frits Sluyter and his team of three assistants. The main duties involved are :

- Organisation of the veterinary coverage for international events (~350 *per annum*)
- Management of the Medication Control Programme (~1100 samples *per annum*)

- Liaison and follow-up on any international disease problems/quarantine etc
- Administration of horse registrations/passports (~3500 *per annum*)
- Organisation and editing of the Veterinary Regulations every 4 years
- Administration of the Veterinary Committee, Medication Subcommittee, Medication Control Programme meetings, Veterinary Courses and Seminars
- Liaison with the Legal Department, particularly on doping cases
- Veterinary aspects of general FEI work (for the Bureau/General Assembly/Bulletin/Annual Report)
- Consultative activities and liaison with International Office of Epizootics International (OIE), Conference of Racing Authorities and the European Union
- Liaison with all FEI Contact and Event Veterinarians

The Veterinary Committee makes a significant contribution to the running of the FEI and the achievement of its goals. It is composed of a Chairman and 4 members who represent as far as possible all the FEI disciplines. The composition of the Veterinary Committee should reflect all key disciplines (jumping, dressage, eventing) and also include academic representation. Preferably, the chairman should hold a university position (i.e. to avoid problems with conflict of interest and provide access to research and literature) and the members should be committed, and well respected in equestrian circles. Recently, the Veterinary Committee has reduced its coverage of the issue of Endurance as a new Technical Committee was established in 1998. This has a veterinarian as Chairman (Dr Hallvard Sommerseth) and at least one other member who is a vet.

The Committee has had a wide range of nationalities in its membership. It usually meets once or twice a year and considers a large amount of business to oversee the work of the Veterinary Department. The committee enforces FEI veterinary policy and provides guidelines for veterinarians or technical committees. It functions as a '*think tank*' to maintain equestrian sports ethically acceptable for the sponsors and the public from a veterinary point of view. It deals specifically with the following matters:

Rules and regulations

- Reviews any proposed modifications to the Veterinary Regulations and discusses their impact as they relate to the application for competition
- Discusses any proposed modifications of veterinary relevance to the rules of the different disciplines (jumping, dressage, eventing, vaulting, endurance, driving). This can refer to veterinary examinations and inspections, the competition format, medication control, dead weight in eventing, and so on

Medication control and policy for treatment

- Reviews and establishes the policy for first aid medication during events and the required treatment facilities on or near the site of the event. It also provide guidelines for emergency treatment of horses during the competition and defines restrictions to limit the possible abuse of this system (e.g. use of flunixin, treatment of lameness and colic)
- Discusses specific therapies, to decide whether these can be considered as medication which can be authorised, thereby not leading to withdrawal of the horse from the competition
- Discusses the protocol and outcome of medication control with the Medication Sub-committee, in order to review if the present system needs to be adapted
- Discussion with the veterinary and legal department, to review the outline for doping control. For example, having a 'clean' equestrian sport in not the same as having an 'acceptable' number of cases per year (to be processed by the FEI judicial system)
- Maintains regular communication with the testing veterinarians, as they sometimes have to work in difficult situations, at the competition site. In addition, these veterinarians do not have their own platform to represent them in FEI discussions, and so require support from the Veterinary and Medication Subcommittee

Events and courses

- Establishes a scientific forum of events, designated at sites where there may be adverse climatic conditions (e.g. Atlanta 1996) or involving long-haul transport (Sydney 2000). From these meetings, research may be promoted and advice given to organising committees and national federations. Sometimes a strategy regarding the health requirements for import or re-entry of participating horses is necessary (e.g. piroplasmosis for competitions in North America)
- Organises courses for veterinarians for which there are two options available:

  - Courses in which FEI funding is provided
  - Courses, mainly in countries at a developing stage in equestrian competitions, where funding is obtained from Olympic Solidarity funds

Veterinary officials

- Reviews any complaints regarding the functioning of veterinary officials during events
- Sets up a mechanism for reviewing the list of FEI event vets, as this list is assembled from entries by National Federations. A system of checking the level of listed events veterinarians is being developed to ensure the best attendance of event veterinarians at internal events
- Discusses the policy for appointment of event officials, to safeguard their level of expertise, the influx of new veterinarians in the circuit, the requirements for these officials to be acceptable, etc. This item also involves the number of officials needed at major events like Olympic Games and the World Equestrian Games

Veterinary involvement in FEI competition

A major part of the FEI Event Veterinarian's role is to act as a facilitator and advisor to the officials and other veterinarians at an event. Their prime function, of course, is to ensure the health and welfare of all horses competing in international events, and this will involve wide ranging and sometimes onerous duties. It is crucial that official veterinarians are experienced equine practitioners, as well as being fully conversant with the discipline(s) at which they officiate. The official veterinarian is a professional and is giving time without payment to assist the FEI and the Organising Committee. Nevertheless, it is an honour to be invited as a veterinary delegate or a member of a Veterinary Commission and the position should never be accepted lightly. There is no doubt that efficient veterinary attendance at FEI events will improve the overall execution of the competition and considerably enhance the reputation of the profession.

It is the official veterinarian's duty to ensure that the FEI Veterinary Regulations are effectively implemented. However, this regulatory and advisory function must always be considered in the context of being facilitatory to the running of the event and not aimed at imposing unwarranted delays or unnecessary restrictions on competitors or their horses. Veterinary delegates must always be available for advice to the competitors, team officials or the Organising Committee, which is why it is important to have experience not only as an equine veterinarian, but also of running the competition itself.

Official veterinarians at FEI events

Event veterinarian

In order to accept an invitation to act as an official event veterinarian at any international competition, the candidate must be formally recognised by the FEI. The veterinarian must satisfy the National Federation that they are sufficiently experienced in equine work and have assisted at a number of previous events. It is also helpful to have attended an official FEI Veterinary Course for event veterinarians. The National Federations then submit lists of event veterinarians to represent them in one or more disciplines for the next two years. These lists are finally approved by the FEI Veterinary Committee.

Veterinary delegate

All international competitions (CIs) must have at least one veterinarian to act as veterinary delegate and be responsible for implementing the Veterinary Regulations. The veterinary delegate will be involved with the organisation of the event and the overall supervision of the veterinary facilities. At the end of each competition, a report has to be submitted to the FEI Veterinary Department within 15 days of the event.

Associate veterinary delegate

It is possible to appoint an additional veterinarian if this is deemed to be necessary (or associate veterinary delegate) to assist the veterinary delegate at some competitions (e.g. Championships or CIOs).

Foreign veterinary delegate

The foreign veterinary delegate is appointed at certain international competitions (e.g. Championships, Games, World Cup Finals, CIOs). The appointment is often made by the FEI and always involves event veterinarians with extensive national and international experience. The foreign veterinary delegate forms part of a three person Veterinary Commission. The other members of the Commission are a President and Associate Member. In some special cases (e.g. Olympics and WEG) more than one Associate member may be appointed, and occasionally more than one foreign veterinary delegate if there is a special need (e.g. Atlanta Olympics 1996).

The foreign veterinary delegate's role is to:

- Check that the Veterinary Regulations are being properly implemented
- Oversee the passport control, and to check and sign each passport
- Assist the Horse Inspection Committee for the Tthree-day event at the 1st and 3rd Inspections and to be in attendance during the 2nd inspection in the halt after Phase C of the endurance test

President of the Veterinary Commission

The President is appointed by the Organising Committee and must be someone with extensive knowledge, experience and authority in the discipline(s) involved. The job involves the supervision of the veterinary facilities and organisation and is the senior member of the Commission.

Associate member of the Veterinary Commission

The Associate member is appointed by the Organising Committee to assist the other members of the Veterinary Commission. It is usual for the Associate member to act as examining veterinarian in the Holding Box during horse inspections/veterinary examinations. This person should obviously have the requisite experience of lameness and equine orthopaedics.

Team veterinarians

Team veterinarians are appointed by their National Federation and are responsible for the health and welfare of team horses. Team veterinarians are not eligible to be members of the Veterinary Commission/Delegate or to act as official treating veterinarians, nor may they officiate in any other capacity or compete themselves. Chefs d'Equipe must report the presence of team veterinarians to the Veterinary Commission/Delegate before they assume their official functions in the care of team horses.

Individual competitors' private veterinarians

The person responsible must report the presence of individual competitors' private veterinarians to the Veterinary Commission/Delegate before they can assume their official function in the care of private competitors' horses. They are not eligible to be members of the Veterinary Commission/Delegate or to act as official treating veterinarians, nor may they officiate in any other capacity or compete themselves.

Treating veterinarians

Treating veterinarians are official veterinarians appointed by the Organising Committee who are in attendance to provide emergency care at the event. The treating veterinarian must liaise closely with the Veterinary Commission/Delegate.

Testing veterinarians

Testing veterinarians are specifically responsible for carrying out the Medication Control in certain geographical areas (e.g. Europe), which the Bureau will indicate from time to time. They must always operate in close liaison with the Veterinary Commission/Delegate.

Examining veterinarians

Examining veterinarians are appointed by the Organising Committee in consultation with the Veterinary Commission/Delegate for certain horse inspections, if provided for by the rules of the relevant discipline. An examining veterinarian is only appointed if this role is not filled by the Associate Member of the Veterinary Commission. They must have specific orthopaedic experience. The role of the examining veterinarian is to provide the Ground Jury/Veterinary Commission/Delegate with an expert opinion on the fitness of horses to compete.

Veterinary participation at FEI events

One of the most important roles of the veterinarians is to advise other officials, competitors and the public on matters affecting the health, welfare and safety of horses. It is, therefore, important that the official veterinarian is available throughout the event. This must be for the whole time the horses are under FEI Rules.

Conflict of interest

The problem of conflict of interest can affect all FEI officials, but it is obviously especially relevant for veterinarians to avoid any hint of improper professional conduct. A new article in General Regulations, Art 162, covers the matter for all officials. Of particular relevance to veterinarians are the following paragraphs:

6. A Team Veterinarian or Individual Competitor's Private Veterinarian may not act as a Veterinary Delegate, a member of the Veterinary Commission or compete at an event.

7. The Veterinary Delegate or any member of the Veterinary Commission may not act as a Team Veterinarian, a Treating Veterinarian or compete at an event.

FEI expects its veterinary officials to refrain from giving any form of medication or treatment to horses at an event. Verbal advice on medication and horse welfare may be provided specifically in the case of authorisation of emergency treatment, but a strict 'hands off' policy in regard to actual treatment of participating horses should be followed. This also applies at 'mixed' events, where both national and international classes are being run. Although FEI rules do not strictly apply to a national class, involvement of an FEI veterinary official in the treatment or horses could lead to confusion and easily damage the image of the sport and its officials.

Horse inspections and veterinary examinations

The official veterinarians have a pivotal role in assessing the horses' fitness to compete by carrying out a series of examinations and inspections. It should be remembered that the veterinarian is there as a professional to advise the judges (Ground Jury). These inspections have recently been standardised so that the same format (i.e. with an Inspection Panel of judges and vets and a holding box) is carried out in all FEI disciplines except endurance riding. The essential question to address is whether the horse is 'fit to compete' (or to continue in the competitions) and all veterinarians who act as officials at FEI events must have the requisite experience to make quick and informed opinions about the state of fitness or fatigue of the horses. The other point to remember is that the official veterinarians do not eliminate horses themselves and must work closely with the Ground Jury. It is therefore vital that the Ground Jury seek and fully respect the opinion of the veterinarian at all inspections. There are a number of important points highlighted by the FEI to both judges and veterinarians:

- A close dialogue and collaboration between the Ground Jury and the veterinarians
- A commonsense approach to the fitness of horses to compete as this should not be considered to be a soundness or pre-purchase examination
- It is clear that no horse that is acutely lame can be allowed to continue; however, some degree of flexibility should be exercised for horses showing only mild stiffness or variation in gait symmetry
- The use of the Holding Box and the subsequent report from the examining veterinarian is crucial in checking on horses deemed to be suspicious by the Inspection Panel
- The Horse Data Form is also a useful way of monitoring the horses' veterinary status and fitness to compete during the event
- It is the safety and welfare of the horses that is paramount
- The ultimate objective is to see as many horses as possible compete to the highest level of their capabilities as long as it does not prejudice their health and safety

A fairly recent innovation into FEI eventing is the use of the Horse Data Form. Much work and advice from colleagues in the United States has gone into the preparation of the form, which provides veterinary information on the horse throughout the event. It has been introduced to monitor the horse's progress from the first examination on arrival through to the final showjumping phase of the competition. These forms have proved to be valuable in assessing the horse's response to the high level of competition under the fairly difficult climatic conditions. In recent years, a good deal of more detailed scientific work in monitoring the horse's vital signs throughout all phases of the competition has been carried out. All this information is currently being evaluated and will provide competition veterinarians and organisers with useful parameters to level of fitness, heat stress and fatigue.

First veterinary examination

This initial examination should be carried out when the horse first arrives at the competition site and before it enters the stable compound. The purpose of an 'examination', as compared to an 'inspection', is for the veterinary delegate to establish the general health status of the horse. The first veterinary examination establishes the identity of each horse from its passport, and verifies that the current vaccination requirements and other details are correctly recorded. The clinical examination ensures that the horse is not suffering from infectious or contagious disease. It may include recording heart rate, respiratory rate, temperature and any other pertinent clinical investigations as deemed necessary. It is not permissible to jog horses during this examination unless specifically requested to by the rider. The entire examination should take <10 minutes. The findings should be recorded on the horse data form which should follow the horse through successive examinations and inspections.

The clinical examination includes auscultation of the heart for rhythm and absence of murmurs, auscultation of the thorax and abdomen, brief examination of the eyes with a penlight, assessment of hydration (i.e. capillary refill, skin tent) and rapid palpation of the limbs. Significant injuries and abnormalities should be noted, especially those that might be questioned by the Ground Jury at the first horse inspection. Particular attention should be paid to palpation of the flexor tendons and suspensory ligaments. Heat, swelling and/or pain on palpation are obvious warning signs and any findings should be discussed with the rider. Potential supporting leg injuries may require investigation by ultrasound or radiography. It is useful to have as much information as possible about supporting leg injuries in order to be best able to inform the Ground Jury of the horse's fitness for competition. Because tendinitis and desmitis may not result in significant lameness at the trot up, affected horses may not be easily identified at the first inspection. It is useful to note the state of the shoeing, as occasionally a horse may lose shoes or require a farrier's attention. It is useful to note possible spur marks and abrasions so that there is a record that these things were present before the competition.

Horses are not eliminated from competition at this examination. Problems with the identification and passport are reported to the Appeal Committee for their consideration and decision on appropriate penalties.

Horse inspections

All horses that compete under FEI rules are required to undergo an inspection for fitness to compete before the events. These inspections are carried out by the FEI official veterinarians and the Ground Jury which act as a Horse Inspection Panel. There is often a great deal of public and media interest in the inspections and it is very important, therefore, that they be conducted smoothly and efficiently. The horses are inspected in hand at rest, and at walk and trot on a firm, level, clean, but not slippery surface (Fig 2). A strict procedure for the inspection should always be used. In cases where there is any doubt about soundness or fitness to compete, the horse is immediately sent to a holding area where the suspected problem can be examined more fully. There is no appeal possible at these horse inspections.

In eventing, the following additional inspections and examinations are included during the endurance requirement of the competition:

Second horse inspection in eventing

The second horse inspection takes place at the halt (i.e. the 10 minute box) immediately after Phase C and before the start of the cross country (Phase D). It is conducted by a committee consisting of members of the Veterinary Commission (or veterinary delegate) and the Ground Jury. The foreign veterinary delegate should always be involved in the inspection in the 10 minute box. The horses are inspected as they finish and then the rider may be asked to trot the horse about 50 metres before dismounting.

Pulse and respiratory rates are taken, along with the rectal temperature, while the animal is being critically evaluated and data recorded. The horse is then allowed to be taken away to be prepared for the cross country. However, it is kept under surveillance all the time and, if the official veterinarian is not satisfied, it may have to be presented again at about 7 minutes for checking the vital signs and a quick trot up. Only horses that are looking well and moving freely are permitted to start Phase D. The committee has the right and the duty to exclude any lame of exhausted horses from the competition and no

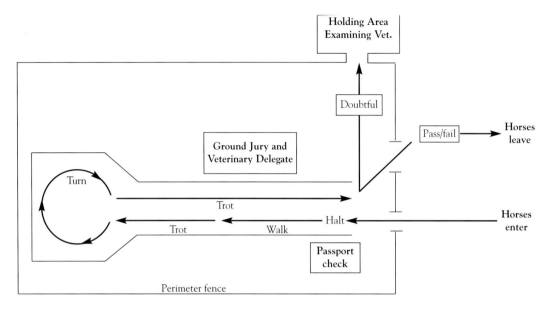

Fig 2: Plan of horse inspections at FEI eventing competitions.

appeal is allowed.

In events where extremes of heat/humidity (e.g. Atlanta Olympic Games) are expected, the organising committee may extend the time of the halt to 15 minutes. In these circumstances, the second veterinary examination after ~7 minutes is mandatory as well as a short trot up to check the gait. Supervision of effective cooling of the horses at this time is also carried out. The information from veterinary monitoring is all recorded on the Horse Data Form.

Second veterinary examination in eventing

At the end of the cross country, the horse is immediately examined by an experienced veterinarian. Horses that are considered to be exhausted can be eliminated by the Ground Jury at this stage. The vital signs are recorded on the Horse Data Form and these may be recorded at one or more intervals until the veterinarian is satisfied that the horse is recovering and can return to the stable area. The examination should not prevent proper cooling of the horses nor stop any medication or fluid therapy as indicated on veterinary advice. Horses can then return to the stables.

Passport control

It is the responsibility of the veterinary delegate/Veterinary Commission to ensure that an official FEI horse passport has been submitted by the persons responsible, for all horses entered in the competition. The identity of each horse must be checked against the details in the passport, as well as ensuring all markings and whorls are properly depicted and recorded. The vaccination status of the animal must be verified that it is current and adequate for the prevailing conditions (e.g. equine influenza at all events; Japanese B encephalitis at some events in Asia).

All horses and ponies for whom an FEI passport, or a national passport approved by the FEI, has been issued, must have the vaccination sections endorsed by a veterinary surgeon, who is not the owner of the animal, stating that it has received two injections for primary vaccination against equine influenza, given no less than 21 days and no more than 92 days apart. In addition, a booster injection must be recorded as having been given within each succeeding 12 months, subsequent to the second injections of the primary vaccination. None of these injections must have been given within the preceding 10 days including the day of the competition or of entry into competition stables.

These are minimum requirements. Both primary and first and subsequent booster injections must be given according to the manufacturer's instructions which will automatically fall within the above ruling. In many cases, booster injections are recommended at intervals more frequent than 12 months.

The details of ownership and National Federation must be checked to see that they are correctly completed and current. The passport must be officially stamped and signed either by the veterinary delegate, or a veterinarian specifically authorised to carry out this function. The details of medication control must also be entered and signed by the veterinary delegate.

All FEI passports are valid for four years and require re-validations for further four year periods. The re-validation stamp can be ordered by the National Federation and obtained from FEI Headquarters. If the veterinary delegate finds an invalid passport, a 30 day warning should be given and this should be stated in the passport.

The main problems with horse passports are:

- Validity of passport
- Incomplete information
- Diagram inaccuracy
- Vaccination problems

Any irregularity is reported to the Appeal Committee, who meet to consider any possible infringement and make a decision. This decision, including any penalty, should be entered in the passport and signed by the veterinary delegate and Chairman of the Appeal Committee.

Medication control

This is a controversial area and a difficult one for all veterinarians, whether they are FEI officials, treating or team veterinarians. The FEI has strict rules concerning anti-doping for all its seven disciplines. Its aim is to keep all FEI competitions drug-free, thereby ensuring that horses perform on their inherent merits without any interference from ergogenic agents or drugs that could affect performance.

The overall programme run by the FEI for medication control is managed by the Veterinary Department at its headquarters in Lausanne. It is set up to be self-financing through the fees charged to Organising Committees. The programme is run differently in different parts of the world. In countries other than Europe, it is left to the Organising Committees to obtain appropriate veterinary assistance to take samples of urine and blood using standard FEI kits. The samples can only be sent to FEI-approved analytical laboratories. The results are sent to the FEI for consideration and any action if samples prove to be positive. In European countries, there is a central medication control programme (MCP) which is run from FEI headquarters (Fig 3). The collection of samples is undertaken by a team of 23 specifically trained testing veterinarians (TVs) from 15 countries. They attend all FEI competitions in the region for all or part of the event and collect the appropriate samples. These are submitted to the reference FEI analytical laboratory. The results are then sent to FEI headquarters. Positive results are referred to the Medication Sub-committee for an opinion on the nature of the substance detected. Their opinion is considered by the Judicial Committee who decide what action and penalties should be imposed. The Veterinary Committee are not involved in this process at all.

Problems with medication control

Veterinarians are faced with the difficulty of advising clients about medication for horses that are going to compete in the near future. There is limited published advice on 'clearance times' of drugs for horses, but with individual variation and complex pharmacokinetics it is difficult to be precise about any drug. Excluding anabolic steroids, it is usually safe to apply the 8-day rule for most drugs.

Another problem involves food contamination in competition horses. Some foods can contain prohibited substances which are unknowingly ingested and result in a positive dope test. Most common in this category have been positives from caffeine and theobromine. It is, therefore, important that competitors always use feed certified free of these substances. Recently, the FEI has included warnings to owners that have been distributed in their passports; this seems to have had a beneficial effect and reduced numbers of positives are occurring.

Other forms of contamination also occur from some types of oral medication. The most common is via powder like isoxsuprine for navicular disease as it can easily be transferred to other horses by inadvertently contaminating buckets, feed, etc. Horses receiving this form of medication should be kept apart and receive their food last to reduce any risk of contamination. Horses may compete with the presence of certain substances in their tissues, body fluids or excreta for which 'threshold' levels/ratios have been laid down, provided the concentration of the substance is less than the maximum levels prescribed.

Results of medication control

The system adopted at FEI competitions is to select not less than 5% of the total horses competing by:

- Random sampling - horses are selected by the testing veterinarian in consultation with the President of the Ground Jury and (foreign) veterinarian delegate

- Mandatory sampling - specific place winners are required in some Championships, World

Equestrian Games and Olympics

- 'Spot' samples - may be requested by the Grand Jury, veterinary delegate or Veterinary Commission at any time during the event

Between 1000–1200 samples are taken within the MCP and ~500 samples in other regions around the world. The details of numbers of samples analysed and numbers tested positive are shown in Figure 4 for the years 1991–1999. The number of positives are given, but the food contamination cases are taken off to give the percentage of the total horses sampled. As can be seen, there is a gradual reduction in positive samples from around 6% in 1991 to 2.2% in 1999. However, this level is still nearly 10 times higher than that recorded for Thoroughbred racing.

There are also considerable differences between the different disciplines in the number of positives recorded (Fig 5). Nearly 80% of positives are recorded in showjumpers, with virtually none in endurance and vaulting.

There is a fair range of substances detected in positive samples recorded from the FEI medication control programme (Fig 6). In the past, there have been serious problems with substances possibly related to food contamination or stable management. For example, in 1997, the highest

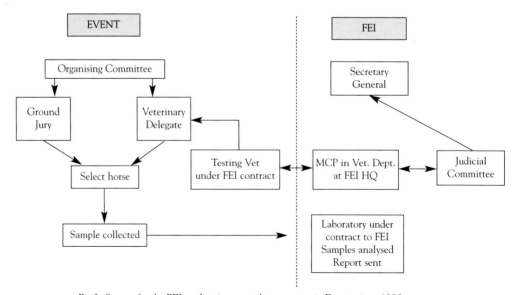

Fig 3: System for the FEI medication control programme in Europe since 1990.

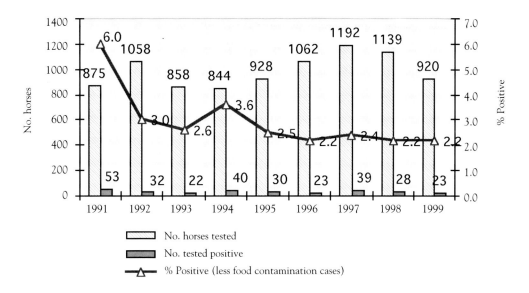

Fig 4: Results of the FEI medication control programme 1991–1999 with the number of horses tested and positive results.

incidence of detections was due to caffeine/theobromine which were thought to be due to contamination of these substances from improperly prepared food. These positives are rarely detected in countries in western Europe, where feed companies are alert to the dangers of these impurities getting in to horse feeds. The FEI has alerted riders to these dangers through notices in the Bulletin and leaflets inserted into FEI passports. There was a substantial reduction in caffeine/theobromine positives in 1998. The potential contaminant is isoxsuprine (circulon), which may be administered inadvertently or from poor stable management (e.g. contaminated buckets, feed or water). Other substances detected tend to be tranquillisers, analgesics and anti-inflammatory drugs (Fig 6).

Treatment of horses during competition

The FEI has established a system whereby horses can, under certain circumstances, receive veterinary treatment during competition for minor illness or injury. The treating veterinarian requests the recommended treatment by completing an official Authorisation Form for Emergency Medication. This is then submitted to the Veterinary Commission/Delegate for their consideration. The veterinary delegate may wish to examine the horse before making a decision and signing the form. After this, the approval of the President of the Ground Jury is required to complete the authorisation procedure.

A review of treatments which have been requested from 1994 to 1996 confirms that there is a need for 'permitted emergency treatment' during competition. Unfortunately, it also reveals that the system is open to some abuse. Horses have been given permission to be medicated that could affect the horse's fitness to continue in competition. These problems arise because:

- The opinion of the rider/owner and their treating veterinarian regarding the fitness of the horse differs from the official veterinarian's view

- The treatment given does not always reflect the existence of a minor illness or injury. For example, allergic reactions, minor lacerations, mild colic, dehydration or conjunctivitis may, after clinical examination, be treated; whereas joint disease requiring intra-articular treatment, colic requiring analgesic administration and lameness requiring nonsteroidal anti-

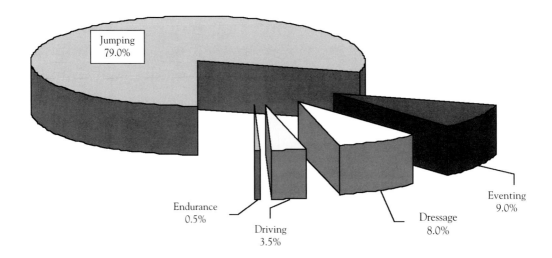

Jumping
79.0%

Endurance
0.5%

Driving
3.5%

Dressage
8.0%

Eventing
9.0%

Fig 5: Results of 250 positive samples recorded in the Medication Control Programme according to the FEI discipline 1990–1999.

inflammatory medication do not fall into the category of non-serious conditions

- Undue pressure to permit treatment of horses which, on veterinary grounds, should be withdrawn

The clearest advice on this matter that can be given is to ensure that horses which suffer from serious conditions **must be withdrawn from competition** to enable them to receive effective treatment without infringing the medication rules.

The whole scheme of medication control has been undergoing intense scrutiny by the Veterinary Committee and Medication Sub-Committee over the last two years. New guidelines have been introduced to cover authorisation of emergency treatment, use of alternative medicine and the administration of medicaments not normally considered to be prohibited substances. It is clear that FEI competition differs from racing and there is the need for some flexibility in permitting medication provided it does not affect performance. The Veterinary Committee is striving to maintain but ensure the welfare of horses during competition. It hopes to stimulate a good deal more research and development in this area to be able to advise the FEI how best to proceed, but maintain the clean reputation of equestrian sport.

FEI development

One of the principal roles of the FEI is the development and encouragement of equestrian sport throughout the world. To achieve this objective it has initiated three distinct programmes:

- Olympic Solidarity Courses - This series of courses is financed by the International Olympic Committee and concentrates particularly on training riders in less developed countries

- FEI Course and Seminars - These courses concentrate on training Judges and officials in all FEI disciplines (including veterinarians) from the most basic to the elite Olympic level

- The FEI World Challenge Series - The FEI World Challenge is a worldwide series of International competitions in the two most popular Equestrian disciplines, Jumping and Dressage. Riders compete under identical conditions against each other while remaining in their own countries. The FEI ensure this uniformity by providing the same Judges for each country in Dressage and by designing identical courses for Jumping. Currently, the FEI World Challenge takes place in 55 countries divided into eight regional groups. In October 1997, the FEI appointed its first

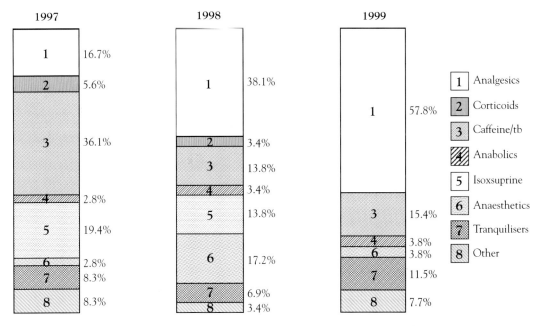

Fig 6: *Detection rates (%) of prohibited substances for FEI anti-doping samples in 1997, 1998 and 1999.*

Development Officer, Mr Michael Stone. A new plan for the development of the sport, especially in non-traditional equestrian regions, is currently under construction.

From the veterinary point of view, this is an exciting time in the FEI with many initiatives and developments underway. These include:

- Improvements to the Medication Control Programme
- New research initiatives involving studies on transportation of horses and abuse from hypersensitisation
- Closer collaboration with the Technical Committees to improve the veterinary profile of FEI competition

- A recruitment drive for more event veterinarians and running more Veterinary Courses around the world for FEI Event veterinarians
- Production of a guide (*aide memoire*) for veterinary officials at FEI competitions

Conclusion

It is clear that the FEI understands the importance of fostering and encouraging greater participation in equestrian sport, not only where it is well established, but in developing countries too. The veterinary profession is very much part of this challenge and is seen by the FEI as essential to the running of its international events.

Equine behaviour: past accomplishments and future directions

KATHERINE A. HOUPT VMD PhD

Animal Behavior Clinic
College of Veterinary Medicine
Cornell University
Ithaca, New York 14853-6401
USA

Introduction

There are three reasons for studying equine behaviour: 1) for the love of it, 2) because horses are fascinating creatures whose every activity is of interest and 3) to assist the owners, handlers and riders of horses in accomplishing their goals without endangering the welfare of the horse or their own safety. The first significant publication on equine behaviour was that of Stephanie Tyler, whose observational study of the New Forest ponies served as a guide to areas of interest for the next generation of equine behaviourists. Very few of the concepts she deduced have been proven wrong; instead, they have been extended to various breeds of horse in differing environments. The areas of equine behaviour that have received the most attention in the past are social relationships, mare-foal interactions, equine learning, sexual behaviour and welfare. In addition, the behaviour of the Przewalski's horse in zoos and now again in the wild has captured the interest of equine enthusiasts as well as conservationists.

Social structure and dominance

Free ranging horses live in small groups, termed bands, which consist of a stallion, several mares and their juvenile offspring. This pattern is found in feral horses in the American West, on the eastern American coast barrier islands of Sable, Assateague, Beaufort and Cumberland and in the unmanaged horses of the Camargue. It had been realised for some time that juvenile colts left their natal group but, more recently, it was found that the fillies, too, usually leave. If they remain in their natal group or if they join a harem group of their half-brother, their reproductive rate is lower than if they join the harem of an unrelated stallion. In most studies, harem groups had one stallion but, in others, there is more than one stallion. The secondary stallions defend the harem from other stallions trying to abduct mares, but sire few, if any, foals. Only a long-term study will determine if the practice of being a secondary harem stallion results in an overall increase in surviving offspring. The factors - climate, population density, etc - that lead to multi-male groups remain to be determined.

Very few domesticated horses are allowed to form the natural groupings described above. Instead, adults are forced to live either in a stall with some release time in a paddock with other horses or are fortunate enough to live in a pasture. The paddock or pasture usually contains large groups, the composition of which is changed frequently. As a result, a new hierarchy is established and it would be desirable to predict which horses will be dominant. Determinants of dominance in groups of horses have been studied in both free ranging and domestic horses. Earlier studies had indicated that males were dominant, but that was not consistently so in our studies of grade ponies or in free ranging Chincoteague ponies. In free ranging mares, age appears to determine dominance, probably because a mare is subordinate to the adults in her band as a juvenile and will remain subordinate if she stays in that band. If she leaves at age two, as most fillies do, and joins another band, the mare of the new band, who are adults, will be dominant to her. Suckled foals show unstable hierarchies, but what little aggression they show results in a dominance hierarchy that is correlated with their age. Upon weaning, when the foals are similar to one another in size, the mother's rank determines dominance independent of sex of the foal.

There is a good reason for all this interest in dominance hierarchies. Although some theorists have questioned the concept of dominance, anyone who has fed a group of horses knows that one horse controls a scarce resource - usually a bucket of grain - and the others acquiesce. If a manager is not careful, one horse will eat too much and the bottom horse in the hierarchy may be malnourished, even though adequate grain for all is available. The subordinate will not only have less access to feed, but will also be expending more energy as he is repeatedly displaced by the dominant animals.

In small groups of horses, the hierarchy is linear, that is, the highest ranking horse displaces everyone and no horse displaces her. The second horse is displaced by the top ranking horse, but displaces every other horse. The bottom horse is displaced by everyone and displaces no other horse. When larger groups are studied, many triangular relationships are seen in which A dominates B and B dominates C, but C dominates A. This probably reflects the unnatural situation of a group larger than six or seven adults - the natural band size.

What most horse owners would like to know is which horse is going to be dominant. That turns out to be a difficult question. It is not necessarily the largest horse nor the male nor the oldest horse. We mix horses so often that age does not appear to be important. Usually maturity is important. A horse less than five years is likely to be subordinate to one older than five. It is probably not a coincidence that young stallions usually acquire a harem of their own at five - the apparent age of social maturity in horses. Aggressiveness does seem to be important. There are a few horses that aggress against others repeatedly but rarely win an encounter. Usually the more aggressive horse wins.

In a food competition, he may continue to threaten with head and heels even when the subordinate has moved away.

Learning

In order to be useful, a horse must be trained, whether the training is as perfunctory as that of racehorses who must tolerate a rider, enter a starting gate and run; or as complex as that of a dressage horse who must respond to subtle rider cues and execute precise and somewhat unnatural manoeuvres. For that reason, there has been considerable interest in measuring learning ability of horses. The earliest studies of learning in horses were comparative, comparing the learning abilities of horses to that of pigs, raccoons, cattle and sheep, horses, donkeys, zebras and elephants. Most of these were visual discriminations in which the animal had to learn that food could be found where a certain symbol was displayed. Horses did not do well in these tests, although they could remember more visual discriminations for a longer time than elephants. In another series of visual discrimination tasks, Quarter Horses were better than Thoroughbreds, perhaps because the latter were more distractable. In an operant task - pushing a lever with the hoof - coldblooded horses learned more quickly than warmbloods.

The next stage of equine learning experiments dealt with maze learning. Quarter Horses could learn a simple one-choice point maze and the reversal when the previous correct turn was now incorrect. The ability to learn that task was not correlated with dominance hierarchy in ponies but was correlated with the speed with which they learned to avoid a painful stimulus. This may indicate an IQ factor in horses akin to that in human intelligence. Foals learned the maze with fewer errors than their dams. When ability of various species - humans, dogs, cattle, possums, etc - to learn a Hebb Williams maze, in which the configuration of the maze changes daily, was tested, horses ranked below dogs but above cattle.

Cynthia McCall and her students have done many studies of equine learning. They found that performance on visual discrimination reversal did not predict the ability to learn to cross a bridge, that 14 trials seemed to be optimum for learning,

Fig 1: The author studying mare-foal behaviour.

and that fairly extensive handling is necessary to improve manageability. Numerous attempts have been unsuccessful in showing that horses learn by observation.

Arabians - the only breed tested - can learn to form a concept. The concept was triangularity. First, the horses learned to tell a black square from a white one, then equilateral triangles from squares, then triangles at different orientation from non-triangles, and then nonequilateral triangles from other shapes. Finally, a hollow triangle was presented for the first time and the one Arabian tested was able to choose it correctly.

Nursing and foal ontogeny

Tyler described nursing bouts of one minute occurring every 15 minutes in New Forest foals, and the same pattern has been observed in Welsh ponies, Arabians, Belgian horses and Thoroughbreds. The most thorough studies of foals development have been those of Crowell-Davis,

who was able to observe Welsh pony foals on pasture for the first several months of their lives. Many of the same mares were observed repeatedly over a three year period. That allowed Crowell-Davis to identify individual differences in maternal attachment that were consistent over the years and did not vary with the sex of the foal.

The changes in foal behaviour from total dependence on milk to a grazing animal takes nearly a year, although grazing occupies 60% of the foal's time by six months. One of the most important findings is that foals grazed when their mother did, which probably results in selection of the same species of plants. The implications of this are that supplemental feeding of foals should be done in such a way that the foals can see their mothers eating. This phenomenon - social facilitation of feeding - is important in adult horses, too. The sight of another horse eating can stimulate an increase in feeding. This can be used to encourage intake in an otherwise anorexic animal.

Imprint training has been practised and popularised by Robert Miler, but there have been few studies of its effectiveness. One week of handling right after birth did not affect manageability, but handling for 15 minutes daily for the first 6 weeks did. Handling for the second six weeks did not result in any improvement in trainability. By examining the management practices of Thoroughbred farms in Japan, where all mare-foal pairs were stalled at night and pastured during the day, Ryo Kusunose of the Japan Racing Association found that the more a foal was led (i.e. the longer distance from stall to pasture), the easier it was to examine as a weanling. Those farms that led, rather than drove, mares and foals from stable to pasture produced more manageable foals. Those farms that removed halters before releasing foals on pasture and replaced them at the end of the day had the most manageable horses.

Future studies of foal behaviour may look at hormonal and breed differences in foal behaviour and, perhaps, take advantage of reproductive technology to help separate genetic (nature) and learned (nuture) influences on foal ontogeny.

Sexual behaviour

What is normal testosterone for a horse? We

Fig 2: Ron Keiper studying feral ponies on Assateague Island.

thought we knew until Dr Sue McDonald found that testosterone values varied with the social situation and are lowest in stallions kept in individual stalls - the manner in which almost all valuable breeding stallions are kept. The levels are high in all-male groups - bachelor herds - and highest in stallions living with mares - harem group. Copulation is not necessary for this effect, because fence line contact with a mare can raise testosterone levels. In the future, more attention should be paid to this factor in treating cases of poor libido in stallions. From a behavioural and welfare point of view, keeping stallions with mares rather than current practice - isolated but with other stallions nearby - would be ideal. There is, however, always the risk that a mare might injure a stallion, so it is more likely that the odour of mares, or even treatment with exogenous testosterone, will be used to treat poor libido.

Another behaviour problem is self-mutilation. This is usually a stallion problem. On the one hand, the stallion - in my experience - has always been housed in a stall. Geldings who self-mutilate, on the other hand, are usually in a social situation and can be helped by removing them from that situation or treating them with the anti-androgen, cyproheptadine. At least one stallion has been cured by putting him on pasture with a mare. In my opinion, the social and sexual frustration of a stallion leads both to an inhibition of testosterone production and to self-mutilation, but, in case the lower testosterone stimulates the stallion to bite himself, it might be worth treating him with androgens.

Trailer behaviour

Approximately 15% of horses have a problem either loading into, or riding in, a trailer. They may kick or throw themselves against the side so they fall or rear and hit their heads as the trailer moves. A series of studies in the USA, Japan and the UK examined the orientation the horse preferred in the trailer and

Fig 3: Lee Boyd with Takhi (Przewalski's horses) successfully released in Mongolia.

the effect of trailering on the horse. The consensus is that horses prefer to stand at an angle to the direction of travel. They stop eating when the trailer is in motion and stand base-wide in an apparent effort to balance themselves. Heart rate and plasma cortisol increase with trailering, but there is no effect on oestrus or pregnancy. A slant load trailer appears to be closer to the horse's preferred - and probably most stable - orientation than the traditional two-horse trailer. Deeper bedding would also be advisable. Horses that fail to load can be retrained using a simple ground work - walk, halt and back, as well as relaxing massage and the popular round pen or free lunging to convince the horse to have confidence in the handler and to be under the handler's control

Behaviour of the true wild horse

Perhaps the most rewarding equine behaviour study is that of an endangered species. The last taki or

Przewalski's horse (*Equus ferus przewalski*) was caught in the wild in the 1950s. For forty years they existed only in a handful of zoos, but their numbers were increased from 12 to a thousand with careful attention to avoiding inbreeding. The behaviour of these horses was observed so that the correct combination of animals would be released into the wild. From the behaviourists' point of view, a zoo population is a desirable one. The behaviourist does not have to pay a *per diem* for care of the horses and, in fact, usually is allowed free admission to the zoo. He, or she, can observe the horses in comfort with film, food, drink and other amenities close at hand - field work without discomfort. The horses are usually managed in a much more natural manner, with foals weaned naturally and a stallion living with the mare. The animals are not often moved or treated because that usually involves chemical immobilisation with a dart gun, a procedure that carries considerable risk.

It has not proven necessary to use artificial means to increase the population of Przewalski's horses, but three embryos were transferred successfully into domestic pony mares. Their behaviour did not appear to differ from that of Przewalski's foals raised by Przewalski's mares but they were weaned at 6 months instead of the normal weaning time of 11 or more months. One of the foals sucked on the ear of her half sister. The problem persisted for over a year and occurred - as cribbing does - in association with eating palatable food such as grain or carrots. This was not a serious problem, but indicates that domestic horses may have been selected for early weaning. Persistent non-nutritive sucking is unusual in domestic horses.

Although the original plan had been to release experienced mares and a young stallion, observations at several zoos indicated that the young stallions were socially subordinate to the mares; and not only failed to breed those mares, but also were inhibited from breeding any mares for the rest of their lives. The plan was altered to release a mature stallion with a small group of mares of various ages. In 1994, after two years of habituation to the environment within a fenced area, the Przewalski stallion, *Khan*, and several mares were released at Hustain Nuruu in Mongolia. Several more releases have occurred and the horses are thriving. Foals are being born and, although some are lost to wolves, the population in the wild is increasing.

Equine welfare

Interest in farm animal welfare is much stronger in Europe than in the US, but equine welfare has been studied on both continents. In the US, transport to slaughter and conditions on urine collection farms have been the two areas investigated most often. Horses lose a great deal of weight and are dehydrated after transport in hot conditions. Watering during the journey helps, but the horses recover normal fluid balance only slowly. Injuries occur during transport to slaughter, the most serious of which are the result not of transport *per se*, but of aggression between horses in the holding areas before loading. Horses in double-decker trailers sustain more injuries; the injuries occur when the horses pass through low and narrow doorways.

In the UK, interest has been centred on stereotypical behaviour or stable 'vices'. Cribbing is the most interesting of these vices because it appears

to be an inherited trait that appears at weaning. Apparently, horses do not ingest the air they aspirate, and instead expire it. There are a number of factors - bedding type, feeding schedule, roughage content and visual access to other horses - which affected the incidence of all stereotypic horses. Stable design is also important because the more openings in the stall, the less weaving. Providing a mirror also reduces the time spent weaving.

The dilemma of equine welfare is that, if no horses were used for a given purpose, no horses would suffer, but then there would be fewer and fewer horses. Much has been made about the welfare of urban carriage horses and, although their care and housing should be regulated and enforced, I would hate to see horses leave the city. Lame horses should be identified and removed from service until they are sound. Carriage horses should not be used when environmental temperature is too high or in areas where horse-automobile collisions are likely to occur.

Similarly, the use of horses for oestrogen production in the pregnant mare urine (PMU) industry has been criticised. Their water was restricted in order to concentrate urine, but a change in company policy has helped to dissuade the PMU ranchers from dehydrating their mares. Another issue was confinement. The mares are kept in straight stalls in order to accommodate the suspended harness used to collect the urine. The frequency of release from the stalls is very variable, so some mares may spend most of the six-month collection period without the opportunity to exercise or roll. The confinement does not appear to be stressful to the mares, although they show compensatory increase in locomotion when released after 2 weeks in the stalls.

The third welfare issue is the fate of the foals produced as a byproduct of the industry. Many are sold for meat. No one has investigated the conditions at horse feed lots, but horses living in groups with free choice food should not be stressed. As noted above, the conditions during transport and slaughter should be carefully monitored. The PMU industry should not be abolished, but the farms should be inspected frequently and the guidelines enforced. Perhaps the most important factor is the availability of forage at all times. That simple management tool seems to promote equine wellbeing more than any other factor.

Future of equine behaviour

Contemplating the future is a subjective endeavour. I would like to think that the money and brain power applied to genomics will be applied to equine behavioural genetics. We should be able to select against those horses that carry a gene for nervousness, aggression, poor maternal behaviour and cribbing, to name a few traits for which genes have been identified in mice and/or human subjects and for which there is evidence for a familial basis in horses.

Horse welfare is receiving some attention now but should receive much more in the future. On one side of the economic scale, very valuable performance horses are kept in luxurious quarters with excellent veterinary care, but the rate of stereotypic behaviours indicates their welfare may be impaired. On the other side of the economic scale are working equids in developing countries for whom owner education about behavioural signs of illness and pain may be as important as free veterinary medical care and cheap, but comfortable, harnesses.

More basic areas for future research include investigation of the sensory abilities of horses. What can they perceive with their olfactory and vomeronasal systems? Can they tell male from female, individual from individual or oestrous from non-oestrous mares? What information is being transmitted when horses breathe into one another's nostrils - and then squeal and strike? What are the critical periods for recognition of the foal by the mare - is it minutes or hours after parturition? What is the true sensitive period for socialisation of the foal? Will different methods of early foal handling have more specific and lasting effects? Can we cure aggression and fearfulness in horses?

References used

Berger, J. (1986) *Wild Horses of the Great Basin*, The University of Chicago Press, Chicago, Illinois.

Boyd, L. and Houpt, K.A. (1994) *Przewalski's Horse: The History and Biology of an Endangered Species*, State University of New York Press, Albany, New York.

Crowell-Davis, S.L. (1986) Spatial relations between mares and foals of the Welsh pony (*Equus caballus*). Anim. Behav. **34**, 1007-1015.

Heird, J.C. and Deesing, M.J. (1998) Genetic effects on horse behaviour. In: *Genetics and the Behavior of Domestic Animals*, Ed: T. Grandin, Academic Press, San Diego, California.

Houpt, K.A. (1998) *Domestic Animal Behavior for Veterinarians and Animal Scientists*, 3rd edn, Iowa State University Press, Ames, Iowa.

Keiper, R.R. (1985) *The Assateague Ponies*, Tidewater Press, Centreville, Maryland.

Kusunose, R. and Torika, K. (1996) Behaviour of untethered horses during vehicle transport. *Jpn. J. equine Sci.* **7**, 21-26.

McCall, C.A., Salters, M.A. and Simpson, S.M. (1993) Relationship between number of conditioning trials per training session and avoidance learning in horses. *Appl. anim. Behav. Sci.* **36**, 291-299.

McDonnell, S.M. and Murray, S.C. (1995) Bachelor and harem stallion behavior and encodrinology. *Biol. Reprod. Mono.* **1**, 577-590.

Tyler, S.J. (1972) The behaviour and social organization of the New Forest ponies. *Anim. Behav. Monogr.* **5**, 85-196.

The Armstrong family

SUSAN PIGGOTT

Florizel
Hamilton Road
Newmarket
Suffolk

Bob Armstrong was born at the George Hotel, Penrith in 1863. One of seven children of the proprietor John William Armstrong and his Irish wife, a Ward from Kildare. Bob showed an interest in horses from an early age. He and his brother Fred hunted, and took part in pony races all around Cumberland, then became Amateur Riders under both rules.

In 1883, Bob started training, and three years later purchased, in his words, "*the best horse I ever had*" at the inaugural Newmarket December Sales. *Dan Dancer*, a two-year-old colt, cost 200 guineas. He won the Ascot Stakes for Bob, but reached the Royal Meeting by a rather circuitous route. Leaving Penrith on 4th June, he headed for Paris, to take part in a big hurdle race on the 7th. Coming to the last, he was well clear - then ran out! Home at Eamont Bridge Stables by the 10th, and looking fairly perky, *Dan Dancer* was dispatched to Ascot, and hacked up at 20/1. Bob's best horse perhaps he was, but it could have been so different.

In 1901, Sir James Miller sent three 3-year-old maidens to Eamont. Bob quickly realised they were useless, and believing honesty to be the best policy, told the owner what he thought. Sir James was offended and sent his horses elsewhere. One of those was *Rocksand*, Triple Crown victor of 1903. In 1912, Bob moved a short distance to Clifton Hill, but was still using the same gallops, which belonged to his main patron, Lord Lonsdale. Two years later, when war broke out, his Lordship was forced to plough the gallops up, which left Bob Armstrong in something of a quandary. The family moved to Ireland and settled into Ruanbeg, on the Curragh. His English owners continued to support him, including Lord Lonsdale, who stayed loyal to Bob for fifty years. Strangely though, the *Horses in Training* books 1914–1920 still show R.W. Armstrong as training in Penrith!

In 1904, Bob had acquired a property, Tupgill Park, situated in the Yorkshire Dales, just outside Middleham. It was rented to a Captain Scott but, in 1920 when the tenant moved out, the Armstrongs moved back from Ireland. Bob and elder son Gerald shared the stabling at Tupgill and later on, younger son Fred, nicknamed Sam, was up the hill at Ashgill. From his earliest days as a trainer, Bob Armstrong had encouraged youngsters who wanted to become jockeys and his first apprentice was R.J. Colling who, when increasing weight forced him to stop riding, established himself as a top trainer; likewise his sons, George and Jack. Bobby Carr, head lad at Clifton Hall, also had a son, W.H. (Harry) Carr, a future Royal jockey. Harry was later to be responsible for something which would have a profound effect on Sam's career as a trainer.

Gerald, a top class Amateur both on the flat and over jumps, suffered two bad accidents and, in 1937, relinquished his licence, having ridden almost a hundred winners. Ten years later, he made a brief return to race riding, in order to clinch his century. This he did at Hamilton Park on a horse he trained, which was owned by his wife. Gerald was also a keen and intrepid aviator. He had his own plane and flew himself to race meetings up and down the country. In 1935, Gerald's *Hyndford Bridge* ran second in the 1,000 Guineas and the following year his tough *Thankerton* won the Jersey Stakes at Royal Ascot, having finished second in the 2000 Guineas and third in *Mahmoud's* recordbreaking Derby. Leaving Tupgill to train in nearby Ferngill, Gerald

Fig 1: Gerald and Bob Armstrong.

finally settled at Thorngill, in 1942, where he was to remain for twenty years, until a serious car accident, in which he was a passenger, forced his retirement. As well as *Hyndford Bridge* and *Thankerton*, the very fast *Como* and *Sailing Light*, who won the Lincoln Handicap, Gerald should be remembered for another training triumph, that of the young Willie Carson, whose first guv'nor he was. Gerald returned to Ferngill to spend his retirement close to sister Doris who lived at Tupgill. None of Gerald's children made their careers in racing, although son Colin flirted briefly with racehorse ownership and became a Director of Ripon racecourse, thus continuing the Armstrong family's long association with that track. He instigated the Armstrong Memorial Cup, run each year at one of the August Meetings. Now Colin Armstrong OBE, he is a highly successful businessman and diplomat, who divides his time between Yorkshire and Ecuador.

In 1920, Frederick Lakin Armstrong left Rossall School and joined H.L. Cottrill at Seven Barrows in Berkshire. Four years later, aged just twenty, he became the youngest licensed trainer when he took over Frank Barbour's private stable at Trimblestown, Co. Meath in Ireland. By 1926 Sam, as he was always known, had returned to Yorkshire and set up at Ashgill. Renting the property from his father, Sam started in a small way, with barely a dozen horses, but within three years this number had more than trebled. In 1936, the name Major L.B. Holliday can be found on the Ashgill owner's list, but in 1937 it is gone! By the end of the decade, now married to Maureen Oates Greenwood (whose Uncle Robin was the ill-fated Antarctic explorer) and father of a baby daughter, Sam was swiftly moving up the trainer's ranks. Then came World War Two.

What with petrol rationing and air raids, racing was greatly curtailed and although, by comparison with southern training centres, Middleham was out of the line of fire, tanks and soldiers roamed all over the moorland gallops. Trainers and their senior members of staff were expected to do their bit for the Home Guard, spending nights on lookout duty at the top of Pen Hill, wearing tin helmets. Taking horses to run anywhere below Pontefract could be a slow and hazardous business. However, despite the difficulties and restrictions, winners kept coming and, during the war years, Sam had an impressive collection of owners, including Sir Woodman Burbridge, then boss of Harrods, flour baron J.V. Rank and South African millionaire Jack Gerber.

But the winds of change were starting to blow from the East. Former Armstrong apprentice Harry Carr, now a successful jockey, was riding in India. He suggested that his main patron, the Maharaja of Baroda, should seriously consider racing in England and recommended Sam to be his trainer. The Maharaja liked the idea and, in 1944, his colours of terracotta and crimson chevrons were carried to victory outside India for the first time. Fired with enthusiasm, the Indian Prince gave Sam *carte blanche* to buy whatever he fancied in the way of bloodstock. This led to the purchase, in 1945, of the full brother to *Dante*, winner of that year's Derby. The colt cost 28,000 guineas, then an unheard of price for a yearling, a record that stood for the next twenty years. Christened *Sayajirao* after Baroda's infant son, he was only one of the several yearlings that were flocking to Ashgill for the Maharaja and other owners. Sam had horses boarded out all over the place. Bigger premises would have to be found. There was only one direction in which to go - south!!

The Maharaja of Baroda paid £52,000 for Warren Place. Set high on a hill of the same name just outside Newmarket, it had been the headquarters of trainer Sam Darling since 1929. On March 20th 1946, a specially chartered train pulled out of Leyburn station, loaded with sixty horses, their lads and a lot of equipment. The move went smoothly, so smoothly that by the end of 1946, F.L. Armstrong had trained sixty-three winners from his new yard. My two-year-old brother, Robert, and I had remained in Yorkshire for three weeks, then travelled down to our new home. We were met at Ely station by Jack Holden, who was to be in charge of all things motorised and become a great family friend for the next fifty-four years. Driving across the Fens, I could hardly believe my eyes, so flat and open after the Dales. And everyone riding bicycles, not a common sight where I had just come from! I was not the only one to feel the change.

My pony, used to the craggy moorland, could not cope with endless vistas of Newmarket Heath and bolted with me. Badly shaken, I refused to ride again for a long time. Years later, as a trainer myself, I would remember that incident and horses that came to me from outside Newmarket, in particular those from the United States, were given a gradual and confidence-building introduction to the wide open spaces of Racecourse Side. Since the beginning of the war, Newmarket had become a sort of club, with families such as Jarvis, Jellis, Colling, Leader, Leach, Waugh and Pratt having the place to themselves and most were now related by marriage. As the first people to move to the town for several years, we were virtual outsiders.

Sayajirao broke his maiden late in July at Hurst Park, then went on to be second in the Gimcrack and third in a good race at Doncaster. He ran only three times at two. The winter of 1946/47 was extremely severe, with heavy snowfall and prolonged freeze-ups. Warren Place was at times cut off from the town. Sam made light of the problems, recalling a time at Ashgill when an intended runner had to be led through deep snow, the four miles to Leyburn Station! But training horses in the early part of 1947 was difficult and, later on, Sam felt that, but for the terrible winter, *Sayajirao* would have won the Epsom Derby, rather than finishing third, which he had also done in the 2000

Guineas. However, the horse did collect two Classics, the Irish Derby and Doncaster St Leger.

Purchased in France, *Lerins* was renamed My *Babu* by Baroda. Winning five of his six races in 1947, he and *Sayajirao* provided His Highness with the rare honour of owning the top rated 2-year-old and top rated 3-year-old in the same year. Also, in 1947, another of the Maharaja's horses, *Diesel*, made history by becoming the first horse to cross the Atlantic by air to race. Flying from Northolt to New York, he ran unplaced in the Belmont. It had been a good year, with sixty-three winners again, and Sam third on the Trainer's List.

Warren Place has a beautiful and quite large house, but although we were living there, it belonged to the Barodas. When the Maharaja, Maharanee, their 4-year-old son and entire staff, came down for racing, we had to keep a low profile. In time, the situation became untenable and we moved to Bassett House on the Bury Road, with Sam commuting between there and Warren Place. Further up the road lived Edgar Britt and his family. Edgar, an Australian jockey who rode for Baroda in India, had come to England in 1946. It was now he who mostly, but not always, wore the terracotta and crimson chevrons. On occasions, the services of Gordon Richards or Charlie Smirke were called upon. My *Babu* fulfilled his promise, winning in record time the 1948 2000 Guineas, and also the Sussex Stakes at Goodwood. He was fourth in the Derby. *Sayajirao* took the Hardwicke and filled second place in the Eclipse. Only once out of the money in fifteen starts, he fully justified his original purchase price. Both horses went on to distinguish themselves at stud. Sam gained two new owners in 1948, Lord Carnarvon, who was to remain for many years and Bernard Van Cutsem, destined to become a top trainer himself in the sixties and seventies.

Sam had always been used to living over the shop and found commuting between Bassett House and Warren Place tiresome. At the bottom of Warren Hill, on the edge of town, stood St Gatien. Built in 1884 by Bob Sherwood, who named it after the horse he trained to dead heat in the 1883 Derby, the yard had lain empty since the outbreak of the Second World War. Sam bought the place, repaired the damage done to the lofts by fire and painted all the woodwork a vivid shade of orange. St Gatien is deceptive to the passer-by. The imposing house, right on the pavement, faces what used to be the horse railway station, at which the Armstrong cavalcade had disembarked in 1946.

But behind the house it's a different story. Sandwiched between two roads, the property comprises three separate yards, with a total of sixty boxes, a cottage, two flats, two paddocks, garaging for horseboxes and cars and a large walled garden. The stable doors are in one piece, so the horses are unable to see out. This perplexed Sam, as he always believed that contented horses made good horses. He devised a replacement door, made of thick wire mesh. On hinges, it could be swung into place very easily. As the yards are well sheltered, these mesh doors, still going half a century later, can be used in all but the severest weather. Sam would find a solution to most problems. A horse who walked his box returned from exercise one morning to find the stable walls painted in diagonal black and yellow stripes. That put paid to his antics! Another could not bear the rain on his head, so Sam sent a 'night cap' to the saddlers, with instructions to extend it as far as the nostrils by attaching a piece of thick plastic. The idea worked perfectly.

By 1950, St Gatien was fully operational, with Sam training for the Aga Khan, Prince Aly and his film star wife Rita Hayworth, band leader Jack Hylton and people from various parts of the world, such as Ceylon (now Sri Lanka) and Brazil, places Sam and Maureen had visited during their winter travels. The Barodas moved their horses, with no prior warning, to George Duller at Epsom and sold Warren Place to Noel Murless. However, it was a long-standing patron from the Ashgill days who was about to take centre stage. As a small child, I had often been led round the yard on a quiet chestnut mare belonging to Jack Gerber, called *Grande Corniche*. In 1950 she foaled a filly by *Niccolo Del Arca*, who was given the name *Bebe Grande*. At two, *Bebe Grande* ran nine times, winning eight, including the National Stakes, Gimcrack, Champagne Stakes and Cheveley Park. Her only defeat came at Alexandra Park, beaten by one of Marcus Marsh's. A tight little track in the East End of London, and known as the frying pan, Ally Pally was one of the first places to stage evening racing. A great favourite with Sam, who trained many winners there, when it eventually closed down, the racecourse executive presented him with the winning post, which until 2001 stood in the paddock at St Gatien. The Maharanee of

Baroda had returned and her *Aquino* won the Ascot Gold Cup and the Doncaster Cup. In addition to inflicting defeat on *Bebe Grande*, Marcus Marsh pipped Sam for Champion Trainer of 1952, but had the title been decided on the number of races won instead of prize money, Sam would have trotted up.

Jack Gerber liked to play an active part in his horse's campaigns and employed a private handicapper, Dick Whitford, formerly a collaborator on Phil Bull's Timeform. Between them they devised a gruelling second season for *Bebe Grande*. It began on April 15th when she was second in the Column Produce Stakes over a mile at Newmarket. On the 29th, she was second again in the 2000 Guineas and two days later third in the One Thousand! Then she went for The Oaks and Willie Snaith, who had ridden her in all her starts but one, was replaced. Ken Gethin took over at Epsom and Gordon Richards was on board two weeks later, in the Coronation Stakes at Ascot. She was unplaced in both. *Bebe Grande's* final race was the King George over five furlongs at Goodwood, with Willie Snaith back in the saddle. She finished third for prize money of £56.10s.

Jack's horses continued to fire. *Royal Palm* won the Woodcote at Epsom; Sam rarely left Derby week empty handed. Then *Royal Palm* took the Horris Hill, but had to settle for third in the Dewhurst. As a 3-year-old he won both the Nunthorpe and the Challenge Stakes. *By Thunder* completed a York double, Ebor (1954) and Yorkshire Cup (1955) in the hands of claimer Wally Swinburn. *Nicholas Nickleby* triumphed in the Royal Hunt Cup. Brilliantly fast but totally neurotic, *Drum Beat* finished second in the July Cup and when he lined up for the 1957 Stewards Cup, another promising Armstrong lad was in the saddle - J. Gifford. Sam loved the big week at Goodwood in July and the Stewards Cup was his favourite race. During the fifties he had won it three times with *First Consul, Palpitate and Sugar Bowl*. The last named, owned by Jack Gerber, scored from the dreaded number one draw. However, Sam always maintained that the shortest route from start to finish over six furlongs at Goodwood was down the stands rail. He felt strongly that with *Epaulette* he could win a second Stewards Cup for Jack and a fourth one for himself.

A handsome son of *Court Martial, Epaulette* did

Fig 2: Susan Piggott and brother Robert Armstrong at Tattersalls October Yearling Sales.

not run as a 2-year-old until October, but managed to win twice. Out early at three, he met with a setback and was off the racecourse for eighteen months. To freshen him up, Sam sent the horse hunting with the Cambridgeshire Harriers and followed this up with a couple of outings over hurdles. *Epaulette* just got beaten at the Kempton Christmas meeting, but obliged at Hurst Park on January 11th 1955, ridden by Colin Casey, a former apprentice of Sam's who got too heavy for the flat. The plan didn't quite work out as, although *Epaulette* won four races that year, he was second at Goodwood. Eventually Sam's faith was rewarded, but sadly he did not benefit from it. In 1958 *Epaulette* did win the Stewards Cup, trained by Paddy O'Gorman.

As a young man, Sam had been a very competent jump jockey, with several winners to his credit. So when, like his father and brother, he started taking on apprentices, Sam had plenty of experience to call upon. Willie Snaith joined the stable at Ashgill as a diminutive youngster, and soon after the war was Champion Apprentice. By 1953 he was stable jockey. During the fifties, on the apprentice front, business was booming. *Curry*, a grand stayer by *Sayajirao* carried Paul Tulk to victory in the Cesarewitch and Great Metropolitan Handicap, then Josh Gifford rode him to win the Chester Cup. Jack Egan spent some time at St Gatien and lightweight Scotsman Charlie Gaston was in great demand. By 1958, fourteen boys were attached to the Armstrong Academy and, although by this time Messrs Swinburn, Gaston, Tulk and Gifford had outridden their claim, there were plenty more waiting in the wings.

Having left school and joined the family firm, it now fell to me to spend hours on the phone, persuading trainers that they could not expect to have winners if they did not use the Armstrong Apprentices! 'Towser' Gosden, father of John, was a good customer, as was Reg Hollinshead, who himself went on to be a kingmaker. Another of my duties, apart from teaching most of them to ride in the first place, was to accompany them to the races and walk them around the track. A yellow van was purchased for the express purpose of transporting the apprentices and me around the country. It was driven by Jack Leafe, a great character, who related his wartime memories as a member of Douglas Bader's ground crew.

All the Armstrong vehicles bore the registration FLA and Sam himself always drove a Jaguar. When I was old enough, Jack Holden started giving me driving lessons. As I did not pass my test until the third attempt, I would head off to far-flung race meetings in Mother's Austin Cambridge equipped with 'L' plates. In the passenger seat was some unfortunate apprentice who already held a driving licence.

My father was a man of high principles. A stickler for punctuality and tidiness of appearance, he insisted all his staff sported short back and sides. When they went racing, the apprentices had to wear a trilby hat, suit, shirt and tie, with their shoes well polished. They must also always take a raincoat. The same dress code applied to those 'leading up' and, as for me, hat and gloves were *de rigeur* and even at the sales, I was never allowed to wear trousers! Naturally the horses had to be every bit as smart and the 'best turned out' prizes usually went to Armstrong runners. A determined man, but at the same time considerate and courteous, Sam lived by two mottoes: *"There's no such word as can't"* and *"It costs nothing to be polite"*. Following Gerald's retirement, 20-year-old Willie Carson enrolled at St Gatien. Three other graduates of the Armstrong school established themselves as successful jockeys only to have their careers terminated by tragedy. Johnny 'Kipper' Lynch suffered severe head injuries in a road accident and Michael Hayes died in a car crash. Fred Dixon, a promising jump jockey, was killed in a fatal race fall. Every year, Yarmouth, another favourite track of Sam's, stages the Fred Armstrong Apprentice Handicap. A fitting tribute.

Many of our owners had studs, and used to breed to both race and sell. From age 11, I started attending the Doncaster Yearling Sales. Back then run by Tattersalls, they were held at the Glasgow Paddocks, in the middle of town. At the end of

August, Father and I did the rounds, checking out prospective purchases at Sledmere owned by Sir Richard Sykes, Marcus Wickham Boynton's Burton Agnes Stud, Mrs Farr's Worksop Manor and Clifford Nicholson's two places, one in Lincolnshire, and the other in Ireland. Once, on the way to visit the latter, we found ourselves near Trimblestown, where it had all begun as a trainer for Sam in 1924. I was given the grand tour! His former bedroom, his office and what horses stood where, in the yard. Luckily, the current incumbent of Trimblestown was very kind and tolerant. As there were one or two French-based owners at St Gatien, Normandy was on our itinerary. It was there I discovered that my Newmarket home shared its name with the airport at Deauville.

Some winters Sam and Maureen went to South Africa. They spent most of their time racing and visiting studs; a bit of a busman's holiday. But one of the new patrons they attracted was diamond magnate, Harry Oppenheimer. As soon as the Goodwood July meeting ended, Sam and Maureen would cross the Atlantic for the Saratoga Yearling Sales. They stayed with one of their biggest owners, Mrs Jo Bryce, whose Mill River Stud was nearby. Racing took place in the afternoon, and the sales, then a black tie affair, late in the evening. All the top names in American racing flocked there, as well as a large contingent from Europe. Sam was now training for a lot of these people, Raymond Guest, Elizabeth Arden, Liz Whitney, Irving Allen and Cubby Broccoli (the James Bond film makers), Mr and Mrs Arpad Plesch, Robin Scully, Stavros Niarchos, Charles Clore, Jim and Meg Mullion and Charles and Edward St George.

Sam also started attending the Florida Breeze-up Sales, held each January at the picturesque Hialeah racetrack in Miami. He was the first British-based trainer to buy there and enjoyed great success with his purchases. The best was probably *On Your Mark*, who won the Great Surrey at Epsom and the Windsor Castle at the Royal Meeting. Sam liked to keep his owners up to date on the progress of their horses and his plans for them. Although he used the phone a lot, he was a great believer in putting things down on paper and spent long hours in his office, pounding away with two fingers on a nonelectric Olivetti. How he would have loved the mobile phones, fax machine and e-mail!

Summer work mornings resembled a military

Fig 3: Sam Armstrong and Lester Piggott.

operation. There were only two lots then, and owners were welcome at either or both. The horse's coats would be buffed to an extra brilliance, thanks to another of Sam's brainwaves - the electric grooming machine. Each visitor was handed a list, showing the order of the gallops. These were typed onto small sheets of buttercup yellow paper, involving the use of copious amounts of carbon paper, photocopiers still being a far off dream. The riders wore different coloured anoraks, making it easier to identify the horses from a distance. The old yellow van roared along the road bordering the Limekilns, changing jockeys and lads from one group to the next.

My job was to accompany the party to where Sam waited, astride the latest in a long line of hacks, always grey, dock-tailed, Percheron cross, rejoicing in the name of Soldier or Sailor. Dressed in a tweed cap, leather jerkin, tan breeches, long socks and polished brown lace ups, he viewed the action through a miniature pair of binoculars, adapted to be worn like spectacles. As well as starting budding jockeys on their way, Sam had, over the years, done the same for trainers. H. Thomson (Tom) Jones was one of the first to benefit from Sam's expertise. Chris Thornton was another. Frank Turner from Italy. Dady Adenwalla from India, Frenchman Jacques Laumain and Tommy Doyle who went from '*doing his two*' to being a top flight trainer in California. Druba Selvaratnam was with both Sam and Robert before embarking on a successful career in Dubai.

The number of horses Sam was sent to train had been increasing steadily over the years, until St Gatien no longer had sufficient boxes to house them all. Sam found an overflow, just the other side of the High Street, along the Fordham Road. Trainer Alf Dalton had more stabling than he needed and, although the Armstrong lodgers were still looked after by Sam's staff, Alf's head lad was in overall charge. The yard in question was Somerville Lodge, destined to become the home of Sam's granddaughter a quarter of a century later. Alf's head lad, Joe Oliver, eventually joined Lester Piggott in a similar role.

I had got married to Lester in 1960 and brother Robert took over my role at St Gatien. I still kept in touch and, in 1963, won the Town Plate on George Tajmindji's *Fulminate*, trained by my father. Whilst at school, Robert had harboured ambitions to make a career in motor sport. Fortunately, as time went on, he abandoned car racing for the equine kind. Seventy-six winners in 1965, the most he had trained in a season, with more than eighty horses in his care, Sam was working harder than ever. Early in 1966, he had a heart attack. Robert was on a skiing holiday when his father was taken ill, but returned home immediately, and took up the reins. Very well he did too, with Mrs Bryce's *Riot Act* winning the Lincoln and Robin Scully's *Catarina*, the Nunthorpe, just two of the highlights among the seventy winners Robert trained that year. At last Sayajirao's 1947 British sale record of 28,000 gns was broken, but not by much; *Rodrigo* made 3000 gns more.

Back at the helm in 1967, with Robert at his side, Sam enjoyed another satisfactory season. He had recovered sufficiently to attend the previous autumn's yearling sales, and brought a nice colt for a new man. *Petingo* cost 7,800 guineas and did very well for Captain Marcos Lemos. Ridden by Lester Piggott, he was unbeaten at two, winning his maiden, the Gimcrack and the Middle Park. Sam Armstrong and Vincent O'Brien had not only been friends for a great number of years, they were also partners in the Pegasus Bloodstock Agency, which they were both now too busy to run. I had just begun to dabble in buying and selling, so took over their office at Tattersalls Park Paddocks.

In 1967, Vincent too, trained a good 2-year-old and both he and Sam had high hopes of classic glory with their respective charges. There was only one problem, the two horses had been ridden by the same jockey - Lester Piggott. He would have to make a choice. *Sir Ivor* had raced only in Ireland, until he went to Paris and won the Grand

Criterium in October. Brilliant as *Petingo* was at five and six furlongs, Lester felt *Sir Ivor* was the one who would stay further than a mile; that meant the Derby, and that clinched it!. Joe Mercer rode *Petingo* to win the Craven and again when he was runner up to *Sir Ivor* in the 2000 Guineas. Later on Lester renewed his partnership with *Petingo* and together they won the St James Palace and the Sussex Stakes.

At the end of 1969, Robert, now married, moved into St Gatien and his parents found a nice house a couple of miles away, which they named Windermere. Sam drove down to St Gatien each morning, rode out with the string, went round stables in the evening and still attended major race meetings. In 1970, *New Chapter* won the Lincoln and *New Member* the Old Newton Cup, whilst 2-year-old *Sparkler* notched up a four timer. The following year *Sparkler* was an unlucky loser in the Irish 2000 Guineas, but won the Diomed and the Prix Quincey.

Robin Scully's *Misty Light* rounded off the season with victory in the November Handicap. At four, *Sparkler* was even better. The Quincey went to him again, along with the Queen Anne at Ascot and the Grosser Pries von Munich, run during the Olympic Games held in the German city that year. Mrs Bryce's *Schoolerville*, successful in the Woodcote at two, added the Temple Stakes and *Steel Pulse*, owned by Ravi Tikkoo, got off to a great start, with four wins, two seconds and a third from seven outings. But Sam's heart problems and the medication he was on were making it harder to keep up the momentum. Late in 1972, he saddled his last two runners. They both won. The following year, Robert took over.

Like the move from north to south, back in 1946, the changeover from father to son went smoothly. *Sparkler* continued to shine, capturing the Lockinge and Prix du Moulin. This time he was second in the Quincey, likewise the Queen Elizabeth II Stakes and third at Deauville in the Jacques Le Marois. When he retired, *Sparkler*, during his racing career, had undertaken thirty-two journeys by air. On these trips he was always accompanied by Derek Duke, travelling Head Lad for overseas runners, of which there were plenty! Derek had been with the Armstrongs all his life, as had his father, Johnny, Sam's first headman. 1975 was the year of the Stable Lads' strike. It began in the spring and reached its peak during Guineas week, when a large contingent of protesters disrupted racing on the Rowley Mile. With so many staff off work, friends and family rallied round. My daughter Maureen and I, several Cambridge undergraduates and Nicky Henderson, could be seen exercising a depleted Armstrong string in those troubled times.

At home and abroad the stable was churning out a steady stream of winners. Three-year-old *Never Return*, unbeaten in five races including the Group 3 St Simon Stakes, followed this up with the Westbury, also a Group 3, the year after. *Al Stanza* took the Princess Margaret and *Noble Saint*, the Voltigeur (Group 2), the Premio Roma (Group 1) and the Yorkshire Cup. Ravi Tikkoo, Lady Beaverbrook and Robert Sangster were doing battle in the Sales ring, with prices frequently exceeding 200,000 guineas, and Company ownership was just over the horizon.

In 1978, I had purchased two colts for George and Elizabeth Moore at the Tattersalls October Sales. They were to carry the red, white and blue colours of Moores International Furnishings Ltd and to be trained by Robert. The first one to strike form was *Moore's Concerto* at Sandown in July. A month later the other colt finished third in a six furlong Newmarket maiden. Robert then sent him to York, his owner's home track, where he won the Convivial. In later years the race was to become the Moorestyle Convivial Stakes. This was the first of thirteen wins in twenty-two starts, and only ever once out of the frame. A great feat of training by Robert and his team.

Moorestyle won the Free Handicap, Prix de la Forêt and Challenge Stakes twice each, Prix de L'Abbaye and Vernons Sprint, Maurice de Gheest and July Cup, in both of which he was also second. Second too, narrowly beaten, in the French 2000 Guineas and the Waterford Crystal Mile. *Moorestyle* was ridden in all but his first outing by Lester Piggott. He cost just 4,000 guineas as a yearling, but was syndicated for over two million pounds to stand at the National Stud, where he died of grass sickness after only a few seasons.

The 1980s began well for Robert. *Mattaboy* secured the Middle Park owned by Ravi Tikkoo, and was respectively second and fourth in the English and Irish 2000 Guineas of 1981, whilst Upali Wijewardene's *Rasa Penang* took the Jersey Stakes at Royal Ascot. Then disaster struck. A Sri Lankan businessman, Upali, had enjoyed several fruitful seasons at St Gatien, until his private jet, with he and some racing friends on board, took off from Kuala Lumpur and disappeared over the Indian Ocean.

Rabdan, having lost his maiden tag in the winter, down at Cagnes-Sur-Mer, went on to collect the Abernant, Meautry, Goldene Peitsche and Seine-et-Oise. *Be My Native*, second in both the Dewhurst and Arlington Million, won the Coronation Cup as a 4-year-old. *Prima Voce*, successful in the Diomed and runner up in the Champion Stakes, brought home the Prix Prince Rose from Ostend and the Cup from Stockholm. Then there was *Never So Bold*. Diadem, Prix de la Porte Maillot, Maurice de Gheest, Temple Stakes, Kings Stand, July Cup and William Hill Sprint, he won them all. Late in his career, *Never So Bold* would go extremely lame after passing the post, recovering completely some twenty minutes later. The cause was eventually traced to bleeding within his knee joint. He enjoyed a long and successful stud career. Both *Rabdan* and *Never So Bold* were bought by Susan Piggott Bloodstock Limited.

Other Group and Listed winners Robert trained during those years included *Gallant Special* (Richmond Stakes), *Dish Dash* (Ribblesdale), *Linda's Magic* (Criterion Stakes), *Miss Demure* (Lowther and 2nd Cartier Million) and *Invited Guest*, unbeaten in four starts at two, with the Waterford Candelabra and Hoover Fillies Mile to her credit. She trained on to win the Prix Physche at Deauville. *Shady Heights* was a tough horse. His 29 starts took him to Ireland, France and Germany on several occasions, as well as the USA and Japan. His seven wins included a Group One, two Group Twos and two Listed, along with enough pattern placings to amass almost half a million pounds in prize money. Robert had a talent for keeping his horses fresh and placing them well, a fact which caught the attention of one prospective owner.

The Maktoum empire was expanding and Robert had become one of Sheikh Hamdan's trainers. He got off to an excellent start with *Mujtahid*, hero of the July Stakes and the Gimcrack of 1990, and *Mujadil* winning the Cornwallis. More success followed, with *Maroof*, Champagne and Queen Elizabeth II Stakes; the good filly *Tajanub* (Princess Margaret Stakes) and *Gabr*. A high-class performer at two, three and four, *Gabr* was sent to race in Dubai and then to the United States. Repatriated to St Gatien, now aged six and better than ever, he had added two Group victories to his record when he suffered a fatal accident on the gallops. *Gabr*, like many of Sheikh Hamdan's horses, was ridden by Willie Carson, whose career had started with Robert's uncle and father. Like them, Robert could spot a promising lad, but finding boys light enough was becoming increasingly difficult, and a lot of them did not stay the course. One who did was Bryn Crossley, a talented lightweight. Paul Tulk, after riding for the stable throughout the 1980s, stayed on as Assistant Trainer, until he took out a licence himself. He was succeeded by Ray Still, another Armstrong apprentice.

Always the globetrotter, Robert had plenty of success to show for it. "Have horse, will travel" could well have been his motto. He broke new ground in 1998 with 6-year-old *Sheer Danzig*. A couple of years before, the horse had won the mile-and-a-quarter Hong Kong Jockey Club Cup at Sandown Park. As time went on, *Sheer Danzig* indicated he could stay further. Second in the Ebor, his next outing was the Melbourne Cup. Sadly, he broke down during the race.

After a most satisfactory career lasting almost 30 years, with a list of owners even more global than that of his father, Robert retired at the end of the 2000 season to pursue other interests. For the first time in 137 years, the name Armstrong was missing from the trainers ranks. Now the only reminder stands opposite St Gatien, where the old horse station used to be. Redeveloped for housing, the area is called Armstrong Close. The Ally Pally winning post has a new home; outside our house!

In the late 1960s, stud land owned by the Jockey Club became available alongside Hamilton Road, with access directly on to the Racecourse Side Training grounds. Doug Smith was the first man to build a yard, followed by Henry Cecil. Although Lester had no intention of retiring for a while, it was an opportunity too good to miss. We built Eve Lodge on a 10 acre site; it consists of a hundred box barn and the usual facilities, all under one roof, with a large indoor school just behind. Four good paddocks and four staff cottages completed the complex. The place was up and running by 1974 and our first tenant was Ben Hanbury.

By 1975 we had built a house for ourselves a hundred yards from the stables, and the move was complete. Ben had bought land just down the road and in 1976 he was replaced by a new tenant, Bill Marshall. Then Bill put up a yard on Hamilton Road, which had now become a Training Centre in its own right! Trainers came and went from Eve Lodge but, in 1984, Michael Hinchcliffe moved in with 77 horses. We had known Mick and some of his owners for several years, so we spent a lot of time around the stables.

When Lester began training in 1986, not only were we familiar with the way the yard worked on a day to day basis, but, as Mick Hincliffe had moved to the Midlands, his head lad, Joe Oliver, joined us. Born in Northern Ireland, Joe was with Paddy Prendergast before coming to England and working for various trainers up and down the country, including of course, Alf Dalton. Having in his time been a jockey and a travelling head lad, he knew the job from all angles. A hard worker himself, he was also a hard taskmaster, but the lads and lasses respected him because he was always fair. Over the years Joe, Ann, his wife, and their daughter Sonia became great friends to all the family.

The build up began in the autumn of 1985. Maureen had swapped a successful eventing career for a life in racing, and she and I set off for the Keeneland September Yearling Sales, where we made a few purchases. Meanwhile, Lester and younger daughter Tracy checked out the one-day Horses in Training sale, which Tattersalls used to hold. They did not come back empty handed, and for a while *Vague Melody* lived in solitary splendour at Eve Lodge. In the Houghton, there were two colts Lester particularly liked. Both chestnuts, one was the son of *Sir Ivor*, the other by *Master Willie*. At Goffs, he spotted an athletic, dark brown filly by *Bellypha*. Fortunately, he got to train them all and *Genghiz*, *Deputy Governor* and *Lady Bentley* turned out to be three of his best horses over the next couple of seasons.

Joe recruited an excellent team, with Charlie Bilham and Craig Stephenson as his assistants, and Malcolm East to be Travelling Head Man. Malcolm had held the same position with Mick Hincliffe, so we already knew each other well. Jennie Goulding was secretary and Lady Rider, with Tony Ives and Bryn Crossley as stable jockeys. Bert Coombes, in charge of maintenance, kept things running smoothly. Lester's parents moved to

Newmarket in 1980, and lived in a house we built behind the stables. Keith greatly enjoyed pottering around the yard, offering advice. Sadly, both of my parents and Lester's mother passed away before he switched to training.

In that first season, Lester had seventy-four horses. His owners included Khalid Abdulla, Lady Clague, Bert Firestone, Karl Fischer, Mahmoud Foustok, Charles St George, Henryk de Kwiatkowski, Bob McCreery, Sue Magnier, Sheikh Maktoum and Sheikh Mohammed, George Moore, Prince Ahmed Salman, Robert Sangster, Sir Michael Sobell, Lord Weinstock and the late Simon Weinstock.

Although the horses were running well, they were not winning and the Press were having a field day! Sheikh Mohammed had sent four maiden 3-year-olds and it was one of these, *Geordie's Delight*, who finally got Lester off the mark at Epsom on 23rd April. After that that there was no looking back. Mahmoud Foustok's *Cutting Blade* ridden by Cash Asmussen landed the Coventry at Royal Ascot. Prince Ahmed Salman's *Deputy Governor* won the Washington Singer and just got beaten in the Royal Lodge, whilst *Genghiz* picked up two races at Newmarket, finished second in the Middle Park and third in the Dewhurst. There was plenty of action abroad too, with visits to France, Italy, Norway and Belgium, where we had a treble at Ostend. By the end of the season, Lester's tally was thirty-three winners, and nine of his 2-year-olds made the Free Handicap. After a good start, more owners asked Lester to train for them, and we were soon full at Eve Lodge. Right next door Derek Weeden had built Calder Park Stables, which we had bought from him. We went into 1987 with 125 horses.

In January, a contingent was dispatched to the South of France, for winter racing at Cagnes-sur-Mer. They did well and when the Riviera season ended in late March, Ian Balding had pipped Lester as top trainer by only a few francs. Back home, *Geordie's Delight* was again our first winner in the Doncaster Shield; *Genghiz* won the Newmarket Stakes and *Deputy Governor* ran a cracking race in the Two Thousand Guineas. It was a busy summer, but our biggest successes were gained abroad, especially in Italy, where *Our Eliaso* and *Brother Patrick* filled third and fourth places in the Derby. Then *Lady Bentley* gave Lester his first classic success with her victory in the Italian Oaks and

Sunset Boulevard brought home the Grand Prix from Brussels.

Lester had a lot of applications from would-be apprentices, male and female, wanting to join the yard. He signed a few of them up. Gary King went on to do well in the Middle East, David Bridgwater made a name for himself as a jump jockey and trainer and Philip Barnard was riding plenty of winners on the flat, until weight forced him to switch to National Hunt. Philip was widely tipped for the top when he met a fatal accident in a hurdle race at Wincanton on Boxing Day 1991. He was 24.

In 1988, I was holding the Trainer's licence. We still had around one hundred horses, but a lot of them were moderate and the 2-year-olds backward. It turned out to be an up and down year. We got off to an early start with Sheikh Maktoum's *Raahin* winning at Folkestone, followed by Bert Firestone's *Javanese* at Newbury, then *Busted Rock* went in at Sandown. We had high hopes for *Moorestyle Girl*, a tough little filly by my brother's champion, but she died from a broken pelvis. In *Dambusters* I could see a future Gold Cup horse. Fifth in the Ascot Vase, he won at Thirsk and then at Goodwood, his owner, Jack Ashenheim's favourite racecourse. The plan was York, for the Listed Lonsdale Stakes, then the Prix de Lutèce at the Arc Meeting. We got as far as York, where he won and, on the rock hard ground, broke the track record. He also broke down and never raced again. I thought things could not get worse. They did, and two days later, I was in intensive care at Addenbrookes Hospital.

I usually rode a rather flamboyant Appaloosa pony on the heath. He frightened the life out of other people's strings! Now and again I would get on a racehorse, and *Versailles Road* was a grand ride. He and I were hacking up the all-weather surface on Hamilton Hill, when he slipped and fell, trapping me beneath. Although wearing a regulation helmet in perfect condition, I fractured my skull in three places and shattered ten ribs. Frankie Dettori has happier memories of *Versailles Road* on whom he lost his five and three pound claiming allowances. During the month I was away, things at home carried on as normal. Maureen was granted the licence and she, Joe and the team trained six winners during my absence. Tracy also did her bit to cheer me up. Now working as a sports commentator in Ireland, she won a charity race at

Fig 4: Maureen and William Haggas with 1996 Epsom Derby winner, Shaamit.

Leopardstown for Kevin Prendergast, in the colours of Sheikh Hamdan.

My dog Grumble was pleased to see me when I got home. She was the daughter of Maureen's Jack Russell, Reggie, who earned his fifteen minutes of fame by eating Derek Thompson's microphone on television. A wonderful companion, she was a popular addition to the yard. I made a good recovery and was back riding out by January 1989. Racing started late that year, on March 30th. As in 1988, we had our first winner at Folkestone, *Northants* in the 3-year-old maiden. It was a steady rather than spectacular year, with several horses, such as old timers *Versailles Road* and *Vague Melody*, along with the 3-year-olds, *Aquaglow*, *Born To Swing*, *Suhail Dancer* and *Saxon Lad*, notching up two or three wins and several placings. *Northants*, opening batsman of 1989, won four times and only just got beaten in a listed race at Ostend by *Turbine Blade*, who I also trained. *Monastery*, owned by Bert Firestone, did best of all. His quartet of victories included a Listed event at Goodwood and a valuable handicap at Newbury. Henryk de

Kwiatkowski's 2-year-olds, *Batzushka* and *Royal Fifi*, each scored a hat trick, and we finished with a total of 34, one of which was on the newly launched all-weather circuit at Lingfield Park.

Nicholas arrived from America towards the end of May 1990. Already a 4-year-old, the handsome little son of *Danzig* had won three times back home. He settled in quickly and was ready to run about a month later. I'd selected Newcastle for his first start, a left-handed track with a very short lead up and a covered saddling yard. I ran him in an American ring bit and booked a jockey who rode Yankee style - Alan Munro. *Nicholas* put up a grand performance to finish second over a distance too far for him. He was running well in decent races, but his first British win, which came in a humble event at Chepstow, will be remembered for different reasons.

Lester had been riding out for some time when he suddenly decided to make a comeback to race riding. Things moved quickly and within a few days of regaining his licence he was in action at Leicester. The following day he got the leg up on

Nicholas, and the rest is history! I couldn't even be there as the Horses in Training Sale was in full swing and we were selling that day. The race was televised and there were more people watching it in the Park Paddocks Restaurant, than there were in the sales ring.

The following summer the partnership won the Group 2 Goldene Peitsche in Baden Baden. *Nicholas* was not only the best horse I trained, but the best of the many good horses Henryk de Kwiatkowski sent to Eve Lodge over the years. Ray Cochrane rode for us on a 'when available' basis for several seasons, but I employed the services of several different jockeys. Alan Munro, Frankie Dettori and John Williams rode for me quite often, also Francis Norton and Jimmy Quinn and I've reason to be grateful to George Duffield and John Reid and particularly, Pat Eddery, for scoring on *Nero*, the only winner I ever owned!

Bryn Crossley was still with us, and quite a few apprentices passed through Eve Lodge. Gary Milligan, an excellent horseman, was a natural lightweight, Sashi Righton, Beverley Brett, Julie Barnicott and Victoria Appleby all spent time with us. Joe Darby was my National Hunt conditional. I enjoyed training the odd hurdler and am very proud to have had a runner at Cheltenham.

In the spring of 1989, Maureen married William Haggas, who trained at Somerville Lodge, where Sam had boarded his overflow, all those years ago. As the 1990s unfolded, things were changing, and life for a trainer was getting even harder. The advent of the all-weather meant year round racing, and then Sunday fixtures burst onto the scene, to mixed reviews. I decided it was time to call it a day, and saddled my final runner at Ripon, late in August 1985. Although I never managed to win the Armstrong Memorial Cup, William and Maureen did, three times before the turn of the century. They also sent out *Shaamit*, Derby winner in 1996. They made an excellent start to the new millennium, by training the top rated 2-year-old filly of 2000, *Superstar Leo*, part-owned and bred by Lester. I too, can claim a tiny part in that success, as I bought her dam.

William and Maureen have two children; a daughter, Mary Anne and son named Sam, after his great-grandfather. Could that be an omen, I wonder?

When amateurs are experts: the story of a foundation mare

LAVINIA LYNAM

Primrose Hall
Gazeley Road
Moulton
Newmarket
Suffolk CB8 8SR

We were complete amateurs at breeding racehorses and our success with *Reprocolor* must be put down to a large amount of beginner's luck! My late father, H.G. (Tiger) Thompson had had fun with a few horses in training, with Bill Elsey in Yorkshire and the late Captain Ryan Price at Findon. The fillies he decided to keep for breeding and, for this, we converted just 26 acres we owned on a South facing hillside at the Southern end of the Pennines in Derbyshire into a studfarm.

Initially, I had my Pony Club knowledge, what I had gleaned from working for Tattersalls (the auctioneers at Newmarket), a TBA Stud Management course and very little else. There was a steep learning curve in those early years. But we were not without our successes, and had a lot of pleasure before it all got prohibitively expensive for the small hobby owner.

Amongst the purchases my father made in 1967 was a yearling filly by *Majority Blue* out of *Hill Queen*, bought at the Doncaster Sales for 600 guineas. A small chesnut filly, with a dipped back and twisted foreleg, we wondered afterwards quite how we had managed to acquire her. She was *Blue Queen*.

Just at that time, her half brothers and sisters began to distinguish themselves. Principally amongst them was *Sandford Lad*, champion sprinter and winner of the Nunthorpe, the Prix de l'Abbaye and the King George Stakes, whilst *Greenhill God* won six races in England, including the Bunbury Cup. A half-sister, *Sandford Lady*, was another good

filly and the dam of winners, including *Gaius*. Incidentally, another of *Blue Queen's* half-brothers was *Doctor Zhivago*, champion National Hunt horse and the winner of many point-to-points. This, and the champion sprinter, from the same mare *Hill Queen*! So the family were on the up and up.

Blue Queen raced, I think, only once at two years, but with her conformation it was doubted she would stand training, and was returned home to us. She was put to quite modest stallions, *Right Boy* and *Town Crier*, in whom we had shares, nevertheless producing winners all the time. *Findon Lad*, five wins in England, won in the USA; *Queen's Message*, two wins, including one at York, to our delight, as it was our favourite racecourse; *Semper Nova*, three wins, and again in America; *Royal Message*, winner and eventual dam of a good horse in Italy, *Flying Postman*.

By 1975 it was clear to me that *Blue Queen* was worthy of much better nominations and could produce something really good for the sale ring if bred to a fashionable stallion, a point my father did not accept. Imagine my disappointment when he purchased a nomination to *Jimmy Reppin* for 200 guineas at the Tattersalls Sales of Shares at Nominations at the Berkley in London! Despite my protestations, off she went to *Jimmy Reppin*.

That June, father died, very unexpectedly, and so never knew the result of his mating plan. So when *Blue Queen* came home empty I was not too disappointed; it had been a late covering to a 200 guinea stallion! But come October, mother, who knew little about horses, but loved *Blue Queen* dearly, announced that she was in foal, and so she was.

The result was a chesnut filly; *Reprocolour*. David Gibson at Barleythorpe Stud actually foaled her down for us, returning the mare and foal at a few days old, as she was not to be covered that year. It is easy to say afterwards that we knew as soon as we saw her walk down the box ramp that here was something special, but we did. She was lovely. We called her '*Lovely*'. There was just something about her. The other foals that year have long been forgotten, but how well I remember her.

She was not a particularly easy filly, being rather highly strung and difficult to keep weight on. Especially when she was parted from the other fillies destined for the October Sales whilst, due to her being late and backward, she was to go to the yearling day at the Newmarket December Sales. We had, at that time, an old character called Riley, supposedly a gipsy, who used to work for us at busy times, and it was he who walked her in preparation for the sales. One day they were gone from the stud for so long we feared she had been kidnapped, and were about to ring the police, when they returned, having been for miles, Riley talking to her in his calming way all the time. My old hunter, *Ranji*, provided uncle-like companionship.

By the time she was ready to go to the sales she looked wonderful, we thought. But would the professionals at Newmarket agree with us? The answer is yes, they did. The more I heard how good she was, the more nervous I became. She was, after all, a chesnut filly, a late foal, by a 200 guinea stallion.

But she could walk. Round and round the sale ring she went, in seemingly two strides. Walking herself into money. Sir Peter Nugent, the auctioneer, did a marvellous job of selling her, finally dropping the hammer at 25,000 guineas. A fantastic price in those days for us. What a proud moment for our little stud, but an emotional one too, as we could clearly hear my father's "*I told you so*".

But she had to be sold, although if things had been different at home she would never have gone. She went to a good and lucky owner, Mr Egon Weinfeld. And to Michael Stoute's yard, where she got the training she deserved, winning the Lancashire Oaks at Haydock, Group 3; Oaks Trial at Lingfield, Group 3; Pretty Polly Stakes at Newmarket, Listed, and placed in both the Yorkshire Oaks and the Epsom Oaks.

After training she returned to us at stud in Derbyshire, before Mr Weinfeld had his Meon Valley Stud ready, as a boarder. She returned again with her first foal by *High Top*, later called *Colorspin*, winner of the Irish Oaks and dam of *Opera House* and *Kayf Tara*.

And the rest is history. She got all the right chances as a broodmare, going only to the very best stallions available.

Now I look at her page in the sales catalogue, devoted entirely to the first dam *Reprocolor*. Chock-a-block with black type. And 'the family' continues to go from strength to strength. She must now be regarded as one of the best foundation mares of her generation.

Nowadays breeding racehorses has become something of an exact science. And expensive too. But sometimes all you need is luck.

Polo

JEREMY ALLEN BA VetMB BSc MRCVS and ALISON SCHWABE MA BSc(Hons)

Department of Clinical Veterinary Medicine
University of Cambridge
Madingley Road
Cambridge CB3 0ES

"Now a polo pony is like a poet. If he is born with a love for the game he can be made. The Maltese Cat knew that bamboos grew solely in order that polo balls might be turned from their roots, that grain was given to ponies to keep them in hard condition and that ponies were shod to prevent them slipping on a turn. But, besides all these things, he knew every trick and device of the finest game of the world, and for two seasons he had been teaching the others all he knew or guessed."

- excerpt from *The Maltese Cat* by Rudyard Kipling.

History

For several thousand years now, man has used the horse's speed, agility and willingness as his legs to play one of the fastest team games in the world - polo. This thriving sport can probably claim to be the first team ball sport ever played, as there are records from over 2000 years ago from ancient Persia.

In the lands that bestrode the valleys of the Tigris and the Euphrates, the horse was an important part of warfare. Kings and nobles commanded vast armies of mounted warriors. Their sport, a version of polo, was called 'chaugan' (the Persian word for mallet)

In the 3rd century BC, the historian Tabari recorded how the Persian king Darius refused to pay tribute to Alexander the Great and, when threatened with invasion, sent him a *chaugan* stick and ball as an insult. The implication was that games were more suited to Alexander's immaturity than warfare. Alexander is said to have replied, *"The ball is the earth and I am the stick"* and later defeated Darius in battle and conquered Persia. Despite Alexander's disdain for the sport, *chaugan* was and remained a favourite pastime of kings and nobility in ancient Persia. Over the centuries it also spread eastwards to China, Japan and India.

It was from Northern India and the people of the mountainous state of Manipur that polo would be discovered and spread to the west. The Manipuris knew the game as '*pulu*' after the bamboo root from which the balls were made. It was popular not only with the Maharajas but also with villagers and tribesmen. They played on small native ponies about 12 hands high which were vital for work in the mountainous way of life. The game was a street game often played between village teams. It was here, in the 1850s, that British Cavalry Officers and Tea Planters came upon the game and quickly developed a passion for it. It spread rapidly throughout the British army in India, being an excellent training for cavalry officers in both horsemanship and teamwork.

It was not, however, until 1869 that polo came to England after officers from the 10th Hussars, reading of this unusual Indian game in the *Field* magazine, decided to have a go themselves. They called for their chargers and experimented, hitting a ball with their walking sticks. Thus polo in the West was born

Those who have played will tell you that polo is an addictive sport, a disease cured only by poverty or death. The 'infection' spread throughout England in the 1870s with London as the centre of the outbreak. It became a favourite affliction of wealthy London society as well as of the cavalry regiments.

Fig 1: Alison Schwabe and Mouldy *at Cambridge Veterinary School.*

It was highly contagious and as reports of the new game reached abroad, so polo crossed the Atlantic to North America and then to South America. It was especially popular in Argentina, whose players now dominate the higher levels of the sport.

The polo pony

The ponies first used in India and England in the early years were small by today's standards. In England stocky Irish ponies were commonly used, whilst in India the small Manipuri ponies of Mongolian origin were ridden, as well as smaller Arab horses. These tough native ponies were usually only 12 to 14 hands high, painting an amusing picture of big men riding small ponies, similar to those ridden by the under 12 Pony Club polo players of today. Indeed the first Hurlingham Polo Club Rules for Polo initially restricted the height of ponies to under 14 hands. It remained this way until after the first World War when the height limit was abolished.

Fig 2: Jeremy Allen.

In South America, the ranch ponies used on the huge estancias to work cattle formed an ideal basis for potential polo ponies. These Criollo ponies, which originated from the imported Barb and Arab horse, had many of the characteristics ideal for polo. They were handy and tough, had congenial sensible temperaments for working cattle, had stamina and a smooth gallop as a good hitting platform. Their training as ranching horses, used to cut out and herd cattle while turning on their hocks, was ideal. The large open expanses of land known as the pampas, the abundance of potential ponies to choose from and the dedication and skill of the South American cowboys, known as gauchos, ensured a plentiful supply of suitable ponies. All they lacked was 'quality' - the pace and competitive nature required as the speed of the game increased. This was added by crossing with imported English Thoroughbreds.

Over the years, Argentina, with a good climate and relatively cheap and skilled labour, has become the largest producer of polo ponies and has produced many of the world's best. Many other countries are now producing significant numbers of polo ponies, in particular Australia, New Zealand, South Africa and the UK. In these countries the racing industries tend to provide an ideal source of potential ponies for polo. Failed racehorses which were either too slow or small for racing are usually cheap and plentiful in supply. Full Thoroughbreds can sometimes be too fine to stand up to the rigours

Fig 3: Howard Hipwood, former Captain of England.

of polo, too hot-headed to remain controllable in the heat of the game or too tall and rangey to turn nimbly. Nevertheless, if they are carefully selected for conformation and temperament, they can make excellent polo ponies.

In England, with the high costs of keeping horses, it has not been economic to breed polo ponies on a large scale, especially when there is a relatively large supply of Thoroughbreds. However, many polo ponies are now bred in Argentina where costs are dramatically lower and the quest for better ponies reaches its peak with the Argentine Open Championships in November. This is the premier tournament in the world, often with 40-goal teams competing (teams composed of four 10-goal players). This is the maximum handicap rating possible. There are usually fewer than a dozen players in the world at any one time with this rating.

Modern breeding methods

In the last decade, with improvements in the manipulation of equine reproduction and unhindered by the ethical and regulatory constraints of the Thoroughbred breeding industry, large-scale embryo transfer has become a reality. In the early years, Professor Twink Allen, from the Equine Fertility Unit in Newmarket, working in conjunction with the Renal family from Argentina, took 14 embryos from top playing mares in Argentina. They were transported frozen to the UK where they were transferred to recipient mares, with 8 subsequent live foals born. Most of these are now playing successfully in the UK and are a good example of what is possible. Hundreds of embryos may be transported around the world in one flask of liquid nitrogen at a fraction of the cost of transporting live adult horses.

Embryo transfer has taken off in Argentina and there are now several very large operations. In the off polo season, the best playing mares are repeatedly inseminated and flushed over a number of cycles and the resulting embryos transferred to recipient mares. The success of such operations has been greatly improved by their large scale. Often they have large herds of several hundred healthy young recipients. Some of the best playing mares are now producing 4 or 5 foals a year via surrogates, while still playing regularly. This has all been made possible by the progressive forward thinking of the Argentinians, making the best use of their natural resources and the desire for better polo ponies.

What makes a good polo pony?

It is difficult to define what makes a good polo pony. In the end it is ultimately a combination of desirable traits which make a player better for whatever reason. Julian Hipwood, Captain of England for some 20 years, and who reached a handicap of 9 goals, once described the ideal pony as a *'hundred-mile-an-hour donkey'*. He also said, *"It should accelerate so fast that it brings tears to your eyes."* The need for speed to get you to the ball quickly ahead of your opponents is obviously paramount but this must be combined with the ability to stop and turn quickly when the direction of play changes suddenly.

Ponies play for periods called chukkas each lasting $7^1/2$ minutes. Each pony may play a maximum of 2 chukkas per game. Heart rate monitoring during play has shown the intensity of work for ponies to be somewhere between eventing and racing and so a mixture of speed and stamina is required. The Thoroughbred is surely unequalled at this level of exercise intensity but is, however, lacking in the strength and sturdiness to carry big men while twisting, turning and bumping into other ponies in the hurley burley of the game. That is why Thoroughbreds crossed with Criollo ponies or other native breeds usually stand up to the rigours of the game better.

During polo, players must be able to concentrate on the game 100 per cent like any other team sport and thus ponies should be balanced enough to work off the bit following only the lightest of aids. Indeed, the best ponies learn to follow the ball and anticipate play, often leaving their riders behind! Ponies must be sensible enough not to lose their heads but remain controllable in the excitement of the game. It is also a big advantage if they have a flat, relaxed gallop so that they make it easier for the rider to hit the ball (no mean feat to master anyway at the gallop). Above all, the best polo ponies, as with all winning competitors, tend to have that extra something, that competitive instinct which will get you to the ball first when it really matters.

Lord Patrick Beresford, many times winner of the Polo Pony Championship at the Royal Windsor Horse Show, describes the qualities of a Perfect Polo Pony thus:

- **Conformation**: a good sloping shoulder, a well set head and neck, a good length of rein, height between 15 hands and 15.2
- **An equable temperament**: therefore easy to play at any level of polo - high, medium or low
- **A light and responsive mouth**
- **Soundness**
- **Action**: smooth and level as opposed to *'choppy'*, so that the rider is brought to the ball at a constant height
- **Handiness**: quick to stop, spin, jump off and accelerate
- **Breeding**: ponies at the top grade today are almost invariably Thoroughbred or at least $7/8$ TB to give the next qualities:
  - Speed plus the stamina to last out a full chukka - and to come back for a second if required
  - Courage and consistency
  - An indefinable air of superiority - the best ponies know they are good and their confidence transmits to the rider

David Morley (renowned trainer of top polo ponies in Sussex):

"Chesney was the best polo pony of his era. He was a winning racehorse with an honours degree brain, who found the perfect partner in Carlos Gracida, rather than working in his service."

(Chesney won the 'Best Playing Pony' award three times in the British Open Gold Cup.)

Henry Brett (currently England's highest handicapped player at 7 goals):

"They've got to look the part to play the part. It's very rarely you see a badly put together champion pony - if ever!"

Polo in the UK

Most polo in Britain today is centred in the South of England, with the major clubs based around

Fig 4: Quantum - best playing pony, Ladies International, owned by Emma Tomlinson. An excellent example of a polo pony.

Windsor in Berkshire, Midhurst in Sussex and Cirencester in Gloucestershire. Here, top level polo is a serious business, with English and foreign professionals playing in teams alongside wealthy patrons. The latter invest huge sums of money just for the enjoyment of having, and playing in, their own team. Prize money in polo is negligible. The competition is fierce in the major tournaments and prices for the best ponies can become astronomical. At the other end of the scale, polo on a more modest level thrives, with many smaller country clubs stretching from Somerset to Perth and Newmarket to Wales. The cost of playing at these smaller clubs is much more modest, with many players enjoying the sport on only one or two ponies. At the grass roots level, polo in the Pony Club is also flourishing with some 500 children competing in Pony Club Tournaments each year. The younger children play on their small, hairy, all-purpose native ponies - referred to as 'Fluffles' - just as was the case with adults a hundred years ago.

Veterinary care and welfare

Veterinary care of polo ponies is not much different from the care of other sport horses. There are a few particular polo-related injuries. The most obvious is known colloquially as 'malletitis'. It is mainly seen in the ponies of less experienced players whose stick control is less than perfect and accidentally hit the ponies' legs. The ponies' legs are protected either by bandages (usually with tendon boots) or by thick boots - the rubberised kind having replaced the traditional leather and felt ones. Most also wear coronet boots to protect against treads and over-reaches. Playing injuries such as localised tendonitis, suspensory branch desmitis and sesamoiditis are common. During play, the frequent requirement to stop and turn quickly from a gallop puts a great deal of stress on the suspensory apparatus. High suspensory desmitis and check ligament injuries are typical of polo. In an effort to reduce such fatigue-related injuries, chukkas, which were originally up to half an hour in length, were shortened to 7 1/2 minutes.

As well as such acute injuries, polo ponies may be treated for more chronic conditions. Ponies usually compete much more frequently than other equine athletes, with practice games or matches

Fig 5: Jeremy Allen (yellow) playing in the 'Old Blues' match 2001.

often 3 or 4 times a week throughout a six-month season. When grounds become dry and hard in mid-summer, ponies, particularly older ones, often become '*footy*' or '*joint-sore*'. As mileage accumulates, fetlock and hock DJD, in particular, are commonly seen in ponies. The Hurlingham Polo Association (polo's governing body in the UK) takes a pragmatic view of allowing a low level of phenylbutazone medication (approximately 1 gram per day for a 500 kg pony), in order to keep older ponies on the road. Its Welfare Committee, however, keep a strict eye on things and lame or injured ponies are not allowed to be played. Drug tests are carried out on both ponies and players.

The term '*polo sound*' is sometimes applied to ponies with low-grade chronic lameness which are still considered to be playable. This term, however, can create tricky complications for pre-purchase vettings as to what is acceptable. Another problem occasionally encountered is eye lesions, especially in Argentinian ponies. These, and other injuries, are often caused by trauma during the traditional rough breaking-in methods sometimes used (called *La Doma*). The animals may be blindfolded and tied up short to a post and beaten in an attempt to '*break their spirit*'. Corneal scars and other traumatic uveal injuries, especially if there is a risk of progression, are very important in polo ponies as ponies blind in one eye are not allowed to play polo. Fortunately the increase in value of good polo ponies worldwide means that attitudes have changed and more care is taken.

As ponies get older they tend to get passed down the level of polo from high-goal to medium

Fig 6: Jeremy Allen receiving the 'Old Blues' Cup 2001 from Professor Twink Allen (his father).

or low-goal. The temptation to pass them to beginners or Pony Clubbers may have to be resisted as these players rapidly improve and soon require faster, hard-working ponies. Many end up umpiring or as hacks, thanks to their reputation as responsive, well-trained, easy-going rides with excellent stable manners.

"That was glory and honour enough for the rest of his days, and the Maltese Cat did not complain much when his veterinary surgeon said that he would be no good for polo any *more. When Lutyens married, his wife did not allow him to play, so he was forced to be umpire; and his pony on these occasions was a fleabitten grey with a neat polo tail, lame all round, but desperately quick on his feet, and, as everybody knew, Past Pluperfect Prestissimo Player of the Game."*

- further extract from *The Maltese Cat* by Rudyard Kipling.

Mill Reef and The National Stud

LT. COL. C. R. DOUGLAS GRAY OBE

Chilcombe, Hook Road
Greywell
Nr Basingstoke
Hampshire RG29 1BT

The National Stud, which had been moved from Gillingham in Dorset to Newmarket in 1966, is the best known stud in England, attracting 20,000 visitors from all parts of the world. In 1963, responsibility and control of the organisation was transferred from the Ministry of Agriculture to the Horserace Betting Levy Board; soon after, it was decided that the policy of keeping fifteen or twenty brood mares at the stud should change and that it should become a purely stallion stud.

When the decision was made to move the stud to Newmarket, the Jockey Club put two farms at its disposal in return for the Levy Board's financial help in the conversion and modernisation of the stands and paddocks on the Rowley Mile Racecourse. This arrangement enabled Mr Peter Burrell, who was Director of The National Stud for over 30 years, to plan from scratch the layout and

The author, Col. Douglas Gray, Director of The National Stud and Michael Bramwell, Assistant Director (right).

design of the new 500 acre stud, one of his main considerations being that there should be a wide dispersal of stable buildings to minimise the spread of possible infection.

In the autumn of 1966, two stallions, the 1954 Derby and St Leger winner, *Never Say Die*, and the successful stallion, *Tudor Melody*, arrived at the new stud and, in April 1967, it was officially opened by Her Majesty the Queen. By the time Peter Burrell retired, in July 1971, the National Stud was firmly established with four stallions - *Never Say Die*, *Tudor Melody*, the American-bred horse, *Stupendous* and the home-bred *Hopeful Venture*.

A short while after Peter Burrell had informed the Levy Board of his intention to retire, Lord Wigg, the Chairman of the Levy Board, invited me to take over as Director, which I accordingly did in 1971.

A regular Indian Cavalry Officer, I had been in Newmarket since leaving the army at the end of Crown Rule in India in August 1947. In 1948, I was invited to manage Hadrian Stud, which had been purchased by Major David Wills. When I left, Peter Player, who had been a stud pupil at Hadrian, succeeded me as the Stud Manager. This was Peter's first appointment in the world of racing, where he has filled many important positions in Newmarket. Meanwhile, in partnership with my wife, Joan, I leased Stetchworth Park Stud from Lord Ellesmere, from where I joined The National Stud as Director.

My five year tenure as Director resulted in considerable expansion and scope at the National Stud. To comply with Lord Wigg's intention to increase the stud's ability to accommodate eight stallions, I felt that the necessary extra buildings

Mill Reef and the author at the National Stud in 1973.

should include four more stallion stables, four more grooms' cottages and one more mares' yard - consisting of twenty-five boxes. As it turned out, all the buildings were designed and completed within one year. In addition, Lord Wigg asked me to appoint and train a younger man to succeed me as the Director when I, in turn, reached the obligatory age of 65 years. Accordingly, I invited Mr Michael Bramwell to join me as Assistant Director.

I had long hoped that the great racehorse, *Mill Reef*, would eventually stand as a stallion at The National Stud - but the opportunity occurred sooner than I expected. One morning, I received an early call from my friend Colonel Robin Hastings - the Managing Director of The British Bloodstock Agency - giving me the dreadful news that *Mill Reef*, in training with Mr Ian Balding at Kingsclere, had sustained a broken left foreleg during a gallop. This was followed by the news that *Mill Reef*'s owner, Mr Paul Mellon, with his American veterinary surgeon, was flying to England for a discussion with Mr Balding and Mr Edwin Roberts, to decide what could be done to save *Mill Reef*'s life.

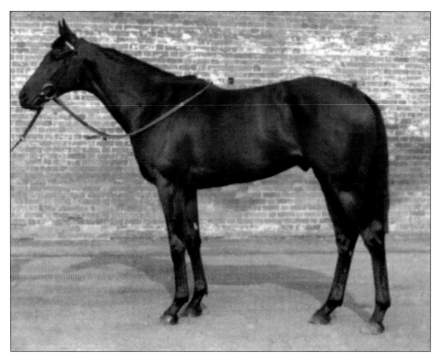

Mill Reef - in training.

Lord Oaksey, the famous former amateur jockey and racing correspondent, in his splendid book 'The Story of Mill Reef', describes exactly what happened on the Lambourn gallops that fateful morning and relates how the great horse was saved as a possible future stallion by the brilliant surgery of Mr Roberts. In this connection, Lord Oaksey has given his consent to quote from Chapter 15, 'Disaster - and Triumph', of his Mill Reef book.

———◆———

Disaster - and Triumph (Chapter 15)

Ian Balding's first thought that morning was that Mill Reef must have split a pastern. That, for a four-year-old, would have been quite bad enough but the truth, as a brief inspection told him, was far worse.

In fact, four separate bones in Mill Reef's near foreleg were gravely injured and, as a result, the whole fetlock joint was left totally unstable. The order in which the injuries occurred can only be a matter of opinion and, in fact, the first warning John Hallum got was a loud crack almost certainly from Mill Reef's cannon bone. But this, the most serious injury of all, may itself have been caused by the total collapse of the inner sesamoid, one of two small bones on either side of the fetlock. If the sesamoid shattered first, the joint would probably have dislocated outwards, throwing an abnormal and insupportable burden on the cannon bone. As that happened, according to this theory, the rim at the top of the long pastern-bone crumpled, the other sesamoid cracked in two and, either then or earlier, a triangular piece nearly three inches long broke off the cannon bone, driving upwards into the medulla and splintering as it did so. The fragments caused by this collision fell down into the crack and would, if not removed, have hindered or prevented reunion of this fracture.

None of this, of course, was known to Ian Balding or John Hallum as they stood in despair that morning, waiting for the horsebox which Mrs Hastings had hurried down to summon.

John's first memory is, as I have said, that dreadful crack, followed at once by a headlong plunge which pitched him up Mill Reef's neck. Even then, on three legs, instinct and momentum carried the horse along for fifty yards and in the end, John had to fling himself off to bring him to a standstill. The wait that followed was agony for both men, but Mill Reef, not yet in serious pain, stood quietly resting his leg and munching grass.

He had still to master the art of walking, though, and it took him nearly half an hour to cover the twenty yards to the side of the gallop. By that time, Bill Palmer and Tom Reilly had the horsebox in position and to all four men, its lowered ramp looked horribly - perhaps impossibly - steep.

For a moment, as Mill Reef stood below it, Ian's eyes met Bill's across his quarters and the same unspoken question was in both their minds: what on earth to do next if he could not get up.

'You could almost see him working it out,' Ian says, 'thinking "I've got to get home somehow".' It was only the first of many strange and painful problems Mill Reef had to face in the next two months and he solved it with typical gallantry.

An awkward three-legged bound carried him on to the ramp and somehow, without assistance, he scrambled up it. But the effort cost him dear and now, shaking and sweating, his distress was heart-rendingly clear. Gently though Norton Jones, the Kingsclere driver, handled the box, the journey down from the gallops must have been a prolonged ordeal, but once in the yard, Mill Reef decided that his own box was the place to be. He hopped off the ramp at once across to the familiar door, and there at last relief was waiting.

Peter Scott-Dunn's assistant, Barry Williams, was ready with a pain-killing injection and as that took effect, he gently applied support bandaging to the injured leg. To him, as he told Ian Balding, the fetlock felt 'like a bag of marbles' and x-rays, taken two hours later by Peter Scott-Dunn's radiographer Mrs Grierson, confirmed that gloomy impression. So, as Barry Williams applied a second, much heavier, plaster of paris support, Ian set in motion the depressing business of telling Mr Mellon, announcing the news to the Press and assembling the experts on whose skill Mill Reef's life and future now depended.

Of the three men chosen, none, as it happened, was in England, but Peter Scott-Dunn hurried back from Germany where he had been attending the British Olympic team, Mr Mellon's own vet, Charles Allen, flew from America for the second time in three weeks, and Edwin James Roberts travelled down from Edinburgh, where he had been attending the BEVA Congress. Mr Roberts, who had only recently resigned from the Equine Research Centre at Newmarket, was, and is, famous all over the world for his pioneering work in veterinary surgery. When, on Saturday 2 September, these three men met at London Airport to examine the x-ray photographs of Mill Reef's leg, it was unanimously decided both that an operation was necessary and that he was the man to undertake it.

Ian Balding was adamant from the first that Mill Reef should not be moved again, so an operating theatre had to be improvised at Kingsclere. As luck would have it, Ian had recently started converting John Porter's old mess room (later used as a chapel) into a gymnasium for the lads. Light and heating had already been installed and the big airy room with its white-tiled walls and a door opening into Bill Palmer's house made an ideal hospital. In one half of it, an operating table was built to Mr Roberts' specifications: straw bales covered in polythene and supported by moveable wooden frames. Ian's brother-in-law, William Hastings-Bass, led the construction team and the frames were so designed that, after the operation, the other half of the room became a cosy straw-lined nest for Mill Reef's convalescence.

All that seemed a long way off when Mr Roberts began, with infinite care and ingenuity, to lay his plans for the operation. His own estimate of the odds was 3-1 on survival of some sort, but only even money a recovery complete enough to let the patient stand at stud.

About midday on 6 September, just a week after the accident, Mill Reef was given a sedative in his box and led slowly along a specially-laid 'tartan' rubber path to the operating theatre. Anaesthetising a horse is a horribly delicate business and, in case he should fall the wrong way, Ian, William, Bill Palmer, John Hallum and Peter Scott-Dunn stood ready with three ropes attached to his neck, his girth and his tail. In fact, their help was hardly needed. Three minutes almost to the second after Mr Roberts had injected the initial dose of Thiopentone into Mill Reef's jugular vein, he gave the signal. So precise was his timing that, with only one gentle pull, Mill Reef subsided gracefully into the exact position planned. For the next seven hours his troubles were over; but those of the men around him had only just begun.

Throughout that afternoon, with only brief pauses for food, Mr Roberts worked unceasingly, assisted by his wife and Peter Scott-Dunn's partner, Anthony Ward, and watched with anxious fascination by Ian Balding and John Hallum. After cutting and folding back a flap of skin to reveal the injury, the surgeon's first task was to remove the fragments of cannon bone which were preventing a proper replacement of the fractured segment. This was then clamped in place and minutely checked for proper alignment. Mr Roberts had decided in advance that to treat the shattered sesamoids

would take far too long and might in any case be unnecessary. The cannon bone was quite difficult enough and for its reinforcement he had chosen a modified buttress plate of the sort used to mend the broken legs of skiers, jockeys and the like. The plate was redesigned to take three screws - two of conventional size but one of the heaviest type available, as big as those used for pinning human hips.

This larger screw ran through the thickest part of the broken segment and into the cannon bone just above the fetlock joint. A second, small, screw secured the middle of the segment and a third anchored the top of the plate to the cannon bone above the fracture. All three screws were set at a slight angle to the leg because Mr Roberts calculated that by following the slope of the broken segment, he would lock it more firmly into place.

Put like that, it all sounds reasonably simple, but holes had to be precisely drilled in advance for all three screws and, at one especially dangerous stage, the clamp holding the broken bone in place was removed while these checks were made. Again and again, x-rays (developed in Bill Palmer's bathroom) were taken to confirm the angle and depth of the drills and the alignment of the bone. And all the while, Mrs Roberts was constantly checking the patient's condition and adjusting the dose of anaesthetic. Mill Reef, in fact, had been - and remained throughout - so totally relaxed that the mixture of oxygen and Fluothane needed to keep him unconscious was only half as strong as that which a normal horse requires. Probably this confirms how right Ian Balding had been to insist on keeping him in his own box until the last possible moment, and certainly it improved his chances of recovery.

In another way too he was an exceptional patient, for when Mr Roberts came to drill the holes above his fetlock he found the bone harder than any in his experience. Since hardness and brittleness do sometimes go together this may explain how the bone came to break in the first place.

Ian and John scarcely left the box throughout the seven hours helping in various ways and stretching Mill Reef's hind legs every half an hour or so to maintain circulation. To them during the afternoon there was brought one cheerful piece of news; as his lifelong friend lay unconscious, Mill Reef's first galloping companion, Red Reef, won an apprentice race at Salisbury in Mr Mellon's colours. To the anxious men standing by the operating table, it seemed at least a hopeful omen.

And then at last it was finished. The final checks were made, the skin was stitched back into place and the

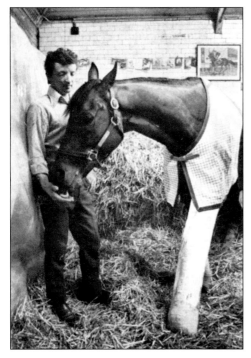

Mill Reef's *splint*.

surgeons applied a full-length plaster, reinforced with an iron splint specially forged by Tom Reilly. Just under an hour after Mr Roberts had completed his marathon task, Mill Reef recovered consciousness. It was a nerve-racking moment, because horses, particularly colts, often struggle to begin with; but with only a little help he rolled over and stood up at the first attempt.

The shock of such a prolonged operation puts a dreadful strain on a horse's constitution, especially on his liver, which has to deal with and dispose of all the accumulated poisons. Serious jaundice can easily set in and for the next three days and nights, struggling with a whole set of strange unpleasant sensations, Mill Reef faced yet another problem. Now, unable to bend his leg at all below the elbow, he had to work out an entirely new method of lying down. Watched day and night by Ian, John and Bill - and when they became exhausted, by volunteer apprentices and Mrs Hastings' two younger sons John and Simon - he tried first one way, then another. Once or twice, Ian offered a helping hand but Mill Reef would have none of that. It was something he had to do alone and in the end he did it. The very first time he was left unguarded, the watchers returned to find him prostrate, fast asleep.

It was some time later, in fact, that Bill Palmer, coming unseen into the box, found how it had been done. Not knowing he was being watched, Mill Reef leant against the straw wall of his 'nest' and then, slowly, with infinite care, slid down it, thrusting out his injured leg. Just once, forgetting, he lay down on the bad side with the plaster under him - and had to be manhandled over before he could get up.

Eating very little but sustained by regular glucose 'drips' and vitamin injections, he battled through the crucial post-operative period and quite soon, John Hallum was able to take him for short walks round the yard. Although the heavy plaster was several inches longer than his other leg, he soon got the knack of swinging it wide and, at this stage, was quite prepared to make full use of it.

From the first announcement of Mill Reef's injury a steady stream of good wishes, 'get well' cards, letters and presents had poured into Kingsclere. More than five hundred cards decorated the walls of his box before he left it and when I visited him one day not long after the operation there were enough peppermints, sugar and assorted goodies at his disposal to stock a fair-sized sweetshop. So many well-wishers sent money for anything he might need or want that, in the end, Ian Balding used the surplus to buy a rocking-horse for the local orphanage. Its name, needless to say, is Mill Reef.

Like most horses, he has always had an insatiable sweet tooth and long before, on journeys to the races, John Hallum and Bill Jennings found him a keen competitor for their sandwiches. Now, when Anne Palmer prepared snacks and breakfast for the apprentices who volunteered to guard him Mill Reef soon asked for - and got - a share of everything. His favourite breakfast, like many sensible civilised gentlemen, was toast, butter and marmalade.

When, forty days after the operation, the plaster was removed, the results were as good as anyone could possibly have hoped. The scar had healed so perfectly that the hair was already growing over it, the broken cannon bone had reunited firmly, the sesamoids were fused in fibrous tissue and the fetlock joint, though almost totally rigid, had not dropped. But now, with only a simple felt support in place of the plaster, Mill Reef no longer trusted his leg. He would only just put the tip of his toe to the ground and although John Hallum massaged them for hours, the triceps muscles of his forearm began to waste. Though prepared to tolerate almost any other form of treatment he still refused point blank to allow the muscle-building Faraday Machine.

A special shoe suggested by Peter Scott-Dunn and built up at the heel helped to some extent, but to make Mill Reef put weight on the injured leg it had in the end to be pulled forward with a rope tied to his pastern. This, as you can imagine, was an agonising period for the little horse's friends. Probably for the first time in his life, he was being forced to do something against his will, and no one at any given moment could be sure how much pain it was causing him. A major problem was replacing the shoes on his other feet, because a horse being shod has one leg in the air and must therefore put weight on the other three. When at last Tom Reilly managed it, Mill Reef was immediately more at ease and progress from then on was rapid. There remained the question of exercise and at first, to make him trot, John Hallum had to run round the covered ride with another lad (usually chosen by Ian because, like John, he was in the stable football team) running behind to provide the necessary encouragement.

Finally, and not without misgivings, Ian decided to let him loose and, as he grazed inside the covered side, the bridle was gently slipped off his head. For several minutes all was well - so much so that Ian left to watch the stable lads playing football in the next-door field. But as he arrived, the Kingsclere team scored a goal and a loud cheer echoed back into the covered ride. It may have simply frightened Mill Reef, but I prefer to think that it awakened memories of half-forgotten days - and of other excited human voices raised to shout him home. However that may be, its effect was explosive. 'Off he went,' John Hallum says, 'at a million miles an hour.

We just didn't dare to look'.

But all was well, and for that brief moment, forgetting all the pain and fear of the past three months, Mill Reef was himself again. As he pulled up sharp and trotted back, there was scarcely a trace of lameness and had Mr Roberts been there he would have been a proud and happy man indeed.

Ever since the operation urgent discussions had been taking place in England and America and across the transatlantic telephone about Mill Reef's immediate future as a stallion. The vets were undecided whether he should go to stud at all in 1973 - and if so, how many mares he should be allowed to cover. In the end, with Ian Balding's strong support, Mr Mellon took the view that there was no great point in waiting. It was decided to limit Mill Reef's first season to twenty mares, a figure which later grew to twenty-three. Mr Mellon kept four nominations himself and gave one to Ian. One went to Lady Halifax and two to American, two to French and four to English breeders. For the remaining six the National Stud, where Mill Reef was to stand, held a ballot, for which there were eighty-five applications, on the basis of £10,000 for a live foal.

With the day of his departure approaching, Mill Reef held his last public audience one bright Sunday morning at Kingsclere. Nearly a hundred cars lined the road outside Park House and in the covered ride John Hallum led his friend through an eager crowd of admirers, young and old. Still lean and light after his

The crowd at Kingsclere to say 'Goodbye' to Mill Reef.

Mill Reef looking at his prospective mares at the National Stud.

long ordeal, *Mill Reef* treated them as ever with perfect courtesy, nibbled titbits of various kinds and allowed himself to be patted, stroked and generally made a fuss of. I spoke to one lady that morning who had driven from Birmingham with two small children.

'We've never seen him before except on TV,' she said. 'And never even backed him once. But we loved him, you see, because he was so brave. Racing just won't be the same for us when he is gone.'

But he had to go and on the morning on 9 January, 1973, the lads at Kingsclere assembled with heavy hearts to watch him board the horsebox for the last time. For many of them too, nothing would ever be quite the same again.

When the box arrived at Newmarket, Ian Balding was waiting, more than slightly anxious about the impression *Mill Reef* would make on his new hosts. He need not have worried.

'He came down that ramp like a two-year-old,' Ian says, 'and stood looking round as if half expecting to see the starting stalls.'

As usual, excitement and novelty had set the adrenalin surging through *Mill Reef*'s veins and as he walked to the new luxurious box with his name and pedigree blazoned on its door, the old jaunty spring was back in his stride. A king had come to claim his new dominion, and no one watching him that day could have dreamt that this was a horse who, three months earlier, had hovered uneasily between life and death.

A small and placid mare was found for *Mill Reef*'s first mating. Her name was *Village Gossip* and she accepted his attentions perfectly, he showing no sign of his injured leg. In all his later matings, *Mill Reef* proved to be a virile horse who could, at times, show exceptional vigour and strength.

I vividly remember one rather frightening incident involving *Mill Reef*, when a coach load of visitors were being conducted around the stud. The stallions were all out grazing in their individual paddocks. After my usual 'spiel' for visitors, the group moved on to the next paddocks to look at *Blakeney*. Unbeknown to me, one visitor had slipped back to *Mill Reef*'s paddock in order to get a better camera angle with the sun behind it. Presumably, the furtive, crouching cameraman irritated *Mill Reef*, who immediately knocked him down and tried to kneel on him. The man tried to protect the back of his head with his camera case and started to scream for help. The stallion man, George Roth, rushed back and caught *Mill Reef*'s headcollar, whilst I held the man's heels and was able to drag him outside the paddock rails. I often thought, what would have happened if *Mill Reef* had killed this stupid man?

In conclusion, I feel privileged to have had control of this great horse who became a legend in the world of Thoroughbred breeding. I was very sorry to hear of *Mill Reef*'s death* a few years after I finally retired from The National Stud.

*Mill Reef was put to sleep as a result of a heart condition in 1986..

From a dream to a reality

LYNDA FREEBREY

International League for the Protection of Horses HQ
Anne Colvin House
Snetterton
Norfolk

"If all these animals could cry aloud with one voice, it would stir the world to do something about it all. One of the most dreadful things about this traffic is that thousands of horses go to doom and agony, trudging along willingly and trustfully and in mute silence. We must be their voice."

- Ada Cole, 1927

Little did Ada Cole think, in the spring of 1911, when she stood on the docks in Antwerp, Belgium, that what she was about to witness would lead to a movement that would continue into the next century. In the midst of the bustle of a busy dockside she noticed old and work-worn British horses shuffling off a cargo boat on their painful journey to death by pole axe in a Belgian abattoir. What she saw that day horrified her so much that she began a campaign that was to consume her for the rest of her life.

Born just outside Thetford, Norfolk, in 1860, into a family of gentleman farmers, Ada had a comfortable and scholarly upbringing which allowed her in her 20s to study to be a nurse.

It was while staying with her sister Effie that she saw the pitiful column of horses on the Antwerp docks and more in the Place de la Duchesse where they stood heads bowed, or collapsed on the cobbles, waiting for somebody to pay a pittance to eke out their last working hours on Belgian soil.

At the time the trade was not illegal, and as the numbers of redundant horses increased due to the rise in urban mechanisation, so did the numbers that were exported for meat to foreign abattoirs.

She lobbied politicians, fundraised and worked tirelessly to heighten awareness of the callous and undignified end that these loyal creatures were having to endure.

"It is your duty to hear," she would point out angrily to people who did not want to listen to her descriptions of the horrifying scenes she had witnessed. *"It is because people do not want to hear that nothing is done. I am going to make people listen!"*

Ada's efforts in raising public awareness to the export of horses for slaughter came to fruition in 1914 with an Act of Parliament that amended an 1898 Government Order and prohibited the

Fig 1: Ada Cole.

Fig 2: From an original drawing by Bryan of Grineau, of horses in a Belgian market (1935).

export of horses unless a veterinary inspector certified the animals *"to be capable of being conveyed and disembarked without cruelty"*. It also stated that every vessel carrying horses should carry a proper humane killer.

Towards the end of the First World War, while working as a nurse with the allied and German wounded, she was arrested for helping allied prisoners escape. Three months in a German prison under sentence of death followed and it was only the armistice that saved her. In January 1919 at the end of the war, at the age of 58, Ada left Belgium to return to Norfolk.

Back in her home county it didn't take long for her to notice that shipments of horses were still leaving King's Lynn for the continent and not only had the 1914 Act remained unenforced during the war, but it had failed to be enacted.

She was enraged; it was not the consumption of horsemeat that infuriated her, but the indifferent and thoughtless treatment of the poor creatures at the end of their lives. But she knew full well that there was little point standing on a dockside, ships or in slaughterhouses complaining, what she had to do was research and gather information as evidence to strengthen her argument. What she needed was political clout, political capital and, above all, political allies.

Through the pages of the Manchester Guardian who published her reports, she gained the ears of influential men and woman and members of parliament.

She lobbied tirelessly for a carcass trade and sought, above all, an act of Parliament that would finally put a stop to the traffic of British horses going for slaughter abroad.

She was tough, impossible to intimidate and countered every argument thrown at her with demonstrable fact. It was this determination and resilience that drew a core of influential friends to her cause.

The struggle for legislation continued and in 1921 The Exportation and Transit of Horses, Asses and Mules Order was passed, designed to improve the welfare of animals on board ship by the provision of adequate water and feed.

It was by then the Roaring Twenties, suffragettes had secured the vote for women and, for some, it was boom time after the austerity of the war years.

Mechanisation was taking over with cars and tractors rolling off factory production lines, machines were replacing horses who were, in turn, sent off to feed the continental appetite for horsemeat.

During this time, another society had been formed independent of the RSPCA or Ada Cole's

Fig 3: ILPH Headquarters in Snetterton, Norfolk.

Old Horse Traffic Committee, as it was then known. At first it was called the National Council Against the Export of Horses for Butchery, founded in Lady Simeon's house in Wilton Crescent, and later became the National Council for Animal Welfare.

Ada recognised that this new society had the money and social influence that she needed and eventually, in 1927, the two societies merged becoming the International League Against the Export of Horses for Butchery.

For the next three years Ada worked tirelessly attempting to bring in her own Bill but was thwarted by the RSPCA when they supplied humane killers for the notorious Parisian slaughterhouse Vaugirard. In the light of the humane killers, the Government rejected Ada's bill on the grounds that the problems no longer existed.

On 17 July 1930, she made a speech to the RSPCA Council, on which she had sat since 1928, which was ruled out of order. She was exhausted, felt beaten by the RSPCA and, on 16 October 1930, she attended her last Council meeting and the very next day, 17 October, she died in her room next to her office at the age of 70.

Lady Simeon wrote of her in *The Times*:

"The death of Miss Cole has deprived the animal world, and especially its horses, of their most dauntless friend - one who was armed at every point with practical and expert knowledge of the work she undertook for them and who literally shared in some of their hardships, crossing the sea with them, and following them all along the road when they were disembarked. As a pioneer in the movement for saving the horses who had worked for us at home from being shipped abroad under terrible conditions, Miss Cole's name should ever be honoured.

It is indeed sad that she had not lived to see its fullest accomplishment in the passing of legislation which will abolish, without leaving any loophole, a traffic in horses sent abroad for butchery, or for a little more work before butchery, which public feeling in this country is unanimous in condemning. Those who knew what her work had been, and that health and family life would have been sacrificed to it, deeply hope that the memorial to her will be the one for which she strove in her last months, the passing of the Bill, Mr Ammons's and later taken over by Mr Broad, which the RSPCA and Animal Welfare Group of MPs - formerly Sir Robert Gower, Chairman of the RSPCA - have fathered."

Her death left 21-year-old Sadie Baum, who had joined her as her secretary *"until the money lasted"*, just three years earlier, to carry on with Ada's struggle.

Sadie, who we know today as Anne Colvin, was a remarkable young woman who took to heart the nature of the work and at her tender age managed to make people not only listen to her but also to take her seriously. She built upon the foundation stones laid by Ada, in her turn working tirelessly to attract into the League people who had clout, both political and social.

Following the publication of a letter about the fate of workhorses for export, written by Geoffrey Gilbey, racing correspondent for the Daily Express, there was a storm of public indignation. Anne was quick to seize the opportunity and asked him to become the first Chairman of the League, an offer he was quick to accept.

This appointment was shortly followed by that of Brigadier General Sir George Cockerill as Honorary Director. Sir George resigned his seat in parliament to take up his position where he remained until his death in 1957.

He was instrumental in drawing up the first draft Convention to protect animals transported by land and sea from preventable suffering. In 1937,

The Exportation of Horses Act came in, which establishes the principle of Minimum Values and the International League Against the Export of Horses for Butchery was renamed the International League for the Protection of Horses.

It is thanks to the dedication and self sacrifice of these two very different women that the International League for the Protection of Horses has become the leading international equine welfare charity it is to day. That the organisation works from such a sound financial base, with the respect of governments both at home and abroad, is tribute to these two noble women who struggled against all the odds to improve the lot of British horses.

Ada Cole would certainly have been surprised to know that in her wake, she would be followed by men and women of real resolve, moved, like her not by sentiment, but by a sense of right and decency and the acknowledgement of a moral obligation.

Through them, the officers and members who give their support, their time and their donations to its activities, millions of horses have felt the hand of the ILPH upon them.

Acknowledgement

With thanks to *Debt of Honour* by Jeremy James. For more information about Ada Cole or the International League for the Protection of Horses, go to: www.ilph.org

Fifty years of racing and breeding

DR CATHERINE WILLS

Sandford Park
Sandford St Martin
Oxford
Oxfordshire OX7 7AJ

When David Wills visited the Newmarket July Course on the Wednesday of the July meeting 1999, to see his homebred *Craigsteel* win the Group 2 Princess of Wales Stakes, it was the last time that he ever set foot on a racecourse; the same racecourse on which, 55 years earlier, his horse *Growing Confidence* had been beaten by a head by *Garden Path* in the 1944 wartime 2000 Guineas, and later ran the unplaced favourite in the Derby held there.

David Wills had no direct family involvement with racing; although he was in with a keen racing set at school at Eton, the only time in his life that he ever bet. He was actually his school house bookmaker. His gambling career ended forever in 1936 when, after large gains on *Mahmoud* in the Derby, he lost all his winnings plus all his 'tuck money' at Royal Ascot a fortnight later, resulting in an extremely hungry second half of the term, in an era when school food without supplements was a serious privation.

Whilst at Oxford University, David Wills rode in point-to-points and was particularly successful on *Bluethorn*, who was only once beaten, due, his rider always said, on that occasion to bad jockeyship. The point-to-pointing naturally ceased with the advent of the Second World War but, on catching polio in Aruba, where he was stationed with his Cameron Highlander Battalion in 1941, David Wills was invalided home and, on recovery, sent to GHQ Southern Command at Wilton House near Salisbury. Salisbury was one of the few courses where racing continued throughout the war. It was also near to several training establishments, so David Wills asked his guardian, Gilbert Dulverton,

if he might be allowed a racehorse (his father had died in 1927 when he was a child and, at that point, he was in his very early twenties). His uncle was not keen, but consented, and gave David the excellent advice never to spend any more money on racing than he could afford to write off and always to count any return as a bonus. Also only to buy well bred yearling fillies which would retain most of their value as broodmares.

The first yearling was then purchased and sent to George Beeby at Compton, Berkshire. She was pessimistically christened *Grave Misgivings* but belied her name and did rather well. A successor was then purchased in 1942 in the shape of a colt named *Growing Confidence*. He came extremely close to winning the 2000 Guineas and at best was top class. By then David Wills was hooked on racing and when the third horse was purchased, *Growing Confidence*'s full brother (by *Blue Peter* ex *Tornadic*), he was named *Great Faith*. *Growing Confidence*'s form was always a little in and out, sometimes excellent, sometimes disappointing. This was subsequently explained by his being a bleeder, the fact of which his trainer had never informed David Wills. When, as a 4-year-old, *Growing Confidence* bled to death on the gallops, David, an extremely gentle man who loved his horses and all animals, was understandably immensely upset and decided that, in the future, he would send his horses to be trained at Newmarket by Jack Jarvis.

Instead of buying any colts, Jack Jarvis only bought fillies for David Wills with a view to building up a band of broodmares. From the start, these fillies were excellent. It was noticeable then, and again when he bought some more fillies for

David in the 1960s, that Jack Jarvis liked buying animals from families that he knew well and had usually trained. These were not necessarily particularly fashionable but they were always tough and Jack set a lot of store by the female line.

He was also a superb judge of a horse's athletic potential. *Unknown Quantity* by *Blue Peter* ex *Firefall*, bought as a yearling in 1947, won the Newmarket and Yorkshire Oaks and the Mornington Stakes and was second in the 1949 1000 Guineas. *Subtle Difference*, by *Admiral's Walk* ex *Riverside* born in 1948 won three races as a 2-year-old and two as a 3-year-old, including the Katherine Howard Stakes at Hurst Park. She was extremely unlucky to be beaten a short head in the 1951 1000 Guineas. It was suggested that David Wills should lodge an objection but he refused to do so, saying that it was not the way to win a Classic.

In 1948, Jack Jarvis bought David Wills a bay yearling filly by *The Phoenix* ex *Bray Melody* who, as a two-year-old, won the Princess Royal Stakes at Kempton Park. Liking this filly *Shrewd Suspicion* considerably, they bought her yearling half sister by *Royal Charger* at the Doncaster St Leger Sales in 1951. Named *Happy Laughter*, she was a top two-year-old before being affected by a severe sinus infection at the end of the season. This necessitated both an operation and treatment by a rare American drug only obtainable in Ireland. After much difficult negotiating with the Irish Government, Douglas Gray, David Wills' stud manager, travelled to Ireland to collect it personally. Finally all was well, and *Happy Laughter* recovered and became the Champion mile filly of her generation in 1953, winning the 1000 Guineas, Coronation Stakes, Falmouth Stakes and Nassau Stakes. She failed to stay in the Oaks, in which she was placed fourth.

Hadrian Stud was acquired by David Wills in 1947 with the help of Jack Jarvis from Sir Alfred Black. It was a fifth part of what, in the 19th century, had been one stud but which had then been sold and divided into five, Hadrian, Derisley Wood, Dunchurch Lodge, Someries and Dalham Hall. A young ex Indian Army Officer, Douglas Gray who had recently returned from India with his wife Joan and was looking out for a job, was suggested by Jack Jarvis as just the person to run the stud. He proved to be an inspired choice of manager and ran Hadrian until 1972 when he was appointed the first manager of the new Newmarket National Stud which had been moved from West Grinstead in Sussex. Douglas started work on 1st January 1948, with just two mares, *Idle Curiosity* and *Dawn Ray* and two men, both Ukranian, who were inmates of the prisoner of war camp at Cheveley. Both men stayed at Hadrian for many years and one of them until retirement.

Gradually, from 1948 onwards, a few mares as well as several more yearling fillies were acquired. The most significant of the former was the superbly bred *Auld Alliance* bought as a 4-year-old in foal to *Blue Peter*. Jack Jarvis had trained her for Lord Roseberry. Placed twice as a 2-year-old she was pretty moderate, only managing to win at Edinburgh as a three-year-old when Jack Jarvis used to take horses up to Scotland to run at the Scottish tracks during the grouse shooting season.

Auld Alliance came from Lord Roseberry's best family, being a half sister by *Brantome* to *Skye*, winner of the Ribblesdale and Princess Royal Stakes, out of *Iona* who was placed in both the 1000 Guineas and Oaks, and was a half sister to Derby and Ascot Gold Cup winner *Ocean Swell*.

The Hadrian Stud policy was to sell the colts, in those days as foals, and to retain the filllies. *Auld Alliance*'s second produce, a colt by *Tudor Minstrel*, born 1956, was sold fairly cheaply at the December Sales of that year to accompany an extremely expensive foal purchase to the USA. The *Tudor Minstrel* colt *Tomy Lee* turned out to be far the better of the two, winning a string of top races as a 2-year-old and the Kentucky Derby and Blue Grass Stakes at three. Sadly, he proved infertile as a stallion.

In 1953, in the wake of *Happy Laughter*'s Guineas success, Jack Jarvis bought a big bay yearling filly by *Big Game* ex *Vertencia* for David Wills. By the time that she came to make her 2-year-old debut, her trainer knew her to be seriously useful so her owner went off in great excitement to watch her run in her first race, which was a small maiden, and for which she was heavily backed, no doubt to a large extent by Park Lodge. She was called *Brave Venture*.

Inappropriately, David Wills, who was a keen fisherman, said to the jockey as he got up, '*tight lines*' which to a fly fisherman means '*good luck*'. Unfortunately, the jockey was not a fisherman and interpreted his instructions literally, so the filly came in a tight held fourth. Jack Jarvis furiously asked the poor jockey what on earth he had been doing, only to be told that Mr Wills '*did not have his money on today*'. Next time out *Brave Venture* won the Molecomb Stakes at Goodwood with ease. In those days it was one of the top 2-year-old fillies' races of the year, so she obviously really should have been a certainty on her debut.

As is well known, with no cameras, in the 1950s it was easy for jockeys to get away with not trying. David Wills often told the story of one of his friends double checking with a top jockey as he left the paddock on a red hot favourite that he was going to win, only to receive the cheerful reply "*not unless the reins break, m'Lord.*"

From the mid 1950s on, David Wills was setting up the Ditchley Foundation whose purpose was, and still is, primarily to promote Anglo-American relations. He had acquired a beautiful and very large Grade I Listed Georgian House for the purpose - Ditchley Park - which was then unfurnished and needed extensive works as well as an endowment. Consequently, in 1958, he decided to sell all except two of his mares, about a dozen in total, to help finance this extremely expensive operation. The retained mares were the 1000 Guineas heroine *Happy Laughter* and the Hyperion mare *High Delight* from the *Vancluse* family, both of whom became useless broodmares. David Wills kept some of the youngstock from the mares sold, in the shape of a few filly foals and yearlings.

Douglas Gray remembers vividly being taken to lunch in Boodles Club in London by David Wills to be told the fairly dramatic news of the impending sale of bloodstock. They chatted away all through lunch and, at the end, David Wills asked Douglas if he would like a glass of brandy, which Douglas declined. David Wills pressed him further but Douglas still refused. Finally David Wills said that he absolutely insisted that Douglas should have a brandy and quickly ordered him a very large one at which point David Wills explained his plans for the mares. Douglas took it all with his usual aplomb and they decided to keep Hadrian going by taking in boarding mares. David Wills loved Hadrian and the wonderful staff who worked there who he wanted to keep employed, and intended to gradually build up his own stud again.

Sadly, when the mares were sold at the 1958 December Sales, although they included *Idle Curiosity*, dam of the 1955 Gimcrack winner *Idle Rocks* and the two 1000 Guineas seconds, *Unknown Quantity* and *Subtle Difference*, they did not make their true value. *Auld Alliance* made a good price on the strength of *Tomy Lee*'s 2-year-old career but obviously, if sold the following year after *Tomy Lee*'s Kentucky Derby win, she would have made a great deal more, which made the whole dispersal extra sad. In fact, some of the mares were bought by Robin Hastings of the BBA for various clients and returned to Hadrian as boarders.

It took a long time to build up the family part of the stud back again from the point of view of breeding top class bloodstock. As mentioned, the two retained mares were no asset. *High Delight*, a small light boned mare bred nothing of any account and *Happy Laughter* had one disaster after an other. The only living foals were a colt by *Aureole*, who was mad and had to be destroyed, a lovely filly by *Tenerani* who was kicked in the head and killed as a yearling, a filly by *Persian Gulf* who was only placed on the racecourse and finally a filly by *Aggressor* whose foaling caused *Happy Laughter*'s death and who was also no good as a racemare. It is noticeable going though the early stud books how many fewer living foals the mares then had and how often they slipped twins or were barren. Modern veterinary science has changed this dramatically.

The youngstock from the 1958 December Sales mares won races and bred winners, but were nothing very special, with the exception of *All Honesty* (b. 1957). A tall, angular spare filly by *Blue Peter* ex *Auld Alliance* she was trained by G.T. Johnson Houghton for whom she won the Sandwich Stakes at Ascot as a 2-year-old. By then the horses in training had moved from Jack Jarvis to Blewbury, which was much closer than Newmarket to David Wills' Oxfordshire home. David Wills, the most tactful of men, had somehow inadvertently managed to upset Jack Jarvis when looking round the horses in training at Park Lodge by suggesting that one of his fillies didn't look well, so the horses went elsewhere for a few years.

By 1963, David Wills was finding it hard to find new and available names in the vein of all his original ones, i.e. nouns with adjectives that qualified them in a particularly characteristic way, such as *Rare Quality*, *Past Experience* or *True Valour*. Having spent a lot of his childhood on the north west coast of Scotland which he adored, David

Wills decided to change his horses' names to those of Scottish place names. Many of the names were, and are, lovely, although some of the Gaelic ones have not been easy for racecourse commentators.

A variety of mares continued to be kept at Hadrian for outside owners as boarders, including some owned by Mrs Arpad Plesch. She had a mare with no pedigree who had never bred anything of any account, called *Duke's Delight*. In 1960, she was sent to *Mossborough*, only known then as the sire of one good horse, *Ballymoss*. The result was a strikingly beautiful chesnut filly with huge presence. Time and again Douglas Gray tried to persuade David Wills to buy her, but her complete lack of pedigree dissuaded him from doing so. The filly in question was *Noblesse*, a brilliant ten length winner of the 1963 Oaks and founder of a dynasty. It is always pointless to think of what might have been. For one thing in this case, if David Wills had bought her, neither *Noblesse* nor her daughters would have been sent to the American stallions that they visited, so the offspring would have been totally different and quite likely much less successful.

In 1960, although continuing to have horses with the Johnson Houghton family, David Wills resumed training with Jack Jarvis. They bought two yearling fillies, as it seemed a good moment to revitalise the stud with some fresh blood. The fillies chosen were *Mingulay*, a *Grey Sovereign* filly, and *Mealasta*, a superb looking bay filly by *Gilles de Retz*. Jack Jarvis knew that *Mealasta* was so good that before she ever ran he rashly told David Wills that he thought she would never be beaten. However, ironically, whereas *Mingulay* won both her 2-year-old races at Newmarket, *Mealasta* was never even placed. Brilliant at home, on a racecourse she seemed to begin to pull herself up approaching the winning post. So convinced of her ability was her trainer that he even ran her in the Oaks, but all to no avail. In disgust, she was eventually sold to Japan.

In 1961, two more yearling fillies were purchased, *Killegray* and *Kerrera*. Sadly, the nicest of the two, *Kerrera*, died before she ever ran, but *Killegray*, a nice tough little *French Beige* filly, won several races. In the mid 1960s, Jack Jarvis trained a colt by *Aureole* ex *All Honesty* (b. 1963) called *Auskerry*, who was potentially a champion. He showed great promise for a strapping great colt of his breeding on his first run in the Chesham Stakes at Royal Ascot, before winning the seven furlong

colts maiden at the Newmarket July meeting on a tight rein by six lengths, breaking the course record, which then stood for the subsequent twenty five years.

Auskerry then won the Hyperion Stakes at Ascot (in those days an important race) in a hack canter. He looked very good indeed. Then disaster struck. He was an incredibly hot favourite in a tiny field for the Doncaster Champagne Stakes. The only other horse with any credentials was the second favourite. So it was an ideal race to fix. The second favourite won and *Auskerry* trailed in extremely distressed and was never any good again. He was undoubtedly doped, although it was never proven. He eventually won two small races in France as a 4-year-old and was sent as a stallion to Chile. He was certainly the most heartbreaking horse that David Wills ever bred, being magnificent looking and so talented.

Some important acquisitions were made in the sixties and seventies. After Jack Jarvis cut down, in 1966, some of his owners, including David Wills and Tom Blackwell, set up Bruce Hobbs as their trainer in Jack Jarvis's second yard, Palace House. Jack Jarvis remained living with his daughter Vivian at Park Lodge, where he had a small string and still trained the odd horse for David Wills until he retired in 1968. Robin Hastings of the BBA was an excellent judge of a yearling. He bought three for David Wills who all turned into good fillies. The first was *Chrona*, a *Princely Gift* filly who won the Cherry Hinton Stakes in 1965 for R.F. Johnson Houghton but who wasn't retained for the stud due to her lack of a really good female line.

Then came two Bruce Hobbs trained fillies, *Hecla* who won the 1970 Cherry Hinton Stakes by eight lengths and who was a half sister by *Henry VII* to the very fast fillies *Mange Tout* and *Rose Dubarry* from the *Mumtaz Mahal* family. Sent to *Sharpen Up* she bred *Famous Star* who, being a colt, was sold as a yearling. Extremely useful, he became a champion sire in New Zealand. Lastly came *Sleat* b. 1969, who won the Sun Chariot Stakes, a half sister by *Santa Claus* to the St Leger winner *Athens Wood*. She was one of the two foundation mares of the modern stud, so more of her later.

From 1964 until the late 1970s, a few horses were sent every year to be trained with Mick Bartholomew at Chantilly. These gave David Wills a great deal of fun and the horses there won lots of races without ever excelling. Probably the best was *Taransay* (bay colt) 1962 by *Narrator* ex *Rare Quality* who was a daughter of *Unknown Quantity*. He won five decent mile races and was placed in class races such as the Prix Perth and Prix Quincey. Lester Piggott rode him in the Prix du Moulin which immediately followed his Prix de l'Arc de Triomphe defeat on *Park Top*. Asked what went wrong, his curt reply was "*the grass was too long*".

Although Robin Hastings' advice on the purchase of yearling fillies was excellent, it proved less successful when it came to stallions and, although some top sires were used, the stud as a whole did not benefit at all from heavy investment in the likes of *Right Boy,* a champion sprinter with no pedigree and a failure at stud, *Sallymount,* bought from the Aga Khan and a hopelessly bad stallion, and *Tutenkhamen,* an elegant *Nasrullah* horse who was an early stallion import from the USA and another disastrous failure as a sire. Even *Sheshoon,* another Aga Khan horse who was stood at the Limestone Stud in Lincolnshire, hardly became commercial, although he sired some good horses.

When Douglas Gray managed Hadrian, he and his wife Joan also ran Stetchworth Park Stud for themselves which they first rented and then bought off the Duke of Sutherland. They lived in their own house '*Homebush*', just outside Newmarket. Whilst at Hadrian, Douglas had various trainee stud managers, in particular Michael Bramwell who went with Douglas to the National Stud and later, just after he came out of the army in 1969, Peter Player. When, in 1972, Douglas moved to the National Stud, an immensely prestigious job, Peter Player took over as the Hadrian Stud manager and lived with his wife Cathy in a house built for them there until the late 1970s. Then Peter's aunt died and left him an estate in Nottinghamshire, Whatton Manor, where he decided to make a stud. This precluded Peter from further looking after Hadrian so David Wills decided to sell the stud, which he did in 1980.

He made a small stud just for his own mares at his Suffolk farm in Bradfield St Clare between Newmarket and Bury St Edmunds, hence the name St Clare Hall Stud. Peter Player was to supervise the new stud which he would visit twice a week, but otherwise it would be run by a stud groom. Many of the old Hadrian staff had retired by then, such as the wonderful old stud groom, Fred Butler and the horsebox driver, George Turner. Some of the others

moved with Peter to Whatton Manor so moving, however sad, was not difficult. With hindsight, it was a good decision. Hadrian had had horses on its ground for over one hundred years and, despite excellent management and rotation of paddocks, grazing cattle etc, the horses had inevitably taken much of the good out of the ground. Several of the last animals bred at Hadrian lacked bone and substance and failed to win. It was noticeable that once the youngstock were moved onto fresher better land they grew more bone and almost without exception won races.

Hadrian was sold to Souren Vanien who sold it to Sheikh Mohammed soon afterwards. He has turned the five studs back into one large one as it was originally, in the shape of Dalham. The stud at Bradfield St Clare, however, was not a success in so far as it was the wrong distance away from Newmarket, too far away for the staff to feel part of the Newmarket scene but too close for them not to hanker after it. Good stud grooms were successively lured away, and as Peter Player became increasingly busy he found it harder and harder to find the time to go there enough. After a few years David Wills decided to sell St Clare Hall and move all the mares to Whatton Manor where they still are, with the exception of four of the young mares who are at Darby Dan in Kentucky in order to benefit from the great choice of stallions available in the USA. This is particularly useful for mares needing outcrosses to *Northern Dancer* blood, of which St Clare Hall has several.

An interesting and enterprising broodmare acquisition, who just missed being a great success, was the 1960 Australian 1000 Guineas winner *Chaise*. Bought by the BBA, she was by a *Dante* horse *Landau* from a good French family and was sent over from Australia by boat in 1964. Her first living foal was an extremely useful colt by *Gentle Art, Affric* (1966). After winning his 2-year-old maiden, he was placed twice at the Goodwood Festival meeting both in the Rous Memorial Stakes and three days later in the New Ham Foal Stakes before being exported and winning a string of races in South America where he went to stud. The next living colt, *Carloway* by *Reliance II,* was thought by Bruce Hobbs to have huge ability, but broke down before he could prove himself. *Chaise* bred more winners but none as good as those first two foals and none of her daughters were good enough to be retained for the stud.

The key mare bought by David Wills in the 1960s was *Margaret Ann* (1956) by *Persian Gulf* out of *Alassio* who was a daughter of *Sun Princess*. She was trained by Jack Jarvis who considered her to be top class. She smashed a front pastern after being third in the Cherry Hinton Stakes and was lucky to survive. She hobbled into the ring at her owner, J.J. Philipps' dispersal sale at the Newmarket December Sales of 1966, but despite making the then large sum of 6,000 gns it was only half what her daughter *Maryland Wood* fetched a few lots later. *Margaret Ann* had already bred an extremely useful animal in the shape of the *Klairon* filly *No Relation* who won the Hillary Needler Trophy at Beverley, and Jack Jarvis strongly advised her purchase. She and *Sleat*, who was very nearly sold to an extremely tempting offer after winning the Sun Chariot Stakes, but luckily retained after determined family opposition to the sale, became the two foundation mares of the present day stud. *Sleat* did not breed any group winners herself but four of her daughters have done so. Despite being half sister to a St Leger winner, all the present black type animals from the family seem to be seven furlong to a mile horses. Conversely, *Margaret Ann*, despite descending from *Mumtaz Mahal*, has become the ancestress of top stayers. This is no doubt because she was sent to middle distance horses herself, as were her retained daughters and grand-daughters. Between them they have created a line in which almost every black type performer stays a mile and a half plus.

When Bruce Hobbs retired, David Wills' horses in training were mainly sent to Henry Cecil. He has done immensely well with the small number, on average two to three a year, that have been sent to Warren Place. These have included the three half sisters, *Coigach*, winner of the Park Hill Stakes in 1994, *Applecross*, second in the Park Hill and Princess Royal Stakes but nevertheless the top rated staying three-year-old filly in Europe of her year, 1990, and *Kyle Rhea*, winner of the Cheshire Oaks in 1997; also *Craigsteel*, winner of the Princess of Wales Stakes 1998. All four are descendents of *Margaret Ann*. He also trained *Ardkinglass*, winner of the 1993 Jersey Stakes and a successful sire from limited opportunities before being exported, who descends from *Sleat*. More recently, horses were also sent to James Fanshawe, a relation by marriage, who principal winner for David Wills was the Group I Prix du Cadran winner of 1998 *Invermark*.

Applecross (*Glint of Gold* ex *Rynechra*), *Margaret Ann's* great grand-daughter, was voted The Thoroughbred Breeders Association Broodmare of the Year in 1998, with winning sons *Invermark* (GpI), *Inchrory* (Gp3) and *Craigsteel* (Listed); a great feat for a small stud which has been operating in various guises since 1947 and which hopefully will continue to be successful well into the 21st century. It was also a wonderful accolade for David Wills after more than fifty years of breeding racehorses.

The Jockey Club Estates

PETER AMOS

Jockey Club Estates Ltd
101 High Street
Newmarket
Suffolk CB8 8JL

History

Jockey Club Estates Limited, known until the mid-1980s as Newmarket Estate and Property Company, owns 4500 acres of land, eighty-five residential and commercial properties, three studs, twelve leasehold training yards and the Jockey Club Rooms. The Jockey Club first began the purchasing of land, previously owned by the Crown and others, in 1808. Since then, other parcels of land have been either bequeathed to the Estate or bought by it. Nowadays included in the property portfolio are the Rowley Mile and July Racecourses, the National Stud, the National Horseracing Museum, the land occupied by the Newmarket Golf Club, tenanted farmland and two Little Chef restaurant and garage sites. The Company also has a managed investment portfolio in London.

Until the early 1960s, the Jockey Club Agent was responsible not only for the Estate and its training grounds but also the racecourse, thereby doubling up as the Clerk of the Course. The position of Agent has been held by famous names such as Captain Marriott (an out and out disciplinarian), Major Gorton, Colonel Gray and

Mr Robert Fellowes. Robert Fellowes was responsible for the introduction of the first generation of modern all-weather surfaces, such as Equitrack and Fibresand. On his retirement, the title of Jockey Club Agent was dropped in favour of General Manager and, subsequently, Managing Director. The present incumbent, Mr Peter Amos, served as a soldier before embarking on a career in farm and estate management. His task was to modernise both methods and attitudes to enable the Estate not only to survive but also to prosper in an increasingly competitive commercial environment.

Current status

Nowadays, the Company is controlled by a Board of Directors and managed on a day to day basis by a small management team based in the Jockey Club Offices in the High Street in Newmarket. The Estate staff profile is shown below.

The Estate's principal role is that of the management and development of its training grounds as a centre of excellence for the training of Thoroughbred racehorses. The training grounds, extending to some 2800 acres of largely naturally occurring heath grassland, provide over 40 miles of

Managing Director

Training Grounds	Administration	Jockey Club Rooms
Training Grounds Manager	Company Secretary	House Manager
24 full-time employees	6 full-time/part-time members of staff	9 full-time/part-time members of staff

Fig 1: The five furlong polytrack surface on Warren Hill.

brought about by the substantial increase in the horse population in the mid to late 1980s, when numbers went from 800 to over 2500. That increase exerted tremendous pressure on the then largely turf gallops and canters, which resulted in modern 'all weather' facilities having to be introduced.

Training grounds

Today the training grounds are made up of:

- Seventeen miles of peat moss dressed turf gallops
- Many miles of turf gallops and canters (18 gallops, 14 canters)
- A one mile watered gallop (equipped with a computer controlled pop-up irrigation system)
- A 5 furlong Polytrack canter
- Two Polytrack gallops - 9 and 11 furlongs in length
- Three ViscoRide tracks ranging from 5 to 9 furlongs
- A 7.5 furlong Fibresand track
- Three woodchips ranging from 5 to 10 furlongs
- Eleven sand tracks
- A 6.5 furlong round sand canter
- A 7 furlong Protrack canter
- Four Plaracon Fibre trotting rings, each measuring 1.5 furlongs
- Two sets of walk-through stalls
- Two sets of six-gated starting stalls
- Six Polytrack surfaced lunging rings
- Over 50 miles of concrete, tarmac and carrstone horsewalks

linear turf gallops and canters, most of which are on a minimum of a two year rotation. Augmenting the turf facilities are some 24 artificially surfaced training tracks. Whilst 'tan' and sand surfaced tracks have been in use for generations, over the last 15 years a range of more sophisticated track surfaces have been developed and introduced to meet the demands

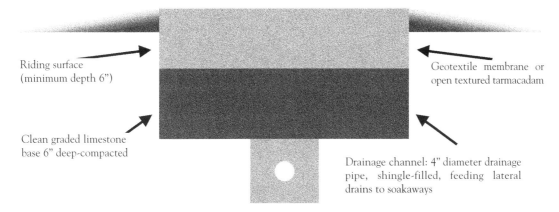

Riding surface (minimum depth 6")

Geotextile membrane or open textured tarmacadam

Clean graded limestone base 6" deep-compacted

Drainage channel: 4" diameter drainage pipe, shingle-filled, feeding lateral drains to soakaways

Fig 2: Cross-section of the base design of an artifical surface.

Fig 3: Harrowing the polytrack surface on Warren Hill.

National Hunt training facilities on the Links

The Estate also manages 300 acres of National Hunt training grounds, providing:

- Log jumps
- Schooling hurdles
- 'Standard' schooling hurdles
- French hurdles (designed and built on the Estate)
- 'Standard' steeplechase fences
- Cultivated schooling track used in dry weather
- Two Grand National-type fences
- A 1 mile turf canter
- A 3 mile turf gallop

The Estate subsidises the Hastings Centre equine pool and contributes towards the cost of a carcass collection scheme.

Artificial gallop/canter surfaces

Whilst most materials referred to above will be recognised, Polytrack, Protrack and ViscoRide might not be. Polytrack is made up of silica sand, rubber chips and 'flock' (woven material, often used in clothing) blended together and dressed in vaseline. Protrack is similar but with less rubber in it. ViscoRide uses silica sand with elasticated fibre and again is vaseline-dressed. The vaseline acts as a bonding agent but has the additional benefit of repelling water.

Modern day artificial gallops are laid on elaborate and very costly drained bases. Figure 2 shows a cross-section of the base design in use at Newmarket.

In the past, tracks were established by removing the top soil to expose the chalk sub-soil and simply laying the riding surface on top of the chalk, making little or no provision for drainage. Consequently, the early tracks often lay waterlogged in wet conditions and suffered from contamination from flints and stones migrating up from the base into the riding surface.

The requirement of an artificially surfaced track is to provide safe, consistent going; the track should be free-draining with little or no surface displacement or kick-back, cushioned and usable in all weather conditions. The latest vaseline-dressed surfaces, correctly prepared and maintained, meet those characteristics. One of the biggest problems experienced with this type of surface is that of contamination. Dust, droppings or dirt carried on to the track, but particularly concentrated at the start, cause the breakdown of the vaseline dressing, soak up moisture and, in cold weather, freeze, making the track unusable in those conditions. Contaminated material has to be removed and replaced with 'clean'.

Artificial surfaces are maintained using a variety of agricultural seedbed makers such as power harrows, rotavators or levelling harrows (Fig 3). Compaction within the riding surface is controlled by operating the maintenance equipment at a depth to re-establish the 'cushion'. Figure 4 shows a cross-section of a riding surface.

The Estate has drifted away from the advice given by suppliers and manufacturers by increasing the depth of the riding surfaces to improve cushion. The additional depth also allows for greater manipulation of the gallop surface to replicate turf conditions.

Turf management

Management of the turf aims to provide trainers with level, safe, consistent going. That is achieved by:

- Hands-on management
- Immediate hand repair of damaged ground
- Closure of ground in very wet conditions
- Good husbandry:
  - Regular soil analysis and timely reaction to results
  - Agronomy advice but minimal input of fertiliser and chemicals
  - Sound cultivation techniques
  - Rotation

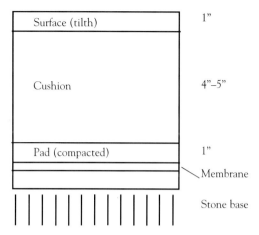

Fig 4: Cross-section of a riding surface.

In practice, when turf is in use, the sward height is seven inches. Immediately after use, the sward is cut down to three inches. The cuttings are then straw-chopped and dispersed. The ground is hand repaired and plugged (using 'plugs' from a 'plug' farm), rolled and spiked. Where necessary, land may be re-seeded using a slit drill with 'Newmarket Mix' seed (a cocktail of grass seed which replicates the naturally-occurring varieties). Thereafter the land is rested and the grass is cut low to encourage 'tillering', then gradually brought up to seven inches prior to it coming back into use.

Relatively small amounts of fertiliser are used but when it is applied it is done so when growing conditions are favourable and in light application. Phosphate is applied where necessary to encourage root growth.

It is not widely known that certain areas of the training grounds have been designated as Sites of Special Scientific Interest (SSSIs). In those areas, rare heathland plants, for example the Lizard Orchid, maintain a foothold in the chalk grassland of Newmarket Heath. Jockey Club Estates works closely with English Nature to protect these sensitive sites.

The trainers

Seventy trainers are based in the town and all of them rightly demand high quality training facilities. Good communications are therefore

Fig 5: The Jockey Club Rooms.

essential and that is achieved by having a management presence on the training grounds every day. However, the Heath Committee, a committee of the Newmarket Trainers' Federation, is the formal link between the trainers and the Estate. That committee meets officially once a year to put forward improvement suggestions for the following year. However, there is regular contact with the Chairman, Sir Mark Prescott, and other members of the committee.

Trainers obtain licences from The Jockey Club in London, and in the case of those based at Newmarket, they have to obtain a permit from Jockey Club Estates to use the training facilities. In effect, the Jockey Club controls who trains here. Furthermore, through its 'Rules and Conditions', the Estate controls the way the training grounds are used. Trainers in breach of the Rules can be fined or banned from using the training grounds. However, it is seldom that any more than a letter is required to bring the offender 'back to heel'.

The Rule that reads '*horses can be galloped on a canter but not cantered on a gallop*' can on occasions cause problems. When a trainer is challenged about his horse cantering on a gallop the answer will often come back as "*Of course it was galloping but that's as fast as the b****y animal can go!*"

As a footnote, it is perhaps worth mentioning that since 1991 the total number of trainers based in the town has remained static. However, since 1991 some fifty-two trainers have, for one reason or another, ceased training in Newmarket and fifty-four have commenced training here.

Fig 6: The statue of Hyperion outside the Jockey Club Rooms, Newmarket (photograph courtesy of Sidney Ricketts).

Health and safety

Every accident, every injury and every near miss triggers yet another risk assessment. Clearly, the responsibility for ensuring that the training grounds are laid out, maintained and manned to minimise the risk of accident and injury to horses, riders and the general public alike impacts heavily on the Estate. Newmarket is, however, fortunate in having a Local Health Authority ambulance based in the town resulting in a quick response to accidents. Furthermore, paramedic-trained doctors from local GP clinics (Mid Anglian General Practitioners Accident Service) also turn out to all accidents. On average, the reaction time to an accident on the training grounds is seven minutes. Heath staff are equipped with handheld radios and all key staff have mobile telephones. There are six strategically sited SOS telephones sited on the training grounds for use by anyone who might see an accident. As a consequence of these measures, reaction time to an accident is immediate.

It is, however, alarming to examine the training ground accident statistics. On average, three riders will be thrown each day and every fortnight a rider will be hospitalised as a result of injuries sustained in a fall. Tragically, every now and again a rider will be killed.

For injured horses, two purpose-built horse ambulances are provided. These ambulances have hydraulic lowering axles, enabling the trailer to be lowered to the ground to eliminate the climb an injured horse has to negotiate to enter the trailer. Furthermore, the trailers were also designed to allow for front exiting. These specialist vehicles were generously funded by the Moller Charitable Trust and are manned and operated by Jockey Club Estates training grounds staff. With two specialist veterinary practices based in Newmarket, veterinary care for the injured horses is pretty well immediate. Regrettably, there are occasions when horses die or have to be put down on the training grounds. It is of some comfort that the number of equine fatalities is on the decline, from 29 recorded in 1992 to 4 in the year 2000. The removal of the carcasses from the training grounds is carried out by a local family-run carcass collection service.

Like all other towns in the country over the past ten years, Newmarket has witnessed a significant increase not only in the volume of traffic but also the speed of that traffic. Where horses have to cross roads, special crossing points have been established and these are equipped with trigger-controlled flashing lights, which are activated by riders to warn oncoming traffic that a string is about to cross the road.

One of the more significant dangers to the general public is that of loose horses. All areas of the training grounds have now been enclosed by fencing to contain the loose horse which would otherwise 'bolt' home.

Visitors

Newmarket, as 'Headquarters', attracts thousands of UK and foreign visitors each year and many of these come specifically to see the training grounds. The Estate also provides educational support to the British Racing School, as well as consultancy advice to horse racing and racehorse training organisations around the world.

The Jockey Club Rooms

The Jockey Club Rooms is rightly recognised as one of the most exclusive clubs in the land with its membership of 600 having just one thing in common - the Thoroughbred racehorse. The Club is home to one of the finest equine art collections in the world, as shown in Figure 5. On race days and sale days it is in use by its members, but at other times of the year it is used for private and corporate entertaining. Members of the Club also have use of 'Rooms' facilities on the Rowley Mile and July racecourses.

Estate property

The Estate property fall into five categories:

- Estate staff housing
- Retired Estate staff housing
- Rent earning housing
- Commercial property
- Tenanted farm and stud land

Jockey Club Estates is one of very few estates in the country that still houses both its serving and its retired staff. Property surplus to those needs is let. With the exception of the land at the National Stud, the land occupied by Newmarket Racecourses Trust and the buildings occupied by the National Horseracing Museum, all other non-residential property is let on a commercial basis.

The Estate is managed to generate a profit and achieves this through:
- Payment of 'Heath Tax' by owners of horses in training at Newmarket.
- Its property portfolio
- Its investment portfolio
- The Jockey Club Rooms

Unlike other companies that would be answerable to shareholders, Jockey Club Estates reinvests profits generated by its trading activities back into the Estate.

The future

The existence of the local authority planning policy for Newmarket, often referred to as the Newmarket Charter, safeguards 'Headquarters'. Jockey Club Estates will continue to support that policy and play its part in the future prosperity of Newmarket in general and racing in particular by providing the best public training facilities in the world.

The day we went to London - memories of the Queen Mother's 100th birthday parade

**TIM R. C. GREET BVMS MVM CertEO DESTS DipECVS FRCVS
(BEVA PRESIDENT 2000)**

*Beaufort Cottage Equine Hospital
Cotton End Road, Exning
Newmarket
Suffolk CB8 7NN*

Since 1968, Her Majesty Queen Elizabeth the Queen Mother has been the Patron of the British Equine Veterinary Association (BEVA). Each year at our Annual Congress she has sent a message of support, which has been read out by the incumbent President. She has also allowed her name to endorse a travel scholarship, awarded under the auspices of the BEVA Trust.

In the Parade of her Regiments, Charities and other Groups in 1990, which she had patronised during her long life, Her Majesty celebrated her ninetieth birthday in fine style with a cavalcade in Horseguards Parade. Ten years on, with the advent of her one hundredth birthday, plans were made to celebrate this unique occasion in a similar but even more magnificent way.

So it was that I, as President of the Association, was invited with a group of people representing BEVA, to contribute to the celebration. Those who had taken part in the extravaganza in 1990 had thoroughly enjoyed themselves. When I spoke to Sir Michael Oswald for advice on the nature of the event, he left me in no uncertainty that the parade was to be held in a relaxed and light hearted spirit.

We decided that the Association should be represented by some of the Board of Management dressed in costume befitting equine veterinary surgeons. Pat Harris, Mark Collins, Alistair Barr, John McEwen, Susanna Majendie and I represented Council and Bob Bainbridge represented the BEVA Trust. In addition, John Fowler would represent the Association, as well as providing some elegant transport for some of the group. Desert Orchid also appeared as a former patient and one of the better known survivors of equine surgery. Finally, Peter and Kim Dun, who run a wonderful equine ambulance in Scotland, drove all the way down for the occasion, to represent another facet of equine veterinary service.

I had not realised that John Fowler was a driving enthusiast. However, he was able to borrow a splendid phaeton and pair, bedecked in magnificent harness. He was ably assisted by 'groom' Richard Jacobs and by a young veterinary surgeon Katherine Hemson, whose elegant attire was a significant improvement on the rather 'variable' appearance of some of the members of the party!

I arrived in Birdcage Walk at our appointed site at just after 9.00 am. We were designated a position right at the front of the procession, with the Jockey Club and the Injured Jockeys Fund, just behind the Royal Corgis which were to lead our section of the parade. Desert Orchid had been allocated a stable in the Royal Mews, the ambulance had been in Hackney and the phaeton was arriving from somewhere in the Home Counties that morning. The whole area surrounding Birdcage Walk, The Mall and Horseguards Parade had been cordoned off, but was swarming with a mixture of police, ambulance people, prospective civilian marchers and an array of military personnel. There were the Coldstream guardsmen allocated as our minders, and servicemen wearing uniforms of every design and hue representing the military element of the parade.

Fig 1: Representing the British Equine Veterinary Association at the Queen Mother's Birthday Parade, 2000 (photograph by kind permission of Sidney Ricketts).

At approximately 9.30 am John Fowler and I lined up with the Injured Jockey Fund standard bearer Jeremy Richardson, a well known Newmarket solicitor. The leaders of each association were issued with a 'Palace-made' plastic sign indicating our name. We stood at the mouth to Horseguards Parade in a long column waiting for our queue to start marching. It was an extremely hot morning in a summer which, until then, had been notable for its dreadful weather. An hour went by with no sign of our being needed. It seemed to me that the various military bands and

horse mounted parades which were being rehearsed could have practised in advance, without keeping us waiting under the hot sun, for our turn to walk through the route.

Another 45 minutes went by. Those of us trapped in the bottleneck leading on to Horseguards Parade were continually having to avoid mounted troops leaving it. The Corgis duly appeared and we started our procession approximately an hour and forty-five minutes late! We, probably quite unjustifiably, felt we were the victims of complete military organisational incompetence. We were informed that our group would be allowed only 10 metres from the front to the back of our group. This had to accommodate the horse ambulance, the phaeton and pair, Desert Orchid, his handlers and the walkers!

As we stood in our allotted spot on Horseguards Parade, we all felt that someone was bound to be killed. There would be the ambulance, four ex-racehorses, Dessie and the phaeton, a landau and six horses, which constituted the Injured Jockeys Fund and our own equine contingent on parade, all crammed into about 10 metres! We were sure that the pipe band standing next to us on one side, the Homeopathy group on the other side, and the Salmon and Trout Fishing group behind us might be in for a rather nasty shock! We stood in the middle of Horseguards Parade listening to the massed choirs and bands, and under constant parade ground instruction from Major Parker. After a while we were dismissed.

We returned to find out how the rest of our group was progressing. The first crisis was that there had been a bomb scare and we had heard that there had at least been one controlled explosion of a 'device'. The result was that much of the West End of London had been shut down including the buses and tube. Some of our contingent were not able to make their way to Birdcage Walk very easily. Nevertheless, eventually they all arrived in dribs and drabs. The horses were camped at the other end of Birdcage Walk but we met up with Susanna Majendie who had struggled halfway across London in a taxi with a rather special picnic and vintage champagne.

At approximately 2.00 pm, the whole Parade reformed for the dress rehearsal. Thank goodness common sense prevailed and the horses and carriages, Desert Orchid and other forms of transport, were only going to be asked to parade in front of the Queen Mother. They were then to be allowed to return via the Mall, where I know John Fowler was looking forward to showing his paces in the phaeton.

In comparison with the chaos of the morning walk through, the dress rehearsal was a much more orderly affair and I have to say how very proud I felt representing BEVA on such an auspicious day.

Eventually it was our turn. Jeremy of the Injured Jockeys and I had decided that we would dip our signs as we approached the Queen Mother, in salute. Then we were on, into the cauldron that was Horseguards Parade surrounded by stands of wildly cheering people. The corgis set an admirable pace and we found ourselves marching at a tempo somewhere approaching the Light Infantry! Having been a perfect gentleman all day, Dessie chose this moment to mess about, but with some extra restraint from the BEVA team and his handler, we managed to settle him sufficiently to pass the Queen Mum without mishap. She looked radiant in pink, and we were past in a flash and moved on round to our designated place on the parade ground.

The parade continued, and hundreds of disparate groups of which she was Patron came to pay tribute to her. I will never forget the cavalcade of vintage Rolls Royces, full of war heroes including several holders of the Victoria and George Crosses. The Parade was wound up by the ever popular Chelsea Pensioners marching to the strains of 'Boys of the Old Brigade'.

This was followed by singing from several choirs, and a few old favourites when the crowd joined in. There was also a spectacular song and dance routine by disabled children. A touch of nostalgia was created by a fly-past of a wartime Spitfire and Lancaster. Then there were more songs and a stirring performance by the combined pipe bands. Sir John Mills, 92 years old himself, finally delivered a short thank you message, and with that she was gone.

The Parade marched out, waving and cheering the crowd for their support and then we all gradually dispersed. Everyone considered it a great success and the Queen Mother was clearly moved by it all. So it was 'all right on the night' despite, or because of, Major Parker's drilling of the unruly civilian rabble. He could put yet another successful Royal event into the file marked 'job well done'!

As for me, I had to dash off to St James' Palace, still clad in my surgeon's gown, to attend a reception. Yet more wonderful canapes and champagne! My only sadness was that I didn't have a chance to chat to the Queen Mother, that really would have been a wonderful end to a wonderful day.

Equine medicine in sixth century China:
Qimin yaoshu 齊民要術

DAVID W. RAMEY DVM and PAUL BUELL PhD
PO Box 5231
Glendale
California 91221
USA

Introduction

China has a rich tradition of veterinary literature. Such literature discusses all aspects of the medical conditions and treatment of various domestic animals, including horses, camels, cattle, asses, mules, pigs, goats, sheep, as well as large animal physiognomy and husbandry. The tradition becomes particularly full after the Song (960–1279), and reaches a high point under the Ming (1368–1644) and Qing (1644–1911).

Within that tradition, the *Qimin yaoshu* occupies a prominent place. This popular farming encyclopaedia is the earliest surviving source, including extensive veterinary materials. It provides witness to the character and content of veterinary medicine as practised in Medieval China, prior to the theoretical systemisation adapted from human medicine present in later texts such as the Ming-Dynasty *Yuan Heng liaoma ji*, 元亨療馬集 '*Yuan and Heng's (Recipe) Collection for Treating Horses*'.

The *Qimin yaoshu* was the work of Jia Sixie 賈思勰, active during the sixth century when he was governor of Gaoyang 高陽 in what is now Shandong (perhaps his home area). Nothing else is known about him. When Jia completed his work is also unknown, but it must have been during the Eastern Wei 魏 (535–562) Dynasty, judging from his office. Eastern Wei was one of several dynasties established in north China by the nomadic Toba, some of whom may have been Mongols.

During this period, north China was inundated by non-Chinese influences. Most stemmed from the Toba and other steppe peoples then dominating the area. Additional non-Chinese influences came from the west, via the Silk Route. As a consequence, there is much in the *Qimin yaoshu* that is not Chinese. For example, the book shows a great interest in fermented milk products that is highly unusual for China (Sabban 1986). Nonetheless, despite such influences, most of the *Qimin yaoshu* is Chinese in focus and concentration. This includes sections of the book dealing with traditionally Chinese livestock and their medical treatment, as well as those focusing on agriculture (the realm of Chinese peasants and not of nomadic conquerors). Since later works take over the lore of the *Qimin yaoshu*, and show similar approaches, the relationship of the work to Chinese veterinary medicine in general seems clear. That is, the *Qimin yaoshu* is not merely reflective of peculiarly Eastern Wei or Toba traditions but documents the Chinese veterinary medicine of its time generally.

Six chapters in the *Qimin yaoshu* pertain to livestock (including fish). Two include medical treatments and recipes: Chapter 56 on horses, asses, mules and cattle; and Chapter 57 on sheep. As a contribution to comparative veterinary medicine, the authors offer our translation of portions of Chapter 56 devoted to the horse. Not translated, in addition to sections on other large animals, are materials on physiognomy (selecting the right horse or ox based upon physical appearance) and passages on large animal upkeep. Or course, this is not to say that these other sections lack interest. Indeed, there appears to be a relationship between the principles of large animal physiognomy, as developed in the text, and certain physiological appreciations and systems found in later works.

Equine medicine in 6th century China

One reason for the *Qimin yaoshu's* interest in the horse was that it had always been a problem animal for the Chinese. First introduced in the 2nd millennium BC, the horse was long used only for elite show, or to draw aristocratic battle chariots. Horses were expensive and difficult to maintain. China also lacked good horse pasture, except in a few frontier areas. Although horses were somewhat democratised when horseback riding appeared, and cavalry to support new mass armies, (circa 5th century BC), the horse remained a rare animal for most Chinese and in short supply[1]. In medieval times the horse was primarily used for military purposes by the culturally mixed militias (*fubing* 府兵) of the northwest. Most of their horses, like most Chinese horses before them, were imported, and with the horses came foreign horse lore (some associated with semi-mythical *Bo Le* 伯樂, a man of Qin state, positioned in the west, nearest Inner Asian trade routes).

The *Qimin yaoshu* contains 31 recipes to treat various equine conditions. These are primarily herbal, something typical of Chinese veterinary medicine to the present day. Although many conditions discussed cannot be correlated with modern counterparts, others can be identified quite clearly. Most of the herbal recipes were practical in application. That is, medical treatments were prescribed according to an easily understood rationale; a condition was identified and treated with a specific prescription. They were not prescribed in accordance with the more arcane, and historically less popular, notions of systematic correspondence theory that appear to have captured the curiosity of some modern veterinary practitioners.

That being said, since Traditional Chinese medicine encompasses a diverse and contradictory belief system including magical, religious and even demonological elements (it is anything but a single, organised system), less rational approaches are also present in the *Qimin yaoshu*. One conspicuous example of a purely magical application is from the cattle section:

> *Recipe for treating stomach distension of cattle when an animal is going to die. Take a woman's pubic hair. Wrap in grass. Feed to the animal. It will recover. This is to treat qi swelling[2].*

Note that a woman's pubic hair is 'yin hair' in Chinese. Since stomach swelling is a *yang* disease, it is susceptible to the magical effect of a balancing *yin* treatment. Some recipes in the horse section also seem more magical than serious veterinary practice. Also seen are combinations of magical and other treatment.

Although treatments in the *Qimin yaoshu* appear quite diverse, they are directed at a relatively few, presumably the most common, conditions. Then, as now, most were either self-limiting or did not have a cure; many possible treatments may have been tried with equal therapeutic success (or failure). With that in mind, it is interesting to look at the recipes themselves[2].

1. Recipe for treating contagious disease of cattle or horses

> *Take otter feces. Decoct and drench the animal. Otter meat and liver are [also] good. If one cannot obtain otter meat or liver, just use the feces.*

Commentary: Of course, it was impossible for the ancient Chinese to distinguish between the many causes of horse disease, but they were aware that one animal could contract a disease from another, as here. General tonics were thus prescribed for any number of conditions. Such prescriptions are typical of veterinary medicine throughout its history, regardless of ethnic roots. They can be seen, for example, in the often-prescribed 'physics' of 19th century European veterinary medicine.

2. Recipe for treating a horse suffering from throat numbness that is going to die

> *Bind a knife [with cloth]. Leave bare a cun 寸 [Chinese inch] of the blade edge. Penetrate the throat. Use [the knife] to break through and*

destroy [the affected area]. The horse will be healed. If the horse is untreated it will die for sure.

Commentary: One wonders whether this is a treatment for a horse with a submandibular lymph node abscess caused by *S. equi*?

3. Recipe for treating horse black sweats

Take dried horse feces. Place on a tile. Cover using disheveled human hair. Roast the horse feces and hair over a fire until they smoke. Put to the horse's nose and fumigate. Direct the smoke into the horse's nose. After a brief time the sweats will be gone.

4. Another recipe

Take fat from a pig's back meat, realgar, disheveled hair; three substances. Position below the horse's nose and roast. Direct the smoke into the horse's nose. After a brief time [the sweats] will be gone.

Commentary: 'Black' here is not a specific colour reference but refers instead to darkness or opacity. The term 'black sweats' most likely means that a horse has sweated profusely, leaving an opaque lather.

5. Recipe for a horse struck by heat

Boil soybeans. After feeding the hot food to the horse three times, it will be healed.

Commentary: 'Heat' usually refers to a condition that is focally 'heating' in terms of the Chinese classification of disease. Here 'heat' may mean no more than that the horse has a generalised fever, a condition easily recognised by individuals attending horses, even though the fever's underlying pathophysiology remained unknown.

6. Recipe for horse sweat chill

Take a sheng 升 *[Chinese pint] of fermented black beans, and a sheng of 'good'[a] liquor (in summer put the mixture into the sun; heat in*

winter). Soak fermented black beans to make a juice. Take hold with the hands and [squeeze] filter to remove the dregs. Irrigate the mouth of the horse with the juice. When a sweat is produced, the horse will be healed.

Commentary: The underlying motivation for this Chinese treatment for 'chill' mirrors closely similar concepts present in ancient Greek humoral medicine. Greek treatments were often based on an effort to do the 'opposite' of symptoms identified. Hence, treatment for fever (too hot) might involve the application of cold, or more aggressively, removal of the fluid identified with heat (blood). Similarly, attempting to make a horse with 'chill' produce 'sweat' would be a rational therapeutic approach.

7. Recipe for treating horse itch

Use realgar and head hair; two substances. Decoct in the fat of a pig of the twelfth lunar month. Make sure the hair is dissolved. Use a tile and scrape the itching [area] until red. Apply medicinals hot. The [itch] will be healed.

8. Another recipe

Wash the itching [area] with hot water. Wipe dry. Cook a fluid dough and apply when hot. Apply hot. The [itch] will be healed.

9. Another recipe

Roast juniper sap. Apply. This will be good.

10. Another recipe

Grind up mustard seeds and apply. The itch will be gone. Itches of all six domestic animals will be healed. Now juniper resin and mustard are both irritants. When the entire body [of the animal] is suffering from itch, one should apply [only] in selected places, here and there, gradually, until [the itch there] is gone. Then apply to other places. If one suddenly applies [the recipe] to the entire body at one time, death will be certain.

---

[a]*Often distilled liquor.*

Commentary: Judging from the number of available therapies, skin conditions were as frustrating for the ancient Chinese as they often are for present-day veterinarians.

11. Recipe for treating a horse suffering from retention of urine

Take salt [lumps], each about as big as an egg's yoke, and put into the two nostrils. Compress the horse's nose until it has tears in its eyes. This will be good.

Commentary: Ancient doctors of all cultures paid close attention to normal bodily functions. As such, 'urine retention' would be identified as a condition growing out of any number of possible aetiologies. Interestingly, 'retention of urine' was still described as a condition of horses in the late 1800s in at least one western veterinary text and the treatment - hanging a cloth soaked in linseed oil, followed by a ball of opium, camphor, linseed oil and molasses - would likely have done as well[3].

12. Recipe to treat a horse suffering from grain [colic]

Grasp the first part of the horse's mane with the hand. Raise it so that the skin separates from the flesh. Repeat this. Use a physician's lancet and pierce the hollow under the [raised] skin. Make [the qi] rush out. If you place your hand next to the incision, it will feel as if something is blowing on your hand, like wind. This is the grain qi. Have someone urinate on [the incision][b]. Also apply salt. Have someone immediately mount and ride the horse for 10 paces. The [horse] will heal.

13. Another recipe

Take some solidified maltose, a [chunk] as large as an egg. Pulverize. Feed to horse combined with grass. It is extremely fine.

14. Another recipe

Take 3 sheng of powdered malt. Combine with grain. Feed to the horse. It is also good.

15. Recipe to treat a horse when a hoof grows extra 'bone' [carbuncle] and it cannot be treated, [when it] enters the knee joint and makes the horse lame

Take mustard seeds, pound cooked; an amount more or less equal to an egg yoke in size. Take three croton beans. Remove the skin and keep the 'navels.'[c]. Also cook the three beans. Pound. Combine with water. Make the mixture cling. Carefully use a knife. If you do not, you may cut your hand. Cut away hair from around the extra 'bone.' Melt wax and press it down around the 'bone.' If you do not do this, the medicine may irritate (and produce) a large ulcer. After the wax has been applied, spread medicine on the 'bone.' Take unprocessed cotton cloth and make a cut at one end. Fold back each end on itself [to make a bandage] and tightly wrap [the 'bone']. Small 'bones' will be done in a night. Large ones should not take more than another night, but one should examine [the bone] repeatedly to avoid damage to good flesh after the 'bone' is gone. When your have observed that the 'bone' is gone, use chilled water to clean and wash the scar. Scratch off [cart] hub grease and form into a cake. Put onto the scar. Also wrap tightly with clean cloth. Remove after three or four days. The area will then grow hair [again] without scarring. This method is extremely good. It is greatly superior to cauterisation. But if the scar is not yet healed, one should not ride the horse. If blood flows from inside the scar, this will become a major illness.

Commentary: It seems clear that this recipe is for a horse with osteoarthritis. It also seems quite clear that the prescribed treatments - topical therapy with a known irritant such as croton bean or cauterisation [firing] - mirror efforts to treat such conditions in western cultures.

---

[b]Urine was used to sterilise; [c]The inner part of the bean.

16. A recipe for treating a horse with a wounded foot

Use guang 穬 barley[d] combined with a paste of food masticated by a child. It will be healed.

Commentary: Here, the use of a poultice-like substance is recommended. Children were thought by the Chinese to be especially healthy and disease-free - hence the recommendation for a child to chew the grain.

17. Horse cauterisation sores

It is not good to make the animal sweat if still unhealed. When a sore is white, and there is a scab, fear a 'wind'. After it has healed one can ride the horse at will.

Commentary: Along with bloodletting, cautery is one of the most time-honored traditions of treating horses in any culture[4]. While the biophysical changes induced by the treatment have been studied only relatively recently, its use persists in the treatment of a variety of lower limb conditions, particularly in racing animals. 'Wind' usually refers to any sudden condition affecting the animal generally.

18. Recipe for treating a horse's ulcerated hoof

Use a knife to pierce the dense hair of the reclining horse's rear foot and make it bleed. The [ulcerated] hoof will heal.

19. Another recipe

Steam and melt sheep's fat and apply to wound. Wrap [it] in a cloth.

20. Another recipe

Take a couple of dan 石 [recently 133.33 lb] or so of salt cake. Drip water on and get one dan, five dou 斗 [recently 316 cu. in.]. Cook [down] in a cauldron to 3 or 2 dou. Cut away

the hair. Clean and wash [the wound] with settled water used to wash rice. When dry, wash with the brine. After three washings, it will heal.

21. Another recipe

Clean and wash [the wound] with hot water. Cauterise. Apply chewed hemp seeds. Wrap in cotton cloth [or] silk. After three treatments it will heal. If the condition persists, use a grain paste. After five or six treatments it will heal.

22. Another recipe

Cut away the hair. Clean and wash with hot salt water. Remove scab. Cauterise. Cook human urine in a broken old pot until it bubbles. Apply hot. It will heal.

23. Another recipe

Use a saw and make a cut right into the middle of the top of the afflicted hoof. Cut obliquely. The cut should be narrow at the top and wide at the bottom, like a saw's tooth. Remove [a piece] as if trimming an arrow notch, to a depth of about 1 cun. Cut with a knife until the [notch] bleeds. The color [of the blood] must be black. Bleed out 5 sheng or so. When bleeding is complete, [the ulceration] will go.

24. Another recipe

First wash and clean with soured water used to wash rice. Then cook a pig's foot soft. Take the juice. Use when hot to wash the hoof. [The ulceration] will go.

25. Another recipe

Take hot water from a steaming low pot. Clean and wash the hoof. Wipe dry with a cloth until liquid is gone. Use glutinous millet to make a thick congee. Use an old cloth about 3 or 4 cun wide, and 7 or 8 cun long. Apply the congee as a paste to the top. Bind the scarred place tightly

---

[d]Guang is a variety of barley with long, fine leaves eaten by horses.

and wrap with free hemp strings. Remove in 3 days. It should be gone.

26. Another recipe

From the middle of a plowed field, take grain stubble facing the east or west (if the land is [positioned] crosswise east and west, take what faces south and north). Take 7 stalks from each mound of earth, 21 stalks from three mounds. Clean and wash. Cook in a cauldron. Take the juice. Cook until black. Cut away the hair. Wash [hoof] with water used to wash rice. Remove scab. Apply the grain stubble juice hot. It will heal after one application.

27. Another recipe

*Soak sheep's dung in urine to make a thick juice. Take domestic sijuecao 四角草*e*. Place on top and roast. Catch the ash in an earthenware basin. Grind up [everything] evenly. Wash the hoof with water used to wash rice. Apply dung [juice and ash]. Repeat three times. The [hoof] will heal.*

28. Another recipe

Cook sour jujube roots. Take the juice and clean and wash [the hoof]. When done, combine wine dregs with water and put into a wool pouch [for pressing liquor]. Soak the hoof [so that the liquid] is absorbed into the wound. After several treatments it will heal.

29. Another recipe

After cleaning and washing [the hoof], pound apricot kernels. Combine with pig fat. Apply. After 4 or 5 applications the [hoof] should heal.

Commentary: Hoof problems were apparently as ubiquitous in ancient China as they are today. Horses affected with such a condition would be likely to recover, no matter what the treatment. Still, one notes that any number of poultice-like applications might have been indicated with little underlying physiological rationale - just like today.

30. Treating a horse when the excrement and urine do not pass, when it is unable to sleep and is going to die, and one must treat it quickly

Untreated, the horse will die immediately. Apply fat to the hand. Seek for grain in the alimentary canal. Remove the impacted feces. Put salt into the urine tract. It will quickly be able to urinate and the bowels will move.

31. Recipe to treat the sudden swelling of a horse's stomach, when the horse sleeps and lies down, and wants to die

Use 5 sheng of cold water, 2 sheng of salt. Grind the salt so that it dissolves [in the water]. Irrigate the horse. It must heal.

Commentary: Clearly, the ancient Chinese recognized colic as a serious medical problem. It is also fascinating to note the attempt to relieve the condition rectally, which indicates both a remarkable observation of the underlying problem as well as a reasonable effort to get at its cause. This method of treatment survived for at least a millennium and is similarly described and illustrated in the *Yuan Heng liaoma ji*.

Discussion

The veterinary medicine of sixth century China was not significantly different from the veterinary medicine practiced in other contemporary cultures. This should not be surprising - ignorance of naturalistic and scientific explanations for medical phenomena made a world-view based on magic and empiricism the only possible one. In addition, concepts of causality would have remained unclear; practitioners gave a medication and waited for a condition to improve. They employed such substances as were readily at hand; indeed, plants and minerals, as well as dung and urine, dominate the pharmacopoeias of ancient cultures.

---

e*This is either* Vernonicastrum cauloptera *or* Lindernia anagallis.

What is conspicuous in its absence among the *Qimin yaoshu's* 31 equine recipes is the complete lack of 'needling' of any kind. There is nothing that can remotely be considered as acupuncture (there is surgical intervention, but with lancets and knives, not needles). Also lacking is any kind of a theoretical construction for horse medicine, as is frequently present in much later texts (other than references to *qi*).

During the Han Dynasty (206 BC to 220 AD), Chinese intellectuals attempted to reduce the phenomena of the world to a limited number of causes and effects. This 'systematic' way of thinking made it possible to try and understand natural processes, as well as influence them. Thus, theories involving ideas such as *yin* and *yang*, *qi* and 'five phases' evolved. They were used to explain normal and pathological human body functions. Apparently these theories had not yet been transposed to animals when the *Qimin yaoshu* was written.

Given the lack of any evidence of acupuncture in the *Qimin yaoshu*, it is then reasonable to question where and when veterinary acupuncture originated. There is, in fact, little evidence that the ancient Chinese ever used the practice. Statements to the contrary notwithstanding, such assertions appear to be based on misunderstanding of the Classical Chinese language. Classical Chinese is as different from modern Chinese as Latin is from modern Italian. Without study of the classical language, it is easy to make factual errors.

One such error appears to be the translation of the word 'needling' (*zhen* 鍼) as 'acupuncture.' In Chinese medicine, the term 'needling' encompasses the widest possible range of interventions using sharp objects, including surgery and therapeutic phlebotomy. The definition of the term 'needling' is not simply a matter of semantics. Indeed, a lack of understanding of ancient Chinese medicine is demonstrated when one asserts that any 'needling' intervention in an ancient text is a variant of acupuncture.

Similarly, translations of the word *xue* 穴, which appears in the ancient texts, as 'acupuncture point,' is simply incorrect. For example, in the *Yuan Heng liaoma ji*, places where internal surgical interventions are to be done are also called *xue*. If cutting into a horse to remove a

tumour, to clear a nasal passage, or drain a cyst on the stomach is acupuncture, then perhaps a broader definition of acupuncture might be in order. On the other hand, if some intervention at some point is acupuncture - regardless of a lack of association with 'meridians,' fine needles, etc - then virtually all of Greek, Arabic, Indian and later Western veterinary medicine, which emphasise bleeding and cautery at specific points, is 'acupuncture,' and these were traditions practiced in those cultures for well over a thousand years before the first Chinese sources mention them. In fact, the existence of virtually identical treatments in other cultures long before such treatments appear in Chinese documents lead us to the strong suspicion that these practices in the early Chinese veterinary material are not even indigenous. Confirmation of this suspicion awaits further translations of original source material. Nevertheless, veterinary acupuncture as currently practiced appears to be a modern invention, rather than a historical practice of the ancient Chinese.

Herbal medicine - not acupuncture - has long been the dominant tradition of China. There are no reliably-dated human acupuncture texts until nearly half a millennium after the earliest document detailing herbal treatments (the *Wushier bingfang*, a probably mid-3rd century BC manuscript found in a Western Han Dynasty tomb) and the overwhelming majority of surviving Chinese medicine texts deal with herbal medicine, not acupuncture. Furthermore, the arcane theories of systematic correspondence had only the most limited influence on Chinese herbal medicine throughout its history and then only during a brief period when such theories were popular: only to be rejected again. There is also clear historical evidence that acupuncture was little popular outside of Imperial court circles (which is apparently one reason why it did not come to the United States with the first Chinese immigrants).

The prescriptions of the *Qimin yaoshu* are consistent with the traditions of Chinese herbal medicine. In this the 31 *Qimin yaoshu* recipes closely resembled those of the *Yuan Heng liaoma ji*, which also calls primarily for herbal treatment, but other influences are also apparent. For example, cauterisation (with hot irons) mentioned in the text is also part of Egyptian, Islamic, Roman and

Greek veterinary medicine. But while cauterisation is present in the *Qimin yaoshu*, it is a minor tradition there. This is quite unlike the recommendations of the *Yuan Heng liaoma ji*, in which cauterisation and bleeding are prominent. But when considered together, the use of such treatments, the fact that the horse is not indigenous to China, and the similarity of treatment approaches and the known contact between Medieval Chinese and other contemporary cultures, strongly underscores the fact that the treatment of animals in ancient China was not completely based on traditions developed from within.

Acknowledgements

The authors gratefully acknowledge the assistance of Professor Françoise Sabban of Paris who graciously read over our draft translations from the *Qimin yaoshu* and made a number of suggestions for their improvement. We would also like to thank Prof. Eugene N. Anderson of the University of California at Riverside, and Medical anthropologist Christopher Muench of Boise, Idaho for their critiques of some of the theorectical points of the paper. Needless to say, any errors that remain are solely our own.

References

1. Cooke, W. (Ed) (2000) *Imperial China: The Art of the Horse in Chinese History*, Lexington, Kentucky.

2. Jia Sixie (1986) *Qimin yaoshu jiaoshi* 齊民要術校釋 Taipei: Mingwen shuju 明文書局. pp286-290.

3. Kirby, F.O. (1883) *Veterinary Medicine and Surgery in Diseases and Injuries of the Horse*, William Wood and Company, New York. p146.

4. McCullagh, K.G. and Silver, I.A. (1981) The actual cautery - myth and reality in the art of firing. *Equine vet. J.* **13**, 81-84.

5. Sabban, F. (1986) Un savoir-faire oublié: le travail du lait en Chine ancienne. *Zinbun: Memoirs of the Research Institute for Humanistic Studies, Kyoto University* **21**, 31-65.

Horseshoeing through the ages

SIMON CURTIS FWCF HonAssocRCVS

The Forge
Moulton Road
Newmarket
Suffolk CB8 8DU

Myths and legends

From earliest times, the art of farriery has been shrouded in mystery. Legends and myths have sprung up about the farrier and his related craftsman, the blacksmith. The horseshoe is perhaps the most potent symbol of good luck. People who have never ridden a horse, let alone seen one shod, regard the horseshoe as an object invested with the ability to ward off evil.

The horseshoe has been with us for over 2000 years. In that time it has changed little. Try to think of another man-made object that has remained so constant in that time. The original iron workers had a vested interest in keeping secret their techniques of extracting iron ore. The farrier also guarded closely his ability to nail a horseshoe onto a living animal. Even today, farriers are constantly asked by non-horse people: *"doesn't that hurt the horse?"*

The first known blacksmith was Tubal Cain. He was mentioned in Genesis and dates from around 3500 BC. By the year 500 AD, farriers had been around for at least 500 years, and the original shoeing smiths, the Celts, had a legend of Wayland Smith. A traditional tale, it told of an invisible smith who replaced lost horseshoes. This was probably based on the Druids, who were not only master blacksmiths but also very secretive.

St Eloy (also spelt Eloi, Eloie, Aloi, Alo, Lo Loye, Loy, Loo and Euloye) is the Patron Saint of Blacksmiths and Farriers. He was born around 588 AD and lived at Chaplelet near Limoges. He became a master goldsmith and was known for his great charity. After his death in 660 AD, he became a cult in Northern Europe. December 1st is still regarded by French farriers as a National Holiday.

Although he certainly existed, it is unlikely that he shod a horse. His symbol was a horseshoe. He is shown, as is St Dunstan, clutching the devil's nose in a pair of tongs. St Eloy is reputed to have removed the leg of a fractious horse before shoeing it and then replacing the leg. Artwork depicting this scene is to be found in the Bologna area of Italy. This is why, when we hear an unbelievable tale, we say that it is 'baloney'.

St Dunstan, born in 910 AD, was a monk who made objects in his forge for the monastery. Legend says that the devil entered his forge for shoeing. St Dunstan inflicted such pain by nailing a still red-hot shoe to his foot that the devil never returned. He is said never to enter a door above which is nailed a horseshoe. Which way round the shoe is hung is open to debate. When the heels are pointing downwards, the shoe is said to staple the devil underground. The Worshipful Company of Farriers has shoes on its coats of arms affixed this way (as has the RCVS). Most people today say that a shoe should be hung up the other way (with heels upwards), to hold in the luck. The luck probably leaks out of the nailholes anyway! Horseshoes also traditionally have seven holes, most probably because seven is the mystical number. The four nailholes are placed on the outside (lateral) branch of the foot and three on the inside (medial).

Long before the horseshoe was invented, the Greeks deified blacksmithing powers. Hephaestus, the son of Zeus and Hera, was the god of fire and of all works in iron. He forged the thunderbolts for his father Zeus, aided by Thor providing shoes for his horses. The theory is often that farriers gained their name from Henry de Farraris, also known as

Wahelim von Ferraris. However, I would suggest that Henry gained his name from farriery, which in turn comes from the Latin *soleae ferreae*, for iron shoe.

From the Romans onwards, many myths and legends sprang up surrounding horseshoeing. It is easy to understand why. Imagine the Celt in his dark forge, the flames from the fire, the sparks flying. The Hindus see the horseshoe as symbolising Nagendra the Sacred Snake.

Many people believe that if you find a horseshoe you should throw it over your shoulder for luck (not lucky for anyone standing behind!). The luckiest shoe is said to be one cast from the left hind of a grey mare. Country girls used to count the nailholes in a cast shoe to see how many years before they married.

The Great King of the Franks, Charlemagne, was said to have shod his own horse and been able to break a horseshoe in two. In 1050 AD, King Alphonso escaped from captivity under Ali Maymon the Moorish King of Toledo. He had his horseshoes placed backwards on the foot to mislead his pursuers. Robert the Bruce of Scotland was also said to have used this trick when escaping from the English on a snow-covered day.

History of horse shoeing

For the last six thousand years, man's history has been closely linked to the horse. His success and development in commerce and war has relied upon a sound and fit animal. Farriery has seen a parallel development in that time.

The first people to shoe their horses were almost certainly the Celts as long ago as 400 BC. However, attention to sound hooves (conformation) would have begun far earlier. The first horses to be domesticated were on the Eurasian Steppes of the Ukraine. By 430 BC, Simon of Athens was describing how a good foot should look. In 43 BC, Marcus Terentius Varro was suggesting ways of keeping mules' feet hard and expressing the importance of cleanliness of the feet.

Contrary to popular belief, it was not the Romans or Greeks who first shod horses. They had little need to. The drier climates of the Mediterranean and Middle East kept the hooves harder and during normal use the hooves would wear at the same rate as they grew. The Assyrians

and Hittites were both equestrian warriors. They also were renowned blacksmiths (workers of iron). Neither of them shod their horses. Occasionally, their inability to shoe caused problems in war. The army of Alexander the Great (356–323 BC) on its conquest of Asia was often slowed because the horses were sorefooted; the army would then have to wait until their hooves grew enough to continue. In the 19th century, a similar problem arose with the North American Indians. Hollywood has us believing in the cavalry arriving in the nick of time to save the circle of wagons. The truth is less exciting, but perhaps more interesting. The renegade Indians would be tracked for days and weeks by the US Army. The Army had one great advantage; its horses were shod and could therefore travel much further before becoming lame.

The domesticated horse arrived in Northern Europe about 500 years before the birth of Christ. What happened next was probably the greatest example of necessity being the Mother of Invention. At the same time that the horse arrived in this damper climate, so arrived the ability to forge iron. The wetter ground softened the hooves and protection was needed. In no time at all, the Celts had mastered the art of nailing a rim of iron to the live hoof. Who knows what mistakes were first made! Horseshoeing had begun. The Celts shod their horses in exactly the same way as we shoe them today. The shoes had a wavy outline and the nails had heads shaped like violin keys but they were indisputably horseshoes. The Romans assimilated horseshoeing along with many other skills. When they conquered Britain, with their usual ingenuity they made subtle improvements. By the time they left these shores, gone was the wavy outline and the nails had become square as today's still are.

Horseshoes, being iron, rust and decay quickly. There are, therefore, few examples of early shoes. The oldest found was excavated at Gloucester and is dated at 80 BC. It is made of titanium and iron and has a white colour. The technique of shoeing horses changed little during the next 1500 years. The farrier's skills spread far and wide during that time. Once the ability to shoe reached an area, then the people living there were able to use horses for draught. Examination of farm records of the 13th and 14th centuries show that many farm horses were shod. These were the heavier types that had been arriving from the continent since the

Norman Conquest.

William the First of Normandy had recognised the importance of hoofcare in maintaining an effective cavalry. He appointed Henry de Farraris to be in control of his farriers and, to Simon St Liz for providing shoes for his horses, he gave the town of Northampton.

The art of horseshoeing may well have spread to the Middle East by the time the Koran was written (610 AD). Was it just poetic licence to describe war horses as *"striking fire by dashing their hooves against stones"*? In 1038 AD, the Greek cavalry under Emperor Michael of Constantinople were shod.

Horseshoes and the nails to attach them became a valuable commodity. The material alone was of a far greater value than today. The Celts, before the Romans arrived, were using iron bars as a form of currency. In 1050, each smith in Hereford was required to make 120 horseshoes for Edward the Confessor from the King's iron. In 1195, Gloucester, known for its horseshoe manufacturing, was taxed annually to pay 100 bars of iron fit to make nails and 36 dacras of iron, a dacrum being 20 horseshoes.

The annual rent of farrier Walter le Brun's forge in the Strand was set in 1235 at 6 shoes and their nails. They are still given in a service on 30th September. The same shoes have been used for the past 500 years! In 1254, the Sheriff of Sussex provided the King with 30,000 horseshoes and 60,000 nails.

The concept of buying large amounts of ready-made shoes is not new. For the Crusades, 50,000 additional horseshoes were made in England between 1189–1199. By 1265, most horseshoes were bought ready-made. One hundred years later, the Flemish were selling their horseshoes in England. These were mainly the wider webbed fullered shoes for heavier horses. By 1590, there were slitting mills operating. These produced bars and nail rods which made shoe and nail manufacture much quicker and easier.

The first manufactured, ready-made shoes appeared in 1800. These were made by Moorcraft and were cast, not forged (casting is when the molten metal is poured into a mould rather than being forged or beaten into shape). In 1809, the first patent for a horseshoe-making machine was registered. Apparently it failed to work. By 1857,

Burden had developed a machine that produced 60 shoes an hour. The effect upon the US Civil War was unestimable. Burden was under contract to supply the Union (North). The Confederates (South) were given orders that, when capturing the Union supplies, the highest priority was to be given to recovering horseshoes. Without steel mills and horseshoe manufacturing, the Confederates were unable to match the Union army.

Although the basic act of horseshoeing has changed little since its advent 2000 years ago, a farrier still needs to reduce excess horn by cutting and rasping, and then fix a metal rim to the insensitive foot; the tools have evolved and the price risen.

In 1265 AD, shoes sold at Dover cost 5 shillings 5 1/4 pence per hundred and nails 9 shillings 3 pence per thousand. Horseshoeing was said at that time to be the greatest cost in keeping a horse (some might say it still is!). In 1270, Walter de Henly calculated the cost of keeping a farm horse in shoes at 1 pence per foot per week.

By 1299, costs had already risen. The shoeing smith was paid 4 pence per day and shoes now cost ten shillings per hundred, nails 1 shilling 10 pence per thousand. The Black Death, in 1348, tripled these costs. In an attempt to control prices, the Lord Mayor of London limited prices to 2 pence a shoe with 8 nails and 1 1/2 pence a shoe for less than 8 nails. Since a smith could buy 30 nails for 1 penny, I should imagine that 8 nails was the norm.

By 1223, a set of shoes cost 2 shillings. During the American War of Independence, the cost of shoeing again rose dramatically. While occupying New York, the farriers there were paid 20 shillings per day. Elsewhere in the colony, the price had risen to 6 pounds per set!

The anvil, with its distinctive shape, was not always so. Before 1268, it was a large block of iron. After that time, in Europe, anvils began to appear with a horn. The horn is the horizontal cone attached to one end. This makes turning shoes much easier. In 1824, a mobile forge was patented which was recommended to '*trainers or gentlemen*' (never to be confused) '*to have on their premises for their smith to use*'. By 1840, every tool needed by a farrier was being manufactured. Prior to this time, farriers had had to hand-make all their own tools. Apprentices trained in this country can still make most of the basic tools. If you thought screw-in studs were a modern invention - James White had the idea in 1802 and, in 1860, S. Morris of London was selling pre-threaded screw caulks for ice traction.

The world of commerce depended greatly on the farriers to keep their horses shod. Without farriers, no shoes - without shoes, no horses. In 1830, a strike by French farriers is recorded and, in 1864, the farriers in the Midlands had a strike which was broken according to the *Veterinarian*. There were some, however, who believed that farriers could be done away with. Between 1880 and 1890, there arose an 'anti-horseshoeing movement'. One Major Rodney had his horses shoes removed in 1886 and presented a paper claiming no ill effects. This theory obviously cut no ice with the RSPCA, who announced it would prosecute anyone on the streets of London who drove a horse without proper horseshoes.

During the last 2000 years, the status of the farrier has changed. His job specification has altered. His various titles have caused confusion. Should a man that shoes horses be called a farrier or a blacksmith, or even a horseshoer or shoeing smith? I have already suggested that the name farrier comes from the Latin for an iron shoe. The name blacksmith comes from the Saxon term to smite iron. So a blacksmith can be an iron worker who never shoes a horse. When a farrier makes a shoe by hand he is 'blacksmithing'. The reason that the horse-owning public in general use the term blacksmith relates back to the time when the farriers split to become veterinarians. Before that time (1791), the term farrier was used to describe someone who cared for animals and also shod horses. The first veterinary school was founded in Lyon, France in 1762, where Chabert taught horseshoeing.

At about the same time, Edward Coleman headed the London Veterinary College. He believed that farriers would be replaced by veterinary surgeons and blacksmiths. He sought to introduce a universal shoe that any workman could use, thereby consigning the thinking horseshoer (farrier) to the rubbish bin. Together with many of Coleman's ideas it did not work, but it has led to great confusion over the years.

The very first farriers must have passed on their craft to their sons (the first recorded female farrier was widow Hendry in 1767) or apprentices. Although this system continued with all crafts for hundreds of years, it was long recognised that horseshoeing was more than an art and craft, but also a science. Apart from the earliest references to the care of hooves, there were attempts to set standards and to study farriery. In 1356, the Fellowship of Marshalls of the City of London was set up to govern the farriers. This later became the Worshipful Company of Farriers, which to this day is charged with that responsibility. In 1674, the Worshipful Company of Farriers was recognised by Royal Charter; this was repeated recently by Queen Elizabeth II. In 1847, the first school of farriery was established in Gotheson, Germany. It is likely that farriery was taught as a subject in Rome as early as 1495, when the first farriery exams took place at *L'Universita dei Ferrari* in Rome. Candidates shod a horse and treated it medically.

By the end of the 19th century there were many schools across Europe and North America. The Worshipful Company of Farriers continued to stimulate education by essays and shoeing competitions. The RSS (Registered Shoeing Smith) examination of basic competence was introduced - now called the Diploma of Worshipful Company of Farriers (DipWCF).

From the middle of the 19th century until the First World War, the horse and farrier were in their heyday. Then the catastrophe happened. Between the wars, the horse all but disappeared. They went completely from the cities. Here worked the pure farrier, who shod horses six days a week. Within a few years, every horse in the city disappeared to be replaced by truck, tram, taxi and car. In the country it was somewhat different. The country smith was a jack of all trades; he mended the ploughs and the tractors, he did a little blacksmithing and maybe one day a week he shod horses. When horse numbers began to revive in the 1960s, he was still there. Older and unwilling to commit himself full-time to an animal that had let him down before, perhaps. Throughout the 1970s and 1980s, horse numbers increased tenfold. The number of farriers to shoe all these horses suddenly could not be found. The other change was the type of horse. Only rarely does a farrier have a working horse to shoe. Nowadays it is all hunting, polo, racing and Pony Club.

So the skills that had taken about 2000 years to develop still existed in old forges across the country. The ancient arts and mysteries of the farrier's craft had been preserved. Now there are plenty of boys and girls wishing to learn the skills, and a willing market for those skills.

Some things have changed. The modern farrier needs to be well versed in the anatomy and function of the foot and lower leg. He (or she) needs to be able to satisfy a horse-owner who is competitive. There has been a sudden increase in the high-tech type of shoes and products. All types of synthetic materials and metals other than steel have been formed into shoes. Hoof fillers and glue-on shoes are now accepted. The farrier may well be asked by a vet to assist in helping remedy lameness. The farrier's skills can be used to apply orthopaedic devices to support or reposition the limb.

Nothing really changes though - for those who believe that the eggbar shoe for treating collapsed heels and navicular disease is new; it isn't! The ring shoe, as it was called, can be found in many 19th century books. As for the heartbar shoe, so controversial in the 1980s, we thought that it had crossed the Atlantic from Texas, USA, but it can be seen on a mosque in India dated 1575!

Further reading

Hickman (1988) *Hickman's Farriery.*
Hymering (1990) *On the Horse's Foot.*
Fleming (1869) *History of Horseshoeing.*

Never a dull day

PHILIP J. BROOK DipWCF

Shrublands
36 East Road
Isleham
Ely
Cambs CB7 5SN

For some, a career path is chosen at birth; many a vet has followed his father or his father's father into the profession. Yet, for me, the progression into the world was far less certain. Like most 'Newmarket boys' I could find myself around a racecourse, but certainly not a horse's foot. It would be wrong of me to say I had always wanted to be a farrier, this simply was not the case. I quite literally stumbled my way into the profession. As a bored warehouse foreman I longed for a new challenging career. My mother, on inspection of a local newspaper, suggested I became a farrier. I applied and thus the ground was laid; all I needed to do was get through the interview.

The interview was an experience in itself. A well respected and renowned Newmarket farrier put me through my paces before offering me a job and a stiff drink. The fact I was offered the job was no surprise, not because of my blinding ability and confidence, but because I was the only one to apply. In the early 1970s, the trade lacked the appeal it has today, in Newmarket at least. Some see it as a dying craft thse days, but most Newmarket training farriers can expect at least three or four applications a week from would-be apprentices.

My apprenticeship was served over four long years, in which I found myself in some 'household name' yards such as Bruce Hobbs and Harry Thompson-Jones. Before I had started my apprenticeship, the only horse shoe I had seen regularly was that attached to a neighbour's door which was said, although I didn't believe it, to belong to a famous Classic winner. Yet, over four years, a slight, child boy was transformed into a fully trained farrier, ready to enter the box of even the most pyschotic Thoroughbred.

A horse I remember, and still carry the bruises of, 'lovingly' needed a strategically-placed broom in its most fragile region before even thinking about approaching it. In a manoeuvre the SAS would have been proud of, a wet behind novice and two 4 foot high stable lads approached with caution, if not fear, gently working our way to the permanently embellished headcollar. A set of four shoes on the delightful animal took a good few hours out of my busy day. This would not have bothered me so much if the horse was a world beater. The truth, sadly, was that it could not win a selling stakes or even a donkey derby at Great Yarmouth.

Coincidentally, two of the most inspirational events of my life occurred on the same day. First, I married my wife, head coach and accountant Rhona. Secondly, I received my qualification papers and announced to family and friends, admittedly after a bit of 'dutch courage', of my plans to 'go it alone'. These days, I have the luxury of competent support staff and apprentices; back in the ABBA-filled days of the 1970s, life was anything but easy. I took on the accounts which no-one else wanted; some kind spirited gentleman farriers, like Bob Walker, took pity on me, and gave work to me. But, it wasn't all 'blood, sweat and tears', especially when I dared venture into the fens!

An instance which immediately springs to mind is when I travelled some distance to shoe just one horse at the end of a long day. The horse was difficult but this was nothing in itself, in fact the day had been surprisingly uneventful. I proudly took the five one pound notes from the owner and proceeded to call my dog, who had decided to stretch his legs.

My attention was taken by the commotion which roared up behind me. I could hear a voice but could not make out what it cried. Somewhat taken aback, I saw a portly gentleman trailing a beanpole-like character with a beetroot face and cauliflower ears. He seemed to be carrying what looked like a duck, while the portly gent was dragging a rope to which seemed to be attached my mongrel.

The beanpole screeched in a strong Cambridgeshire accent "T-T-Th-Thats h-him farrther". I looked back in shock as the man exclaimed with a stutter he would not let me go. I enquired into what I done to upset him so much. He replied with a stronger stutter fuelled by his anger, that my dog had killed his prize-winning duck. I, somewhat bemused, offered to pay for the duck, father responded in no uncertain terms that my offer was to be taken up and I owed five pounds. Thus, I had driven many miles, worked hard for a couple of hours for what, a prize duck? Well no, in fact not a prize duck, the son, so emotionally distraught by the bloody murder, would not hand over the fowl for my five pounds. So me and my criminal pet, who had failed to catch a cold before his duck hunt, returned home tired, hungry and empty handed.

As has already been seen, I have in my career met my fair share of characters on my travels, but as my youthfulness deserted me, and my responsibilities became firmly bedded in Newmarket, I decided to do away with my rounds. Instead, I decided to centre my non-horseracing work at a permanent base in the nearby village of Higham. Thus, a whole new chapter of funny instances and interesting people was opened. The forge was an old building which had not been used for its proper purpose for years. Instead, it stood as an ancient store full of 19th century machinery and tools.

I gleefully looked forward to bringing the building into the 20th century. The electrical wiring I had been assured was in good working order and so I called in the local electricity board to connect everything up. On the day of the grand opening it took the man from the electricity board just two minutes to burst my bubble. He took one look at the wiring and turned to me slightly bemused and amused, but probably more of the following. He stated he has never seen anything quite like it; the wiring was prehistoric and could under no circumstances be used.

The forge needed to be rewired, not a problem in itself. A horse was booked in to be shod but I had a fire and an old bellows; no problem, or so I thought. The horse arrived on time with its lifelong pal, a strong-willed donkey. The horse's owner, a woman no more than five foot high, her six foot two husband, who towered over her like the Eiffel Tower, and her father, dressed for a grouse hunt in a deerstalker hat and his trousers sportingly tucked into his socks, had found their way to Higham. Everything was going OK, the 'three musketeers' and I made our way into the forge, accompanied by the animal. Two men were working on the ceiling repairing wires and connecting everything up. Yet, disaster was just around the corner.

The donkey, with traditional stubbornness, had managed to place itself right in my way and was not keen on moving. To tempt the awkward animal out of my way I gently tapped it on its backside. The animal took offence and decided that neither it, or the owner's father, who was holding it, was going to stay in the same building as someone as rude as me. It shot out of the open door, too late to bolt it, across the road and into a hedge. All that could be seen from the road was a donkey's backside and swishing tail sticking out of the hedge. The father, deerstalker and all, had been quite literally dragged through a hedge backwards. He lay, dazed and confused, still holding onto the lead rein for dear life. And for the workmen, the commotion attracted the attention of one of them; seeing the poor old gent dragged through a hedge he burst into laughter. Then, in a swift turn of fate, the man who had found everything so funny was now in a sticky situation himself. He had laughed so much that he had lost his footing and started hurtling towards the ground at pace. He managed to regain his composure and grabbed onto a protruding beam. He hung there still laughing. His workmate, who had nipped away for a coffee, came in to help him but he could not, he was temporarily paralysed by laughter. The horse stood quiet and still, patiently waiting for its next shoe.

Throughout my career I have met many influential characters. However, none have been as influential as Mr Lawrence Pullen. 'Lawrie' is well known in farriery circles as an expert in the profession and helped me learn and develop a love for the art of the trade. He opened my eyes to the importance of my role in the development of the horse. He showed me that the profession was about more than just shoeing as many horses in the quickest possible time. I'm sure my career would not have been as long and as fruitful as it has been if he had not shared his wisdom with me. Yet, Mr Pullen is not just an incredibly knowledgeable man; he is also very entertaining with a sharp sense of humour. Lawrie often brought sections of real horse's feet with him when he visited, which he used to help me understand the foot better. One particular day he had arranged to meet me in a famous, if not infamous, racing yard. There was a horse in the yard which was talented but had terrible feet, and it attracted our attention. The horse was due to race the next day, so we decided to check on its feet. It was at this moment that Lawrence hatched one of his most devious plans.

The yard had a very charismatic head lad who was the victim of our trickery. As I approached him I could see that he already looked upset and stern-faced. He saw me approach and knew something was wrong. He asked me what was the matter. I told him that we had a problem and held out a horse's foot and explained how it had fallen off one of the best horses in the yard. He, believing my story, launched a torrent of abuse at me, letting me know in no uncertain terms that we were both for the 'high jump'. By now, he was very hot under the collar and I was trying very hard not to laugh. He had just finished calling me the last name under the sun when out of the corner of his eye he saw Lawrence. The head lad realised he had been set up and he then repeated the long list of obscenities, this time at both of us; and a bit more cheerfully than he had done before!

There is never a dull day in my job. I thrive on this, the hours are long and the work physical but never ever boring. The job is made interesting, not just by the horses but also the many characters that accompany them along the way. Would I swap it all for a 'nine to five' job which would be easier on the back? No, of course not, I would not swap it for the world.

Thoughts on the veterinary/farrier relationship

MARK J. MARTINELLI DVM
San Luis Rey Equine Hospital
Bonsall
California
USA

Introduction

As *'Guardians of the Horse'*, the equine foot is one realm of great concern. Not only is care of the foot critical to soundness, but it represents the shared jurisdiction of the veterinarian and farrier. For this reason, the topic of veterinary and farrier interaction is often discussed within the horse industry. It is of paramount importance to the ongoing and future success of our two professions that a greater interaction and mutual communication develop between farriers and veterinarians. Our clients are more knowledgeable and are taking a more active role in the decisions regarding their horse's health care. They have access to a multitude of information by attending special lectures, reading journals or through the internet. Clients are demanding more from their horse and from the professionals who serve them. For these reasons, it is imperative that the veterinarian and farrier join forces to provide the very best service to our clients and their horses. This may be easier in theory than in actual practice, since the two professions have had their differences. Perhaps the root of some of the problems over the years resides in the background of the two professions. In order to understand more fully the similarities and differences between them, it is essential to explore their beginnings.

History

The history of veterinary medicine and farriery are closely interwoven. The two professions, or occupations as they were first known, very closely followed the ever-increasing role of the horse in civilisation. Domestication of the horse rapidly changed civilisation by providing a beast of burden for work and transportation. These ideas were adopted rapidly by the military sectors of society, who realised that a mounted strike force in the form of a cavalry would introduce mobility and power to an otherwise ambulatory army. Early evidence of veterinary medicine exists in most of the literate civilisations of the day, although the Greeks and Chinese seemed to have the most advanced understanding of the time. Some of the conclusions of Aristotle and Apsyrtos regarding equine medicine may have been erroneous, but the Greek logic was impressive for the time. During the reign of the Roman Empire, veterinarians were mentioned as an integral part of keeping the cavalry and transportation horses healthy. At that time in Roman society, the veterinarian occupied a status quite low on the social ladder and they were often considered to be unscrupulous characters. The name *'veterinarian'* is often ascribed to be a conversion of the name *'Vegetius'*, a Roman layman and author with a significant interest in the horse. It should be noted, however, that the Romans also used the term *veterinarium* for the place that pack animals were kept and *veterinarius* for an animal caretaker. There are no specific references to farriers during that time, although proper foot care was deemed essential in maintaining a sound horse. The feet were trimmed and sometimes treated with a hardener on the sole surface prior to long journeys on hard roads. It was also noted in Roman writings that the stabling environment should be kept clean in order to maintain hard feet. It appears that the

Romans did invent one of the precursors to the modern horseshoe in what was called the 'hipposandal'. It is speculated that these iron foot coverings were tied onto foot-sore horses to keep medications in place.

The Dark Ages provided a curious backdrop for the progression of the equine industry. After the Fall of the Roman Empire, the horse continued to escalate in its role as an essential machine of war and societal development, but its medical care advanced little during that time. The religious beliefs of the time served to squash much of the medical intellect, since many bold thinkers were subject to persecution as heretics. The Dark Ages did produce one of the most important technological advances in equestrianism with the invention of the nailed-on iron horseshoe by the Celts, probably sometime during the first century AD. These first hoof aedifiers were a major advancement on the mobility of the horse and were credited with aiding William the Conquerer during the Norman Conquest in 1066 AD. Because of the massive demand for iron horseshoes, the farrier became the most sought-after craftsman and the entire well-being of the horse, including veterinary care, became his domain. During the sixteenth and seventh centuries, however, ignorance in the equine industry continued to reign, as evidenced by the work of the English author Thomas Blundeville. Although not a farrier, veterinarian or even a horseman, he wrote the major work of the day on shoeing and veterinary care. While he is credited with originating the concept of fitting the shoe to the foot, his complete lack of practical experience simply served to propagate the myths, fallacies and cruelties of the day, thus preventing the craft from advancing to professional status in the public eye. In another book from 1696, *The Gentleman's Compleat Jockey with the Perfect Horseman and Experienc'd Farrier* by A.S. Gent, one chapter is entitled *The Whole Art of a Farrier* and deals with curing diseases, while the next chapter contains the *Methods of Shoeing*. Such works illustrate the dual role of the farrier at that time.

The next major era in the history of the veterinary/farrier relationship seemed to be the establishment of formal veterinary schools in the eighteenth century. The first was founded in France in 1762. It focused solely on the health care of the horse, and its founder, Claude Bourlegat, was a major innovator in the design of horseshoes. The French school turned out graduates from all over Europe who were instrumental in establishing veterinary medicine as a science. One of these French graduates, Vial Sainbel, was commissioned in 1791 to help establish the first veterinary school in Britain. One of the early advocates of the London-based school, Granville Penn, found it absurd that the animal care was entrusted to the horseshoers. He equated that with allowing human medicine to be practised by cobblers. The initial admission standards preferred students with a strong educational background, especially those from the human medical field. After the untimely death of Sainbel, 18 months after the establishment of the school, the second principal relaxed the school standards significantly. Although Edward Coleman had himself a proper medical background, he shortened the veterinary programme and was said to have preferred the practically trained students to the scholarly ones in favouring the sons of farriers to those of surgeons. The programme was criticised for concentrating solely on the horse and Professor Coleman, lacking in practical experience, perpetrated some of the shoeing inaccuracies of the day. This only served to confuse the farriers and horseowners in Britain further. One of the London graduates, William Dick, the son of a farrier himself, established the veterinary school in Edinburgh in 1823, specifically to train the intellectually-oriented blacksmiths in anatomy and clinical medicine. Although the veterinary schools attempted to bring science and organisation to the care of horses, many practically trained farriers and 'horse doctors' continued to practice medicine, in spite of the formally trained veterinarians.

The interactions between the two professions continued over the years with veterinarians, many of a military background, influencing the practice of horseshoeing. Finally, an official split between the two professions resulted when specific licensing laws were enacted and voluntary registration and certification was carried out. In the veterinary profession in Great Britain, the Royal College of Veterinary Surgeons received its charter in 1844, but a testing programme did not come into existence until 1870 and The

Veterinary Surgeons Act finally gave legal protection to the profession in 1881. Although the Worshipful Company of Farriers had been formed as a skilled trade guild in London in 1356, it was not until 1890 that they conceived and instituted their own registration and examination programme. The initial qualifications were basic, but more advanced levels were added in the early 1900s. In the 1970s, acts were passed to promote good farriery and ensure a higher skill level among the farriers of Great Britain. In the veterinary profession in the United States, the first Veterinary Medical Association was formed in 1863 and they adopted a code of ethics in 1867. The organisation became the American Veterinary Medical Association in 1898 and continues to provide ethical guidance to the profession, while licensure to practice veterinary medicine is granted by each individual state. For farriers, the International Union of Journeymen Horseshoers was formed in 1874 and the American Farriers Association in 1971. Certification tests, similar to those in Great Britain although not mandatory, were adopted by the AFA in 1979.

Practical aspects of farriery

Having discussed the situation with well-respected individuals from each profession, it seems that many of the misunderstandings and ill-feelings of today emanate from discrepancies between medical training and practical experience. It stands to reason that the farrier must, at least, possess a thorough knowledge of horsemanship, metal working, and anatomy of the foot. Today, many farriers are also quite well versed in the basics of radiology, lameness diagnosis and general disease processes. On a practical level, the sheer number of feet encountered in the everyday practice of the horseshoer would transform almost any neophyte over time into an experienced farrier with knowledge unparalleled by any other professional, including the veterinarian. Without the repetitive, practical experience known only to the farrier, it is unrealistic for the veterinarian to expect to acquire such a thorough understanding of the external equine foot or to become as proficient in the use of the farrier's tools.

Current veterinary education

By the same token, the equine veterinarian undertakes a very rigorous medical training programme which serves to prepare the individual for a career in the diagnosis and treatment of medical and surgical disorders of the horse. The thorough training in anatomy, physiology, pharmacology and pathology follow the prerequisites of mathematics, physics, biology and chemistry which can be assimilated only through many years of study and hard work. Each of these disciplines can then be applied to the different species, bodily systems and disease processes in an attempt to prevent and treat disease. Specific training in foot diseases and farriery varies between veterinary schools. Most schools in both the US and UK include some concepts of farriery in a general musculoskeletal lameness or surgery lecture. Some schools further this training in specific elective classes that may even include a practical class with an experienced farrier. It is unrealistic to expect an average veterinary student to accumulate enough knowledge or practical skill in such a curriculum to enable them to become proficient with even the most basic trimming procedures. As discussed earlier, these skills can only expect to be mastered by the repetition of the farrier's training course and routine practice.

A feasible approach

It would now seem appropriate to propose a feasible approach to effective interaction between the two professions that would be mutually beneficial to both the horse and owner. It is of paramount importance to the relationship that each party understand and appreciate the strengths of the other as presented above. Neither the veterinarian nor the farrier should profess, or assume, complete jurisdiction over the equine foot, but rather work to symbiotically manage the challenges present in the field of equine podiatry. Put into the most practical terms, it is inappropriate and illegal for the farrier to diagnose independently or treat specific causes of lameness, prescribe drugs, or perform surgery. It is proper for the farrier to comment on lameness, changes in foot conformation or the presence of other medical problems which may require the attention of a veterinarian. The relationship that most farriers enjoy with their clients is often more conducive to the maintenance of health than that of veterinarians because of the inherent need for frequent and scheduled visits. The farrier will often be consulted and be able to identify the very early signs of diseases and lamenesses related directly to the foot and musculoskeletal system as well as those related to the general health of the horse. The farrier may see subtle changes in foot shape over time such as contracting of the heels or atrophy of the frog that may indicate a change in weightbearing related to lameness in that limb. He/she may notice shoe wear patterns consistent with dragging the toe or landing on the outside of the limb. Routine paring of the sole may reveal bruising of the sole anterior to the apex of the frog, while trimming the foot may expose pending hoof wall separation or old abscesses. Trimming may also provide information about hoof growth and quality which may then reflect nutritional or metabolic alterations in the horse. Other information gleaned during the process of shoeing may not be directly related to the foot. For instance, the farrier may notice that the horse had become more reluctant to lift its hind legs for trimming, which may be a sign of such problems as distal tarsitis or pelvic problems. Often, inexperienced horseowners will ask the farrier for advice about weight gain or loss, signs of infectious disease such as coughing or nasal discharge, or management of wounds, before even consulting their veterinarian. For these reasons, farriers can serve as a valuable source of information to their clients and should be cultivated as an ever-present sentinel of lameness and disease.

Although the farrier is often the first professional to see the horse, there are times when the veterinarian may be the first one consulted for a foot problem. In a similar way, it is at the very least inappropriate, if not illegal, for the veterinarian to create a situation that requires the farrier to function as a diagnostician or surgeon or administer drugs without proper interaction between the two. This may require a joint visit to see the horse, or at least effective communication. In this way, the veterinarian may not physically have to carry out the procedure on the foot, but the farrier would be acting under the direct guidance of the veterinarian. Further quality interactions between the two professionals may also require the

veterinarian to be sensitive to the observations of an experienced farrier in relation to subtle changes in foot conformation or way of going as a preliminary indicator of impending lameness. In such cases, the farrier may have recommended to the client that they seek veterinary intervention and it would be inappropriate for the veterinarian to dismiss the case without a thorough investigation. Finally, it may be more suitable when dealing with corrective trimming and shoeing for the veterinarian to discuss the diagnosis, possible aetiology and therapeutic goals with the farrier rather than prescribe a specific recipe for accomplishing the goals. Such therapeutic goals may include general treatment concepts such as shortening the toe, hastening breakover, adding posterior heel support or protecting the sole. The farrier may then provide a preferred method of accomplishing the goal and an informed discussion may follow. In this way, the veterinarian uses their training properly while also allowing and encouraging the farrier to use their acquired and respected expertise.

Future trends in veterinary education

The trend exhibited over the last several years, which appears to be gaining momentum, especially in US schools, seems to indicate that fewer veterinary students will come from rural backgrounds and, therefore, less practical experience may become more common in future large animal or equine practitioners. While this is in direct contrast to the concept that most veterinary schools were founded on, it is, nevertheless, a fact of modern veterinary education. Another, no less concerning issue, is that the veterinary curriculum seems to be shrinking. This issue does not seem to be related to a shorter programme or less class time, but most likely to an ever-increasing volume of relevant clinical material that must be covered in a fixed period of lecture time. This, along with the concept of species tracking at some schools in the US, may mean that even less time may be available in the formal curriculum to devote to specialised topics such as farriery. This issue has been addressed recently by a number of veterinarians and farriers in both the US and UK. The professional organisations of these countries have combined to institute different levels of acquiring farriery experience or 'seeing practice' with a competent farrier for interested equine veterinary students. Most veterinary schools employ or at least interact with a competent farrier full or part-time to work on pertinent clinical cases. Such an individual can be a valuable asset to the training of veterinary students and may provide the necessary practical experience. In this author's opinion, the decision to pursue such a hands-on experience in farriery must be made by each student on an individual basis, but this kind of professional interaction should be highly encouraged. It is imperative, in this author's opinion, that the prospective equine veterinarian at least be competent with a hoof knife and at pulling shoes. There seems to be no other way to gain these skills and the practical knowledge of the farrier than by experiencing the trade first hand.

On the continuing education front, there appears to be more interaction between veterinarians and farriers. Recently, both the American Association of Equine Practitioners and the British Equine Veterinary Association have included farriers as speakers in some of their educational programmes. There are also meetings, such as the annual International Bluegrass Laminitis Symposium in Kentucky, that specifically target the common ground between our professions. These interactions seem to be well-received by the veterinary profession and should continue to be encouraged. While interpersonal interactions in general, and specifically the veterinarian/farrier relationship, remain controversial and difficult to implement and maintain, a co-operative approach would be best for all involved, especially our equine patients.

Further reading

Butler, K.D. (1985) *The Principles of Horseshoeing II*. Doug Butler Publishing, Maryville, Missouri.

Dunlop, R.H. and Williams, D.J. (1996) *Veterinary Medicine: An Illustrated History*. Mosby-Year Book Inc., St. Louis, Missouri.

Hickman, J. and Humphrey, M. (1988) *Hickman's Farriery*. J.A. Allen & Co., London.

Alternative medicine and scientific methods

PETER D. ROSSDALE OBE MA PhD DESM FRCVS

Beaufort Cottage Stables
High Street
Newmarket
Suffolk CB8 8JS

In this volume, authors have contributed articles on ancient and alternative medicine for horses. The thread that binds them is that their origins can be traced way back before modern conventional medicine began in the 15th and 16th centuries.

The phrase *alternative medicine* has been coined to describe procedures of therapy not normally practised by medical and veterinary clinicians, nor taught within their *curriculum vitae*. However, many forms of alternative medicine practised today have their origins in the mists of time. In all walks of life, systems are developed which gain the label of authenticity by becoming organised into what we call professions or societies. The gates of entrance are guarded by those appointed within the profession to set standards by which those seeking entrance may be judged.

The veterinary profession has adopted this way since its formation in the early 19th century (for a full description see the first volume of *Guardians of the Horse: Past, Present and Future* pages 38–42 and 43–47). In order to graduate, an individual has to go through 5 or 6 years of training and pass yearly examinations in order to proceed.

Professions are, largely, self-regulating bodies and exclusive to those who pass their examinations and conform to standards laid down by senior members. The objective is to ensure that the end product of service meets high standards. In veterinary practice, this entails adhering to scientific principles of medical and surgical procedures. Briefly, this means that the diagnostic approach and opinion, therapeutic intervention and all methods are based upon information tested under proper conditions published in text books and peer review journals. The protocols and disciplines of science, developed since the mid 19th century, are rigorous and challenging; a necessary process to ensure that the truth of all claims for efficacy are fairly and rigorously determined.

Alternative medicine is currently progressing along the same pathway, but there is some way to go in this respect. Alternative medicine is highly regarded among many owners of horses and demand for its application is substantial.

This book contains articles on osteopathy, acupuncture, homeopathy, animal therapy and equine shiatsu; and each of these disciplines has their proponents and opponents. They are based on the principle of providing assistance and care towards the welfare of the horse; and for this alone must be respected both as a method and for the dedication of those who apply the means to the end.

The attitude of veterinarians covers the same spectrum as their medical counterparts, from scepticism to enthusiastic support. Most vets, as with the general public, have only a passing knowledge of each subject and it is in this respect that it was considered important to include these chapters in *Guardians*. Knowledge is the key to understanding and, although each writer is the enthusiastic proponent of the material they present, reading their views and knowledge of the subject can only progress the debate as to the pros and cons of usage.

Healing has always depended upon art and science. The art of healing is based largely on the empiricism of applying the means towards the ends of improvement of the human or animal condition, whether the means involve the laying on of hands or the administration of herbs and other potents. If the patient feels better and/or the condition resolves following therapy, it is reasonable to suppose there has been a cause and effect relationship in the same way that assumptions are made with regard to traditional medical interventions.

The term science is derived from the Latin *scientia*, meaning knowledge. Veterinary science therefore denotes the knowledge of a particular kind relating to animals; and equine veterinary science, that applying to horses. However, knowledge itself may extend from osmology to the migration of birds or from virology to mental processes.

The one element which binds all knowledge is whether or not it relates to facts that have been demonstrated beyond doubt to be true. Frances Bacon set forth, in his *Advancement of Learning* in the 16th century, the belief that, in any field of knowledge, the facts must be collected according to an accepted and pre-arranged plan; and then passed through a logical process from which correct judgements could emerge.

Briefly, modern scientific method dictates that knowledge or facts should be based upon a system of testing whereby cause and effect can be linked to observations collected and annotated under strictly controlled conditions and, increasingly in recent times, verified by means of statistical analysis.

What does all this mean? It may best be explained by an example. A new remedy for migraine is developed; the remedy may be a drug, the laying on of hands, hypnosis, acupuncture or the withholding of certain foods. In order to demonstrate the cause and effect relationship of any improvement in those suffering the condition, there has to be rigorous analysis of possible variables, i.e. factors which might accidentally or incidentally interfere with the interpretation of the results.

First of all, migraine sufferers have to be defined in a way which relates as accurately as possible to the actual condition. Migraine has particularly wide-ranging symptoms which differ from one individual to another. However, by setting out specific criteria of headache, sickness and/or visual signs a group of sufferers may be identified. There are other variables that then have to be taken into account, e.g. age, sex, time of year, climatic conditions (sunlight may be a triggering factor) or diet (cheese or chocolate may also be a trigger).

As far as possible, therefore, each individual should be subjected to the same external conditions of diet and activity or, at least, when two groups of sufferers are constituted, each group should contain identical numbers of similar properties.

The two groups to which I refer are the selection at random of individuals; one group to be put on the treatment and one not. The trial, therefore, consists of observations made of the two groups as to the cause and effect of treatment and relief of symptoms.

It is essential, however, to avoid as much bias as possible from the results. At the level of the patient, the individual should not know whether he or she is taking the drug or receiving the treatment, so they are unaware of into which group they fall. In order to help in this process one group will receive a *placebo*, i.e. treatment which is similar to the actual treatment (e.g. a powder) but does not actually contain the treatment drug.

Again, bias must not be introduced by those assessing the outcome being aware into which group each individual falls. This is known as a blinded study, i.e. the observer of the endpoint is blind to whether or not the patient has fallen into the treatment or *placebo* group.

When applied to horses, the same assessment must be made, although the use of *placebo* on the horse itself is not necessary, as there is no conscious awareness of what is happening. Assessment of the endpoint must, however, importantly, be blinded and the observer not have knowledge of whether or not treatment has been applied or the type of treatment followed.

There are increasing efforts for the audit of equine veterinary procedures at all levels of medicine and surgery. Questions are and must be asked; for example, as to whether carpal surgery for a chip in the knee is better than conservative treatment and rest. Scientific principles apply in this, as in any other assessment of the benefit of cause and effect.

There are always problems with this assessment, particularly in the field rather than under experimental conditions. If a therapy is thought to work, the clinician and the owner are unhappy at withholding the treatment in order to establish that it actually works. We ourselves would not wish to withhold benefits of a drug in order to prove that it has worked! Nevertheless, such observations, across sufficient numbers of the population, are essential if progress is to be made and the scientific method applied. Over time, there have been great benefits while, on the other hand, some false impressions have been made and harm done by assumptions that a treatment works when in fact it does not.

Alternative medicine does not lend itself readily to appraisal by scientific method. The reason, given by the writers in the accompanying chapters, is largely that many of the techniques and drugs supplied are part of a process personal to the operator. Nevertheless, in human as well as in animal medicine, complementary or alternative medicine has rightly and necessarily come under scrutiny in recent years. The House of Lords Science and Technology Select Committee produced a report on the subject in the year 2000. An editorial in the *Journal of the Royal Society of Medicine*, commenting on the report, was of the opinion that it provided something for everyone! The writer recounted the story of the two men, both thinking that one was cheated by the other, who appeared before a judge for arbitration. After the first man had presented his case the judge said, "*You are right*". When the second man had recounted his side of the story, the judge said, "*You are right*". "*Hold on,*" commented a third man, "*they cannot both be right*". The learned judge contemplated for a while and responded, "*You are right too*".

This story is something of an aphorism, as we clinicians and veterinary or medical scientists, on the one hand, look critically at alternative medicine as it has not been properly tested by scientific method, whereas there are many horse owners and others in the general population who wish to use alternative medicine, especially where traditional methods have failed. This is another reason for presenting the chapters in this section of *Guardians*; reading and understanding both the advantages and disadvantages of the methods is the basis of making progress in future.

Finally, I give a personal opinion. I believe that one of the weaknesses of alternative therapies is often that those who practise them are not sufficiently aware or take account of the absolute need for diagnosis before therapy. Medical and veterinary clinicians appreciate that therapy without diagnosis is often misdirected and may be dangerous, even life-threatening. It is for this reason that those who practise alternative medicine must do so in consultation with veterinary clinicians. Horses would otherwise be put at risk. There are, fortunately, moves being made to register those who practise physiotherapy and other forms of alternative medicine; and to promote a good relationship between equine clinicians and practitioners of the arts of alternative medicine. There should be no need for ill-feeling or friction, provided these harmonising avenues are followed and, particularly, that modern scientific diagnostic methods are used before any therapy, traditional or alternative is applied.

Shiatsu for horses

ELAINE LIECHTI MA MRSS, JACQUELINE COOK BHSAI and LIZ EDDY BSc

Glasgow School of Shiatsu
South Hourat Farm
Dalry
Ayrshire KA24 5LA

Origins and theory

The therapeutic mode *shiatsu* originates in Japan, where it is widely used in the human population for muscular pain, digestive upset, headache and migraine, and other common ailments. The word '*shi-atsu*' means 'finger pressure' in Japanese. This aptly describes the basic technique of the therapy, which involves pressure with fingers, thumbs or palms on areas of pain or sensitivity. Rotations and stretches also form an integral and important part of the treatment, which seeks to stimulate the body's own self-healing ability through increased blood circulation, lymphatic flow and activation of both divisions of the autonomic nervous system.

In the UK, *shiatsu* for humans has been gaining in popularity since the 1970s. Equine *shiatsu* was pioneered in the US by the American practitioner Pamela Hannay, and has been taught in Britain since the mid 1990s. As yet, there is no professional organisation for equine *shiatsu* practitioners, but approaches have been made to the Shiatsu Society, the main professional body for *shiatsu* therapists in the UK, and several of the teachers of equine *shiatsu* courses are Members of the Register of the Shiatsu Society. The Society's code of ethics and practice has clear guidelines on the use of *shiatsu* for animals. It is hoped that in the future there will be either an independent register of equine *shiatsu* practitioners, or that the major professional organisations for *shiatsu* will provide a listing.

The underlying theory used in *shiatsu* is similar to that of traditional Chinese medicine (TCM), familiar in the West as acupuncture theory. For equine *shiatsu*, we take such aspects of theory as are relevant to horses and apply them accordingly. The basic premise of all oriental medical philosophy is that the body (human or animal) is an *energetic* entity whose health and personal harmony are dependent upon a smooth flow of *energy* (*Qi* in Chinese, *Ki* in Japanese) to all internal organs, body tissues and systems. *Ki* (sometimes known as *life force*) is present throughout the body but condenses more strongly in *meridians*, or energy pathways, and *tsubo*, acupoints. The *tsubo* (Japanese for acupoint) are spots on the body, often close to nerves, joints or major arteries, where *Ki* can be accessed effectively, either by puncture with needles, pressure or application of heat. *Tsubo* are often sensitive or tender to the touch, and may become definitely painful if energy is out of balance, either excessive or deficient. The meridian pathways join *tsubo* with a similar quality or which are known to affect a particular organ or body system. *Meridians* are thus named after different organs, e.g. the Heart meridian (HT), which governs heart and circulation, and the Liver meridian (LV), which governs storage and distribution of nutrients and energy.

In equine terms, the overall strength of *Ki* can be seen in the brightness of the eye, the lustre of the coat and general alertness. Specific imbalances within particular *meridians* can be observed in the relative build-up or loss of musculature, freedom of movement in particular limbs and by palpation of specific acupoints situated some 2–3 inches lateral to the spine (depending on the size of horse).

Although *shiatsu* and acupuncture share a common theoretical basis, the way of working and indeed the purpose of treatment are often quite different. TCM, as a therapeutic system, is designed to work on 'what is wrong', i.e. the aspects of pain, imbalance or disharmony. Needles are inserted into specific *tsubo* in order to regulate and rebalance a problem; these points are chosen because of their known effect on the condition and may be close to the site of the problem or distant from it. *Shiatsu*, on the other hand, focuses on 'what is', i.e. the areas of both weakness and strength in the health profile. It can be used for general relaxation and toning, as part of a health maintenance programme, as well as for specific ailments. The accent in *shiatsu* is on working the entire length of *meridians*, and this can identify areas of tightness and lack of muscular tone whilst also enabling the practitioner to home in on particular *tsubo*, which may be of assistance in a specific problem such as lameness or colic.

As with human subjects, *shiatsu* in horses can be extremely useful in those cases that lie in the grey area between sickness and health, when things are not definitely 'wrong', but are 'not quite right' either. In oriental terms, this would be interpreted using *Yin-Yang* theory, which proposes that *Yang* individuals are constitutionally more robust and active, assertive and physically stronger, whereas *Yin* individuals tend to be quieter and less physically developed (a typical bottom-of-the-herd poor doer). Touch technique would then vary according to the horse's needs. Meridian theory focuses on the more technical aspects of imbalance, e.g. the Stomach (ST) meridian deals overall with digestive problems and *tsubo* on it are helpful during colic and to assist with sluggish metabolism. A horse with an imbalanced ST meridian may have a tendency to be greedy and bolt his food or he may be a worrier and find it hard to assimilate food, especially if under pressure.

An aspect of theory widely used in both acupuncture for horses and *shiatsu* is the '*Theory of Five Elements*'. This ascribes various energetic attributes found in nature to individuals (both human and equine - useful in establishing compatible horse and rider partnerships!), on all levels from the physical to the emotional. For example, *Wood* energy is rising and expansive, like the powerful upsurge of nature's energy in springtime. The *Wood*-type horse is generally muscular and well proportioned, enjoys work and becomes angry, impatient or naughty if not given plenty to do. Looking at him, there is a sense of contained strength and energy; when imbalanced, this has a tendency to explode into aggressive outbursts. Muscle, tendon and ligament injuries are a common problem. *Metal* energy, on the other hand, represents the downward and inwards movement of autumn, with *Ki* being conserved within boundaries and structures. The typical *Metallic* horse, similarly, does not exhibit great presence, but appreciates the regularity of a structured environment and routine. He is not overly emotional or affectionate, but will work steadily and honestly in exchange for fair and honest treatment. Health problems may arise with his lungs, skin or gut - the boundaries between inside and outside. Each of the five elements governs a pair of

Fig 1: Applying pressure on the meridian lines by leaning in to the horse using the practitioner's bodyweight.

Fig 2: Stretches and rotations are used to loosen up the limbs.

meridians, e.g. *Metal* governs lungs and large intestine; with the exception of the *Fire* element, which governs four. Therefore, there are 12 meridians that run bilaterally. In addition, two run on the midline dorsal and ventral, making a total of 14.

Typical *shiatsu* session

A typical *shiatsu* session begins with the practitioner taking a case history, including questions on the animal's attitude to work, social position in the herd and emotional outlook, as well as physical details. Usually this will be followed by some time observing him being walked and trotted up, even worked under saddle if appropriate. All this information provides pointers towards the overall energetic and meridian imbalance and will help the practitioner choose on which of the 14 meridians it is most appropriate to work. The session then starts with sweeping the hands all over the horse's body to accustom the horse to the giver's touch, and to explore for any areas of sensitivity, heat or cold. Pressure on the meridian lines is effected by first using the palm of hand and then the thumb or fingers, and leaning in to the horse using the practitioner's bodyweight (Fig 1). There is no sense of 'prodding' or 'jabbing'; it is more a feeling of applying 'an inquisitive finger' to see what you can find. One of my teachers (of *shiatsu* for humans) used to say: "Shiatsu is 50:50, let their energy come to you". So, pressure is applied for three to five seconds to each point, using the weight of the giver's relaxed arm. The amount of

pressure used obviously varies depending on the animal and the area being worked; large thigh muscles usually enjoy deeper stimulation, whereas touch on the face, in particluar around the eyes, has to be gentle. A length of meridian, say the Bladder meridian in the back or the Liver meridian in the hind leg, would be worked several times, with extra attention being paid to sensitive or needy points, then the next part of the meridian would be stimulated, until the whole channel has been covered. Stretches and rotations are used to loosen up the limbs, with angles of stretch being varied to work different meridians. This is an aspect of the treatment which horses particularly enjoy and can enter into with enthusiasm (Fig 2). Because of the 50:50 nature of *shiatsu*, quite often we as practitioners are also stretching when they are, and there is a sense of doing *shiatsu* 'with' the horse rather then 'for' it. This means the horse can also choose how much he wants to let himself go into the stretch - definitely non-invasive and encouraging the 'patient' to participate in treatment.

Even if the object of a session is to focus on a particular problem, say stiffness in a hind leg, the whole body will be worked, although some parts just briefly. Often a session will end with relaxing techniques on the face or tail, and sometimes the horse will look quite sleepy during and at the end of treatment. This is often attributed to the release of endorphins, or the stimulation of the parasympathetic division of the autonomic nervous system. Usually a session lasts between 30 minutes and an hour - depending on the wishes of the

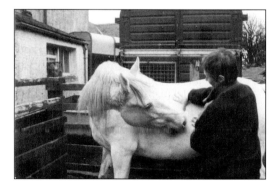

Fig 3: Horses may 'point' with the nose, indicating where they may prefer attention to be directed.

receiver! As a practitioner of *shiatsu* on humans of some nineteen years experience, I have never had a patient get up off the mat before their time was up, but some of my horse clients do wander off around the box as if to say "*I'm fed up with that technique, could you do something else, please*". This is occasionally accompanied by 'pointing' with the nose (usually to an area of the back), offering a part of the neck or even backing up to present their tail or rump (Fig 3).

Personal experiences

My personal involvement in shiatsu with horses has grown out of my shiatsu practice, in contrast to my colleague whose clinical experiences follow, who was primarily a 'horse person' and got into shiatsu as a method of helping her own horse. As a shiatsu practitioner, I know that the therapy is extremely effective for human patients and can successfully help with a wide range of conditions from severe back pain, through migraine, irritable bowel syndrome (IBS) and multiple sclerosis (MS), to depression and anxiety. Thus far in my training with horses (I am two-thirds of the way through a three level course which has taken me two and a half years), I have found shiatsu helpful for stiff and elderly horses, to promote relaxation, both physical and mental, in horses coming back into work, to alleviate boredom in a pony on three months box rest, to assist with nervousness, and for minor lameness of muscular origin. Nothing spectacular, but enough to make me think shiatsu on the horse can be a useful addition to the general health maintenance programme. The owner of an event yard I visit regularly feels that shiatsu relaxes and eases the horses: "I think it does help physically and mentally. Their muscles are softer when they come out to work." On my own horses, I have used tsubo for colic (point ST25: 2–3 inches lateral to the umbilicus, held for several minutes at a time, produced breaking wind and then dung within 15 minutes); also Ahshi (locally sensitive) points on the spleen and liver meridians around the stifle for a torn medial meniscus. The case histories which follow come from practitioners with greater clinical experience than mine and illustrate how shiatsu may be used to help balance more complex cases.

Case history

Presented by Jacqueline Cook, BHSAI, Level 3 practitioner Shiatsu for Horses

Client Name: Liz Cousel
Horse's name: Bosworth Field ('Bozz')
Breed: Cleveland Bay x TB
Length of ownership: 15.5 years
Date: August 2000
Date of birth: 1984
Sex: Gelding
Height: 17.3hh

Current environment: Country, in a DIY livery yard. Turned out with 15hh gelding. Other paddocks with a variety of horses and ponies surround their paddock.

Current/past work: At present, Bozz is in light to moderate work. Previously, he has done hunting and BHS Horse Trials to Intermediate standard. When he was unable to stay at this level, he did Pony Club activities with Liz's daughter.

Brief history: Bozz had strangles at the age of 5. He then developed *Purpura haemorrhagica*, with a 10% chance of survival. For the last eight years, Bozz has had a lot of problems with his forelimbs, with a variety of vets looking at him, performing many x-rays, scans, nerve ending tests etc, all giving a similar comment: "*He's not lame, but he's not sound either*".

Visual observation

As Bozz was taken from his box to be walked up for me, my first impression was how bolt upright his head and neck were, with a tremendous amount of inflammation at his atlas/axis region which was transmitting tension and lack of elasticity further down his spine. His tail was clamped. He also seemed to be unaware of who or what he was standing on or over.

When moving at a walk he could not track up, demonstrating the lack of movement in his lumbar region and that his quarters were extremely weak. He was lame on all four limbs, indicating that the musculoskeletal and biomechanical function was under excessive stress. His circulation was also very poor.

Bozz's whole constitution was very depleted; visually, you could see this particularly in his quarters where the muscle was showing deterioration. He was showing a reluctance to move forward, and a lot of general fatigue.

Observation through touch

A session of *shiatsu* always begins with 'hands over hands' introduction, stroking the horse all over. This prepares the horse for a session and helps the practitioner to discover more about the horse, i.e. hot spots/places (indicate inflammation, too much energy) or cold spots/places (not enough energy, will often be seen as a weak area, muscle deterioration). It also gives the practitioner a chance to pick up any previously unseen lumps or bumps.

Bozz was very unhappy about being stroked all over. He found even this simple technique too sore to bear, particularly around his poll region. His tail was rigidly clamped and his legs were stone cold. His hair was quite coarse to touch where it was standing on end. His muscle structure would brace against the touch.

Body type

Bozz is a *Wood* element type, with more *Yang* constitution then *Yin*. His problems were very much in relation to his type:

- General muscle soreness
- Neck tension - headaches
- Joint, tendon and ligament problems

                    YANG - Gallbladder

- Circulatory problems
- Hind leg stiffness
- Muscle strain/inflammation
- Eye problems

                         YIN - Liver

Meridian work

The main meridian pathways that I worked on with Bozz were:

1) Gallbladder - For general muscle soreness; neck tension, joint, tendon and ligament problems; headaches.
2) Liver - Hind leg stiffness; circulation problems; muscle strain and inflammation; eye problems.
3) Bladder - Hind leg soreness and stiffness; neck pain; back pain; general fatigue; clamped tail.

Meridian point work

The following points were used during Bozz's sessions;

1) Gallbladder - Point 21. To relieve shoulder pain; softens tense muscles; used for hock problems.
2) Gallbladder - Point 29. To relieve disorders of the hip joint.
3) Stomach - Point 36. To relieve fatigue and helps restore the immune system.
4) Stomach - Point 2. Relaxes muscles, tendons and the body in general. Excellent pain relief point.
5) Large intestine - Point 4. To relieve pain from any part of the body.
6) Bladder (large intestine association point) Point 25. Relieves pain in the neck, shoulder and lower back.

Response during sessions

His first session was very difficult as his body was extremely sore and deep pressure could hurt him. I used only palm pressure at this stage, with soft, subtle movements. He found it very pleasant and some relief was pleasing for him. He was unable to do any leg rotations and stretches.

It was after his first session that Bozz blossomed with the work. The tension and soreness eased, to be replaced with muscle that became fuller, and the elasticity had returned within the whole body structure.

Initially Bozz had three treatments, each a week apart. This was followed by three fortnightly sessions. By this time, the root of the problem had been sorted and he then went on to monthly maintenance. Bozz had to be shown how to move again as he had been compensating for so long that he was moving incorrectly according to his conformation. This was achieved through rotations and stretches, encouraging him to be aware of his body in motion.

Today, Bozz is the picture he should be for his

breed and size; a big, beautiful, powerful horse who has good active hock action, fluent movement and who is in control of his body - and he is now sound.

Vet's report on case study: Bosworth Field ('Bozz') Samantha Stock BVetMed, MRCVS

Bozz was presented in June 2000 with a 3/10 degree of lameness at trot in his left forelimb, with the toe area of the hoof being positive to hoof tester pressure. The area was explored but no infection was found, only mild signs of inflamed laminae. The lameness improved to almost sound with a bilateral abaxial sesamoid nerve block. The horse had a history of front foot pain a few years earlier, which had been improved with bar shoes, plus he had moderately poor conformation of the forefeet with broken back hoof pastern axis, collapsing heels and flat feet. In light of this, front foot radiography was advised to rule out any bony pathology.

Radiography showed no bony abnormalities, so bar shoes combined with low dose phenylbutazone were prescribed due to foot conformation and possible early mechanical laminitis. After 4 weeks (and off the phenylbutazone), Bozz's lameness had improved to sound on a straight line but persisted at 3/10 lame on the left fore on the left rein and 1/10 lame on the right rein. More time was allowed and further anti-inflammatory treatment given, as well as keeping him shod with bar shoes.

Another month later, the left rein lameness was persisting. The left foot was no longer sore to the hoof testers and it was beginning to look like Bozz was suffering from a secondary problem. His large size and unusual conformation of higher quarter compared to front assembly with a weak back made it likely that past and recent lameness problems may have left Bozz with stresses and strains on various areas of his back and other parts of his anatomy.

Bozz's owner was keen to try complementary therapy and certainly something to help bring his body 'back in line' and working as a unit was indicated. Shiatsu therapy was suggested and we decided that we would see if it could help, as conventional medicine had done what it could. Jacqueline Cook, a local Shiatsu with Horses practitioner, was contacted in August and Bozz has had regular sessions ever since. Bozz has steadily improved, both in his lameness and physical ability as well as his mental attitude, becoming a much happier and more relaxed horse, indicating a relief from pain. At his last check up in mid-December, he was sound in a straight line and on both reins on the lunge as well as having built up muscle in areas where he was weak as a result of a gradual exercise programme suggested by Jacqueline to go along with her shiatsu therapy. Bozz still has his bar shoes on at this stage and these may eventually be removed only if the foot conformation improves sufficiently.

This case highlights how conventional and complementary therapy can work hand in hand to improve and resolve a chronic lameness. This case resolved because of good professional communication between all three parties involved, with each person having an open mind as to how to help Bozz and treating him as a whole horse, with appreciation that a problem in one leg can have a knock-on effect on other body areas.

Owner's comments
Liz Cousel

In the last eight years or so, there have been long periods when Bozz has not been quite sound. He has been x-rayed (by different vets) on several occasions. Apart from general wear and tear, nothing was diagnosed until recently when I was told he had mechanical laminitis. I was advised to avoid trotting him on roads, and told he would probably have to be on 'bute' indefinitely. I did not like this, so I asked Jacqueline to come and give me her opinion. Six months later, thanks to Jacqueline and her shiatsu, and my vet Sam, who agreed it would be a good idea, Bozz is now as sound as a bell and looking better then ever before. Treatment will go on a while yet, but it has all been worth it.

Conclusion

Shiatsu is a hands-on therapy which may be used both for specific health problems and as part of a general health maintenance programme. It differs from massage and physiotherapy in that it is based in a rich tradition of medical philosophy which has been in use in the Orient for centuries. Shiatsu can be applied to both horse and rider: how often do we see horses compensating for their rider's physical imbalances? This shared experience can help to foster a sense of horse and rider being in the same team. One of the aspects of *shiatsu* which is so appealing is its very simplicity - everyone has hands and can be taught to use them to help their horse. *Shiatsu* also has a holistic approach. Keeping our animals happy, healthy and in balance is the goal of all horse 'caretakers', whether our charges are family pets or top-level competition horses. *Shiatsu* appears to be a means of maintaining this balance for an increasing number of owners. For example, Mrs Caro Haddow, whose daughters compete at Pony Club Inter-branch level, Elementary dressage, and international Pony Eventing, commented that regular *shiatsu* can report on the general state of things and can pick up little things the owner might not.

"We like it for the horses when they are competing, because shiatsu can pick up quite quickly if they are sore. The horses like the stretches. They become more self-aware and more amenable. We also like it because it is non-invasive - if the horse doesn't want to do a stretch it doesn't have to."

She regards their practitioner, Liz Eddy, as 'one of our props'.

On a more humorous note, I notice my horses applying practical *shiatsu* to each other in a scratchy sort of way very frequently, especially when it is coat casting time. The bladder meridian, which runs along the back close to the spine, appears to be their favourite channel to work. If they are already doing it to each other, why should we not assist, with a little more technical knowledge?

As a healing art, *shiatsu* shares the same ancient lineage as Chinese acupuncture. Despite its poetic terminology, oriental medicine has a precise internal logic and hundreds of years of experience in applying an energetic viewpoint to the art of healing the sick, whether human or animal.

In our modern world, the pressure to succeed is greater than ever, and this can put a lot of stress on horse and rider. When practitioners of different healing disciplines, be they scientific or esoteric, work together to complement each other's skills and expertise, then much may be done to bring about profound results and relieve the pressures of modern life. I hope that the experiences above may encourage readers to regard *shiatsu* as a possible complement and adjunct to orthodox medical treatment.

Further reading

Touching Horses by Pamela Hannay, J.A. Allan Ltd, London.

Equine Acupressure by Zidonis, Soderbery and Snow, Tallgrass Publishers, Denver, Colorado.

Complete Illustrated Guide to Shiatsu by Elaine Liechti, Element Books, Dorset.

Traditional Shiatsu for Horses by Sue Hix, Kenilworth Press.

The *Shiatsu* Society: www.shiatsu.org

Jacqueline Cook: www.shiatsu-for-horses.com

Liz Eddy: www.equestrian-shiatsu.com

The sport of endurance

TONY PAVORD BVSc MRCVS
Lower Penygraig Farm
Llanfoist
Abergavenny
Monmouthshire NP7 9LE

Endurance riding - what is it?

Not for nothing did the sport of endurance riding earn its name, although for decades its strenuous, and often emotive demands, were well disguised under the aura of an eccentric, fringe activity on the general equestrian scene. At one extreme, it was considered cruel and contrary to the welfare of the horse and, at the other, an afternoon hack for genteel ladies who were afraid of jumping. Only those whose dedication and determination made them aficionados knew its true challenge and fascination. Even today, endurance tradition has its myths and legends, its unique history and its special challenges to which all may aspire - such as the '*four buckle club*' which to this day has not received a single member, although several riders must now be close. To be accepted, the aspirant must successfully complete all three of the World's great 100 mile endurance rides - the *Tevis Cup* in America, the *Tom Quilty Gold Cup* in Australia and *Florac* in France, as well as winning a world championship medal.

The powers of endurance and fortitude of the horse in helping the development of human civilisation need not be recounted. However, modern equestrian endurance sport truly began in 1955, when Wendell T Robie and his friend Lloyd Tevis, a President of the Wells Fargo Company, set out to prove that modern horses possessed the same strength and stamina as those of the great pioneer days. With a few other friends, and supreme horsemanship as their goal, they set out to ride 100 miles through the Sierra Nevadas of Northern California in no more than 24 hours, bringing their horses home in good condition. The idea fired the imagination of others and so the Tevis Cup was born.

In Australia, entrepreneur and horseman R. M. Williams heard of the feats in California and persuaded his friend Tom Quilty to put up the prize for a similar event in New South Wales. The Tom Quilty Gold Cup, purchased for one thousand pounds in 1966 contains more gold than the Melbourne Cup and now resides in the Stockmans Hall of Fame at Longreach, Queensland, the winner each year receiving a handsome replica. That first Tom Quilty Ride almost never happened, due to animal welfare activists and the opposition of the RSPCA. However, it was eventually run with such regard and attention to the well being of the horses that all protests were overcome and endurance in Australia today is renowned for its religiously strict veterinary judging. As one vet observed to a rider who protested that his horse had been like that all through the ride and was only a little bit lame: "*You can't be a little bit pregnant either!*"

Within a few years, the experiments in the US and Australia were being repeated in France, where two rides, *Florac*, in the Lozere and Montcuq, in the wine growing region around Cahors, still dispute which was the first to be established. *Florac*, which is renowned for its dizzying ascents and descents over sharp, rocky going, follows the classic 100 miles in 24 hours principle. We cannot leave Florac without mentioning two of its greatest proponents. Local rider Denis Pesce, who has also represented France on numerous occasions, has achieved legendary status in his own time, by winning the event no

Fig 1: Kerry Ridgeway in action at a UAE ride.

less than ten times. Also involved in breeding top horses from pure and part-bred Arabian strains, Denis is usually mounted on a son or daughter of the great Arabian stallion *Persik*, who for many years has stood in the Parc de Cevennes at the home of Yves Richardier. Twice a winner of the *Florac* ride himself in 1975 and 1976, *Persik* has sired over 100 offspring that have been successfully placed in endurance competition. Nearly 30 have won major championships or competed in international teams, including the gold and silver individual medal winners at the 2000 World Championships, Varoussa and Dynamik.

Les Deux Jours de Montcuq, however, presents its own special challenge, with 200 km (120 miles) to be covered in two days. The ability of horses to finish 60 miles on Day one, then come out fresh, sound and fit to tackle the same feat next day, never fails to impress those who make the regular trip each year to the picturesque French village, overlooked by its historic '*donjon*'. To see the winners canter up the main street and under the '*Arrivee*' banner, with all traffic stopped, is awe-inspiring.

Britain, in more sedate fashion, evolved the *Golden Horseshoe* ride as a set-speed competition in the mid-1970s, under the auspices of the Arab Horse Society and then the British Horse Society. The Horseshoe settled down in its Exmoor home at Exford, but changed format several times until in 1988 it became a two day, 100 mile set speed event,

with gold, silver or bronze awards going to the successful competitors. In the first year of the new Millennium it is about to change again, amid controversy between the progressives and the traditionalists, as it becomes an FEI sanctioned endurance ride, with a 'first past the post' winner. This represents a major shift in the emphasis of the British Endurance Riding Association, to bring its premier ride into line with international competition and underline its role as the representative body for endurance sport in Britain.

For many years, the *Summer Solstice one-day* 100 mile ride, run by the alternative Endurance Horse and Pony Society, has been the country's established 100 mile endurance event. However, it suffers from lack of international recognition and, until the current negotiations for the dissolution of the existing organizations and the formation of a single new body to run the sport in Great Britain are concluded, it will be difficult for British endurance riding to make serious further progress.

On the international scene, the role of endurance in the FEI has been revolutionised by the rapid development of interest from the countries of the Arabian Gulf, spearheaded by Sheikh Mohammed bin Rashid Al Maktoum of Dubai. Unprecedented levels of sponsorship worldwide, a hugely increased calendar of rides, an influx of wealthy buyers into the endurance horse market leading to fortunes being made by some

Fig 2: Endurance is not all flat desert.

sellers and an incentive to breed top quality athletes for the sport, have all combined to bring endurance riding to a prominence far from its original eccentric, fringe image.

The World Championship in the United Arab Emirates in 1998 was officially recognised by the Guinness Book of Records as the biggest equestrian sporting event ever held, with 37 nations and 175 horses taking part.

Two years later, interest continues to grow, as other middle eastern countries take up the challenge, with rides having been held in Syria, Egypt, Jordan, Saudi Arabia and Bahrain to name a few.

In classic terms, endurance was run over tough, often mountainous terrain, in all weather conditions. The nature of the Gulf countries and the competitive nature of the Arab psyche however, has led to rides over the flat desert sands and average speeds that would have been considered beyond the physiological capability of the equine athlete, a few years ago.

The current developments are exciting, awesome and seriously challenging to the vets who have to control and judge the sport, ensuring that the welfare of the horse is not compromised by increasing pressures brought on by professionalism and vested commercial interests. In this whirlwind scenario of change, it is comforting at least to know that the great traditional rides, the Tevis and Quilty, can each still draw 200–300 competitors

annually and that their special challenge of horse and rider against the elements and terrain, will continue to exist. Meanwhile it is necessary to look at the rules that have developed to govern this most fascinating of equestrian sports and to protect the horses that participate in it.

The rules and veterinary involvement

In the development of any equestrian sport the rules that are necessary for that sport grow with the sport. In the early days of Endurance it is quite evident that groups of people from all around the world started of with the idea 'wouldn't it be nice to ride from point A to point B', a good example of one of these ideas was the Vienna to Budapest ride. Once the idea was born then rules had to be set up to manage even rides with this simple philosophy. The rules had to cater for horse injury, rider injury, horse welfare and competition.

One of the first rules that came into being, probably in the USA where modern day endurance started, was that the horse should, at the end of the competition, be able to continue. The phrase 'fit to continue' became the focal point of endurance competitions. It became quickly apparent that veterinary surgeons were the only people with the knowledge, expertise and impartiality to make this judgement. From this early decision the involvement of vets in the running of an endurance

Fig 3: Ardennaise: *is she ready to present to the vet?*

ride has grown. He, or she, now decides if the horse can start the competition, if the horse can stay in the competition which can be over one day or be multi-day, can consist of many stages and last up to 24 hours in one day, and finally decide if the horse can finish. Although every one of the founder countries developed much the same overall concept of how endurance should be run, it was inevitable that the type of competition, and the rules used to control the sport, evolved in different ways. An international body was needed to rationalise these differences into a set of rules and regulations that could be applied throughout the world.

This was supplied by the Federation Equestre Internationale (FEI). Endurance riding became one of the special equestrian disciplines in 1984 and was promoted to a full discipline in 1998. Endurance riding could now be considered the top level of the sport and can be defined as long distance horse racing, over distances up to 100 miles in one day on one horse, subject to strict veterinary supervision. The welfare of the horse is paramount at all times and due to the comprehensive veterinary controls the equine safety record is unsurpassed by any other horse sport.

In a short paper such as this it is inappropriate to go into the present day rules in any great detail. Those interested can find them on the FEI web site at '*www.horsesport.org*'. The principles behind the rules are fundamental, however, and are summarised in the FEI code of conduct which is:

1. In all equestrian sports the horse must be considered paramount.
2. The well being of the horse shall be above the demands of breeders, trainers, riders, owners, organizers, sponsors or officials.
3. All handling and veterinary treatment must ensure the health and welfare of the horse.
4. The highest standards of nutrition, health, sanitation and safety shall be encouraged and maintained at all times.
5. Adequate provision must be made for ventilation, feeding, watering and maintaining a healthy environment during transportation.
6. Emphasis should be placed on increasing education in training and equestrian practices and on promoting scientific studies in equine health.
7. In the interests of the horse the fitness and competence of the rider shall be considered as essential.
8. All riding and training methods must take into account of the horse as a living entity and must not include any technique considered by the FEI to be abusive.
9. National Federations should establish adequate controls in order that all persons and bodies under their jurisdiction respect the welfare of the horse.

Fig 4: Persic at the age of 30, 3 years before his death.

10. The national and international Rules and Regulations in equestrian sport regarding the health and welfare of the horse must be adhered to not only during national and international events, but also in training. Competition Rules and Regulations shall continually be reviewed to ensure such welfare.

The veterinary control of the competition

This can be divided into a series of inspections. The initial examination takes place as soon as possible after the arrival of the horses at the stables of the ride. The aim is first to establish the horses' identity (passports, registration documents) and second to establish their health status. The first inspection should, whenever possible, take place on the day before the start of the competition. Its purpose is to determine the fitness of the horse to compete and is performed by the Veterinary Commission, together with the Ground Jury. Heart rate, respiratory rate, and temperature are recorded and general parameters noted. Each horse is trotted up on a flat, firm surface and his gait observed. Any horse with abnormal metabolic parameters or with an irregularity of gait consistently observable will be eliminated.

At each compulsory halt, five being the recommended number during a 160 km ride, each horse must be inspected against its veterinary card, completed at the first inspection. The inspection will determine the fitness of the horse to continue the competition. Horses with a heart rate above the parameter of the ride - normally 64 beats/min after a maximum of 30 minutes rest - and horses showing signs of excessive fatigue, heat stroke, colic, myopathies and severe dehydration or abnormally high temperatures must be eliminated. Lame horses as defined above must also be eliminated.

The final inspection must take place within 30 minutes of the finish time. As above, the pulse and other parameters must be taken and registered on the veterinary card. This inspection is to determine whether the horse is still fit to be ridden after a normal rest period and it will include the same control as the inspections during the course. At all inspections, the decision to eliminate a horse must be made by a majority of votes of at least three members of the Veterinary Commission in the presence of at least one member of the Ground Jury.

The competition takes place over natural ground on a marked route composed of different phases, each phase finishing with a veterinary inspection carried out at a prepared area commonly known as a vet gate. As mentioned the number of phases varies and can span multiple days but the distance of each phase should not be more than 40 km. The competition is a race, the first horse past the winning post that satisfies the criteria of the final inspection wins or, put another way, the horse that successfully completes the course in the shortest time is the winner. At the end of each phase, after a successful veterinary inspection, the horse and rider undergo a compulsory hold period where they can rest and refuel. Food and water is essential if a horse is to complete a 160 km course at the speeds we are seeing from modern day horses. Riding times in the region of eight hours have become commonplace in the last few years over the flat, hazard-free courses of the Middle East.

Race time does not stop until the horse presents for a successful inspection that must occur within 30 minutes of arrival at the vet gate of that phase. The faster the horse can be prepared for that inspection the greater the advantage he gains in overall riding time. This preparation procedure, called crewing in Europe and America, strapping in Australia, has become a highly specialised job the aim of which is to reduce the recently exercised heart rate as fast as possible to a level at or below the rate of the day. By controlled exercise and aggressive cooling a skilled crew can reduce a heart rate beating above 150 beats/min to one at or below 64 beats/min in 2 or 3 minutes. This of course requires a superbly trained horse, an experienced rider and excellent crew. Correctly done it can confer an time advantage of 5 to 10 minutes over a less skilled team.

How veterinary inspections have changed

From the very early days of endurance, it was apparent that considerable skill and experience was needed by officiating veterinary surgeons in order to protect the horses competing in this discipline. The lame horse was no problem in terms of welfare. Judgement of lameness is a subjective act, especially in the constrained area of a vet gate and the vote to eliminate a horse for a gait abnormality is often a two to one decision and it is commonly said that if the vets cannot agree whether a horse is lame, then to allow it to continue is hardly likely to be a welfare issue.

Metabolic issues are another matter. During the 1970s and 1980s, it was not uncommon for horses to die following an endurance ride Even today, in less experienced countries, where horses and riders are poorly prepared for the rigours of

competition, horses are still dying. Invariably, these competitions are not being run according to the modern FEI rules. The veterinary knowledge, infrastructure and funding is usually also inadequate. It is only too easy to take the supreme equine athlete, let alone the inexperienced horse, beyond his ability to cope with the metabolic demands put upon him by climatic conditions, ill-judged riding tactics or poor preparation. Again, in the early days, we endurance vets working in the field thought we had metabolic excesses under control - of course we could tell if a horse was in trouble and successfully treat it!

Perhaps that was the case in temperate northern Europe but as we met colleagues from France, Australia and America and learnt from their experiences, it quickly became evident that we were wrong. We needed more tools to help us identify the horse that satisfied the official parameters at one or other of the vet gate inspections but was already under metabolic stress.

Dr Kerry Ridgway, an eminent American ride vet, also a successful rider, started looking for such a tool. He had noticed, with the help of the new onboard heart monitors, that the heart rate of fit horses dropped rapidly once exercise stopped, 30 to 50% in a few minutes. He also noticed that a rested horse, rested in the context of a vet gate, when trotted for a short distance, increased his heart rate by 50 to 75% but within a short time returned to the rested level or below. However, when tired or compromised horses exercised over the same distance, the heart rate remained above the resting rate. These observations he developed into a procedure commonly called the cardiac recovery index (CRI). This procedure has become common practice at all major rides and has undoubtedly enabled us to identify horses that would have passed the official parameters only to collapse later on in the ride.

In the last few years, however, experienced veterinary surgeons, especially those working in the Middle East, were becoming worried about the increasing number of horses that passed the metabolic parameters of the ride with no evidence of cause for concern, only to collapse on the track or at the next vet gate. Also some of us realised that it was slightly ridiculous to pass a horse that had been expertly prepared and presented in two or three minutes and then not see that horse again, until the next vet gate. How well had this aggressively cooled horse actually recovered during the following hold period? Work done by a group of French endurance vets gave us the beginnings of an answer. They conducted an exit inspection just before the horse left the vet gate. They found that the majority of those horses that either had a high pulse or a positive CRI index at this inspection failed to finish the ride. This extra inspection has been used in Great Britain and the UAE since 2000 and already has enabled us to remove horses from competition before they are compromised.

Without the cadre of vets who are as dedicated to the welfare of the horse as they are the sport and its future development, endurance riding would pose unacceptable risks and dangers to the horse.

What does the future hold?

Olympic gold is the ultimate aim of every aspiring sportsman and woman, and the more progressive proponents of endurance riding share this high ideal. They are pressing for inclusion in the Olympic Games, even while the other horse sports' position in the Olympic field is threatened. Others are not so sure, seeing a threat to the traditional ultimate challenge - the self reliance of horse and rider in covering 100 miles in one day in remote, often inaccessible terrain, fired by the pioneer spirit and un-enhanced by teams of highly skilled crew people to aid the horse and rider at every turn. At the end of the day the questions remain unanswered: *What is the ultimate test of equine endurance* - fast and flat, or steep and strenuous? *How far and how fast can these horses really go?*

Reminiscences of a Chantilly *vétérinaire*

ROBERT LESAFFRE DVM

La Garenne aux Gres
Bois Saint Denis 60500
Chantilly
France

My long professional career lasted for most of the 20th century and this implies, by its very nature, that I am one of the rare living witnesses to the important revolutions that happened in my profession during this century.

Before I became a vet, I rode horses in training or at racecourses, and I was often in contact with my predecessors who looked after my father's horses. This was the focal point of a calling centred on racehorses.

These developments were two pronged. Firstly, by events as dramatic as they were unbearable; the two world wars in which millions of people tragically died. Secondly, the scientific discoveries in health care which changed the world's destiny. These were revolutions that aimed to ensure the continuity of the human race, counterbalancing the destructive capacities of war or the splitting of the atom nucleus.

The peaceful revolutions were the development of sulphonamides and antibiotics. They saved the lives of not only millions of human subjects but also those of animals and modified, from top to bottom like a magic wand, every aspect of our professional lives.

Between 1932 and 1935, Gerhard Domagk discovered the antimicrobial value of sulphonamides including Prontosil. Tréfuel and Fourneau completed this work at the Institut Pasteur de Paris.

In 1928, Alexander Fleming was immortalised by his discovery of penicillin. In 1939, Ernst Boris Chain and Howard Walter Florey studied its activity and toxicity and fine-tuned production methods.

I have lived, been informed, followed and benefitted from the evolution and results of this work. I can conclude that our profession has also benefitted from this evolution in terms of surgery, which before these events was almost infantile in its execution.

At the beginning of the century, in Chantilly and the region surrounding it, there were around 500 to 600 horses in training. This figure has grown to about 2,500 at the present time. In that period, animal medicine was nothing more than empirical; the medicines were limited, with oxygenated water, iodine, potassium permanganate and opium amongst the most popular. As for surgery, more often than not it consisted of more or less scientific '*carvings*' which were normally fatal, as the vital importance of the discoveries from the Pasteur Institut concerning antiseptics were assimilated too late. Also, knowledge of the noxiousness of bacteria and other pathogens was limited. Veterinarians at the time did their best considering their meagre therapeutic means.

I began using penicillin from 1944 when I was the vet for the highly successful Marcel Boussac (120 horses in training). This great owner imported unstable penicillin from the United States at his own cost in frozen containers. The temperature could not exceed 4°C and the preparation had to be extemporised and the injection given immediately with a dosage of 5,000 units twice a day. We were 'miles' away from current dosages. It was an adventure and an expensive one at that, but the results were immediate and worth it.

Now that we had an antibiotic cover, and following scrupulously the strict observation of aseptic guidelines, we could give free rein to our surgical concerns.

I was particularly interested in surgery. I can state that from 1944, our professional capacities developed at an astonishing rate in every country where horses were important.

Frédérick Chapard was the first veterinary surgeon to leave his mark on Thoroughbreds. He practised until the First World War and was an innovator. His surgical endeavours and successes gave him a reputation which crossed frontiers.

At the same time, two professors at the Alfort School, Cadiot and Almy, published two important papers on surgical treatments. These works were ahead of their time, so much so that I find surgical techniques which they had already discussed, in scientific papers today.

The first vet in Chantilly to practise in a professional manner during the First World War was Doctor Geslin Bouchet. He was initially based in Creil with a predominantly rural clientele. He was interested in horses and moved to Chantilly in 1915, where he joined forces with Gaston Cavel. The latter quickly abandoned his veterinary clientele and specialised in transporting horses with automobile horseboxes. He started, together with Léopold Bara, the Sociéte des Transports Hippiques, which is still active today. This company works hand in hand with Hipavia, which specialises in airline horse transport. I am no longer involved in this company, which I created in 1947.

André, Bouchet's son, a veterinary student at the time, injured his leg and became partially crippled during the first few days of the First World War. He finished his studies at Alfort and then spent a year at the Royal Veterinary College, London, and set up practice in Chantilly in 1918 with his father, who promptly retired and left the reins to his son. He began a lifelong friendship with Dr Williams, in Newmarket. He had achieved fame with his remarkable work on the paralysis of vocal cords and the fine-tuning of ventriculectomy.

At that time, the Chantilly Training Centre held about 2,000 horses. Another veterinary surgeon, Mr Carnus, worked at the centre but was nowhere near as competent as the Bouchets, father and son. Other vets, belonging to the teaching profession, came and went but the three or four local vets could not cope with all the work. I joined the group in 1944 when I became an associate of André Bouchet.

Our interesting work involved not only treating Thoroughbreds but also looking after a number of draught horses and a large troop of Friesian dairy cattle. Also, in the fifties, the specialisation of medicine for small animals was still undeveloped, and so we also had to treat them. In our town, there were many cats and dogs, especially hunting dogs. This versatile activity has slowly disappeared, although not without leading to some strange stories.

One of my colleagues, Doctor Pollet, a fine surgeon and an inveterate hunter, would use, in all seriousness, a 'pendulum' as much for diagnosing as for indicating which would be the best part of the forest for finding wild boars. He had his own clientele, proof that *'all tastes are in nature'*.

Airline horse transport - 1946

One day in 1946, at the Auteuil racecourse, one of my clients, Mr Marcel Boussac, who managed the Chantilly Training Centre, called me via his manager, who was none other than François de Brignac. He made me an extraordinary proposition:

"We've sold 4 stallions to the USA… but the buyers demand that the horses be delivered as soon as possible. We have therefore decided to send them by plane, and as we know that you have a lot of experience with transporting horses by plane, we would like you to quickly organise this trip to the States. Can you please give us your reply as quickly as possible."

It should be noted that aviation was still in its infancy then. We had never transported horses to the States by plane and we only had propeller-driven airplanes. A journey by boat took about fifteen days. It was a real expedition, but I had previously already organised several of them.

The risks were great, the crossing of the Atlantic would be very long, plus the 36 hours to New York, and the planes were not very reliable. They were Boeing DC4s, most of which had been used for transporting troops and material between the United States and England for the Normandy Landings. The engines were in a worrying, dilapidated state. This safety concern would give me numerous problems in the future. Furthermore, we were in the dark regarding the repercussions that such a long plane voyage could have on Thoroughbred horses, particularly stallions in full strength.

I decided to accept Mr Boussac's proposition, despite all the obstacles and risks, not the least of my problems being to convince both my wife and my mother. My enthusiasm was not shared by my family, especially my wife. In 1946 there were no jet airplanes and we would be using old DC4 freight planes that the American army had sold to TWA. There were few passengers at the time; it was not like today when a plane ride is the equivalent of riding a bicycle in bygone days. I began preparations for a scheduled take-off in the middle of November.

We would be leaving from Orly airport. I injected the horses with a buccal tranquilliser; a hydrate of chlorine-based solution, to relax the four stallions during the trip. I had enough of the solution for the 40 hour long Atlantic crossing. The flight was scheduled to end at Lexington in Kentucky with four stopovers: Shannon in Ireland, Meeks in Iceland, Gander in Newfoundland and finally La Guardia in New York.

This is where we were met by Customs, no easy task in America, but all the paperwork was in order and we were held up for only two hours. We then headed for Lexington in Kentucky. As soon as we landed, I noticed the presence of a large crowd, including the stable lads who would look after the horses as soon as they left the plane. There were also a lot of cameramen. The media wanted to see these expensive stallions which had come all the way from France. Their names were *Goya*, *Priam*, *Adaris* and *Hieroclès*. The latter was not an easy horse. I had even spent 48 hours at the studfarm to familiarise myself with him and to learn from the stable boys how best to deal with him without risk.

When we landed, I gave instructions to the stable boys who were taking the stallions to their studfarm. The horses left in a caravan of horseboxes, and my participation in the expedition was over. I immediately telephoned Paris to inform Marcel Boussac of the successful journey. I owe a great debt to him as he allowed me to stay in America for a month. I made valuable contacts in the horse world, especially with fellow vets. I spent those thirty days in operation theatres or in their clinics. I learnt a great deal. I became a member of the 'American Association of Horse Veterinary Specialists' (now AAEP) and for the next 30 years

I attended the Association's annual Congress nearly every year. This enabled me not only to develop my contacts but also to increase my knowledge. This episode was to have a great bearing on my professional career.

The transportation of racehorses by plane across the Atlantic was a first and a great media event. But the repercussions were not only journalistic or professional, as soon a number of owners contacted me to ask me to organise transatlantic crossings for their horses. I was a private pilot and was knowledgeable in this field, but I was not an airline pilot and, although I had flown multiple engine planes, I was not qualified for this work. Therefore, I contacted one of my friends from Mans who was available and was a good manager, and created the company which I baptised Hipavia.

I looked after the promotion and the technical aspects of the flights, and he was in charge of the financial and management aspect. I remained in the company for five years, but left because of other projects and the competition from other jets. I am very proud of the success of this company, which came under American control and broadened its base of activities by taking over the STH company (Société des Transport Hippiques). I sometimes wonder if I was right to leave, but I had other adventures in store.

Hipavia specialised in short flights to countries such as England, Italy or Germany and we had a contract with Nord Avion, whose headquarters were in Bourget. This airline owned twin-engined planes that were perfect for transporting horses. The planes were Bristol Freighters derived from gliders used in the Normandy Landings and which had front opening and loading.

Naturally, such planes could not cross the Atlantic and we still used the old American Boeing four-engined planes. It has to be said that I took considerable risks. I flew about twenty transatlantic return trips in these planes and, in at least half the cases, I was not sure of returning. The trickiest part of the journey was between Ireland and Newfoundland, the longest stretch. We would fly over the south of Greenland, over numerous icebergs and, when the weather was clear, we had the most delightful view. On four frightening occasions, one of the engines caught fire; fortunately, the Pratt and Whitney engines, however ancient, were equipped with extremely efficient fire extinguishers.

Another time, we were ready to land in Newfoundland in a blizzard the likes of which I had rarely seen. The weather was so overcast that the pilot attempted four times to find the runway. These were not the only incidents which happened during my many crossings, and I cannot resist telling you about the most extraordinary adventure I ever had.

One day, an owner telephoned to ask me to accompany one of his horses to the United States. He had just sold it to some Americans and wanted the trip to run as smoothly as possible. The horse would not be paid for until it landed in America in perfect health. I was relatively free at the time, so I accepted. As usual, I organised the trip with great care and, on the scheduled day, we found ourselves at Bourget airport next to a plane that had just arrived from Frankfurt.

It was an old TWA cargo freight plane. As always, I went aboard the plane to see whether everything was installed properly and to check that every precaution had been taken so that there would be no accidents when the horse got onto the plane or during the flight. I saw that the installations for the horse were on the right hand side of the plane at the top end. On the left side, I noticed a crate of about 2 m long by 1 m wide, covered by a green tarpaulin. I presumed that it was an engine that was being returned to the US.

There was straw, hay and blankets aboard, along with tinned foods in case of a crash landing; that is, if we managed to stay afloat. As everything seemed in order, I decided to bring the horses on board as the crew were waiting for us before taking off.

It was November and pretty cold, about -4°C (25°F), but I was comfortable in the plane. I was ready to spend the next 35 hours on board this plane with only the horse to keep me company. I had not met the crew and for good reason, as three beautiful TWA air hostesses were being flown back to the States and had immediately gone to the crew section with comfortable beds. The plane was equipped with a very efficient automatic pilot system, which enabled the crew to spend the long flight doing 'navigation exercises' in which pleasure was more important than the maps and rulers.

I, on the other hand, had only the crate as a bed

and I did my best to make it comfortable by placing some straw on top. I undressed and lay down on this bed which was obviously too uncomfortable for one of the hostesses to share with me, even for an hour or two. Furthermore, the smell of a horse is not quite as seductive as Chanel No. 5! I was not going to 'get lucky' on this trip. I fell asleep, only waking up during the stopovers to feed my passenger, and extending artificially its semi-lethargic state. I am cutting this story short, as 35 hours of flight is a long time indeed. As usual, we stopped at Shannon in Ireland, Meeks in Iceland and Gander in Newfoundland, and this time the flight was pretty much incident-free, until we arrived at Idlewild Airport, now Kennedy Airport, in New York.

In 1947, none of the buildings we now know had been built. There was an enormous plain with several runways. As it was November, and we were high up in altitude, and the landing was at 11 o'clock in the morning, the winter sun shone very brightly. The weather was fine and clear. After quickly getting dressed, I looked out of the porthole.

As the engines were cut, I was staggered to see the most incredible scene below me. A red carpet, around 20 m long, had been rolled out from the entrance of the plane and, at the end of the carpet, there were two companies of American solders in ceremonial uniform with their silver helmets, with weapons at the ready. An orchestra was playing the national anthem. The rest of the airport was deserted. I was stunned, as they were facing just a broken-down airplane which held only a horse of no great value, accompanied by a young vet who, however brilliant he might he think he was, could only wonder why such a troop movement had been deployed.

My mind was racing as I was sure this ceremony had not been organised for the horse, the plane or the crew. What was the reason? Suddenly my head began to swell and I started to think that maybe I was the centre of attraction. I had just been to war, but I knew that my 1940 campaign had not been an illustrious one or so unforgettable that a regiment of American solders would be deployed when I entered their country. Neither did my speed in retreating (with weapons, mind you) with my troop from Sedan to Cahors deserve such honours.

So I told myself, it was probably because I was

Marcel Boussac's vet and that our stables were winning all the great races in Europe at the time. I had become a star. I was still watching, whilst I filled my head with fanciful thoughts, for no more than a couple of seconds, when brutally the door was opened by two gorilla-type American solders, who shoved me back towards the back of the plane and swore: 'son of a bitch'. They headed straight towards the crate on which I had spent such a comfortable night, all the while continuing to swear at me. They removed the tarpaulin, the straw and hay covering it. They opened one of the sides of the crate to extract a coffin that was taken with a great deal of care and consideration towards the troops who were presenting the honours.

I was already shaken, but there were more surprises in store. We waited for the troops to leave with my unexpected passenger so that we could bring the horse out. The owner was waiting 100 m away, next to his horsebox. He lifted his arms up, smiling and said, "You didn't know who you were travelling with, did you?". Naturally, I replied that I had no idea, probably a high-ranking officer. He told me that he had asked the soldiers and it seemed that it was General Patton. This information did not make me feel either proud of myself or more comfortable. I must admit that I did not try to check whether the information was true, but it did seem credible. Afterwards, I was astounded that the body of such an important general was flown over to America in such a careless manner. However, it should be noted that, at the time, General Patton was not held in the high esteem he is today. He had had problems with the American press during a hospital visit when he slapped two solders who told him they refused to go back to the front.

But in the end, whether it was General Patton or another high-ranking officer, I have bad memories of this journey, snugly sleeping on a corpse, even if he was covered in stars and medals. My return in a brand-new Air France Constellation plane and in first class to boot, was an altogether more agreeable experience. I have to confess though, once I was home, several nights in a row, before sleeping, I would look furtively at the bed to assure myself that it was free of any unseemly bodies.

Sir Winston Churchill and *Colonist*

My relationship with England goes far back. Already in 1935, before taking my A-levels, I had travelled to Newmarket with a horse called *Nightcap II*, trained by Henry Count. He raced in the Cesarewitch and was second by only the shortest of heads behind *Sibritt*. Before that, I had spent several months with the famous trainer for Lord Derby, Cole Leader. I learnt English training techniques whilst galloping along the Downs every morning.

Then, for five years during the Second World War, I lost contact with a lot of my English friends, several of whom died fighting for our freedom.

Looking back, I cannot help but think of Fred Rickaby, who flew his Spitfire with glory and was decorated with the DSO by King George VI. Others were less lucky and died either during the Battle of Britain or on land, fighting for the English army.

After the war, my contacts with my British colleagues grew to such an extent that some of them came and worked in France for their owners, and I often went to England to look after the affairs of mine.

One of my colleagues who became a close friend was Carey Foster, who was based at Epsom. One day he telephoned me to say he was arriving in France soon and asked me in the meantime to find a good horse for Winston Churchill. It seems as if the 'Old Lion' was willing to sacrifice himself sportingly to please HM The Queen.

I knew of a good 3-year-old owned by Eugène Nominé, who ran the Bréviaires studfarm near Rambouillet.

He was in training at Charley Cunningham's stables in Chantilly. He had had a small problem with his fetlock when he was a 2-year-old but had recovered well during the winter. I told Carey of the horse and advised him to come quickly as others were interested.

He arrived 48 hours later with Christopher Soames, Churchill's son-in-law, who would later become the English Ambassador in Paris. Things went quickly, as the horse was exactly what the Great Man was looking for and, besides, he was not expensive. Carey and Christopher lunched at the house and took the plane back to return to

Fig 1: Winston Churchill and Colonist, *winner of the Gold Vase, Ascot, 1948.*

Epsom. The horse was called *Colonist*. He won quite a few major races for Churchill, including the Gold Cup at Ascot in the presence of HM the Queen.

I received, in thanks, an autographed photo of Mr Churchill, stroking his horse and every year until his death, 25 of his famous cigars. I believe he was the only racehorse Winston Churchill ever owned. I am quite proud to have discovered it for him.

Chantilly on Thames

Since Louis XIII, the fashion for racecourses had crossed the Channel and, although Pigalle did not exist then, the British aristocracy was already irresistibly attracted to Paris. Large stakes were at hand, races were run over all distances, but the English won regularly as, unlike the French, who wanted to mount their horses themselves despite

their heavy weight, they used 'lackeys' for their smallness and their lightness. The notion of a handicap was born, and we had to accept our incompetence in comparison to the talents of the jockeys and their English masters.

It was after the Restoration, in 1830, in the period of the 'Three Glorieuses' and under the rein of Louis Philippe, that the wave of British immigration which was invading the horse scene in France was most keenly felt.

This flow of horse knowledge has not stopped since. The contribution of British trainers, for the most part very capable, is of irreplaceable value to the racecourse industry in our country. The majority of the families of this peaceful friendly invasion have laid roots in our country and still to this day we have numerous friends with British-sounding names, even though they have been French for several generations.

A lot of them have fought in the great wars in

which France and Great Britain have been involved. A lot of them died, such as Alec Carter, the top jockey of his time, who died in the fields of honour during the first few days of the First World War. It is not possible to name all the families or all the trainers who have come to France to offer us their talents. I will mention the most important ones: the Carters, the Cunningtons, the Bartholomews, the Heads, the Counts, the Clouts, the Carvers, The Harpers and the Swanns, to name but a few.

Many of these families still live or work out of Chantilly and a few of them figure at the top of the lists of winning trainers or jockeys, such as the Heads, the Cunningtons and Clouts. Despite having English-sounding names, they are in fact French. The only breach in tradition is that we prefer to speak to them in French rather than the language of Shakespeare.

New professionals from Britain arrive and live here year after year; we welcome them with open arms, people like Hammond, Gibson and Pease, whose success no longer surprises us. Thus, the tradition continues.

Amongst all the families who have immigrated to France, the Carters have illuminated the French turf for nearly a century and deserve special mention here.

The Carters

There is no family more closely linked to horse training in France than the Carters, as their name has been associated since the first races in our country. The first of them, Tom Carter, came to live in France in 1830, after having served an apprenticeship at Newmarket with the famous trainer, Robson.

Lord Seymour took him on board and he was the architect of all the great winners of this horseowner. At the time, he was based at the Rue de Ferme in Neuilly. After Lord Seymour retired, Tom Carter managed Baron Nathaniel de Rothschild's stables, where he trained *Annetta*, *Anatole*, *Drummer*. He then set up his own operation at Lamorlaye, where one of his best horses was called *Bounty*.

He had three brothers, one of whom, Elijah, trained for the King of Italy, and his son William

went to India, along with another brother, Jonathan, whose job was at Tattersalls in England. He had a son, Tom, who became a distinguished trainer for Mr Fould, then the Duc de Castries, the Baron of Soubeyran. He was associated with great horses, for example, *Saxifrage* and *Little Duke*. His son, Willy, trained enthusiastically for Mr Espous, Olry Roederer and then left for Italy.

Tom Carter's third brother, Richard, trained horses in Belgium and France, at first in Viroflay and then in Royallieu, to look after the Compte de Lagrange's studfarm. He was a great hunter and his son-in-law, Tom Jennings, trained the horses in the stable before his son, also called Richard, took over the mantle.

The second Richard Carter, called Richard Carter senior, also looked after the Say and Ephrussi stables, and in particular he trained the famous stud *Codoman*. He had a son, Charles, who managed the Brissac, Liénart, de Gheest and Cohn stables, training such horses as *Killarnay*, *Imbroglio* and *Mon Petiot*.

I knew Charles Carter well and, when I first met him, he was about fifty years old, married to Flo, the sister of another trainer, Henri Count. However, the two men did not get along and had a major legal dispute because of a business transaction, which ended badly.

He spent his whole professional training life at Avenue de Jonville in Bois Saint-Denis. His training stables still exist under the expert care of Emmanuel Chevalier du Fau. I often visit it for professional reasons, and always feel a stab in my heart. In the middle of the courtyard there is a huge chestnut tree, under which, when I was five years old, Charles Carter let me ride my first horse, a Shetland pony. But enough of me, let me recount some stories which made him famous in the French horse world.

Charles Carter had many qualities but he had one major fault; he was rather too fond of whisky, especially VAT 69. In those days, cars were exceedingly rare and most people travelled in horse carriages, either a Tilbury or a Tonneau. Charles Carter had a Tonneau with a medium-sized horse, like a cob.

The Tonneau (the French word for a barrel) was a square-shaped, low-cut horse carriage, with two large wheels, a floor that nearly touched the ground and it opened from the back. It was very comfortable and about 1.20 m deep. Each night, after evening stables, when horses were bedded down and the trainer made his rounds, Charles would harness his Tonneau and, whip in hand, would head for the town. His itinerary never changed.

He went on a bar crawl, always beginning at the Café de la Gare, and then he would stop off at the Condé. This bar was where the guests of the Grand Conté Hotel would drink. After the Second World War, it was transformed into flats and the bar has since become the exhibition centre of the Renault garage.

More often than not, Charles stayed longer at the Condé bar than the others did, as it was fashionable with the horse set; on any given night you would find the best trainers and the best jockeys. The nights were long, as at the time there were very few radio sets and television was just a pipe dream. The 'Veillée des Chaumières' was held there in those days. When Charles left, or should I say when Charles's horse carriage left, or should I say when the horse pulled his carriage, he would head to the next bar. This was the Manor House, at the corner of the Rue Connétable and the Avenue du Bouteiller.

Another whisky stop and Charles would begin to have problems stepping into his carriage; the horse would then take him to his last stop, which was the Hotel du Château, at the end of the Rue Connétable, and which still exists today. After this final stop, Charles would be the worse for wear and would often be helped into his carriage by the barman. That night, he untied the horse's lead and shouted out "Home", and the horse, armed with a sort of perfect psychological radar, obeyed and headed off home.

The horse, as usual, knew perfectly the way back home to his oats. He trotted up the large avenue, under the Porte Saint-Denis, and then along the racecourse, before taking the Avenue de Joinville all the way to the stables. However, this time, Charles, instead of holding onto the seat, slipped towards the bottom of the barrel and fell into a deep sleep. The horse, as it normally did, entered the barn under the first stable boy's flat. The stable boy, hearing the horse's hoofs on the cobbles, walked down to unharness the horse. He could not see in the dark that his boss was sleeping at the bottom of the carriage, as normally Charles got off at his door and then let the horse make his own way to the barn. The stable boy unharnessed the horse, parked the carriage and took the horse into his box, and then went back upstairs.

Normally Charles got home at nine o'clock and so, by half past ten, Mrs Carter started to get worried. She questioned the first stable boy who told her that the carriage had arrived safe and sound but that he hadn't seen the boss. The poor lady, sick with worry, phoned the police, the hospitals, and everyone in any way connected to horses in a desperate bid to locate Charles Carter. She rang everyone she could think of, she rang us as we were friends and neighbours, and my father joined the others in the hunt for Charles. They retraced his route that night as his 'evening crawl' was well known.

At two o'clock in the morning everyone went home, despite Charles' continuing absence, leaving the job to the police. At six o'clock in the morning, Charles having slept off his whisky, woke up, stumbled out of the carriage and roused the house, shouting and insulting everyone because they had let him spend the night at the floor of the carriage. Finally, everyone was reassured, but this did not serve him a lesson as it happened again, except this time it ended well.

Old timers in Chantilly can still remember the pond, located between the main road and the Petit Chateau, that was used as a drinking trough. This drinking trough, which had been very useful for centuries, sloped gently and was roughly 30 m wide and 40 m long. Its maximum depth was about 50 m. One night, in the middle of a heatwave, Charles, thirsty as usual, had drunk a prodigious amount of whisky. He had not collapsed into the carriage but was sleeping deeply on the seat. It was still very hot but Charles was no longer thirsty; this was not the case of the horse who, since the beginning of the night, had been tied up without drinking at the doors of several bars whilst it waited patiently for its owner.

As it was passing the drinking trough, it probably thought to itself, "He's no longer thirsty, but now it's my turn to cool off"; and calmly entered the drinking trough step by step until he was breast high and drank his fill. Naturally, the water flooded into the carriage and the cold water awoke our friend who, in his drunken state, did not have the strength to dig himself out of this hole, and, what's more, he did not know how to swim.

He tried to pull on the reins but the horse, well grounded in the mud, refused obstinately to move and carried on drinking nonchalantly the fresh pond water. At this time of night there was not much traffic and the Chateau road was not very busy. He would no doubt have drowned if, by chance, one of his colleagues, Charley Bartholomew, had not been passing by and heard Charles shouting. Seeing his predicament, he walked shoulder high into the pond and helped him out. He took the horse in hand and led him back to the stables.

On their return, the wives' welcome was a little frosty to say the least. My memories of Charles Carter are not all funny anecdotes. It should be remembered that the gentry of Chantilly were mostly made up of families of British origin, and an English lifestyle held sway.

Charles Carter had two beautiful daughters, Hilda and Olga, aged 17 and 18, respectively. I was 7 years old and head over heels in love with Hilda, to such an extent that I wanted to marry her. Along the east wall of the training facilities Charles had built the only clay tennis court in our region. Hilda and Olga were excellent players and, every Wednesday, Mrs Carter, Flo to her friends, would invite British youngsters to play. Nearly everyone was involved in horses and at teatime we could have been in Newmarket!

They also played cricket on the small lawn of the racecourse, but especially tennis that the British in Chantilly played so well.

Richard Carter senior's brother, T. R. Carter, found fame in the Delamarre stables which he ran for fifty years, training *Vermout*, *Bois Roussel*, *Friandise*, *Verte Bonne*, *Vasistas* and *Kasba*. He had three sons, Fred, Richard and Arthur.

Fred Carter worked for the André and Aumont stables, training such horses as *Mlle de Senlis*, *Fra Diavolo*, *Ténébreuse* and *Monarque* (the second). He

had a son, Alec, who despite the passing of time, no one in horseracing has forgotten. He was a well-known jump jockey who died in the first days of the First World War. I have already spoken of the families of British origins whose children gave their lives for France. A lot of us knew his other son, Frank. He was the famous trainer of the greatest horses of the first part of the century: *Belfonds*, *Mon Talisman*, *Dorina*, *Hotweed*, *Pearlcap*, *Mistress Ford*, *Samos*, *Clairvoyant*, *Victrix* and *Le Ksar* for the Martinez de Hoz, Saint Alary and Esmond stables.

Richard Carter junior, Fred's brother, ran the Lefevre, Caillault and Belmont stables amongst others, with notable successes with *Perth*, *MacDonald II* and *Cherie*. He was the father of Percy Carter, the last trainer of the dynasty, who married Rita, Frank's brother. They had one son, Rooney, who died recently and had never been involved professionally with horses. He was a decorator for a renowned Parisian firm. He was the last remaining member of this illustrious family, and died practically destitute, surviving only thanks to the help of The Administrateur de L'Institute de France, who hired him as an interpreter guide for British visitors to the Chantilly Castle.

There is no need for me to mention, after this overview of the Carter family tree, the invaluable part they played in the French horse industry for over 160 years. Each of them was involved with the greatest horses bred here in France. Now that the Carter dynasty is over, I can only rejoice in the immense service they gave to the development of horse racing in France. They were the leaders in the training of numerous French professionals.

It is true that the Carter dynasty has disappeared but, during all those years, their descendants or their relations made alliances with other English families and even French ones. Thus the lineage is not completely extinct.

Family dynasties: equine and human

ALEXANDRA SCROPE

6 Church Road
Moulton
Newmarket
Suffolk CB8 8SF

It has been my good fortune to spend my life surrounded by the best and finest of horses; it was a happy accident of birth. My maternal grandfather, Sir Mark Sykes, died many years before my arrival on the planet and it was my grandmother, Edith Sykes, who maintained and improved the stud at Sledmere. Her dominance there left a lasting mark on the Thoroughbred breed through the great foundation mares **Mumtaz Mahal**, **Lady Juror**, **Straitlace** and **Teresina**.

My father, Adrian Scrope, returned from a period in New Zealand in 1927 to take over the management of the Sledmere estate and stud from my grandmother's cousin, Henry Cholmondeley. He was 21-years-old when he took over the management of the estate and it covered some 24,000 acres. Throughout his working life my father farmed from a horse, always Thoroughbreds, never more than 16 hh. Among his hacks, which I was later to remember (both notoriously difficult rides), were *High Stakes* (Fig 1), by *Hyperion* out of the Oaks winner *Pennycomequick*, who had won 32 flat races for his breeder, Lord Astor, and *Barleycorn*, a witchy little mare by *Hyperion* out of *Schiaparelli*, who was later to found a dynasty for Baron Guy de Rothschild (it was odd that *Hyperion* became known for the difficult and often unpleasant character of his stock for he was the perfect gentleman, the only stallion my sister Tessa and I were permitted to approach as little girls to offer him his favourite treat of fresh dandelion leaves).

It was not long after his arrival at Sledmere that my father began to be regularly accompanied on his long rides over the Yorkshire Wolds by my mother, a most elegant side-saddle rider, who was a year his junior. She loved farming and was a wonderful judge of stock of all sorts, cattle, sheep, horses, pigs. My father never bought a horse, be it a hunter or a mare, without her approval. They were married a week after her 21st birthday and survived to enjoy their diamond wedding with all seven of their children.

It was not long before Henry Cholmondeley grew bored with his retirement and asked my parents to buy him a mare of his own. He had bought *Trustful* for Sledmere some years before. Her first daughter, *Jury* by *Hurry On*, had been sold at the Doncaster sales and my parents thought it would be nice to track her down and try to buy her back for Henry. It transpired that her purchaser had been bankrupted and the filly sold in York market place for a derisory sum. Through the auctioneers they traced her to her new owner, a sheep farmer from Lincolnshire. They contacted the farmer and asked if he still had the mare. He did and it was arranged that they should meet him at Goole livestock market where he was to take some sheep the following week.

The mare was tied to a sheep hurdle by a hessian cow halter and wearing a jute sack for a saddle which was secured with binder twine. She was very thin and carrying a coat like a highland cow in her role as shepherd's hack. My father offered £100 for her but the farmer gave him a beady look and said *"Tha thinks I don't know 'er bruther topped Doncaster Sale. I'll 'ave £1500"*. It was a princely sum at the time but, the farmer knew what he'd got and *Jury* returned to Sledmere for Henry until he went blind some years later when my father bought her back for the stud. On Papa's advice, his friends Lord Halifax

Fig 1: Lt. Colonel Adrian Scrope riding High Stakes, *Lord Astor's 1942 gelding by Derby winner* Hyperion *out of Oaks winner* Pennycomequick, *winner of 32 flat races including the Ormonde Stakes, Lowther Stakes (Newmarket) twice and the Great Yorkshire Stakes twice.*

and the Duke of Norfolk bought her daughters *Epona* and *Inquisition* who, in their turn, became foundation mares for them.

In 1937, the parents moved from Sledmere to Stanley House where my father took over the management of Lord Derby's bloodstock interests. At Newmarket the property extended from Side Hill and Longholes studs on the Cheveley Road to Stanley House and the racing stables on the Bury Road, across private gallops to Woodlands Stud, the mixed farm at Hatchfield where much of the forage was grown, through to Plantation Stud on the Ely Road. In addition, there was the Thornton Stud in Yorkshire (where Hyperion and we children were briefly hidden when invasion by Hitler seemed imminent) and Knowsley Hall near Liverpool, the Stanley family home.

In the first few years of my father's influence at Stanley House, the famous black jacket, white cap of Lord Derby won the 1942 Derby with *Watling Street*, the 1943 1,000 Guineas and St. Leger with *Herringbone*, the 1944 2,000 Guineas with *Garden Path* and, in 1945, the 1,000 Guineas and Oaks with *Sunstream*. I still have my father's letter, written to my mother from 8th Army HQ in Northern Italy just after VE Day, when he had received the news of *Sunstream's* 3 length victory in the 1,000 Guineas setting out his hopes that she could win the Oaks and thereby complete the sweep of the Classics.

Throughout my childhood, our house at Newmarket was open house and race weeks and sale weeks produced many distinguished (as I later found out) foreign visitors. Among my favourites were Elizabeth Couturie, a school friend of my mother and breeder of great note. Her *Right Royal V, Tahiti, Tyrone* and others made a lasting impact on French breeding. Her trainer, Etienne Pollet, dapper and meticulous, who once made a spectacular appearance at the top of the stairs wearing a hairnet and perfectly pressed blue pyjamas after discovering my chinchilla, Ambrose,

Fig 2: Marguerite Vernaut *1957 by* Toulouse Lautrec *out of* Mariebelle, *bred and owned by Marchese Mario Incisa della Rocchetta (Dormello Olgiata), winner of the 1960 Champion Stakes.*

in the bottom of his bed… *"Il y'a une bête dans mon lit!"* We thought this a tremendous success. He brought such magnificent horses as *Sea Bird, Hula Dancer, Never Too Late, Grey Dawn* and many others to race in England.

Marchese Mario Incisa della Rochetta, partner of the legendary Federico Tesio in the Razza Dormello Olgiata and later, after Tesio's death, an exceedingly successful breeder (for which successes he was never really recognised in his own right), was my favourite. A very funny man, he was highly intelligent with great curiosity on a wide variety of topics; an amateur in the true sense of the word. He once complained to me that he was a man with no identity, first he was known as Tesio's partner, then as *Ribot's* owner. I have to say, there was some truth in this and he deserved better. Aside from the splendid horses he bred on his own account, he was a connoisseur of art, headed the World Wildlife Fund in Italy, really founding nature conservation in that country, created probably the finest wine in

Italy, Sassicaia; he was a man of broad interests which he pursued with passion.

Mario Incisa came for the December Sales one year. The Dormello horses which were in England were mostly trained by Jack Clayton. An old friend of Mario's, Comte Foi, was staying with Jack Clayton and his sister Jane at Bedford House. A mare in the catalogue had caught Mario's eye, she was named *Mariebelle* and, though by *Mieuxce*, she was also in foal to him and a crib-biter. They thought this a huge joke and bought her for 230 gns. By dinner time, Bastien Foi found it a lot less humerous so Mario Incisa bought him out. Poor *Mariebelle* looked like Don Quixote's *Rosinante*, all ribs with no neck and a belly like a kettle drum. The resulting colt foal went on to race without distinction in Italy but, in 1957 she foaled an immense chestnut filly by the homebred Gran Premio d'Italia winner *Toulouse Lautrec*; the world was to know her as *Marguerite Vernaut* (Fig 2), the 16.3 hh

Fig 3: Ribot *1952 by* Tenerani *out of* Romanella, *undefeated winner of 16 races at 2, 3 and 4 years, including the Gran Criteriun, Gran Premio di Milano, Prix de l'Arc de Triomphe twice, King George VI and Queen Elizabeth Stakes, with Alfonso.*

chestnut filly with the raking stride, who came from Italy to beat Etienne Pollet's 1,000 Guineas and Oaks winner, *Never Too Late,* in the Champion Stakes. *Marguerite Vernaut* won nine races; she had been champion 2-year-old in Italy and had won the Gran Premio d'Italia before coming to Newmarket. Her descendants were to produce two more Gr. 1 winners for Dormello Olgiata over the coming years.

Papa had been a great friend of Tesio through whom he had come to know Mario Incisa and for many years my parents made annual visits to Italy to see the yearlings and to shoot wild boar at Bolgheri in Tuscany where I was eventually to work for Mario Incisa for a year. Tesio died in 1954 when the mighty *Ribot* was a 2-year-old so it was for Mario that he raced. My father went twice to Italy to watch this phenomenal horse work, on neither occasion did *Ribot* finish with a rider on his back!

On the first occasion, in Milan, as the horse swept round the turn, all could see that something was amiss with his rider who was rolling badly in the saddle. Watching the work with Mario Incisa

and my father was Mario's doctor. In the straight, the work rider rolled off completely. Inspection by the doctor revealed that he was dead having suffered a heart attack while on the horse. *Ribot* on the other hand was very much alive and enjoying his liberty. Eventually he was encircled by the string trained by Luigi Turner and recaptured. On the second occasion, at the end of his career, an exhibition gallop was arranged to pacify the Roman crowd who had never seen their great champion race. As the horses came into the straight and *Ribot* swept majestically past his workmates, he spotted an object ahead on the track, propped, unshipped Enrico Camici and was free once again.

Ribot (Fig 3) stood his first season at Stanley House - between *Hyperion* (Fig 4) and *Alycidon* (Fig 5). He was a difficult character and did not relish human company. In later years at John Galbreath's Darby Dan Farm in Kentucky, he apparently became savage but, for his first season in 1957, he arrived in state at Stanley House accompanied by a retinue of four delightful Italians, Alfonso, Alfio, Giovanni and Benito. Alfonso was stallion man and then, for many years, stud groom

Fig 4: Lord Derby's Hyperion, *1930 by* Gainsborough *out of* Selene, *winner of the 1933 Derby and foundation sire, photographed at Stanley House in his old age with Mick Ryan, who was stud groom there for many years.*

at Dormello until a crippling stroke when his place was taken by Alfio. 'The Italians' were housed in a converted stallion box near our house and treated us children to immense plates of spaghetti and played cricket with us in the summer evenings.

I came to know Dormello when I joined the French shipping firm of Hipavia. Mario Incisa loathed flying and would not allow his horses to fly either. The journeys made by *Ribot, Botticelli, Marguerite Vernaut,* etc. were marathon journeys by road and rail. My father had purchased part of Plantation stud especially to house the Dormello mares which used to come to England on two year rotations. At the end of the stud season the mares and their foals would travel by road and ferry to Paris where they were loaded onto a convoy of cattle trucks. The trucks were each divided into three with special gates creating a large loose box at either end each housing a mare and foal, with plenty of room for a groom and the forage by the

sliding doors in the middle section.

It fell to my lot to travel to Italy several times with these convoys, long sunny days spent lying in the straw with a book and a box of fresh peaches and a couple of French saucissons for sustenance. The tricky bit came on arrival at the huge marshalling yards in cities like Turin where one had to fetch water for the mares. There were literally hundreds of tracks and thousands of trucks.

The train would be split up, trucks shunted to the top of a ramp and slipped loose to rumble free down the slope and onto the back of the appropriate train. A railwayman would be waiting with a metal shoe to throw under the wheel to brake the truck before it hit the back of the stationary train. We used to mark our wagons by sticking straw out of the side doors but it was quite possible for your truck to pass you more than once as you hopped across the lines with your two enormous buckets of water.

Fig 5: Lord Derby's Alycidon *(left, rearing), 1945, winner of the 1949 Ascot Gold Cup and Goodwood Cup, with Alec Notman, who went on to become manger of Dalham Hall Stud for the Hon. James Phillips and later for Sheikh Mohammed bin Rashid al Maktoum. On the right is* Never Say Die 1951, *by* Nasrullah *out of* Singing Grass, *winner of the 1954 Derby, and stallion man John Lomas.*

On arrival at Dormello, dirty and tired, I would be ushered into the Villa at Dormello by the butler. In the evenings I would dine with Donna Lydia Tesio and she would show me the magnificent book in which she had meticulously recorded Tesio's opinions of every foal, yearling, horse in training and mare they produced. The following day, Alfonso or Alfio, my old friends, would take me up to the paddocks on the hill above Dormello to see the horses.

Much later, in 1977, I spent a year working for Mario Incisa. My brief was to see if I could discover any developing nicks among the up and coming bloodlines. I spent most of that year in a little office in the attic of Il Poggio, the magnificent villa on the Bolgheri estate in Tuscany, surrounded by books of pedigrees which I coloured with pencils to try to establish any patterns. *Nearctic*, mostly through *Northern Dancer*, was the newest flavour and it was fascinating to see patterns emerging out of all proportion to their population. Even then it was clear that the very old and seemingly dying Teddy line of broodmare sires was re-emerging through *Nearctic's* influence. *Nijinsky*, *Storm Bird*, *Danzig*, *The Minstrel*, were eventually amongst *Northern Dancer's* most influential sons. All carried this cross, in fact were mostly inbred to it, and even nowadays with the Teddy mares almost extinct, *Linamix* is holding the line.

When I left Bolgheri at the end of that year, Mario Incisa was kind enough to give me the work I had done. Its development eventually provided the foundations of a new career for me working with a new generation of owner breeders and a new generation of magnificent racehorses.

Racing is an expensive business

RORY MacDONALD

The British Racing School
Snailwell Road
Newmarket
Suffolk CB8 7NU

Introduction

The average price of yearlings in 2000 at the Houghton Sales was £160,000 and at the Tattersalls October Sales was £29,000. Across Europe, The Racing Post, in their Bloodstock Review, reported that the prices at the seven leading sales in Europe during 2000 totalled £84 million. This was an increase of 27% on 1999. As owners will testify, the cost does not stop there. In addition to trainers' fees, there are additional costs from farriers, vets, chiropractors, back experts, nutritionists and others. At the same time, considerable investment is being made to improve the facilities on racecourses and, in 1999, the Horserace Betting Levy Board provided £12 million in loans to racecourses for capital projects and £20.1 million for improvements.

However, racing is a partnership between man and horse. Poorly trained staff can ruin any horse. In 1999, The British Horseracing Board commissioned the Stable Staff Resources Group to 'carry out a full analysis of existing human resources and working practices in training yards' at a time when there was general concern amongst trainers of staff shortages. The annual accounts of The Racing and Thoroughbred Breeding Training Board (now The British Horseracing Training Board), in March 1999, indicate that the Horserace Betting Levy Board provided a grant of £296,000 towards training and education and the trainers provided a further £321,000 from prize money deductions under Order 194. In total, therefore, this equates to the price of four average-priced yearlings at the Houghton Sales. The question, therefore, has to be asked whether sufficient priority is being given to staff training and development given the problem which racing faces in this area and the significant sums of money which are spent elsewhere within the industry.

The context

Before consideration is given to possible solutions, it is important to understand the environment in which the racing industry in Britain operates. The national economy is healthy. Unemployment in June 2000 was 2.5%. Within this, some areas are even lower. For example, Forest Heath, which includes Newmarket, had a rate of only 1.4%. Wage rates nationally have risen steeply as affluence has cascaded through the workforce. The average gross weekly earnings for full time employees in Britain in June 2000 was £405 a week which equates to £21,000 per annum. Traditionally, racing has looked to school leavers as its main source of potential stable staff. However, currently 80% of 16-year-olds stay on at school or college to continue with their education. Other competitors have also appeared. Many of what were the old agricultural colleges have now diversified into equine training, offering qualifications up to degree level. Colleges are also attracting students with seemingly appealing subjects such as Media Studies and Leisure and Tourism. It is also apparent that younger generations are taller and heavier than previous generations.

The present Government remain committed to education and training. They have laid down National Targets. The current targets are that, by 2002, 85% of those aged 19 will have achieved a National Vocational Qualification (NVQ) Level 2, 60% of those aged 21 will have achieved an NVQ

Level 3 and that 50% of the adult workforce should have achieved an NVQ 3 or equivalent. For racing there is, therefore, a great deal to be done before we come near to meeting these targets.

The problems that racing faces are shared by other industries. The building industry, for example, is apparently having difficulty finding trainees for its craft trades such as bricklaying, plastering and plumbing. The care industry, involving hospitals and care homes, is also experiencing staffing problems. It is felt that young people are drawn to the service and technology sectors, which offer regular and social hours.

Similarly, if racing is seen within the context of other sports, the comparison is less than favourable. Sports Lottery funding has had a huge impact in improving facilities and improving the access to sport for a wide group of people. Football, in particular, is involved in a wide range of community projects aimed at attracting more young people into the sport. Whilst racing is included in the list of sports eligible for financial support, priority has been given to those sports which are contested at the Olympics. Britain is not alone in experiencing these problems. Ireland was always assumed to have a surplus of people who wanted to work with horses. However, with a booming economy, the phenomenon has appeared of Irish trainers advertising in Britain for staff. This would have been unheard of, even a few years ago.

Current training provision

Currently, staff training in Britain is the responsibility of The British Horseracing Training Board (BHTB). The delivery is the responsibility of The British Racing School (BRS) at Newmarket, the Northern Racing College (NRC) at Doncaster and The British Stud Staff Training Scheme (BSSTS), also based in Newmarket. Under the Stable Staff Training scheme, established in 1993, it is mandatory for those under age 19 to undergo training if they want to work in a trainer's yard. Both Schools operate similar schemes which are based on Foundation Modern Apprenticeships (FMA). This training is eligible for Government funding under the Young Persons Workbased Training Scheme.

The BRS at Newmarket is the main training provider for the industry and is its Centre of Excellence. The School was opened in 1983 on its present site. The original remit was to develop potential jockeys following the Jockey Club's Marriage Report which identified a dearth of home grown talent. Since then, the range of training offered in support of the racing industry has developed greatly. Courses are now provided for jockeys, trainers, groundsmen, head lads and others. However, the main stream of activity is training stable staff.

Currently, the School offers 180 places a year. Courses are run throughout the year with a new course starting each month. Trainees spend nine weeks at the School, at the end of which they are guaranteed a job in the industry. This training is provided free of charge and is open to complete beginners. Entry is by interview or following a trainer's recommendation.

The training at the School is demanding and aims to prepare the trainee for the realities of the job. To achieve this, the facilities are tailor-made. The main part of the training are the 52 horses. The majority of them are horses out of training but, in order to cater for those with limited experience, the School has two ponies and a couple of non-Thoroughbreds.

The School offers a marvellous second career for horses that have had a successful career on the racecourse. Currently at the School are Group 2 winner *Decorated Hero*, *Three Cheers*, who was placed in the Ascot Gold Cup, listed winners *Spanish Grandee* and *New Capricorn*, as well as old favourites such as *Knobbleknees*, *Mweenish*, *Hebridan*, *Nakir* and *Land Afar*.

The School has purpose-built facilities including all-weather gallops, an indoor school and grass gallops. Use is made of technology where appropriate and, for example, all outdoor riding instruction is provided using a radio system which allows trainees to hear the instructor at all times. The aim is to give trainees a sufficient level of competence in their riding and stable management to allow them to be a valuable member of staff to a trainer and to allow them to complete their qualification in a trainer's yard.

The training also covers wider subjects which hopefully develop them as individuals. This includes, for example, first aid training, training on computers and a programme aimed to help them to make the transition between home and working life. Trainees come from all parts of the country and all sorts of backgrounds. Currently the split is about 65:35 female to male.

Great emphasis is put on quality and, in particular, the quality of the training. The School received an excellent report from The Training Standards Council, who are charged with inspecting all work-based Government funded training. It has achieved recognition for the British Standards Institution Standard ISO 9001. This was particularly notable, since the only other organisation in sport to achieve this accolade is Chelsea Football Club. The School was also fortunate enough to win a National Training Award for '*the excellence of the training provided*'.

Further training beyond the FMA is available through the Advanced Modern Apprenticeship. This is aimed at those who have the ability to progress to positions of responsibility in yards. Currently, only about 10% of trainees continue with this level of training, which is demanding.

In Ireland, training is centred on The Racing Academy and Centre of Education (RACE) based at The Curragh. RACE takes 30 trainees a year on their Pre-Apprentice Jockey Course. The course lasts 42 weeks. It includes an NVQ in Racehorse Care, in common with British trainees. In the second and third terms, trainees have an opportunity to ride out for trainers. In addition, RACE is the designated training body for the Irish Turf and is responsible for delivering mandatory training of jockeys and trainers. Financing of RACE is provided by grants from the Irish Horseracing Authority, sponsorship and a percentage of prize money from horseracing.

Conclusion

In Britain and, probably, elsewhere in Europe, the emphasis put on staff training and development is inadequate. The problems of inadequate staffing levels cannot be solved without an acceptance across the industry that staff must be properly trained and managed if they are to fulfil the role required of them in the industry. This means a comprehensive change of attitude to gain common acceptance, especially from trainers, that people matter and that if they are to be retained, they need to be properly rewarded and managed. Only by developing the employment package that trainers are willing to offer their employees will sufficient individuals be attracted to positions within the racing industry.

This is not simply an issue of pay. Employees need to have a means of progressing to the limit of their skills and ability. They need to feel valued as individuals. The solution will have many facets. It will involve improved recruiting, not just of 16- to 18-year-olds but also of part-time staff and older age groups. It will involve professional development for stable staff so that they can feel valued. It will involve improving the way staff are managed in yards, especially by the Head Lad and Trainer. It will involve rectifying the identified reasons why people leave racing. This is no easy task.

Some progress has been made through The Stable Staff Resources Group. However, it will take a much more integrated and radical approach if the real roots of the problems identified are to be met. Such a large change will take time, but it means that everyone in the industry has to accept the value of good staff to its future and prosperity. If this cannot be achieved, then this will have a serious effect on the future and prosperity of the industry. This message is probably not new, but the longer it is ignored and tackled in a disjointed and inadequate fashion, the more far-reaching will be its consequences.

The Utrecht Veterinary Faculty

P. RENÉ van WEEREN DVM PhD DiplECVS DiplRNVA
and MARIANNE M. SLOET van OLDRUITENBORGH-OOSTERBAAN DVM PhD

Department of Equine Sciences
Faculty of Veterinary Medicine, Utrecht University
The Netherlands

"If the world comes to an end, I'll go to Holland for there everything happens 50 years later", the famous German poet Heinrich Heine said in the 1830s.

The start

It can be argued whether the above statement was generally true in those days and more so whether it still holds today, but it was certainly true with respect to the development of veterinary medicine. The first veterinary school was opened in France in 1762 and many followed all over Europe in the first few decades after that year. By the end of the 18th century, centres of veterinary education had been formed in all leading European countries, but not in the Netherlands. During the French occupation (1796–1813), rather far-developed plans had existed to construct a veterinary school in the town of Zwolle in what was then the 'Département de l'haute Yssel', but the fall of the Napoleonic empire halted this development.

After the liberation from the French and the 1815 Conference of Vienna when the political map of Europe was redrawn, together with many other changes, the southern and northern parts of the low countries were united to form the Kingdom of the Netherlands (present-day Holland, Belgium and Luxembourg). The country rejoiced in a new vitality under the forceful and efficient leadership of the 'king-merchant' Willem I. It was strongly felt that the country could not fall behind with respect to formal veterinary education which had already proven its value elsewhere in Europe for over half a century.

In Holland, which had always been a state of merchants and had not boasted any significant military successes, except for those by the navy in the 17th century, it was the great losses caused by the cattle plagues of those days (principally rinderpest and contagious pleuropneumonia) that urged the foundation of a veterinary school, more than the need for good horse doctors in the army. Nevertheless, the horse was then so important for military purposes that the choice of Utrecht as seat of the Veterinary School was determined by both its central position in the country and the fact that it was an important garrison town.

After long and tedious preparations, a 17th century mansion was purchased that lay about a mile east of the then still existing medieval walls of the city of Utrecht. On the premises of this mansion, in 1814, a cotton printing factory had been built that had gone bankrupt shortly afterwards. These two buildings served as the nucleus of the veterinary school that officially opened as 'State Veterinary School' in 1821. A few stables and a forge were constructed and under the leadership of van Lidth de Jeude, a zoologist who in 1826 was succeeded by Alexander Numan, a medical doctor who would hold the helm until 1851, the education of veterinary students began.

The early 19th century

The new veterinary school had a good start, with 24 first year students in 1821. The influx of students decreased thereafter, but soon stabilised at around 15 during the first decades of the school's existence. In 1830, the southern part of the Netherlands segregated to form the independent kingdom of Belgium. This meant a decrease in the

Fig 1: View of the entrance of the State Veterinary School in the 1840s.

potential number of students (in Belgium the first veterinary school, in Cureghem near Brussels, was opened in 1832). Most of the students who entered had an agricultural background. The threshold to enter the school was not high and the newly qualified vets had great difficulty in maintaining themselves in a field that for centuries had been dominated by empiricists of varying backgrounds. Public esteem for the profession was low and could by no means be compared to the medical profession, which was taught at an academic level. This fact, together with the very slow technical progress in the profession, led to a drop in interest from potential students. During the 7 years from 1848 until 1855, no more than 8 (!) students in total began to study veterinary medicine. In those days, the course took 4 years and was divided in 8 semesters: 4 so-called winter courses and 4 summer courses. The disciplines that were taught included anatomy, physiology, botany, pharmacy, toxicology and 'practical veterinary medicine'. Despite the name of the last subject, the course was largely theoretical. There was little, if any, practical training of the students, which gave the young vets an enormous handicap in the field.

The rather disastrous situation at the veterinary school did not remain unnoticed. In 1850, the Minister of Home Affairs stated in parliament that *"The significance of veterinary medicine was very little and did by no means justify the high costs of the education"*. In 1851, Numan was substituted by Wellenbergh who, again, was not a vet. Things began to change, and the numbers of students and patients began to rise slowly (in 1861/1862 a total of 467 horses, 18 cows,

4 donkeys, 20 goats, 12 pigs, 300 dogs and 15 cats were treated), but the breakthrough came when MacGillavry took over in 1872.

Revival in the 1870s

MacGillavry was not just a vet but also a medical doctor. He was the first director who saw the importance of practical training in veterinary medicine. Whereas Wellenbergh had looked upon the veterinary profession with contempt, MacGillavry contracted good veterinarians as teachers and gave them much more influence than they had ever had under the former, rather autocratic directors. He also initiated extensive new constructions on the school premises.

Another, independent development that enabled veterinary medicine to flourish was the revolutionary scientific breakthroughs in the 1860s and 1870s in the fields of microbiology and pathology. Pasteur and Koch provided the clues for many diseases that had so far been of mysterious origin. The brilliant pathologist Virchow laid the basis for a cell-based pathology that broke with the old humoral theories. These discoveries had enormous implications, not only for human medicine, but also for the veterinary sciences. In fact, for the first time, great successes thanks to veterinary intervention became evident. The great cattle plagues, rinderpest and contagious pleuropneumonia, came under

Fig 2: Alexander Numan, director from 1826–1851.

Fig 3: Lameness examination by Dr Schimmel around the turn of the century.

control. In the horse, the causative agent of glanders, then the greatest plague of this species and, as a potentially fatal zoonosis, a constant threat to man, was isolated by Schütz and Löffler in 1886. All these developments boosted the interest in veterinary medicine and emphasised the importance of the profession.

With the exciting developments in the profession, and the internal changes initiated by MacGillavry, the Utrecht Veterinary School made a good re-start. When MacGillavry was appointed as a professor at the University of Leyden in 1878 and the first vet, Wirtz, took the helm, expectations were high. In the end, the Veterinary School was to be governed by vets as was, logically, the rule everywhere else in Europe. Unfortunately, things turned out to be different. Wirtz was a good clinician, a hard worker and an excellent administrator. However, he completely lacked the social capacities a good director should have. Within a few years he was at war with the council of the school and all his fellow teachers.

A new period of stagnation followed that only ended in 1909 when Wirtz (at the age of 73!) was succeeded by the most senior teacher, Schimmel. In the late 19th century, other protests were heard than those against the autocratic director. Slowly, animal welfare was becoming an issue. Throughout the 19th century it had been a tradition to practise surgical interventions on living horses. Up to 84 operations were performed on the same horse, until the 1880s without anaesthesia. The public began to protest and the government intervened. Most practical training from then on had to be done on cadaver specimens. Only specific surgeries, such as bleeding and tracheotomy, were still permitted in living horses.

Schimmel proved to be a good director who had a good relationship with his staff members. Apparently he had not forgotten the many years he had suffered under Wirtz. After his death in 1914, a system with a yearly rotating directorate was adopted until 1918, the year when the most important thing since the foundation of the State Veterinary School happened; the promotion to an institute of higher education. Finally, after almost a century, veterinary medicine in the Netherlands had outgrown its infancy.

The Veterinary High School (1918–1925)

The first serious attempt to raise the standard of veterinary education in the Netherlands was made in 1904. However, the Minister for the Maintenance of Dikes, Roads, Bridges and the Navigability of Canals and of Commerce, who was then responsible for the State Veterinary School, did not think the matter of sufficient importance and refused any change in status of the school. Things changed a year later when an independent Ministry of Agriculture was formed which took responsibility for the school. Already, in 1908, a plan was launched to raise the academic level of both the agricultural schools and the veterinary school and, in 1913, a bill was introduced in Parliament. Because of the First World War (in which Holland remained neutral, but which of course had a great impact on the country as all its neighbours were at war and tens of thousands of Belgian refugees flooded the country), the bill was not passed until the end of 1917.

On 16th March 1918, the new, independent Veterinary High School was inaugurated. Large celebrations took place, including a dinner with HRH Hendrik, Prince of the Netherlands and husband of HM Queen Wilhelmina, as special guest of honour. The new High School was governed by a Senate that consisted of full professors and was presided over by a Rector, a position that changed from year to year. Like a university, the new High School had the right to bestow PhD titles. In the preceding years, many vets had obtained a PhD title abroad, mostly in Berne, as it had not been possible for vets to obtain

Fig 4: The seals of a) the State Veterinary School (1821–1918); b) the Veterinary High School (1918–1925); c) the Faculty of Veterinary Medicine (from 1996).

this title in the Netherlands.

Until that time, the official seal of the Veterinary School had been the national arms (a climbing lion) with 'State Veterinary School' written around it . The new High School chose a new logo, based on ancient mythology: Androcles and the Lion. The story is that Androcles, who was slave to the Roman proconsul in Northern Africa, fled his master and hid in the cave of a lion in the desert. When the lion came home, it was severely lame because of a thick thorn that had pierced one of its feet. Androcles removed the thorn and continued his flight. Later he was found, arrested and condemned to death in the lion pit. However, when he was thrown into the pit, the lion that was released to kill him happened to be the same lion that he had helped earlier. The animal recognised him and, instead of killing Androcles, hugged him. The proconsul was so impressed by this behaviour

that he set both Androcles and the lion free. The two became inseparable and lived together from that moment. As the story nicely symbolises the bond between man and animals, it was chosen as the inspiration for the new logo.

The new Veterinary High School made an impressive start, not least because of the generous financing by the Ministry of Agriculture. Staff members (including faculty and all other personnel) of the old State Veterinary School had totalled 45 in 1900. In 1910, this figure had risen to 60. In 1918, the new High School had 110 staff members. The various full professors now received a budget of their own that they could dispose of in the way they thought best for their discipline. Teaching and scientific research flourished as never before. In 1921, the 100 year jubilee of veterinary education in the Netherlands was celebrated extensively. However, dark clouds appeared on the horizon. Economic depression caused state finances to become restricted and pressure on the Veterinary High School to cut back the budget increased. Already, in 1922, it was noticed that the independent Veterinary High School was far more expensive than the comparable faculties at Utrecht University. This was true and was partially caused by the increasing separatism of the various disciplines. The solution was all too easy and became unavoidable in the following years. In September 1925, only 7 years after the start, the independent Veterinary High School ceased to exist and was replaced by the Veterinary Faculty of the University of Utrecht. The Veterinary Faculty was the sixth faculty of this University, which was Holland's second oldest, being founded in 1636. Veterinary education had reached the position it essentially still holds today.

Part of Utrecht University

Incorporation into the University led to some changes in the curriculum. Most lectures in the first, propaedeutical, year were now given simultaneously for students in veterinary medicine, medicine and dentistry. Of course, the school's own Senate and Rector disappeared, but in other respects the Veterinary Faculty became a largely independent and rather solitary part of Utrecht University. While the new organisation of the

Utrecht Veterinary Faculty took its course under rather favourable economic conditions in the late 1920s, this situation would not last long. The crash in Wall Street in 1929, and the ensuing worldwide depression, began to take its toll in 1932. Utrecht University had to lower its budget by over 10% in a single year. Although no faculty was closed and the existence of the Veterinary Faculty was never threatened, conditions became harsh. Investments were hardly made and the budget continued to be cut during the mid 1930s. In the field, the situation was grim too. Practising vets saw their income fall and forecasts about possibilities of employment for young vets were gloomy. In fact, there was pressure from the College of Veterinary Surgeons to demote potential students as the influx of first-year students (around 30 during this decade) was deemed too high.

Towards the end of the 1930s, economic conditions slowly improved. Immediately, the Veterinary Faculty started to make plans. In 1938, a report was published that described the deplorable state of veterinary education in the Netherlands in comparison to neighbouring countries such as England, Belgium, France and, especially, Germany, where large investments had been made in the past. If Holland were not to lose international competitiveness, drastic changes must be made. The curriculum had to be prolonged to a 6-year course. New personnel was needed and, not unimportantly, vast improvements had to be made with respect to the buildings. The last new large construction dated from 1923 and, in some disciplines, the situation was hardly bearable. Back in 1930, the new professor of reproduction, van der Kaay, had accepted his appointment only on the condition that he would get a new clinic in the foreseeable future.

Had the 1930s been a decade of complete standstill? Certainly not; international scientific progress had been substantial and, at a local level, post-academic education had been formalised with the introduction of the so-called 'Veterinary Week', during which new techniques were shown and discussed at the Faculty premises for an audience of graduated vets. Further, new disciplines such as radiology had been incorporated into the curriculum. Nevertheless, investments had forcibly been well below what was actually needed and the time now seemed ripe to compensate for the delay. However, an event that would shock the entire globe and would change the history of mankind was to frustrate these plans, some of them for more than 50 years; the outbreak of World War II.

The Veterinary Faculty during World War II

Holland had remained neutral during World War I and had optimistically thought to follow the same policy during the years of increasing international political tension in the late 1930s. However, the expansionist German Nazis had other ideas and, in the early hours of May 10th, 1940 German troops crossed the frontiers. The weak Dutch forces could not halt the well-equipped invaders and, after the Luftwaffe had bombed the city of Rotterdam on May 14th and threatened to do the same thing to other towns, including Utrecht, the Dutch forces surrendered.

In the Veterinary Faculty, the occupation at first meant normalisation as all equine vets, who had been mobilised for the then still large cavalry, returned. The attitude of the occupier towards the universities seemed friendly at first. The Rector of Utrecht University was told on May 25th that the university would be able to continue its duties as before and that nobody would have to fear for his or her position because of political opinion or racial origin. It soon became clear that the reality was different. In September 1940, a decree was issued that no Jews could be appointed in government positions. Those who already had a position were to be suspended. These measures were completely against the Dutch tradition of tolerance. In Leyden, the law professor Cleveringa held a speech in which he vehemently denounced the measures. The reaction of the occupier was quick and clear; Leyden University was closed and remained so. At the other universities, including Utrecht, most people felt that keeping the universities open was in the interest of the country. Therefore, the decrees and directions from the occupying forces were followed, though reluctantly. At the Utrecht Veterinary Faculty, the chair in physiology had been held since 1927 by Professor Roos, who was of Jewish origin. He was suspended in November 1940 and officially

Fig 5: Professor G.M. van der Plank.

dismissed 3 months later. In June 1942, Roos was arrested and transported to Mauthausen concentration camp where he was murdered in October 1942.

As the friendly approach that had been adopted at the beginning of the occupation did not lead soon enough to the desired 'Nazification' of society, the attitude of the occupier became harder. Because of the participation of some students in the Resistance, in March 1943 a decree was published that obliged all students to sign a declaration that they would refrain from any unlawful action against the occupying forces and respect all laws that had been declared valid in the occupied territories. Not signing the declaration would imply dismissal from the university. The decree caused much unrest. Most students did not want to sign, but many professors were afraid that the whole academic world would come to a standstill and that the occupier would close all universities if the so-called Loyalty Declaration was not signed by the majority of the students.

At the Veterinary Faculty, opinions were divided. There were a few collaborators among the staff who had been appointed by the German authorities or had already shown Nazi sympathies before the war. They, of course, were in favour of the declaration, but they formed a tiny minority that was completely ignored by the other staff members. Some others, for example, the Professor of Animal Husbandry, van der Plank, were vehemently opposed to signing and told their students so. However, most of the professors thought the continuation of veterinary education more important than the political situation and advised the students to sign. They were repudiated by their students who showed a braver attitude; less than 20% of the veterinary students eventually signed. The vast majority disappeared into hiding as did most of the students of other faculties and universities. After this, teaching virtually came to a halt, but the Faculty remained open for patient care and some research was still done.

As the war went on, supplies went down. Most, if not all, articles became scarce. The situation worsened quickly after the allied invasion in Normandy in June 1944. In September 1944, liberation seemed near, but the battle of Arnhem was lost which meant for all but the southern part of the Netherlands another winter under occupation of the Germans. These did not become friendlier, with the growing awareness that it was inevitable that they would lose the war. The winter of '44–'45 was exceptionally cold. Fuel and food supplies had fallen to completely inadequate levels and in the Western, urbanised part of the country, 25,000 people died of starvation and cold. At the Veterinary Faculty, all work had come to an end. Although some of the employees were forced to perform slave labour for the Germans, the overall situation remained bearable. Some people were kept in hiding from the Germans on the Faculty premises. Gradually, the stock of experimental animals fell victim to 'highly contagious diseases'; so read the official reports in order not to raise suspicion. In fact, they were illegally slaughtered and served as very welcome extra rations for the faculty personnel. It even came to the point that the Pathology Department inspected animals that had been illegally slaughtered by German soldiers (who, in the very last phase of the war, themselves began to starve), charging, as a fee, a substantial part of the carcass.

Finally, the German occupational forces in the Netherlands surrendered unconditionally on May 5th, 1945. The first allied troops entered the city of Utrecht from the east, thus passing the gates of the Veterinary Faculty, at 10 am on May 7th. Holland was free again.

Building a new Faculty

Directly after the war, van der Plank was made president of the Faculty, being the professor who had shown most courage during the difficult years of the occupation. The few collaborators were dismissed and punished, and the professors who had advised the students to sign the Loyalty Declaration were forced to apologise in public. Some of the students were excluded from the Faculty for a shorter, or longer, period because of their behaviour during the war.

Slowly, life returned to normal, although many goods remained scarce during the rest of the 1940s. The housing situation of the Faculty, which had been a matter of intense concern before the war, was even worse now. In 1947, one of the professors broke his foot because the floor of his laboratory broke down. However, as a large part of the country lay in ruins and the economic situation was dreadful, the government thought, not without reason, that there were more urgent matters to worry about than the Faculty of Veterinary Medicine. Nevertheless, economic conditions improved and there even was a boom from the mid-fifties onwards. The economic revival had an impact on all parts of society, including the Veterinary Faculty. New chairs were created, such as those in pharmacology, nutrition, immunology and virology. In 1958, government permission was finally obtained to construct an entire new Faculty that was to be built to the east of the city of Utrecht.

Thus, history was to repeat itself, as the original State Veterinary School had also been built to the east of the town. However, the city had encroached on the Faculty, leaving no room for further extension. Plans were made and many faculties abroad were visited. In December 1964, a start was made and on October 25th 1967, HRH Prince Bernhard, the spouse of HM Queen Juliana (and, in a certain sense, the successor of HRH Prince Hendrik, who had assisted at the Inauguration Banquet of the Veterinary High School), opened the newly built Large Animal Reproduction Clinic. van der Kaay had his new clinic after 37 years. He would retire in 1968. In the years thereafter (1968–1970), the clinics for Surgery, Internal Medicine and Small Animals followed. The

Fig 6: The travail-bascule *being operated. For surgical interventions, the horses were only locally anaesthetised.*

improvements when compared to the old situation were huge. Large Animal Surgery, for instance, moved from an outdated single operation theatre where the old 'travail-bascule' was still operational to two fully equipped ultramodern operation rooms with hydraulic operation tables that were moved around by electric trolleys. The housing capacity of the Large Animal Hospital had more than tripled and the buildings were so large that people had to resort indoors to that typical Dutch way of transport; the bicycle.

Economic booms tend to fade out and to be followed by depressions. The boom of the sixties was no exception. In the early 1970s the oil crisis followed, and the building programme was suspended for many years. The Faculty would remain divided over 2 locations for more than 20 years. Only in 1980 did the Faculty Administration get a new building on the new premises, and it was not until 1988 that the last disciplines were moved from the old site to the new one, exactly 50 years after the 1938 report that stated the urgency of improving the housing conditions.

The 1960s did not bring changes only with respect to material things. The curriculum changed drastically and was thoroughly modernised. The number of staff members grew constantly. In 1964, the total number of personnel of the Faculty was 379; in 1970 this figure had almost doubled to 634 However, the number of students had grown more quickly. In the 15 years after the war, the number of first-year students had averaged about 75. In the year 1968–1969, this number had grown to 244, causing severe capacity problems. Not only had the number of students grown, but their attitude had changed.

The 1960s were the decade of protest and 'revolution'. The students' revolt in May 1968 in Paris was followed the next year by similar actions at the Dutch universities. In Amsterdam, the administrative building of the University of Amsterdam was occupied by students, causing great public upheaval. The veterinary students were, however, not in the forefront. They had always formed a rather closed and very loyal community with little, if any, political activism. It may be exemplifying that in the days that people like Daniel Cohn-Bendit stood on the burning barricades in Paris, a professor of the Dutch Veterinary Faculty complained that students behaved so badly these days. He had been addressed by one of them simply as 'Sir' instead of the customary 'Professor', and some of them did not step aside when the professor drove his car onto the Faculty premises!

One item should not remain unmentioned in this paragraph; the call for differentiation in the curriculum. During the 1960s, many conferences had been dedicated to the ongoing changes in the veterinary profession. It was becoming clear that the vet would have to become more than just the general practitioner he used to be; the classical country vet of the 'James Herriot' type who knew a lot about all species and diseases, but who had no in-depth knowledge in specific areas. It was predicted that in the near future more specialists would be needed in various areas. Inevitably, this would be at the cost of the classical broad scope of the vet. Should the Faculty anticipate these developments and offer a differentiation in, for example, the last part of the curriculum? A majority of the Faculty thought so and proposed a Clinical line and a Public Health line. Diplomas would be different, but it would be possible for a 'clinical' vet to do an extra course in Public Health in order to become double-qualified.

The College of Veterinary Surgeons strongly opposed the idea and, although formally they did not have a say in veterinary education, advised the Minister in a negative sense. A compromise proposal was made in 1967; differentiation in the last half year of the curriculum with no influence on the diploma. Even this plan failed, due to strong opposition from vets in the field. Evidently, the time was not right. It was not until more than 15 years later that an almost identical plan to the 1967 compromise was indeed implemented. Another 10 years later, differentiation comprised the whole last year of the curriculum and plans were already made for different 'study paths' that would start in a very early phase of the curriculum.

The only constant thing is change

In the early seventies the Government had regulated student numbers, which also exceeded capacity for a number of other studies, such as medicine and dentistry, by a kind of lottery system. The Veterinary Faculty was assigned a fixed number of 175 first-year students. This figure should be seen against the background of approximately 1,000 applicants each year. As

Fig 7: Aerial view of the clinical departments after their completion (1970), located in the countryside.

everywhere else in the world, the ratio of male to female students started to change. From the very start, the veterinary profession had been an exclusively male affair. In the 19th and early 20th centuries, the emancipation of women still had to start, and also the job could be very physically demanding. The first female student was welcomed in 1925 and graduated in 1930. It took another 10 years until the example was followed, but, from then on, there was a steady influx of female students that stabilised at about 10% until the early 1960s. From then on the percentage rose to 20–25% until the end of the seventies, to explode thereafter. In the year 1999–2000, 80% of the first-year students were female.

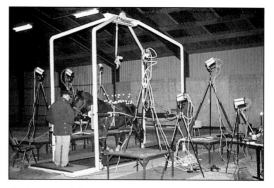

Fig 8: Research being conducted in the Equine Biomechanics Research Laboratory.

The last 25 years of the Faculty of Veterinary Medicine were characterised by many more changes than the sex ratio of the student population. Modern audiovisual techniques were being used in teaching. As everywhere else, computers invaded the Faculty from the mid 1980s onwards and now form an indispensable part of everyday life. In the clinics, new imaging techniques were introduced, such as ultrasonography, computer tomography (CT) and magnetic resonance imaging (MRI). New clinical techniques such as endoscopy, arthroscopy and laparoscopy became commonplace. Not unimportantly, scientific research was given a much more prominent place than it used to have.

Research had been performed since the days of the State Veterinary School, but the attitude towards it had been somewhat ambivalent. The dictatorial director Wirtz, although he had been quite a good researcher himself in his younger days, forbade his staff members to perform research as their tasks were 'teaching and patient care'. Later, the climate for research became better and some people, like the chemistry professor Sjollema in the 1930s, who caused a breakthrough in the treatment of milk fever by recognising the importance of calcium, had made significant contributions to veterinary science. However, particularly in the clinics, the old adage that patient care and teaching were the most important tasks for a clinician was strong-lived. Research was carried out in spare time only, and was directed mainly by the interest of the individual researcher. Therefore, it forcibly had a somewhat haphazard aspect, as strong research lines failed to exist. These lines had in the meantime been created by the pre- and para-clinical departments and had led to widespread international recognition, especially with respect to virology and immunology. It was not until the 1980s that the attitude towards research started to change in the clinical departments too. In the equine field, forces were joined between the Departments of Anatomy, Surgery and Internal Medicine in order to set up an Equine Biomechanics Research Laboratory. In 1992, a fully equipped laboratory with treadmill, force plate and kinematic analysis equipment, was inaugurated. Research on equine exercise performance by the Department of Internal Medicine related well to this line of study. Later, other lines of research were established, such as those on articular cartilage-related disorders including osteochondrosis (OC).

All these investments had been made possible by the strong determination of the Faculty management to upgrade the standard of veterinary education and research in the Netherlands and to increase international competitiveness. The days of stagnation had now long gone and recognition came. In 1973, the Faculty was granted accreditation by the American Veterinary Medical Association (AVMA) as the first (and for more than 25 years the only) veterinary faculty outside the US and Canada. Every 7 years, a visitation committee arrived to inspect the Faculty to give recommendations for improvement and to see to what extent earlier recommendations had been implemented. Whereas the AVMA criteria are based largely on the educational programme and on the facilities, an independent international visitation committee that visited the Faculty in 1999 and focused on scientific research ranked the

Utrecht Veterinary Faculty among the top 5 in the world. The increasing self-consciousness of the Veterinary Faculty was symbolised by the adoption, on the occasion of the celebration of 175 years of veterinary education in the Netherlands in 1996, of a logo of its own. A choice was made, again, of Androcles and the Lion.

These accomplishments could only be made thanks to the efforts of the staff to improve the quality of their work and to adapt to often radical changes. The atmosphere of change peaked in the late 1990s and is still very prominent today. In 1995, a completely new curriculum was adopted, based on problem-oriented teaching. In September 2000, the contingent of first-year students was raised to 225. In September 2001 the next curriculum started, in which differentiation from a very early phase in the form of various 'study paths' is implemented. In 1999, a sum of approximately 100,000,000 Euros became available over a 10 year period to entirely facelift the clinical departments which were then 35 years old. In relation to this, on January 1st 1999, the whole clinical section was reorganised and adapted to developments in the field. The old discipline-oriented approach was abandoned and replaced by a species-oriented approach. This led to the formation of an independent Equine Clinic, comprising all clinical disciplines, and led to profound changes for many of the (senior) staff members.

The ambience of permanent change enables adequate adaptation to the rapidly changing outside

Fig 9: Aerial view of the present-day Utrecht Veterinary Faculty. Slowly, the Faculty is being surrounded again by blocks of buildings.

world and, therefore, seems unavoidable under the present conditions. It is, however, felt as a heavy burden by many people; a burden that may become excessive and will undoubtedly be counteracted in the future. However, it can be stated that if Heinrich Heine lived today and were to judge the situation in the Netherlands by the state of affairs at the Veterinary Faculty, he would not opt for Holland as a safe haven when the end of the world was near.

Further reading

Dunlop, R.H. and Williams, D.J. (Eds) (1996) *Veterinary Medicine. An Illustrated History*, Mosby, St. Louis.

Kroon, H.M., Paimans, W.J. and Ihle, J.E.W. (1921) *Een eeuw veeartsenijkundig onderwijs - 's Rijks Veeartsenijschool - Veeartsenijkundige Hoogeschool 1821-1921*. Senate of the Veterinary High School, Utrecht.

Offringa, C. (Ed) (1971) *Van Gildestein naar Uithof - 150 jaar diergeneeskundig onderwijs in Utrecht. Part I. State Veterinary School (1821-1918) and Veterinary High School (1918-1925)*. State University of Utrecht, Utrecht.

Offringa, C. (Ed) (1981) *Van Gildestein naar Uithof - 150 jaar diergeneeskundig onderwijs in Utrecht. Part II. Faculty of Veterinary Medicine (1925-1971)*. State University of Utrecht, Utrecht.

Wester, J. (1939) *Geschiedenis der Veeartsenijkunde*, Hoonte, Utrecht.

"One of life's greatest pleasures…"

JAMES GIVEN BVetMed MRCVS

Staffords Yard
Northfield Lane
Willoughton
Gainsborough
Lincolnshire DN21 5RT

Most trainers think they are vets and most vets think they are trainers. This may be a somewhat cynical view of how two professions view each other; however, there are few of us who have the privilege of being both. Some may say that we are Jack of all trades and masters of none. I feel some of my abilities as a vet have waned as I have spent time away from normal practice. However, I am confident that I am vastly more experienced over some issues particular to Thoroughbreds in training. I also know when I do not have the facilities or ability to deal with some situations and then I refer to specialists without delay.

When I went for my interview at the Jockey Club, the panel asked me to have a look at a basic anatomy test of the lower limb of the horse. All interviewees were asked to do this and, when they asked me what I thought of the difficulty of the test, I replied that I would expect the majority of trainers to be able to answer it correctly. It was a surprise, but perhaps a lesson to me, when they told me that of the last 57 applicants, I was the first to get it right. I have not forgotten this and whenever I am asked if I think it helps being a vet as a trainer, I cannot help but consider that an understanding of anatomy and physiology, amongst all other knowledge we learn at vet school, has to help one be a better trainer.

When I was young I did not have a grand plan for my life, although from my mid-teens I wanted to train as a vet. Throughout my childhood I wanted to learn to ride but never had the opportunity. On qualifying, I took a position as a small animal House Surgeon at the Royal Veterinary College, which was thoroughly enjoyable, and continued my education. Most of the specialised skills I learned during this time I no longer use; but the general medical and surgical approach to cases I still find useful.

It was only when starting to work in a mixed practice, in Yorkshire, that I was able to indulge my lifelong ambition of learning to ride. It was a little strange in a riding school populated by teenage girls who seemed more proficient than me! I thoroughly enjoyed riding and was soon invited to join a team-chasing team. Fortunately, I had a generous horse who followed the lead horse all day and taught me a great deal. I was again lucky enough to buy a horse who was an excellent schoolmaster for me and we had four happy years eventing and showjumping. I became very involved in my hobby to the extent that I found that my day job was getting in the way.

After a particularly annoying morning in the practice I, by chance, saw an advert for an Assistant Trainer and Veterinary Surgeon to work for Mark Johnston. The job could not have been written better for me and I applied, although I thought that without any racing background I would not have a chance of getting the job. In hindsight, it was perhaps this lack of experience that encouraged Mark to employ me. Three valuable years learning training skills and experience led to my winning the Alex Scott Memorial Scholarship for Assistant Trainers. This sponsored me for a month in Dubai, which opened my eyes to many different approaches to training horses. Not only did I learn about track style training and racehorse management, but it made me question the validity of some of the dogmatic approaches I had learned.

Fig 1: I Cried for You *winning the Cambridgeshire at Newmarket (2001)*.

Even if you come back to agree with a particular approach, it is a valuable exercise to question it and to explore the options.

On my return from Dubai I did a locum job to keep the wolf from the door and it also confirmed, after a four-year absence from practice, that it was not for me. During this period I applied for my trainer's licence, looked for a yard and tried to encourage some prospective owners. It seemed at times that a head in the sand and plough-on attitude was necessary, because if I stopped and reflected on what I had undertaken it sent icy shivers down my spine.

I started training on the track at Wolverhampton with six horses and, very soon, had some lessons in the harsh realities of training. One owner who had two horses with me only paid for ten days, then never again. Another horse broke its pelvis, so my string was rapidly diminishing.

Fortune favours the brave they say, and I was lucky enough to meet my now business partner, Andrew Clarke, who bought into the business and prevented me getting into trouble with Customs and Excise and the bank. We moved to Willoughton and, in the two and a half years since, have expanded the business to have both our yards full with 56 horses, with another 25 resting and waiting to come back in. I would never have been able to cope with this rapid expansion without a partner to deal with running the business. He has left me free to train the horses and look after the owners, and the hard work has reaped its rewards in big winners at the festivals and our first Group winner, *Jessica's Dream* in Milan.

My training as a vet has been invaluable to my understanding of training racehorses; however, other skills, such as public relations and shrewd business sense, are also essential.

My school careers master spent the entire twenty minutes of my careers interview trying to dissuade me from becoming a vet; similarly Geoff Wragg and Peter Calver kindly took time to advise me and tried to persuade me not to take up training racehorses. I may not always have made what appear sensible decisions or taken easy options, but I am grateful for where my life has led me. As Sheikh Mohammed said, *"One of life's greatest pleasures is doing what others think you cannot"*.

I thoroughly enjoy training and feel honoured that the care, management and racing of these magnificent animals is entrusted to me.

The evolution of the French veterinary ethos

ROBERT LESAFFRE DVM

La Garenne aux Gres
Bois Saint Denis 60500
Chantilly
France

Scientific equine associations have been born; the AAEP in the United States, BEVA in Great Britain and I helped to create the AVEF in 1966, in France. These Associations and their annual Congresses are a major factor in the development of our knowledge. Furthermore, many of our profession trained in foreign countries. Professor Raker at New Bolton in Philadelphia trained me; I worked with my distinguished British colleague Mr Jim Roberts and with Mr Fackleman, who specialised in tendon transplants. I also studied under Professor Wheat at Davis University in California and Professors Sevelius and Petersen in Sweden.

In the last 50 years, much has changed, although the number of horses in training in the Cantilienne region, i.e. Chantilly, Gouvieux, Lamorlaye and Saint Leonard, has remained pretty stable. This figure has fluctuated between 2,000 and 2,300 racehorses in training. This figure does not take into account the 300–500 trotters, together with the sporting horses in the Equestrian Clubs and Centres, three-day eventers, hunting, harness carriages and riding horses for private pleasure. There is every type of horse imaginable in our region, although Thoroughbreds, both for jumping and flat, form the majority of the horses. There are about 3,000 horses in the local region. We all know, in France, as in other countries, that this animal arouses a real passion amongst its owners. It is almost as if it is a transfer, a return to nature in all its aspects to counterbalance the invasion of mechanisation, or modernism in all its more aggressive aspects for the *homo simplex* that we are, whether we want to admit it or not. This sentimental attachment, coupled with the incredible veterinary advances in medicine and surgery, has greatly increased our workload.

It should also be noted that one of the causes, and not the least of them, is the development of communications in all its forms, often positive, but occasionally negative.

This observation of a return to all things natural, is true not only with regard to horses. In 1960, on one of my journeys to Moscow, I noticed the existence of numerous floral shops, as well as an unexpected number of veterinary clinics for small animals, whose existence were motivated by pet shops. A large market for pets had, in fact, developed in this country where the atmosphere was particularly sombre, as I could testify, and did not really incite people to invest in pets. However, it is well known that the Slavs are very sentimental.

In France, veterinary teaching took into consideration the considerable modifications occurring, not only in the countryside, but also in towns, and began to concentrate more and more on horses and pets. At the same time, we created a fourth Veterinary College in Nantes, adding to the pool of vets.

Further to this phenomenon, the application of the Treaty of Rome for the free circulation of people within Europe and the recognition of diplomas, has encouraged a lot of young vets to set themselves up in France where they can often achieve a better standard of living. This trend will only grow with the European Community increasing to 27 countries and the entry of the Eastern European countries with uncertain economies. This will no doubt lead to difficulties in both France and other European countries.

Since the 1950s, the number of practitioners at the Chantilly Training Centre has grown to 17 or 18. In 1950, we were only 3 vets for the same number of horses. It should also be noted that, in parallel to this growth of practitioners, the range of medicinal and surgical interventions has increased steadily.

Since 1945, I have made numerous professional visits to the United States, Sweden or Germany to further my knowledge. At the time, only Edouard Pouret and I were members of the AAEP and I decided on a long plane trip back from a congress in Los Angeles to create *The Association Vétérinaire Equine Française* in order to share this desire to increase my knowledge with fellow vets. The scientific enrichment that I had acquired after spending four days at the Congress and a month or so working all over the States made me feel a moral obligation to create this Association, whose aims would be to develop training and teaching facilities and to establish and increase contacts within the profession.

The French Equine Veterinary Association was created in 1966 with the valuable collaboration of Roger Bordet, Professor of Surgery at the Ecole Nationale Vétérinaire d'Alfort. As the Honouree Founding President, my heart is filled with joy that the objectives which Roger Bordet and I set have been achieved. The incredible work of the active Presidents has contributed to this success.

The Association now has more than 450 members and its annual congresses are hugely successful. I am honoured to have been the initiator, promoter and organiser of the frequent and friendly contacts with the British Equine Veterinary Association. Regular meetings between professionals in France and in England can only be beneficial to our mutual scientific enrichment and thus subscribe to the objective of the publication of this book with the evocative title '*Guardians of the Horse*'.

I would also like to mention that our British friends should know that they are the inventors of Thoroughbreds, a quality that none of us would dare contest in any way, we quickly followed in their footsteps and we strive to be their equals in the veneration they bring to '*the most noble conquest of man*'.

In the south of Paris, at Boissy Saint Léger, there is a huge estate, called Grosbois, which was purchased fifty years ago by the Société du Cheval Français with the aim of creating an ultra modern training centre for trotters. It is a model of its type and I strongly suggest readers visit the next time they travel to France.

I had for a long time had the idea of setting up a state of the art veterinary clinic using as a model the best American installations. This clinic would be used by colleagues to carry out cutting edge surgery and medicine. I contacted the management of the Société d'Encouragement (the holding company which runs all the flat and jump racecourses in France, now called France Galop).

It received a frosty reception, although Professor Godfrain, the Inspector General of the Veterinary Colleges, and who was present at the meeting when my project was proposed, received my proposition favourably.

It should be stated that, at the time, the managers of the racehorse courses had an attitude which I could describe as '*static and dusty*' and '*whatever you do don't make any waves*'. For some strange reason, our profession was looked down upon. Fortunately, things have changed greatly since then, now that is run by genuine businessmen.

One day, when visiting Lexington, I saw the Kentucky Derby in Louisville at the Churchill Downs racecourse and had the opportunity to observe the '*starting boxes*', which were commonly used in the States at the time. I had ridden a lot of races before the war, and had rued the numerous occasions when I had lost a race because of a bad start, due to either the elastics or the Australian Starting Gate. I wrote an article from Lexington, which was published in the great and unique racing newspaper of that era, the *Sport Complet* (the equivalent of Paris Turf today). I wrote at length about the advantages of this starting technique and suggested there should be a fact-finding mission to explore the possibilities of using this system in France. Once again, I was hitting my head against a brick wall and the reason given for the refusal was that the Australian system was the best. We now know how things ended up but how many years did it take us to realise it? It is true that we are often blamed for being right the first time!

However, I was stubbornly convinced of my idea for a surgical clinic despite all the problems I had encountered. I turned to the managers of the Société du Cheval Français in charge of the trotters and, in particular, President Ballières. The project to set up a clinic in the Grosbois estate took immediate effect. It was achieved in a couple of months. Jean Plainfossé, one of the collaborators, is well known to British vets. Its success continues today and is expertly run by Richard Corde, an eminent member of AVEF and his team.

Its success was so rapid that, in 1969, '*Horse and Hound*' magazine sent one of its reporters, Howard Brabyn. I had the privilege to receive him and gave him a guided visit of the clinic and one of my clinical interventions. This long interview included photos and was published on Friday February 1 1969, at 1s 6d per edition.

Thanks to the AVEF, relations between fellow vets have become dignified and friendly. It pleases me that the younger generation have understood that competition is necessary and unavoidable, that being courteous, whilst undeniably efficient and competent and available at all times, is the way forward.

One of our projects is to create a research and training institute, the '*Centre d'Etudes de Formation et de Recherches et Equines Sportives*' (CERES), under the aegis of Professor Lekeux of the Ecole Vétérinaire de Liège, of Patrick Langlois, the current president of AVEF, of Michel Péchayre, a practitioner at Chantilly and several leading such trainers, such as Christiane Head.

The Annual General Meeting was held on the 17 November 2000. Madam Christiane Head was elected President, with Professor Lekeux and Michel Péchayre elected as Vice-Presidents and Patrick Langlois as treasurer. We also created '*L'Association des Vétérinaires Equins de l'Aire Cantilienne*' in order to regroup all the practitioners in the Chantilly region interested in using the services of *CERES* and to speak as one voice if needed.

I am pleased to say that every single vet in the region joined this Association, proving once again our desire to work together. As we enter the third millennium, the equine veterinary movement here in Chantilly has shown its vitality as well as its sense of responsibility, both privately and professionally.

This constructive attitude is extremely satisfying; it indicates to racehorse owners and other professionals in the equine world that our profession is increasingly conscious of its responsibilities, despite a multitude of constraints which have arisen in the industry, together with its growing administrative complexities. The only way in which we can surmount these obstacles is for everyone within the equine profession to have as cordial relationships as possible and for there to be an absolute trust between the people involved in these activities. This is the behaviour that all the veterinarians in Chantilly have adopted. This bodes well for the future. I am sure our fellow British colleagues will be in complete agreement and I would like to take this opportunity to send them my warmest greetings.